DATE DUE

Developing Minds

Developing Minds

Challenge and Continuity
across the Life Span

Michael and Marjorie Rutter

BasicBooks
A Division of HarperCollins*Publishers*

Library of Congress Cataloging-in-Publication Data
Rutter, Michael.
    Developing minds: challenge and continuity across the lifespan /
by Michael and Marjorie Rutter.
        p.   cm.
    Includes bibliographical references and index.
    ISBN 0-465-01037-7
    1. Psychology, Pathological. 2. Developmental psychology.
I. Rutter, Marjorie, 1937- . II. Title
RC454.4.R87   1992
155—dc20   92-52739
                                                                 CIP

First published by
Penguin Books Ltd
27 Wrights Lane
London, England

93 94 95 96 RRD 9 8 7 6 5 4 3 2 1

Contents

Preface

The idea of writing this book goes back many years. One of us, Michael Rutter, has taught courses on development for psychiatrists in general training for a quarter of a century. From the start, the lack of adequate texts was frustrating. It was not that there was any shortage of excellent books on child development, but that none of them considered development in terms that placed emphasis on the issues of most relevance to clinicians, and most gave more information than appropriate for this group. Also, most stopped in adolescence with little, if any, consideration of the ways in which developmental concerns may be relevant for what happens in adult life. Our good friend, Fraida Sussenwein, was experiencing similar frustrations in teaching development to social workers, with most of the books aimed at that audience being very light on empirical research findings and rather heavy on outmoded theories. She urged the need for a readable, non-technical, book that would fill these gaps and, over the years, she tried repeatedly to persuade Michael Rutter to take on the challenge. A dozen years ago, he edited an academic book (*Scientific Foundations of Developmental Psychiatry*) that sought to cover some of this ground. It was generally well received but it fell short of the initial aspirations of integrating developmental and clinical perspectives and of providing a life-span approach; moreover it also aimed to be an academic textbook, leaving the need for a less technical presentation. During the 1980s, Marjorie Rutter started to teach a course on development for nurses and to integrate developmental perspectives into her teaching on psychosexual and well-woman counselling. Joint discussions between us made us appreciate that the same needs applied to this audience and that her viewpoint, as someone clinically involved with adults, added a valuable complementary perspective. At the same time, Michael Rutter had moved in a major way into life-span developmental research and began to feel more ready to take on Fraida Sussenwein's challenge. Accordingly, we started to plan this joint volume, an enterprise strengthened by our joint teaching of a short course on developmental psychopathology across the life span organized by Albert Einstein College of Medicine, where, in 1961–2, Michael Rutter received training in child development with Herbert Birch, the comparative psychologist, who first excited his interest in the importance of approaching clinical problems from a developmental perspective.

Marjorie Rutter wishes to record her view, not shared by Michael Rutter, that the joint writing of this book has been a rather uneven division of labour. Certainly, it is the case that the developmental concepts, and the review of the empirical research findings, has been mainly the responsibility of Michael Rutter. However, the overall approach presented here represents the joint thinking of two people, one (Michael Rutter) whose clinical work is mainly, but not entirely, concerned with children and one (Marjorie Rutter) whose clinical work is with adults. In writing together, it has been necessary also to blend the knowledge and experience of an empirical developmental researcher (Michael Rutter) with those of a clinician who kept bringing him back to the issue of how research was relevant to work with clients and patients. We might have incorporated the term developmental psychopathology into the title, as that is the approach we have espoused. However, we did not, because the main emphasis is on developmental concepts and findings, rather than on psychiatric disorders as such. The joint writing of the book has been fun, as well as illuminating, in forcing us to clarify our thinking about what was involved in the process of development and why it was relevant across the life span, and not just in childhood. We hope that the result proves to be of both interest and assistance to clinicians of all disciplines who are concerned with psychosocial difficulties in young and old.

Organization of this book

Anyone who writes about development is faced with the dilemma of how to organize the discussion of ideas and research
findings in order to convey the most realistic impression of what
is involved in developmental processes. Because the most important goal is an understanding of the mediating mechanisms, we
have chosen a tripartite structure for the book. The first three
chapters focus on principles and causal processes that apply
broadly across different domains of development (emotions,
cognition, etc.) and across time periods (infancy, adolescence,
etc.). The first of these chapters sets the scene in terms of the
main concepts that apply to development as a whole and the
next two chapters provide more detailed accounts of specific
mechanisms. Although written in non-technical language, Chapters 2 and 3 inevitably involve the introduction of a set of ideas
that may be unfamiliar to many readers. Accordingly, in order
to aid an understanding of what is involved, they are returned
to, with fuller examples, in the next two sections of the book.
The middle section takes three broad domains of psychological
functioning and considers their course of development across the
life span, in order to emphasize the complex mix of continuities
and discontinuities that operates. The third, and last, section
seeks to note the interconnections between different facets of
functioning as they apply to transitions and turning-points in
development by considering three age periods in greater detail.
In order to emphasize life-span considerations, post-childhood
age periods have been chosen for this purpose. The last chapter
ends by a brief bringing together of a few of the main underlying
concepts that have had a key role in earlier chapters. It will be
apparent from this outline of our approach that the book is
meant to be read as a whole.

A further dilemma, in covering as wide a territory as we have
in this book, has been the problem of deciding how to reference
the many empirical studies that form the basis for our conclusions. To list them all would have resulted in a hopelessly long
bibliography and would have cluttered the text with references
to an extent that would have interfered with readability. Never-

theless, as empiricists, we regard it as most important that readers should be able to access the evidence and judge matters for themselves. Our compromise has been to cite specific studies when we have wished to emphasize a particular research point, or when more general reviews have not been available, but otherwise to reference review books or articles that consider the evidence from many studies in more detail. In many cases, such reviews have appeared as chapters in multi-authored edited volumes; in these cases we have referenced only the book as a whole, but have indicated the authors whose chapters we have cited. Because our emphasis is on those aspects of development that are particularly important in their clinical implications, we have mainly relied on reviews that reflect that perspective. This has meant a greater use of Michael Rutter's reviews than would otherwise be warranted.

Acknowledgments

We are unusually fortunate in having as friends and colleagues some of the most creative thinkers and empirical researchers in the field of life-span development, and it is obvious from our frequent references to their work throughout this book that we are indebted to them in ways that are far too numerous to list. We would like to place on record our very great appreciation of the immense amount that we have learned from them over the years. Four individuals, however, require special mention: the late Herbert Birch, who first fired Michael Rutter's interest in the interface between development and clinical issues; the late Jack Tizard, who introduced him to the importance of an epidemiological approach to developmental questions; Robert Hinde, who, over the last two dozen years, has been immensely influential in shaping his thinking about developmental matters; and Norman Garmezy whose ideas on vulnerability and resilience have done so much to create the field of research into risk and protective factors in development. It is obvious, too, that both of us have learned much from our patients; indeed to a large extent it is clinical issues that have forced us to think about the role of developmental factors.

An earlier draft of this book was reviewed by Simon Baron-Cohen, Robert Goodman, Dale Hay, Christine Rutter and Emily Siminoff, and we would like to express our great thanks to them for their many helpful suggestions and incisive comments. As with many previous books, Joy Maxwell was immensely helpful in preparing figures, chasing down references, and in making valuable suggestions on wording. Her contribution has been invaluable.

We are also grateful to the following for permission to reproduce previously published material:

Academic Press Inc. (London), Ltd (6.2, 6.3); Academic Press Inc., US (9.8); American Association on Mental Retardation (6.5); American Psychological Association (3.5, 7.3, 7.4, 8.4); *Australian Journal of Psychology* (8.8); Avebury, Ashgate Publishing (2.12); Basil Blackwell Ltd (4.2); Cambridge University Press (8.7); Cambridge University Press and Dr Anders Ericsson (9.9, 9.10); Cambridge University Press and Professor N. Kreitman (9.5, 9.6); Castlemead Publications (7.2); *Child Development*, Society for Research in Child Development (6.6, 6.7); Cornell University Press (8.2, 8.3); *Family Planning Perspectives*, Alan Gutmacher Institute (7.5); Gower Publishing Group (2.11); Harvard University Press (3.6, 7.6); Haworth Press Inc. and Springer Publishing Co. Inc. (9.4); Her Majesty's Stationery Office and Professor David Farrington (5.2); *International Audiology*, S. Karger AG, Switzerland, and Springer Publishing Co. Inc. (9.7); *Journal of the American Academy of Child and Adolescent Psychiatry* (2.7, 2.10); *Journal of Child Psychology and Psychiatry* (3.7, 4.1); *Journal of Child Psychology and Psychiatry* and Professor Rutter (3.12, 3.13); *Journal of Marriage and the Family* (9.1); *Journal of Pediatrics* (3.2); Lawrence Erlbaum Associates Inc. (3.8); *Nature*, Macmillan Magazines Ltd (2.8); Open Books (3.3); Oxford University Press, Inc., New York (2.1, 3.9, 3.10); *Pediatrics*, American Academy of Pediatrics (3.4); Penguin Books Ltd (8.1); Plenum Publishing Corporation (3.1); Policy Studies Institute (2.4); *Scientific American* (6.1, 7.1); *Social Psychiatry*, Springer-Verlag, Heidelberg (9.3); *Society for Research in Child Development* (2.13); University of Chicago Press (5.1); University of Chicago Press and Springer Publishing Co. Inc. (9.2); University of Minnesota Press (2.3); John Wiley & Sons Ltd (3.11, 9.11); Williams & Wilkins Co., Baltimore (2.2).

Developing Minds

Chapter 1

Introduction:
Concepts of Development

The development of children is a never-ending source of wonder to all fond parents and grandparents. The sources of that wonder are, however, many and varied. Sometimes it is the extent of change, as children acquire language or gain control over their environment. We are forced to question how on earth children extract enough sense out of the 'booming, buzzing confusion' (as William James described it) of their external world for them to learn to speak and, moreover, to acquire complex language skills so amazingly rapidly. Sometimes, it is the extent of individuality that astounds us. How can two children brought up apparently in the same way by the same parents be so incredibly different? Why is John such an ebullient, outgoing, confident boy when Peter is such a timid, shy, solitary child? Alternatively, we may ponder over questions of continuity and discontinuity. Is our brash, assertive adolescent son really the same person as the compliant, cooperative boy that he seemed to be a mere couple of years ago? Are the troubles that Jane is experiencing in keeping her friends at age twelve a consequence of her parents' divorce when she was three?

Traditional theories of development have tended to focus on the first of these questions. Often psychological growth has been viewed in terms of a systematic progression through a series of stages, which occur in a predetermined order, which all children pass through, and each one of which takes the child nearer to the maturity represented by adult functioning. For the most part, there has been a concentration on the universals of development, rather than on individual differences. Thus, Freudian theory emphasized psychosexual stages: oral, anal, phallic, latency and genital. Piaget, by contrast, focused on cognitive mechanisms in the progression from the sensorimotor stage of infancy through the preoperational and concrete operational stages of childhood to the formal operations stage (in which logical reasoning comes to the fore) of adolescence onwards. Kohlberg extended the approach to moral development, with stages representing different levels of moral maturity (preconventional, conventional, etc.). Gesell charted development in terms of a series of milestones in physical, motor and perceptual domains. Erikson, too, saw development as a progression through stages, but differed from the others in his emphasis on the importance of interactions with society and in the extension of development into and through adult life. His focus was on psychosocial transitions, with stages characterized by age-defined social tasks and crises involving features such as identity, intimacy and generativity.

Each of these pioneers, and many others, contributed greatly to our understanding of the various processes involved in development.[75] Thus, Gesell drew attention to the extent to which function is determined by biological maturation; Piaget to cognitive mechanisms; Freud to children's inner mental life involving both strong emotions and the interpretation of experiences; and Erikson to social events, many of which did not occur until after the years of childhood. Nevertheless, despite their central place in most textbooks of child development, these are not the issues or ideas to which we will pay most attention in our discussion of personal development. In part, that is because we want to focus on the questions of individuality and of links over time rather than the universals of growth. However, in part, too, it is because the 'big' theories provide such an inadequate portrayal of what development is all about. By concentrating on stages, they imply a mechanical predictability that is out of keeping with the dynamics of change, the extent of the flux over time and the degree of individual variability that seem to be the case. Moreover, the assumption appears to be that there is just one developmental path that is followed by everyone and that there is a fixed end-point of normal maturity. That does not fit with what we know about socio-emotional development; it is likely that children take a variety of paths, and adult outcome cannot sensibly be reduced to mere differences in levels of maturity.

However, there are three other major limitations to the 'big' theories that deter us from making much use of them. The first is that no one theory constitutes anything like a complete explanation of developmental processes. Most pay lip-service to the role of genetic factors in development, the importance of biological maturation and the relevance of brain pathology. However, usually these influences are passed over rather rapidly as variables to be invoked as playing an unspecified role when other explanations have failed to account for everything. Only very rarely is there any attempt to provide even the most elementary form of integration. The second is that most theories seem to ignore children's social life despite the fact that personal relationships are such a crucial part of our heritage as social beings. Friendships with other children, play, relationships between brothers and sisters, and love relationships all play a fairly minor role in Freudian, Piagetian and Eriksonian concepts of development. As a consequence, there has been a need to develop new concepts; for example, those put forward by writers such as Kagan,[236] Stern[459] and Dunn and Plomin.[128] Psychosexual and operational stages have given way to a focus on attachment,[52,53] on the ways in which one relationship influences others,[208,211] on the development of social understanding[126] and on the ways in which children make inferences about other people's thoughts and beliefs (see Astington *et al.*,[7] Dodge[346] and Whiten[499]). The third point is that each of the 'big' theories has been shown to be wrong, or at least seriously lacking in some of the concepts that are central to the theory.[267]

For all these reasons, no one theoretical perspective shapes our account of personal development. Even so, throughout the book we will be seeking explanations in terms of underlying processes. The mindless collection of factual information is not the way that science proceeds and facts in themselves are of no use to the clinician unless they can be used to infer mechanisms. Accordingly, at all times, our aim will be to seek to bring conceptual order into factual chaos. In order to do that we will place particular reliance on experimental approaches, both contrived and natural,[397] and on the use of longitudinal data to study changes in individual behaviour over time in relation to specific experiences,[406] as both are needed to test hypotheses on mechanisms. The result is not the science fiction of a tidy comprehensive model. However, research has certainly clarified our understanding of some of the processes involved; also some of the answers challenge long-established preconceptions. Our goal is to convey something of the interest and excitement of the new ideas and to do so in ways that are relevant to clinicians and practitioners working with adults as well as children.

In that connection, it has been necessary to broaden the focus on individuality. We have to ask whether clinical disorders and problems represent the extremes of dimensions that apply to everyone, or categories that are different in kind. No general answer to that question can be expected. We know for sure that some disorders *are* qualitatively distinct from normality. For example, it is clear that the causes of severe mental handicap are quite different from those that account for variations in intelligence within the normal range. In most cases the handicap is due to some overt disease or damage to the brain. Thus, Down's syndrome is the commonest single cause and this is the result of a chromosome anomaly. Although there are partial cases of Down's syndrome, for the most part a person either has or doesn't have the condition. It makes no sense to think of everyone having the syndrome to varying degrees.

However, there are many psychological disorders where it is quite plausible to suggest that they might constitute extreme variations of abnormal traits or exaggerations of a normal developmental phase. Thus, almost everyone sometimes feels sad or miserable; but are depressive conditions extreme varieties of this tendency? Or, many adolescent girls in our society worry about their body shape and adopt extreme diets in an attempt to become thin. Is anorexia nervosa merely an extreme manifestation of this phenomenon or does the fact that it sometimes leads to death make it different? Of course, similar questions apply in adult life. Is alcoholism the next stage on from 'normal' heavy drinking or is it a disease that is quite different? In most instances, firm answers are not yet available to these questions. However, it is important to seek answers because they are likely to shed light on the mechanisms involved and hence suggest ways of helping the individuals suffering from the problems.

Two points need to be made at the start. First, the relevant dimension may take a number of different forms. It may concern some characteristic that operates at all ages as it is thought to apply to temperamental variables. Some people are, by their nature (however caused), much more timid and fearful than others. Are anxiety states or phobias mainly a function of someone being extreme on that trait? Alternatively, the dimension may apply to a developmental phase such as the moodiness and unhappiness that seem to become more common during adolescence. Is the rise in depressive conditions and in attempted suicide that takes place at much the same age period part of the same phenomenon or does it have a rather different set of causes? The second point is that within an overall group of disorders, the answer may be different for sub-varieties. Thus it could be that the severe types of depression that lead to hospital admission, and which may alternate with periods of manic excitement (so-called 'bipolar' affective disorders), are qualitatively distinct, whereas more ordinary 'out-patient' types of depression consti-tute extremes of normality. The possibility of a major difference between these two broad types is suggested, for example, by the finding that genetic factors are very important in the former but play only a minor role in the latter.[300] Because some psychologi-cal disorders may represent, as it were, extremes of normality (in which both genetic and environmental factors play a role), we shall discuss development with an eye to the possible implications for disorder.

In the chapters that follow, many specifics of development are considered. However, in order that the details may be seen in the context of the whole, we need to begin by outlining some general principles and concepts.[408] The first derives from the points already made about psychological disorders: namely, that there can be no presupposition that normal and abnormal develop-ment do, or do not, show the same mechanisms; or do, or do not, exhibit the same qualities; rather there must be a concern to use empirical research to test for similarities and dissimilarities. It is to be expected that both will be found.

Second, we shall be adopting a life-span perspective, in which developmental concepts are extended beyond the years of childhood into adult life. It is a mistake to assume that development stops with the attainment of physical maturity; it does not. We are social beings and our psychological functioning is influenced by the interactions and transactions we have with our social environment. Because social experiences such as marriage or childbearing tend not to occur during the childhood years, social development needs to be considered in relation to what happens during adult life as well as in relation to the happenings of early life. However, there are several other reasons for a life-span approach. As we shall argue in the next chapter, experiences in adult life have a history and background and do not just happen by chance. It is necessary to ask, not only what are the psychological effects of marriage, but also why did the individual marry this particular person at that time? How did the experience arise? Also, we have to consider whether the way in which an individual deals with a specific adult experience is influenced by past experiences. Finally, with any experience (whether internal or external), it is necessary to ask *how* it brings about its effects and to inquire whether the sequelae are of a kind likely to be evanescent or carried forward into future years. As we shall see, this perspective has implications even for old age, where some of the changes thought to be an inevitable direct consequence of physical ageing prove not to be so.

Third, our perspective will be biological, as any discussion of development has to be. Biology, of course, comprises an emphasis on both intrinsic and experiential influences on development. Genetic factors play an important role in shaping both individual differences in psychological characteristics and also the pattern of their development over time. The physical maturation of the brain will have necessary consequences for the working of the mind. Also, physiological transitions not primarily involving the structure of the brain, but which involve major changes in hormonal output and in bodily configuration (as is the case with puberty), will have psychological consequences. However, development is also affected by environmental factors that are not accompanied by any somatic alteration (other than that which is intrinsic to learning). Thus, experiences within and outside the home have been shown to make an impact on intellectual and behavioural development.

The next three considerations also derive from a biological perspective. The fourth, very basic, concept is that both continuities and discontinuities are to be expected. The process of development is concerned with change and it is quite unreasonable to suppose that the pattern will be set in early life. The growth of cognitive skills and understanding, physiological alterations (such as those associated with puberty) and new experiences will all serve to shape psychological functioning. In some cases, the effects will be so radical and far-reaching that to some extent they constitute a break from what has gone before. However, continuities will also occur because children carry with them the results of earlier learning, and of earlier structural and functional change.

Fifth, the *timing*, as well as the nature, of experiences is likely to influence their impact on development. The importance of timing arises for several different reasons. To begin with, the effects on neural structure and functioning will be influenced by what is happening at the time in neural development. Examples of this are provided by the effects of prenatal sex hormones on brain organization and sexually dimorphic behaviours in later life and by the varying effects of brain damage at later ages. Also, the effects will be influenced by sensitivities and vulnerabilities deriving from the psychological processes that are emerging at that age. Thus, it is probable that very young infants are relatively protected from the ill-effects of separation experiences because they have yet to develop strong selective attachments to other people; older children are protected because they have learned how to maintain relationships even when the other person is not physically present; but older infants and toddlers are most at risk because attachments are first becoming established at this age and because they lack the cognitive skills required to maintain a relationship during an absence.

In addition, timing may be important because experiences may be felt differently, or give rise to different societal responses, if they arise at non-normative times (i.e. times other than those that might ordinarily be expected in the culture). For example, this may apply to the links between teenage pregnancy and difficulties in parenting; to the increased risk of divorce associated with marriage at an unusually young age; and to the greater stresses associated with forced redundancy in middle life compared with voluntary retirement in old age.

Sixth, it is crucial to appreciate that children, as well as adults, are *active* creatures. It makes no sense to conceive of experiences as external forces impinging on a passive organism. This is seriously misleading because of two rather different considerations. On the one hand, people are not completely at the mercy of fate; to a considerable extent they are able to select and shape their own experiences. On the other hand, given any particular experience, it is necessary to consider how people deal with it. Events, challenges and life transitions do not just happen to people. People respond to them, and cope with them, in different ways, so that it is necessary to focus on the process of *negotiation* of life experiences and not just on their impact. This negotiation comprises not just what people *do* about the experience but also how they *think* and *feel* about it. Were they oppressed by the increased responsibilities associated with promotion at work or were they invigorated by the new challenges? Did they see the exam failure as a reflection of their general hopelessness or as an indication of a specific problem that needed to be tackled in another way?

A seventh consideration is the need to take into account individual differences in the meaning of, and response to, such transitions. Thus, parenthood that arises as an unplanned and unwelcome outcome of casual sex or rape at the age of fifteen will not be the same as a wanted child being born to a young adult in the context of a happy marriage, and both of these will differ from the experience of having a first child after more than a decade's unsuccessful attempts to conceive even after multiple medical and surgical treatments for relative infertility. All three will differ yet again from parenthood as a result of artificial insemination by donor, or adoption, or fostering.

A further principle to be borne in mind when examining development over time is that continuity may be heterotypic as well as homotypic. In other words, we must recognize the possibility that behaviours may change in *form* while still reflecting the same *process*. The butterfly looks nothing like a caterpillar, yet we know that the one developed from the other. If we had not seen it, would we envisage a tadpole growing into a frog? The issue, then, is whether there are similar (albeit less dramatic) alterations in form during the course of psychological development. There are numerous methodological difficulties in testing for this possibility. For obvious reasons, the mere fact that one behaviour is regularly followed by a different behaviour at a later age does not mean that the latter grew out of the former. In infancy, sitting is regularly followed by talking but no one supposes that the mechanisms involved in the two are the same. Nevertheless, there are some well-demonstrated changes in form that are known to reflect the same underlying process. For example, this is the case with the continuity between social isolation, peer rejection, odd unpredictable behaviour and attention deficits in childhood, and the emergence of a schizophrenic psychosis in adult life (see Rutter and Garmezy[204]). Within the field of normal development it probably also applies to the link between attention in infancy and problem-solving intelligence in later childhood.[45]

A ninth issue is that it is necessary to consider both risk *and* protective factors, together with interactions between them. Both good and bad experiences influence development. However, it is also crucial that some experiences that seem negative at the time may nevertheless be protective. It is obvious that this is so with respect to somatic functioning. Thus, resistance to infections does not come from positive healthy experiences but rather from 'successful' encounters with the infective agent either naturally or deliberately by creating exposure to the bacterium or virus in a modified or attenuated form (the basis of immunization). Similarly, resistance to acute specific stress comes from experiencing such stresses and coping successfully with them, *not* from avoidance of stressful experiences. It may well be that the same applies to people's responses to chronic psychosocial adversities. For example, Elder[133] found that many older children who had to take on family responsibilities during the economic depression of the 1930s, and who did so successfully, emerged from the experience psychologically strengthened by it.

A fundamental developmental consideration, especially from a

life-span perspective, is that often continuities derive from indirect chain and strand effects, as well as from direct influences.
What this means is that in many cases the long-term impact of
some experience, or intrinsic change, in early childhood may lie
more in the fact that it sets in motion a chain reaction than in
any persistence of the immediate behavioural consequence. For
example, academic success at school is likely to increase the
chance of better living conditions and a well-paid job in adult
life – *not* because passing exams alters personality but simply
because academic credentials open the door to career advancement, which in turn is associated with a range of social advantages
in adult life.

A basic concern in any study of development is the elucidation
of the processes and mechanisms involved in such indirect and
direct continuities over time. That means that if we are to make
practical use of knowledge of risk and protective factors, we
need to know *how* they operate. For example, there is good
evidence that adaptive psychosocial outcomes are more likely if
children have a high sense of self-esteem and a positive social
orientation; if their family exhibits warmth, harmony and cohesion; and if adequate social supports are available. However, if
we are to be able to bring about this happy state of affairs in
order to foster normal development, we must go on to ask *how*
self-esteem develops, which experiences or biological qualities
are most likely to foster it and by which mechanisms it operates.
The last point is important if we are to differentiate between risk
indicators and risk *processes*; a crucial consideration in planning
successful preventive or therapeutic interventions. For example,
a comparative study of mental hospitals a generation ago[64]
showed that one of the best indicators of a poor institution in
which patients did badly was a lack of personal toothbrushes.
Obviously, this was because it represented a pervasive lack of
concern for the people as individuals; no one would suppose
that, if nothing else was done, it would make much difference to
distribute toothbrushes to all patients. However, very frequently,
it is not so obvious whether or not an association directly reflects
a risk process. For example, poor living conditions are associated
with an increased risk of child psychiatric disorder. Does this

mean that the risk would be reduced by the provision of improved housing? Experience suggests not, at least not necessarily so. It is desirable in its own right to improve housing conditions, but whether or not this has psychological benefits will depend on whether the new housing is associated with better or worse *social* circumstances.

Our round dozen of developmental concepts and principles is completed by noting that age is an ambiguous variable. Developmentalists naturally focus their attention on the ways in which people change as they grow older. There is an accompanying temptation to assume that increasing age *explains* the developmental process but obviously it does not. That is because age indexes so many different features. This is so even if attention is confined to 'internal' characteristics. Is it the structural and chemical maturation of the brain that matters, or is it the altered patterns of sex hormones or is the crucial feature the increase in cognitive skills and understanding? But, of course, age does not only reflect intrinsic maturation, it also represents changing social experiences. Is it these, rather than the intrinsic bodily changes, that are responsible for the psychological developments? Again, if we are to make *use* of knowledge on age changes we must know what they mean. This is no academic matter, as the connections between these different facets of age vary enormously. For example, the father of one of us left school in the early years of this century to start work at twelve, well before reaching puberty; by contrast our son had his first regular job only after completing medical training in his mid-twenties, many years after reaching physical maturity. How did their psychological development differ as a result of the very different pattern of disjunctions between biological maturity and economic independence?

With these considerations in mind, we need to turn to some of the specifics of development. Because our focus throughout will be on the ways in which people differ in their development, we start with a discussion of some of the possible reasons why people are so different from one another.

Chapter 2

Why are People So Different from One Another?

Maturation

In seeking to understand why people differ from one another, it is appropriate to begin with the notion of biological maturation as, in a real sense, that has to constitute the basis of growth. It is not, of course, just a question of children growing bigger, or of their physical and mental capacities increasing. Maturation also involves qualitative change. That is obvious in the case of the major alterations in physique and the development of primary and secondary sexual characteristics that accompany puberty. But there are numerous other, less obvious, examples. For example, the body's immune system alters as a result of exposure to infectious agents; moreover it does so in different ways according to the age at which the infections are encountered.[42] Also, the normal development of the visual cortex of the brain is dependent on visual input. Experimental studies of the cat have shown conclusively that if one eye is blindfolded or cut off from patterned input (as by wearing an opaque lens), the visual cortex of the brain fails to develop normally (see Blakemore[42]). There is one very important medical consequence of this phenomenon. If children have a strabismus (squint) that is not corrected in the early years of childhood, binocular vision will fail to develop. These examples bring out a most important consideration; namely, that biological maturation is influenced by experience. There is a two-way flow between soma and psyche. This applies, not just to maturation, but to functioning throughout life. There is sometimes a tendency to assume that once a biological abnormality has been established, it must be basic to, and causal of, the psychological disorder with which it has been found to be associated. Of course, often (probably usually) it is, but the causal arrow may run in the other direction, or in both directions. Rutter[403] cited as an example that an increase in the level of the male sex hormone, testosterone, leads to a rise in assertive behaviour but, equally, defeat (as in a competitive game of tennis!) leads to a drop in hormone levels;[379] also one study[356] showed that getting patients to act as if they were depressed or manic led to the biochemical changes associated with depression or mania.

These findings indicate the need for caution in any assumptions that maturational influences must be primary. Nevertheless, it is clear that psychological development must be heavily dependent on biological maturation. The functioning of the mind has to be influenced to a major extent by the structure and organization of the brain. The question is whether maturational variations play a significant role in individual psychological differences. The possibility is certainly there because it is well established that children vary greatly in the pace of their maturation. This is readily apparent in the timing of puberty. Many textbooks on development have striking pictures of two children exactly the same age but of wildly different physique – two fourteen-year-old boys, one of whom is a well-built six-footer looking very much a man whereas the other is a five-foot stripling who still has the appearance of a young boy, or two girls of twelve or thirteen, one of whom appears a mature woman whereas the other is still a child without any indication that she is about to enter puberty.

Could comparable differences in the maturation of the brain explain, say, why some children have quite an extensive vocabulary at eighteen months whereas others are only just beginning to talk at the age of three? Or why some boys are still wetting the bed at fourteen whereas others are out of nappies at two? Doubtless that is the explanation in some instances. It would be surprising if it were not the case. There are known to be substantial individual differences in all aspects of biological maturation (thus, the variations in age of puberty are paralleled by variations of equal degree in the timing of the eruption of teeth). It must be expected that these biological differences will have some functional implications.

Nevertheless, there are very considerable difficulties in sorting out the role of maturational factors in individual psychological differences. The first problem is that knowledge is lacking on just how brain structure and function interconnect. That they are connected is not in doubt, but the question is *how*. It cannot be assumed that all delays in psychological development represent normal variations. We know that they do not because some children with specific delays in language never fully catch up (see Rutter and Mawhood[415]); because some children with early damage to the brain mainly exhibit sequelae in the form of specific delays in development (see Casaer *et al.*[415]); and because extreme environmental privation can cause serious developmental delays (see Puckering and Rutter[506]). A major constraint in studying the links between structure and function lies in the adequacy of our tools to investigate the workings of the brain during life. Of course, the new brain imaging techniques have greatly increased our ability to do this but there is still a long way to go.

The second difficulty is a reflection of the first. Because we lack direct measures of brain maturation, there is a tendency to rely on chronological age as a proxy measure. However, quite apart from the fact that this conceals huge individual differences in rate of maturation, age indexes far more than maturation.[407] Let us take the rise in depressive feelings during adolescence as an example (see Rutter[166]). The details are discussed in Chapter 7, but at this point we may note that there is a considerable range of possibilities to consider. Is the rise a result of the hormonal changes of puberty, of a switching on of genes, of cognitive maturity, of a loss of social support (as the young people develop independence from their parents but have yet to have a love relationship), or of an increase in life stressors (with national exams, starting work or unemployment, broken love affairs, etc.)? It is obvious that the mere finding of an association with age tells us nothing about the mechanisms. Age is an ambiguous summary variable and it is necessary to break it down into the numerous facets of maturation and of experience that age represents before causal processes can be inferred.

It must be added that the stimulus and the causal mechanism underlying the psychological feature need not be the same. Two very different examples may serve to illustrate this very important point. Stattin and Magnusson[286,458] found that Swedish girls who reached puberty unusually early (menarche under the age of eleven) showed a much higher rate of misbehaviour (getting drunk, staying out late, taking drugs, etc.) at the age of fourteen than did girls who matured either late or at the usual time. There was every reason to suppose that this was a true association, with early puberty as the stimulus. However, further analyses showed that the mechanism was social, even though the stimulus was physiological. The increase in misbehaviour was shown to be a function of the fact that many of these early-maturing girls went round with groups of much older girls. Those whose friends continued to be of the same age did *not* show any excess of norm-breaking behaviour.

The other example concerns the observation that the sequelae of organic abnormalities of the brain already present in infancy may not become manifest until adolescence. For example, it has been found that about a fifth of autistic children develop epilepsy, but the usual time for epileptic seizures to begin in autistic individuals is not until adolescence or even early adult life.[115,390] Of course, in this example, there has already been one consequence – autistic behaviour – but it appears that some aspect of brain maturation may need to take place before this is accompanied by a high risk of epilepsy. Something similar may apply with schizophrenia. It has been found that schizophrenia is associated with both structural abnormalities of the brain and possibly also abnormalities of the mother's pregnancy (see Murray[42] and Jones and Murray[301]). There is some doubt as to whether the latter are a reflection of a genetic abnormality or an indication of something going wrong in the womb or the birth process but, either way, they seem to index some form of organic risk. What is interesting is that this is not manifest in the form of schizophrenia until the psychosis develops in adolescence or later. We do not know why this is so but it has been suggested that the answer is related to the maturation of neuro-transmitters; the brain was damaged much earlier but this did not show in behaviour until sufficient maturation had taken place for the functional results to be evident.[491] We are only just beginning to understand these brain processes, but the implication of both examples is that some aspect of brain maturation may, as it were, unmask the consequences of damage or disease already present from many years earlier.

We may conclude that it is indeed likely that maturational influences play a role in psychological functioning, probably more so than is sometimes appreciated, but by the same token their effects are quite complex and far from easy to unravel.

Genetic Influences

In the past it was usual to divide influences into two components: genetic and environmental. For years there was vigorous and impassioned debate over the relative importance of nature and nurture. During the 1950s, 1960s and 1970s many social scientists sought to argue that environmental influences were overwhelmingly more important than genetic ones. For example, Floud and her colleagues[157] argued that 'it is well known that intelligence is largely an acquired characteristic' (p. 65). The dismissal of genetic factors arose for a variety of reasons: a wholly appropriate concern to improve the lot of socially disadvantaged children; a fatalistic view that nothing could be done about genetic effects; a distrust of the genetic evidence; and a distaste arising from the misuse of genetics in support of racist policies. The last concern was much fuelled by Jensen's seminal article in 1969, in which he argued that Headstart had failed and that the lower IQ scores (on average) of blacks in US society, as compared with whites, were genetically determined. His position was not intended to be racist but his arguments (which were mistaken in certain key respects)[401,411,416] were certainly used by racists. As a consequence, anyone in the 1970s who attempted to suggest that genetic factors might be important influences on any psychological function was likely to be greeted by abuse from their audience.

All of this has changed during the last decade and genetic research constitutes one of the major growth areas in psychology and psychiatry. The change has come about first because improvements in traditional genetic research strategies led to convincing evidence of the importance of genetic factors in a wide range of human behaviour, both normal and abnormal.[350,414] That that is so can no longer be in serious doubt. The strength of the evidence stems from the degree to which different research strategies all point in the same direction. Each strategy has the objective of separating the effects of nature and nurture, but does so in different ways. The classical method involved the comparison of identical (monozygotic or MZ) twin pairs with fraternal or non-identical (dizygotic or DZ) twin pairs. MZ pairs have all their genes in common whereas DZ pairs share, on average, half their genes. In so far as MZ pairs are more alike than DZ pairs, this suggests the importance of genetic factors. However, it is possible that this could arise from parents being more likely to treat identical twins in the same way. In fact, the evidence suggests that, to the extent that they do, this is because they are *responding* to similarities in the twins' behaviour rather than causing them (see Plomin[350] and Scarr and Kidd[190]). This is shown, for example, by the finding that when parents are mistaken in their belief that their twin children are MZ or DZ, the twin similarities are more a function of *actual* zygosity than of perceived zygosity; by the evidence that the extent to which they are treated similarly is not related to their resemblance on most characteristics; and by the high correlations, in IQ, for example, found between MZ twins reared apart.

Adoption provides a rather different method of separating nature and nurture. In this case, the extent to which children resemble their biological parents who did *not* bring them up suggests genetic influences, whereas the extent to which they resemble their adoptive parents, with whom they have no blood relationship, suggests environmental influences. There are numerous variations in research designs that can help test genetic and environmental hypotheses. What is striking is that where it has been possible to use a wide range of genetic strategies (as, for example, with both IQ and schizophrenia), the result has been the demonstration of a substantial genetic influence. The strength of the effect varies somewhat according to the particular psychological characteristic being considered but, overall, it seems that genetic factors account for some 30–60 per cent of the variation between individuals in the general population.

However, a more positive approach to genetics was not just a consequence of the strength of the evidence on genetic effects: it was also fostered by a realization that a fatalistic view of genetics was seriously misleading and by an appreciation that genetic research strategies constituted some of the most powerful tools for demonstrating the reality of environmental influences and were highly informative in pointing to some of the specifics in environmental effects.[411]

We began this section by referring to the division of influences into genetic and environmental in the past tense. That was not because the separation has ceased to be informative; on the contrary, it remains a crucial methodological step in research into individual differences. Its placement in the past stems from the evidence that the polarization of nature and nurture is a seriously mistaken notion. There are two main reasons why it is a misleading way of viewing things. The first is that some genes operate mainly through their effect on susceptibility to environmental influences. This is most obvious in relation to certain medical diseases. For example, phenylketonuria (PKU) is a metabolic disorder due entirely to a single major gene. It would be correct to say that it is 100 per cent genetic; environmental influences have a zero effect on the presence of the underlying biochemical abnormality. However, it would also be true to say that its effects are almost entirely environmentally determined! That is because the abnormality comprises an inability to deal with a particular food substance, phenylalanine. Because that substance is part of all ordinary diets, all PKU children show some degree of mental impairment, often severe, if untreated. However, the simple expedient of markedly reducing phenylalanine in the diet largely restores the IQ to normal. The condition is wholly genetic but its effects are wholly environmental (or nearly so, as it is probable that some slight and subtle deficits remain). It sounds paradoxical but it isn't really. That is because the gene operates through its effect on the body's response to the environment. We do not know how much this applies to genetic effects on psychological characteristics. Some findings suggest that those concerned with criminality may operate in this way in part[72] and it is quite possible that others do, too.

Two interconnected types of evidence point in this direction for criminality. First, there is the finding from Scandinavian studies that there was a very low rate of criminality in adopted children for whom neither the biological nor adoptive parents had a criminal record, a marginally higher rate when only an adoptive parent was criminal, a rather higher rate if a biological parent was criminal, but a substantially higher rate if both were (see Cloninger and Gottesman[303]). Second, there is the finding from a couple of studies that adverse environmental factors had an appreciable effect *only* for children who were genetically at risk by virtue of criminality in a biological parent.[73,106] Of course, the occurrence of criminality in the father or mother constitutes a most imperfect index of genetic risk, the range of environmental risks studied has been quite narrow and there are only a handful of adoption studies that enable genetic and environmental influences to be separated in ways that allow interactions to be examined. Accordingly, only tentative conclusions are possible; however, these do suggest that some genetic effects on psychological functions may operate through their influence on susceptibility to environmental adversities.

It has proved difficult to test for gene–environment interactions (the term applied to this altered vulnerability effect) in human psychology.[353] However, the pervasiveness of person–environment interactions in biology generally (a point we discuss below) indicates that they are likely to be found if examined in relation to specific measured environmental influences in the segments of the population to which they apply.[421] The practical importance for these considerations lies in the fact that if genes operate through making people more vulnerable to environmental stressors, the individuals who are most at risk genetically are those who are most susceptible to psychological damage from environmental hazards.

The second reason why nature and nurture are not as separate as once thought is that genes are likely to be important in determining people's exposure to risk environments.[351,431] At first sight the notion that genes could 'cause' the environment seems both troubling and implausible. Of course the environment is not itself caused by genes. Nevertheless, it is quite likely that genes do truly play a substantial role in determining the particular environments to which people are exposed. This arises in three somewhat different ways. First, there is what may be termed a *passive* correlation, such that parents who pass on a particular set of genes will also provide a particular type of environment. Thus, highly intelligent parents will not only transmit genes that affect intelligence but they are also likely to provide a home environment that is more conducive to intellectual development. Similarly, highly musical or sporting or scientific parents will pass on both the genes related to those skills and also an environment in which children are exposed to the exhibition of these skills in ways that may enhance interest and/or provide practice that aids their development.

Second, genes may act through their influence on behaviours that *evoke* particular reactions from other people. For example, children with a very sunny, easy, cheerful disposition are more likely than miserable, difficult children to elicit harmonious, friendly interactions with other people. Thus, we found that when parents were depressed and irritable they were much more likely to snap at, shout at and criticize those of their children who had 'difficult' temperamental styles.[392] It is a commonplace observation that some children are much easier to love and like than others and, in part, this is influenced by genetic factors.

The third way concerns the *active* selection of environments. To a very important extent we choose our environments (or they are chosen for us on the basis of our perceived characteristics). For example, highly intelligent children who read easily are likely to read more books than those for whom reading is a struggle; as a consequence they will have much greater opportunities to learn from reading. Similarly, intellectually gifted children are more likely to be placed in academic schools which, in turn, may provide an environment that is more conducive to scholastic success.[296,399] Naturally extrovert children will go to more social occasions than will children who are less outgoing in temperament. It is curious how little attention up to now has been paid to the crucial question of where life events and experiences come from. Part of the answer lies in genetic effects but there are other explanations, as we argue below. However, the importance of the possibility of gene → environment effects is that it points to the need to consider how far genetic effects operate through an influence on environmental risk factors. In so far as this effect applies, it means that the functional consequences of the genetic influence may be, at least partially, preventable.

Person–Environment Interactions

Most discussions of environmental influences on development tend to assume that they have much the same effect on everyone. Yet it is obvious with ordinary life circumstances that individuals vary greatly in how they respond to the same stress stimulus. Some people have a very short fuse and blow their top at the least frustration or aggravation; others respond calmly, in a matter-of-fact fashion, even when severely provoked. Some people are able to concentrate well on whatever they are doing in spite of a hubbub of noise about them; others can do so only if they have real peace and quiet. The same applies to physical stimuli. We all know people who get an upset stomach with the least change in diet and others who seem to be able to eat almost anything. These everyday observations are borne out by the results of systematic research reviewed by Rutter and Pickles.[421] It is well recognized that there are very marked individual differences in people's susceptibility to infection. There are many reasons for this variability. They include previous exposure to the infectious agent, nutritional state, intercurrent disease and genetic influences. Sometimes one disease may actually protect the person against another. The best-known example of this is the finding that people with the sickle-cell gene in heterozygote form have a much increased resistance to malaria. Another probable example of a protective genetic effect concerns the flushing response to alcohol seen in some individuals of Asiatic extraction. It is known that Asiatic people have a lower rate of alcoholism and it is thought that part of the reason for this is that many Asians experience this unpleasant flushing response to even small amounts of alcohol.

Person–environment interactions also apply to the effects of diet on cholesterol levels. The media frequently emphasize the importance of diet in coronary artery disease and, as a result, many people make strenuous efforts to reduce the cholesterol in their diet. However, for most people, this makes very little difference to the cholesterol levels in their blood; they are able to handle ordinary amounts of cholesterol in their diet and their blood levels are well within the normal range. But people vary greatly in their response to low and high cholesterol diets and in the few who cannot handle dietary cholesterol satisfactorily, diet may be very important. It is known that there are important genetic influences on lipid metabolism and, although the extent to which they operate through modifying responses to dietary variations is not known, it is very likely that this constitutes part of the process. However, it is not just genetic factors that influence the body's response to diet. Studies in baboons have shown that breast-fed and formula-fed animals differ in their response to high cholesterol diets in adult life. The diet in infancy may shape sensitivities to diets in later life (see Mott et al.[42]).

Another example of variations in susceptibility to environmental hazards is provided by the very well established greater vulnerability of boys, compared with girls, to a wide range of physical hazards – spanning malnutrition, infection and irradiation.[130] In many respects, other than in muscle power, males are the weaker sex, although they may not like to think so! The examples that we have given serve to illustrate the general point that across a very wide range of circumstances, individual differences in people's susceptibility to various environmental factors are the rule, and often they are marked.

Does this conclusion apply to psychological, as well as physical, stressors? Almost certainly it does, although the evidence is less extensive than one would like. Perhaps the effect is seen most easily with respect to people's immediate response to stress situations, although the principle probably extends to long–term reactions as well. In recent times, there has been a lot of interest in the marked individual differences between children in their response to unfamiliar, challenging and stressful situations.[237,238] Some young people hang back and appear shy and timid; others seem confident and uninhibited from the outset. This behavioural characteristic has physiological parallels; inhibited children show a brisker autonomic response (as shown, for example, by a larger increase in heart rate). Much the same has been found in monkeys (see Higley and Suomi[251]). One interesting facet of this temperamental feature is that it is not very apparent in ordinary circumstances; it is mainly revealed in challenge situations. The key aspect of individual variability, in this instance, lies in differences in response to environmental stressors. Another way of expressing the same point is that what is disturbingly stressful to one person is pleasantly challenging to another. This temperamental feature shows a moderate degree of consistency over time, but it is influenced by both genetic and environmental factors and is by no means fixed. So far, there is very little evidence on the clinical significance of behavioural inhibition, but it seems that children with this characteristic may be more likely to develop anxiety disorders when they are older.[380]

Lest it be thought that it is only excessive responses to stress that carry risks, we need to note that the reverse also seems to apply. A variety of studies have shown that persistent delinquents or criminals tend to have a *reduced* physiological reactivity to stress (see Venables[303]). The precise meaning of this finding remains uncertain but it seems very likely that it taps into features associated with a greater risk of showing socially disruptive behaviour. The alternatives include the possibility that it reflects a reduced tendency to learn from experience (because there is a diminished responsivity to negative consequences) and the suggestion that the risk derives from an increased tendency for sensation- or excitement-seeking activities (because risks that are unpleasant for most people are positively stimulating to less reactive individuals). Further research is needed to sort out the processes involved but, whatever they prove to be, they seem to involve characteristics that regulate aspects of people's reactivity to their environment.

These considerations lead us to the question of how genetic influences operate in shaping people's behaviour. One of the main blocks to many people's acceptance of the notion that genetic factors may be important is a reluctance to accept that you *could* inherit a tendency to steal or to be bad-tempered or miserable. The reluctance is well based. It does not seem at all likely that specific patterns of behaviour are inherited. With a few possible exceptions (such as autism or schizophrenia or bipolar manic-depressive conditions), it is equally unlikely that psychiatric disorders as such are inherited. It is unlikely because genetic factors rarely predominate – as we have mentioned, they account for about 30–60 per cent of the overall variation in the general population – and because most psychiatric disorders do not show a sharp demarcation from normality. For most of the commoner disorders, it is probable that genetic factors operate through their influence on broader behavioural tendencies of some kind (see Plomin et al.[90]). Moreover, many of these tendencies may be characterized in terms of responsivity to particular features of the environment. Knowledge about these processes is extremely limited at the moment but what *is* evident is that it would be seriously mistaken to assume that the presence of a major genetic component means that some particular out-come is predestined. It is not.

Do Genetic Influences Lessen as We Grow Older?

It is commonly assumed that genetic effects must be maximal at birth, with environmental influences increasing steadily with time. At first sight, it would seem obvious that this must be the case. After all, the genes are all present at birth whereas in infancy the environment has had scarcely any chance to operate. By adolescence the environment has had a dozen years to exert its effects and it would seem to follow that this must mean that genetic effects will have become less important. It therefore comes as a bit of a surprise to learn that, on the contrary, for many psychological features genetic factors become rather *more* important as children grow older, at least up to middle child-hood.[350]

Probably this comes about for several rather different reasons. First, although all DNA is indeed present at birth, this does not mean that genes exert their functional effects at that time. To begin with, it is known that some entirely genetic diseases do not become manifest until middle age. The best-known example is Huntington's disease, in which dementia is the most striking feature, but there are others. The gene, as it were, seems programmed to 'switch on' only after many years have passed. Similarly, the timing of the menarche is fairly strongly influenced by genetic factors but it does not occur until adolescence.

Second, some psychological functions take time to become manifest. Thus, language is not present at birth; rather, children's first words usually appear some time after the first birthday, with language skills growing rapidly over the course of the next few years. Because the early manifestations of language (or intelligence or personality) include only a portion of the final set of skills or attributes, it may be that genetic factors operate to a greater extent on the later appearing features. In so far as that is the case, the impression of increasing genetic factors will be an artefact of measurement. In other words, the measures of cognition or intelligence at, say, eighteen months, have a quite different mix of components to those at, say eighteen years.

Third, the environment does not begin at birth; experiences in the womb also have effects. For obvious reasons, these are much more evident in infancy than later in childhood. In some circumstances, their impact can overwhelm genetic influences for a while. For example, the differences in birth weight between identical twins are *greater*, on average, than between non-identical twins. That is because identical twins may sometimes share their circulation (whereas non-identical twins cannot) and this may lead to one twin 'taking' much of the blood that should be going to the other twin (the so-called foeto-foetal transfusion syndrome).

A fourth reason is that genetic factors play a major role in controlling the developmental process itself (and not just the end-point), whereas this is less the case with environmental influences. Identical twins tend to show the same pattern of ups and downs in development whereas the timing and extent of developmental variations tend to be different in fraternal twins. The consequence is that genetic effects accumulate over time whereas environmental effects show this tendency to a lesser degree.

However, there is also a fifth reason why genetic influences may increase as children grow older; namely, the interplay between genes and environment. On the whole, as pairs of identical twins grow older they continue to show roughly the same degree of similarity. By contrast, non-identical twins tend to grow further apart. Figure 2.1 shows the findings for height (a strongly genetic characteristic) from the Louisville longitudinal twin study.[191] Identical twins tend to become even more alike as they grow older whereas fraternal twins become increasingly different with age. In part this is likely to be due to the cumulative effect of genetic influences. However, the finding also suggests that genetic factors may play a role in moderating environmental effects. It may be inferred that two processes are likely to be operating; first, genetic effects on susceptibility to environmental influences (gene–environment interactions); and second, genetic shaping or selecting of environments (gene–environment correlations). In both cases, the genetic forces will pull environmental effects identically for identical twins but, to a substantial extent, differently for non-identical twins. This latter effect needs to be considered in greater detail under the more general topic of why children differ in their environmental experiences.

Why Do People Differ in Their Experiences?

There is a vast literature on how all manner of environmental stressors and adversities may influence children's behaviour and development. As we shall see, those effects are real enough. However, much less attention has been paid to why some children have a stable, harmonious upbringing whereas others encounter a seemingly endless stream of environmental hazards. Of course, chance must play some part in this variation. Its operation is most obvious with respect to the major natural and man-made disasters such as earthquakes, volcanoes, floods, plane crashes and shipwrecks. However, it is not likely that chance constitutes a sufficient explanation for variations in people's experiences of the more ordinary types of psychosocial stressors such as family discord and break-up, parental depression, scapegoating, overcrowding, homelessness, unemployment, personal rebuffs and lack of social support. Indeed, it is clear that systematic factors of several different kinds are operative.

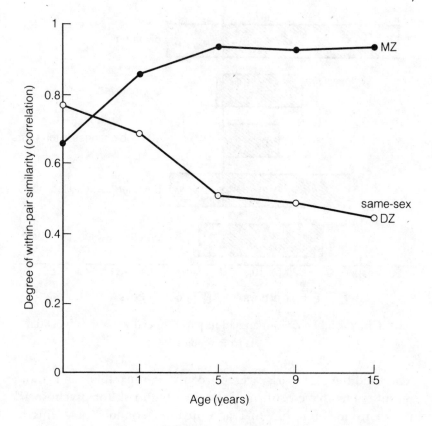

2.1 Within-pair correlations for height (Louisville Twin Study).
Data from Matheny.[295]

Effects of People's Behaviour in Shaping Their Environment

The effects of people's behaviour in shaping their experiences may be seen in both the short term and long term. As the latter are the more dramatic, they may be considered first. Among the stressors in adult life associated with onset of depression are unemployment, break-up of a marriage and lack of friends. Robins's[372] classical follow-up of children who attended a child-guidance clinic showed that antisocial boys were ten times as likely as controls to be unemployed when seen as adults; seven times as likely to have been divorced at least twice; and four times as likely to be practically without friends (see Figure 2.2).

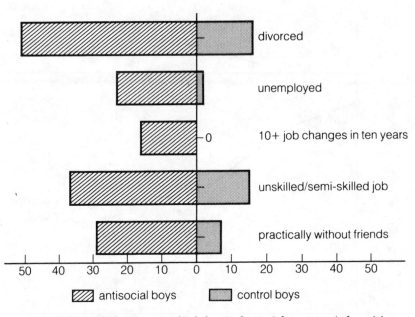

2.2 Childhood behaviour and adult psychosocial stressors/adversities. Data from Robins.[372]

The findings for girls were broadly comparable, and more recent studies have confirmed the very high risk for psychosocial problems in adult life that accompanies conduct problems in childhood.

Usually these results have been considered as showing that the childhood disorder frequently persists into adult life in the form of widespread impairment in social functioning, or personality disturbance. That is a very appropriate way of conceptualizing things, as there is every reason to suppose that the disorder has persisted. However, the point we wish to make is equally applicable; namely that the disorder takes the form of maladaptive ways of dealing with other people and with social roles and tasks. As a consequence, the very features that index personal social maladaptation may also be viewed as 'external' stress experiences. The fact that, to an important extent, the individuals have acted in ways that have brought about those experiences does not make them any less stressful. This is most easily appreciated by thinking of instances where the environmental risk factor operates on the individual through a mechanism that is clearly different from that by which the person brought about the environmental risk.[403] Smoking constitutes a particularly striking example. People choose whether or not to smoke so that they determine whether or not to expose themselves to the carcinogenic (and other) risks of smoking. However, the fact that they have brought about the risk by their own actions in no way diminishes the effect of smoking in very markedly increasing the risk of lung cancer and several other serious diseases. The same principles apply to the effects of childhood conduct disorder in leading to stress environments in adult life. Not surprisingly, antisocial adults are more likely than other people to experience feelings of depression (see Cadoret et al.[375]). Moreover, the evidence from adoptee studies shows that this association is environmentally mediated; genetic factors play a role in bringing about adult antisocial behaviour but the risks of depression are not due to those genetic factors.

It is not difficult to envisage how these effects may come about. Boys with conduct disorder show their disorder in the form of quarrelsome, aggressive, disruptive behaviour. It is scarcely surprising that this makes it more difficult for them to maintain friendships, love relationships and jobs. Indeed, the effects are evident in what happens in the here and now as shown by both naturalistic and experimental studies. For example, Brunk and Henggeler[67] trained ten-year-old boys to act in compliant or oppositional ways. Not surprisingly, these forms of behaviour elicited different responses from the adults who interacted with them. However, what was less predictable was the finding that, within minutes, the boys established 'reputations' that led adults to respond differently even to neutral behaviour. That is, even when oppositional boys were behaving well, other people tended to assume that they might be about to be difficult or aggressive and therefore responded negatively; the reverse applied to compliant boys. Because the boys were acting a part, we may conclude that the effects stemmed from their behaviour rather than from other features of them as individuals.

Dodge[117,118] has shown much the same thing in his observations of interactions between boys playing together. Aggressive boys not only behave more aggressively themselves but they also *elicit* more hostile behaviours from other boys. Their actions in a way create a vicious circle of negative interactions. When coercive or unpleasant behaviour brings about a hostile response, this makes it more likely that the coercive behaviour will continue.[343] This is very evident in family interactions. Minor acts of misbehaviour are much more likely to blow up into a family row if uninvolved members of the family chip in with negative comments – 'Oh, shut up, Bob' or 'It's your fault again, Peter' or 'Leave him alone, Mary.' Retaliation all too often follows and what started as a minor incident rapidly escalates into a flaming row.

The examples we have given so far concern behaviours that are clearly deviant in some way. However, the effects of personal behaviour in shaping other people's reactions extends more widely than that. We have mentioned already the finding that temperamentally difficult children (meaning those who tend to be non-adaptable, emotionally intense, likely to withdraw from new situations, generally negative in mood and unpredictable in their pattern of eating and sleeping) are more likely than others to be the target of parental criticism and hostility.[392] But, perhaps the most striking example is provided by gender rather than temperament. There are many ways in which people treat boys and girls differently. There is a tendency to think of this differential treatment only in terms of parents trying to encourage their sons to be 'masculine' and their daughters to be 'feminine'. Of course, this does indeed take place. In many families the boys are more likely to be given toy cars or a football whereas the girls receive dolls. Similarly, boys are expected to be tough and assertive, whereas girls are allowed to cry and be comforted.

In part, of course, people are *responding* to differences in the ways that boys and girls behave but that is not the whole story, as is shown by the so-called 'baby X' experiments.[446] In these studies, toddlers aged about a year or so are dressed in snowsuits (or some equivalent clothing) that are unisex in design so that you cannot tell who is a boy and who is a girl. The children are then given names that indicate gender, the names coinciding with their own true gender half the time, and half the time not. The children are then looked after by adults who play with them. By design, half the time the adults play with 'Mary' or 'Sue', thinking 'she' is a girl whereas in fact the child is male (or with 'Peter' or 'Bill', who are actually girls). The results of several such studies have shown that adults treat even very young children somewhat differently according to whether or not they *think* they are dealing with girls or boys; however, some of the variations in adult handling are a consequence of differences in the actual behaviour of male and female infants. In this way, upbringing tends to reinforce cultural expectations regarding masculine and feminine behaviour.

However, such gender-related differential treatment also takes more subtle forms. For example, a series of studies by Dweck and others[204] showed that the teachers tended to treat poor scholastic performance differently in girls and boys. With girls, teachers tended to be understanding and accepting, saying things like 'Never mind, you did the best you can.' By contrast, boys were more often told that they should have done better – the failure was because they weren't trying hard enough, or were misbehaving, or hadn't done their homework properly. On the face of it, boys were being treated more harshly but the implicit message was that they had the necessary capacities and that the solution lay in their own hands. The expectations were lower, on average, for girls, and they were led to believe that they could not do anything to improve their performance. The implication is that this form of teacher response may have the effect of getting at least some boys to strive harder and may also encourage them to develop a sense that they can cope with challenges. Girls, on the other hand, may be more likely to come to feel that they have to accept things as they happen. Obviously, not all teachers showed this pattern of differential behaviour and the effects are likely to vary from child to child. However, what is clear is that the upbringing of boys and girls differs in all sorts of ways that are not obviously related to cultural stereotypes and which carry the potential for long-lasting effects.

A rather different example is provided by the findings on people's physical appearance, names and ethnicity. It has been found that an unpleasant appearance is associated with social rejection (see Barden[258]). Similarly, deformities (especially facial ones) make it more likely that people's initial reaction will be negative. Interestingly, in Western societies marked fatness in children is viewed negatively in much the same way. Even peculiar names may constitute a risk factor. Much the most obvious social prejudice is concerned with ethnicity. Experimental studies have made it clear that a black skin or a foreign-sounding name leads to gross discrimination in relation to both housing and employment.[59,110] Of course, this is illegal, but it is easy for people to say that the house has now been let or the job has just been filled. We know that these are often lies or excuses because the studies have shown that, *after* this has been said, white applicants are offered the house or the job. Unfortunately, religious and racial discrimination is still all too prevalent. Personal charm may overcome these prejudices but initial social reactions are shaped to an appreciable extent by the 'surface' characteristics of appearance and the preconceptions with which they are associated.

These varied examples show the importance of personal characteristics as determinants of social experiences. However, they also bring out the important point that the relevant 'characteristics' include not just people's actual behaviour (although certainly that is very important) but also preconceptions based on stereotypes of various kinds and by personal reputations based on how we have behaved in the past. The reactions we encounter from others are shaped both by how we behave and how they *think* we will behave.

Effects of Past Experiences in Shaping Current Experiences

For many years there was a general belief that personalities were largely shaped and fixed by experiences during the first few years of life.[48] It seemed obvious that that must be the case because of the frequency with which really bad early experiences were followed by psychological problems in later life, and by the relative persistence of these problems in spite of later good experiences. However, it is now known that the sequelae of even adverse or depriving experiences in infancy do *not* fix personality development.[93,394,408] Provided later experiences are really good, the ill-effects of early deprivation or adversity are surprisingly evanescent in many respects. The *impression* of lasting effects stems from the very high probability that a poor early upbringing will be followed by a poor later upbringing. The persistence of behavioural sequelae is largely a consequence of the persistence of the damaging experiences. Although this conclusion ran counter to most people's previous assumptions, there is no doubt that it is largely correct. There are some exceptions, which we consider in the next chapter, but, by and large, early experiences do not have an over-riding importance that is independent of later experiences. That they do not is shown most dramatically by the achievement of normal intelligence in severely deprived children who have been rescued from their appalling circumstances only at the age of six or seven. Thus in the Koluchova twins[93] an IQ in the 40s at seven years of age increased to 100 at fourteen; similarly, Dennis found an increase of some 30 points in Lebanese orphans moved from a poor to a better institution at the age of six. Findings such as these led some social scientists to dismiss the early years as of no special importance and to regard people's behaviour as largely determined by the experiences of the moment rather than by happenings in the past.[237]

Recent research has forced something of a rethink on the matter, as evidence has accumulated demonstrating a rather complex mix of both continuities and discontinuities.[408] It is not that the findings of remarkable recovery with major changes in environment have been disproved. On the contrary, they remain solid. Rather, it is that there has been a growing realization that the wrong question was posed. The key issue is *not* whether early experiences have a permanent effect that is independent of what happens later. Instead, we need to focus on the observation that it is exceedingly uncommon for early and late experiences to be independent of one another. One reason is that people's behaviour shapes their environment, as we have seen already. A second reason is that early experiences tend to determine later experiences. Of course, to some extent this is just a matter of environmental continuity. Children who are born into poverty, or into a discordant, quarrelsome family, are likely to go on experiencing similar environments as they grow up because poverty and family discord tend to persist over time. However, it is also the case that environmental advantages or disadvantages tend to persist even when there has been a radical change in life circumstances. That is because one sort of 'bad' environment tends to make it more likely that other different sorts of 'bad' environments will also be encountered; the same applies with advantageous circumstances. For example, Brown and his colleagues[60] showed how, in girls, stressful family separations in childhood increased the risk of lack of adequate parental care, which in turn predisposed to a premarital pregnancy, which then made it more likely that the woman would land up with an undependable husband. The specific environments changed but adversities of one kind or another persisted. Similarly, children from a privileged home are more likely to go to a superior school. The home and school environments are separate but advantages in the one tend to predispose to advantages in the other. Numerous other examples could be given, but once one thinks about it, it is obvious that there is substantial continuity in advantage/disadvantage.

Effects of Social Structure in Shaping Experiences

A further main source of variations in people's life experiences lies in the structure and organization of society, together with the effects of one level of the environment on the other levels. Bronfenbrenner[57] used a biological parallel in expressing this notion as an ecological perspective. He described the ecological environment as a set of nested structures, each inside the next, like a set of Russian dolls. The basic idea is that the interactions between two individuals, say a mother and child, are influenced by the social context within which the interaction takes place, say the family. Similarly, the functioning of the family is in turn influenced by the broader social setting (with respect to features such as income level, overcrowding, racial tensions and so forth). Equally, the social setting will be shaped by political influences – on, for example, the availability of housing or income distribution. Sociologists have focused especially on the last of these effects – the ways in which structural aspects of society constrain and bias opportunities. Family therapists who use systems approaches, by contrast, have focused on the first – the ways in which dyadic relationships are shaped by relationships outside that dyad but within the same family group. However, whatever the focus, the basic idea is the same; namely that the environment is made up of a complex set of interactions between its different elements, so that a change in one tends to have repercussions on the other parts of the social system.

Two key considerations arise out of this ecological (or social-systems) perspective. The first is that the balance of society, like that of nature, is dependent on a complex set of interrelationships at all levels. Quite often the same feature has both positive and negative functions and if you seek to eliminate the latter you may inadvertently remove the former as well. In medicine, this is particularly obvious in terms of the side-effects of antibiotics taken by mouth. The normal gut needs bacteria for a variety of purposes and if the 'good' bacteria are removed along with the ones causing the infectious disease the result can be devastating. Lewis Thomas,[473] the biologist, in an amusing, cynical essay 'On Meddling', applied the principle to social systems, arguing tongue in cheek that 'You cannot meddle with one part of a complex system from the outside without the almost certain risk of setting off disastrous events that you hadn't counted on in other, remote parts' (p.110). His point was not really that it was always wrong to interfere with nature (he emphasized the benefits of medical advances), but rather that if social interventions are to be beneficial overall, it is necessary to understand the social system as a whole and not just the bit that you want to alter. Conservationists learned this the hard way as they discovered that putting out all forest fires was not such a good thing after all, because fires were needed to clear the undergrowth that inhibited the growth of big trees like the giant redwoods of California. Later in this chapter we consider some practical consequences of these considerations with respect to the effects of stress and in Chapter 4 we discuss them in terms of the interconnections between different types of personal relationship.

The second implication of the ecological perspective is that

the broader environment, including the structure and organiza-
tions of society, plays a role in shaping personal experiences.
This is apparent in all sorts of ways. For example, the Black
report noted that cigarette smoking was two to three times more
common among unskilled manual workers than among professional workers.[480] Similarly, child deaths from injuries to pedes-
trians by motor vehicles were half a dozen times greater in
children from socially disadvantaged families than in those from
professional families; these differences apply to physical experiences but the same effects are seen with psychological stressors
and adversities. For example, the Newcastle 1000 Family
Study[250] showed that multiply deprived families experienced
significantly more family accidents, arguments or tensions, adult
difficulties with the law and deterioration in finances than did
non-deprived families. On the whole, children living in chronic
disadvantage were more likely to experience acute stressful experiences. National surveys, too, have shown that socially disadvantaged children are more likely to experience family break-up
and to be taken into group foster care.[428] There are also important geographical differences. Thus, all sorts of family adversities
were found to be more commonly experienced by children in
inner London than on the Isle of Wight.[393,426] In adult life as
well, stressful experiences such as unemployment and marital
breakdown are most frequent in socially disadvantaged segments
of the population.

There are many reasons for these associations between broader
social circumstances and negative personal experiences. In part
they reflect the mechanisms already discussed. Thus, for example,
Robins's[372] long-term follow-up showed that antisocial boys
were more likely to land up in unskilled jobs as well as experience
higher levels of unemployment and marriage breakdown. In this
case, one of the most important connecting links lay in the
consequences of their own behaviour. However, there are also
effects associated with the structure of society and with living
conditions at the time. Thus, unskilled jobs tend to carry less
security of tenure than do professional jobs; as a consequence,
periods of unemployment are more frequent. Also people in
local-authority housing are more likely than those in affluent

private housing to live in a high crime area, so that they are more likely to experience muggings and break-ins.

In summary, it is apparent that the huge variations in the extent to which people undergo stressful experiences is not just a matter of chance. To a substantial extent it is explicable in terms of the effects of their own behaviour in shaping their experiences, the continuities between environments and the effects of social structure and overall living conditions.

Environmental Influences

We have already noted that the same research designs that have demonstrated the importance of genetic influences have also shown the major impact of environmental factors. What we need to consider now is *which sorts* of environmental influences matter most for personal development, and *how* they make an impact. There are various rather different ways in which environmental influences may be subdivided but, from a developmental perspective, perhaps it is most appropriate to start with those that affect the development of the brain itself, as these will have consequent effects on the working of the mind.

Effects on Brain Structure and Development

Before considering the effects of environmental influences, it is necessary to say something about what is involved in brain development. The first point to note is that the brain differs from most other body organs in having its growth spurt during the prenatal period and the first few years after birth (see Figure 2.3). As early as six months, the brain has reached half its final mature weight, whereas the body as a whole does not do so until about the age of ten years. Indeed, the brain reaches 90 per cent of its final weight by the age of five. One implication of this timing is that the brain is in some respects most vulnerable to damage during this phase of rapid growth occurring early in life. This variation in the pace and pattern of growth of different body organs is paralleled by similar variations between different parts of the brain. For example, the occipital cortex (dealing with vision) matures well before the prefrontal cerebral cortex (which, amongst other things, deals with particular types of

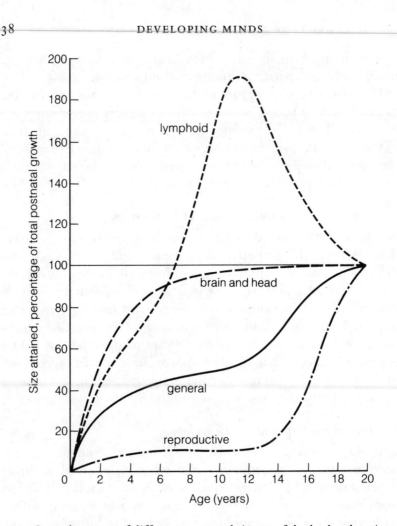

2.3 Growth curves of different parts and tissues of the body, showing the four chief types. All the curves are of size attained, plotted as a percentage of total gain from birth to age twenty, so that size at age twenty is 100 on the vertical scale.

Data from Tanner.[468]

learning), which, in turn, matures well before the cerebellum (the part of the brain dealing with coordination and balance). The implication is that the effects of damage are likely to differ according to *when* they occur.

The process of brain development goes through several overlapping phases (see Goldman-Rakic *et al.*[190] and Goodman[415]). To begin with, there is the formation of the main structure of the brain followed by a proliferation of nerve cells. Soon after the nerve cells have been formed, they migrate to their final destination, which may be quite some considerable distance away. At the same time, there is continuing elaboration of the neuronal network in the brain with an increase in the number of synapses (cell junctions). Finally, there is an extensive subtractive phase during which some half of the neurones die off; this selective cell death seems to serve a kind of fine-tuning function and continues for many years after birth (in some parts of the brain up to late adolescence). This fine tuning seems to be associated with an increasing specialization in the function of different parts of the brain. The development of these specialized functions is influenced by sensory input relevant to the functions subserved by the reorganized neurones (see below). In parallel with this development of neuronal networks, neurotransmitters also develop. Different neurotransmitters develop at different times and over time there are considerable changes in the balance and topographical distribution of these chemical messengers.

Several key implications stem from the complex pattern of brain development, of which five may be singled out as having particular practical importance. First, damage to the brain prenatally or very early in life tends to be *less* likely to result in specific deficits but *more* likely to lead to a general lowering of intellectual and scholastic abilities. There are a variety of reasons why this may be so but it is likely that one concerns the greater powers of neuronal reorganization in early life. This enables undamaged parts of the brain to take over functions that they would not serve ordinarily (hence the reduced rate of specific sequelae). By the same token, this greater potential for regrowth in infancy may result in more *mis*connections and unhelpful 'rewiring' of the brain, which could interfere with function. It used to be thought that the main consequence of brain damage was the functional deficit resulting from a loss of brain substance. It now seems that the *mal*function stemming from imperfect repair processes may be at least as important.

Second, the cell migration and altering pattern of neuronal

organization mean that the same part of the brain may serve
different functions at different phases of development. As a
consequence, a fixed lesion of the brain in early life may have
quite different functional consequences as the person grows
older. For example, delayed-response learning in monkeys depends on different parts of the prefrontal lobes at different
developmental stages – the orbitomedial portion in early life but
the dorsolateral portion in childhood (see Goldman-Rakic *et
al.*[190]). The consequence is that damage to the dorsolateral
region in early life has no measurable effect at the time, but
when the monkeys reach adulthood impaired/delayed response
learning is apparent. This consideration means that there may be
late effects of early damage to the brain. The scholastic difficulties
seen in some very-low-birth-weight infants of normal IQ (see
Casaer *et al.*[415]) may constitute an example of this kind. It also
suggests that apparent changes with age in functional deficit
need not necessarily reflect any change in the underlying brain
abnormality. Goodman[415] has suggested that this may be the
explanation of why some autistic children seem socially responsive in the first year of life but are obviously grossly
impaired socially later. This could arise if social functioning is
served by different parts of the brain in early infancy from those
responsible thereafter.

Third, the 'driving' role of sensory input in organizing neuronal development means that a lack of the relevant experiences
can have a lasting effect on brain development. We have noted
already that the well-known and serious medical consequence of a
squint that is uncorrected in infancy is a permanent loss of
binocular vision. What remains quite uncertain is whether the
same crucial organizing role of experience applies outside the
field of vision.[415] The partial impairment of language development sometimes associated with transient hearing loss in early
childhood resulting from recurrent ear infections could reflect
something of the same kind, although the effects are far less
clear-cut, and not so lasting, as those seen with vision. Even
more speculatively, this type of mechanism could account for
some of the lasting sequelae of an early institutional rearing (see
Chapter 3). Fourth, the organization of brain structure and

function is susceptible to other 'external' influences, of which hormones and other chemicals seem the most important (see below).

Fifth, as Goodman[301] has noted, it is necessary to consider the role of chance in brain development. It is clear that the precise migration of individual nerve cells and the formation of billions of synapses could not be genetically controlled. There are insufficient genes for this to be possible and, in any case, that does not seem to be the way in which genetic instructions are translated into neuronal organization. Rather, what happens is that general principles allow a highly developed neuronal organization to come about through the combination of proliferative and subtractive processes which enable a remarkably precise degree of selective honing to take place. One implication, however, is that there must be a degree of chance in what takes place – something equivalent to the random Brownian movement of intracellular particles. Goodman drew attention to several examples in which chance is thought to play a role in human development. For example, females have two X chromosomes, of which one is inactivated; which one it is seems to be random. Similarly, there is a genetically determined abnormality in ciliary motility which puts embryos at equal risk for having their internal organs the normal way round, or the opposite way. Which path they follow appears to depend on chance. It is quite unknown whether this chance element in brain development has any functional implications, but it could have. Goodman suggested that this may account for the fact that with strongly genetic disorders, sometimes only one of a pair of identical twins is affected.

With these implications in mind, we turn to some of the main environmental influences on brain structure and organization. To a very considerable extent, nature has ensured that, while it is growing in the womb, the foetus is protected from inadvertent damage. Nevertheless, it is subject to a variety of influences, both normal and abnormal. Hormones constitute one important class of influences; these may stem from either the foetus itself or the mother. While in the womb, males and females differ in their sex-hormone pattern and it is likely that this has an effect on brain development. Experimental studies in animals have shown that sex hormones affect the pattern of brain development and, as noted by Swaab,[415] there is some indication that this may also apply to humans. There are subtle structural differences between the brains of males and females, and it may be that these are brought about by prenatal hormonal influences. Research findings suggest that these biological differences may have functional implications. Thus, girls exposed to abnormal levels of the male sex hormone while in the womb tend to be rather more tomboyish than other girls.[366] It is quite difficult to be sure of these effects in humans because, necessarily, the opportunity to examine them only arises in abnormal circumstances, but it seems probable that the effects are real, albeit slight.

Most attention has been paid to the implications for sex-typed behaviours as summed up in the terms 'masculine' and 'feminine'. However, the effects on other aspects of functioning may be greater. One set of animal experiments showed that males and females differed in their response to early brain damage and that this was a function of hormonal exposure (see Goldman-Rakic[190]). It is well demonstrated that boys are more likely than girls to suffer from a wide range of developmental disorders (such as speech delay or reading difficulties) and it has been suggested that this might be due to prenatal sex-hormone effects on brain development.[164] It cannot be claimed that these prenatal hormone effects are at all well understood but there are well-established sex differences in rates of many psychological disorders[130] and it seems very probable that early biological influences on brain development play a major role. Other hormones may also affect the maturation of the brain. For example, either too much or too little thyroxine (the hormone produced by the thyroid gland) has been shown to influence the development of the cerebellum in rats, with consequences for adult behaviour.

During recent years there has been a growing realization that many drugs taken by the mother during pregnancy can have deleterious effects on the foetus. Of drugs commonly taken, alcohol is the most clearly damaging.[355] During the first ten weeks of pregnancy, alcohol is toxic to brain cells, causing a deficiency in brain growth; in mid-pregnancy there is a transient disorganization and delay of the migration and development of brain cells, and interference with neurotransmitter (the chemicals involved in transmission of messages in the brain) production, leading to neuroendocrine abnormalities. The behavioural consequences in childhood include intellectual impairment, hyperactivity and attentional difficulties. These effects are well demonstrated with very high alcohol consumption but the extent to which they apply with moderate drinking remains uncertain. Although there is no clear threshold below which the drinking of alcohol is 'safe', it seems likely that the consequences of light drinking are negligible. Of course, alcoholism in mothers is likely to be associated with many postnatal environmental disturbances and it is difficult to separate out foetal effects, but there is no doubt that damage before birth can have consequences that persist.

Smoking provides the other common drug effect on the foetus. Numerous studies have shown that it is associated with a lowering of the birth weight, with its associated risks. There are some long-term implications for cognitive development but the effects are slight because of the numerous other influences on the growth of intelligence.

Marked anxiety in the mother can have effects on the foetus – both immediate with respect to foetal activity level and possibly longer term in terms of an increase in birth complications.[226,231] However, it seems likely that the effects are usually transient and of little long-term significance.

Probably there has been the greatest focus on the brain damage associated with pregnancy and birth complications. In the past, this was thought usually to be the result of 'birth injury', damage during the process of being born. It is now clear that most instances of supposed 'birth injury' did not arise during birth, but rather much earlier in pregnancy. Also, as we have noted, it may well be that sequelae derive as much from abnormal 'rewiring' as from loss of function as such (see Goodman[175,415]). Much has been made of the greater plasticity of the brain early in its development; neuronal regrowth is still possible and functions normally subserved by one side of the brain may be taken over by the other half. This recuperative potential is real and it does have benefits. For example, it is unusual for damage to just one side of the brain, when it occurs very early in life, to result in permanent language impairment, whereas this is common if the damage to the dominant hemisphere occurs in adult life. However, this potential also has the disadvantage that it may result in *mis*connections in the brain.

With respect to the effects of brain damage after birth, Goodman[415] has suggested that it is helpful to distinguish three main developmental phases: early infancy (and the prenatal period), childhood and adult life. The acquisition of specific skills may be remarkably normal (although general intelligence may be impaired) after either bilateral or unilateral damage in the first period. During the middle phase, covering the rest of childhood, recovery from bilateral damage may be just as poor as that in adults, but recovery for some skills after unilateral damage can be much better. After mid-adolescence, both unilateral and bilateral damage is likely to result in some lasting deficits in specific skills, although some degree of functional recovery is probably the rule rather than the exception. The main reasons for these age differences have already been outlined.

Shared and Non-shared Psychosocial Experiences

Traditionally, geneticists have divided environmental influences into those that are 'shared' and those that are 'non-shared'. 'Shared' influences are those that impinge similarly on all children in the same family. Overcrowding, poverty and family break-up are examples of this type. By contrast, 'non-shared' influences are those that impinge *differently* on each child in the same family. This will be the case with experiences that involve only one child, as when only one child is admitted to hospital or when two brothers go to different schools. Influences will also be 'non-shared' if they discriminate between children within the same family – as with favouritism or scapegoating. Most research concerned with psychosocial influences has concentrated on family-wide shared influences and, hence, it has come as a bit of surprise to most people that the genetic evidence suggests that, for most psychological characteristics, 'non-shared' environmental influences are much more important.[128,352]

With the appropriate calculations, the relative importance of the two broad types of environmental influences can be quantified. However, a general 'feel' for the evidence can be obtained by considering the implications. If shared influences were all-powerful (after taking genetic factors into account), the effect would be to make children in the same family very similar to one another and very different from children in other families. For most characteristics it is obvious that this is not the case. Children within the same family are often extremely varied in their personalities and in their abilities. The same applies with many psychological disorders. For example, quite often only one child in the family suffers from depression or fears or anorexia nervosa. The lack of impact of shared environmental influences is seen most strikingly in the findings on adopted children. When two adopted children are brought up in the same family, they are usually very little more alike when they grow up than any two people picked at random from the general population.

If, on the other hand, non-shared influences were the most important ones, then we would expect just the substantial within-family variation that has been found. Also, however, it should follow that the differences between children in the same family will be associated in a systematic fashion with differences between the children in their experiences. There is very little research that has examined that question directly but there are a few findings that offer support for the proposition. These are well summarized by Dunn and Plomin[128] in their splendid book *Separate Lives*.

They argue the need for a major shift in view of how families influence children's development. Thus, they maintain that family-wide influences such as socio-economic status or marital discord 'cannot influence behavioural development' unless their impact is experienced differently by each child in the family. This is quite a revolutionary idea. As they recognize, and as we emphasize later in this chapter, the sweeping claim that family-wide influences have no effect on development needs very considerable qualification. Nevertheless, we need to take on board the evidence that non-shared influences are considerably more important than has been appreciated in the past.

Three main implications have a particular practical impor-

2.4 Exam scores at sixteen in three schools according to reading levels
at age twelve using variance components model

School	Reading Score at age twelve		
	40 (− 1 s.d.)	*75* (mean)	*110* (+ 1 s.d.)
12	− 2.35	0.78	3.91
22	− 0.83	3.48	7.79
32	1.05	6.82	12.58

From Smith and Tomlinson.[447]

tance. First, there is the possibility that experiences *outside* the
family of rearing may be quite important. Research findings
show that this is indeed the case. For example, there are now
several well-designed investigations of the effects of the particular
school attended by children.[312,399,447] The usual design employed has been to assess children's behaviour and scholastic
attainment at the time they enter a school and again some years
later. The consistent finding has been that children's scholastic
progress varies greatly according to the school they attend. In
some schools, progress is great whereas in others there is huge
individual variation, but the differences between schools are
quite substantial enough to make a real difference.

Figure 2.4 shows the findings from Smith and Tomlinson's[447]
study of secondary schools. They are presented in the form of
the average exam scores at age sixteen in different schools for
children from a skilled manual background with below average,
average and above average reading skills three years earlier. The
results show dramatic differences in attainment according to the
school attended − representing a difference between schools of
four grade C passes at O level. It is obvious that this difference
could make a marked difference to children's subsequent careers.
Figure 2.5, from the Mortimore *et al.*[312] study of primary
schools presents the findings in a different way − in terms of
school differences in the *progress* in reading made between first
and third years of junior school (roughly between eight and ten

2.5 The difference between the most and the least effective school in promoting pupils' reading progress

	Difference in raw score points	Percentage difference from average
Most effective school	+ 15	+ 28
Least effective school	− 10	− 19
Overall average for sample	54	

(Overall school effect on progress accounts for 24 per cent variance, compared with 6 per cent variance due to background factors.)

From Mortimore et al.[312]

years of age). Taking 'average' children from a similar background in each school, the attainments at age ten were 19 per cent worse than average in the least effective school and 28 per cent better than average in the most effective one. Schools were *four* times as important as family background in accounting for variations in progress over these years. At first sight, that seems very surprising and completely counter to the extensive evidence that, overall, family influences are more important than school influences with respect to scholastic attainment. However, the contradiction is apparent rather than real. That is because the results are being expressed in different ways. At the end of the day, families *do* account for more of the variation in attainment than schools do. That is because there are already very marked differences in attainment between children at age eight. For obvious reasons, schools cannot have influenced children's attainment before they enter, but what Mortimore et al.'s[312] findings show is that they have a big effect on progress during the time the children attend the school. These findings concern scholastic attainment, but findings for behaviour also demonstrated marked school effects. Thus, Mortimore and his colleagues found that children's behaviour improved in some schools but got worse over time in others. Overall, in the most effective schools the behavioural changes were 32 per cent better than the average whereas in the least effective school they were 15 per cent below average.

The peer group constitutes a further important extrafamilial influence. It is not easy to sort out just how much difference the peer group makes because, of course, to a very large extent children choose whom they go around with. However, some estimate may be obtained in circumstances where external factors control the peer group to an important extent; two examples of this kind are provided by the composition of the pupil body in schools and the effects of a geographical move. In a study of twelve inner London secondary schools, Rutter *et al.*[420] showed that delinquency rates were substantially higher for children in schools with a marked preponderance of academically less able children (this difference applying *after* taking into account the individual child's *own* characteristics). The implication is that children were influenced in a delinquent direction by the overall mores of the peer group, who were relatively unengaged in the academic enterprise. West[495] in a prospective longitudinal study of working-class boys, also in inner London, showed a substantial reduction in delinquency among those who moved away from the metropolis – a drop not explicable in terms of their prior characteristics. It seems likely that a change in peer group played a large role in this change, although a reduction in opportunities for crime outside London probably played a part as well.

The second implication from the finding that non-shared experiences are very important is that *relative* differences between children in the ways in which they are treated may often be more important than absolute differences in level. There is remarkably little evidence on this important point, but the findings from one study of siblings[129] showed that children's behaviour at home (as reported by mothers) was associated with differences in maternal affection and control. Those children who received less affection and more control than their siblings tended to show more problem behaviour. Dunn and Kendrick's[127] earlier study in England of first-born children's response to the birth of a younger brother or sister also showed the importance of jealousy and rivalry. It is clear that children both notice and respond to differences in the ways parents treat them compared with their siblings. Dunn and Plomin[128] argued that the overall pattern of findings suggests that parental discrimination is likely to be much more influential than the overall characteristics of the family environment. In other words, they suggest that it may matter very little whether children are brought up in a home that is less loving or more punitive than average whereas it may matter a lot that one child consistently receives less affection or more criticism and punishment than his brother or sister. There is too little evidence for any firm conclusion that this is so, because we lack direct comparison between these two types of influence. However, it certainly seems probable that relative scapegoating within families is much more influential than is sometimes appreciated.

It is obvious that this point has a parallel with the recurrent political discussion of whether relative or absolute poverty or privation matters most.[419] In the UK, the Tory government has taken pride in the fact that average income (in real terms) has risen during the decade or so that it has been in power. The opposition, on the other hand, has expressed concern that the divisions within our society have widened markedly, with the rich being much richer but the poor being scarcely better off at all. Which matters most? Of course, the answer will depend on what outcome criterion is taken. However, from a psychological perspective, it is apparent that people do not mainly compare their current situation with some circumstance in the past, but rather they consider how they are faring compared with other people whom they know. In this connection, it should be noted that the comparison made is *not* usually with society as a whole; instead the comparison is with other members of the group of which they feel part – what social psychologists call their reference group.[241] This tendency to compare oneself with others is a very basic human tendency. People's satisfaction with their lot in life depends to a considerable extent on what they have been led to expect and who they compare themselves with.[387] Because comparisons with brothers and sisters in the same family are unavoidable and because they are almost bound to be felt as important, they are likely to make a substantial psychological impact.

The third implication is that, even when there are important family-wide influences, we need to be concerned with each child's *micro*-environment (in other words, non-shared influences). Studies of families troubled by serious discord or by mental disorder in one parent show that not all the children suffer to the same degree or in the same way.[142,409] Some parents are skilful in protecting their children from involvement in family problems; they try to avoid embroiling children in their quarrels or enveloping them in their depression or irritability. Equally, within any individual family children vary in the extent to which they become caught up in family rows or other difficulties. When parents are feeling miserable, it is very common for one child (often a daughter) to be used as a source of solace and comfort, and equally common for one child (often a son) to be the target and focus of their anger and irritation. Although inadequately studied to date (because so few investigations have compared siblings within the family), it appears that this micro-environment may well be more important than the overall family situation, or macro-environment. We emphasize this point because the non-shared-environment findings do *not* just apply to siblings. It is not just differential treatment among siblings that matters but also the specifics of interactions with an individual child in one-child families.

Having underlined the very considerable importance of non-shared environmental influences, it is necessary to go on to emphasize some crucial qualifications and exceptions. The first is that there are some psychological characteristics for which the shared environment is very important. Most obviously this applies to juvenile delinquency and probably to aggressive and antisocial behaviour in childhood and adolescence more generally (see Plomin *et al.*[273]). Figure 2.6 gives the twin concordance data pooled from several twin studies of juvenile delinquency (see McGuffin and Gottesman[417]). There is a slight difference in the concordance for MZ and DZ pairs (87 per cent and 72 per cent), suggesting a modest genetic component. However, the very high concordance in DZ pairs, in nearly three quarters of which both twins were delinquent, points to major environmental influences that are affecting both twins (i.e. a shared influence). These twin data are consistent with the widespread observation that it is common for several children in the same family to be delinquent and with the extensive evidence that delinquency is

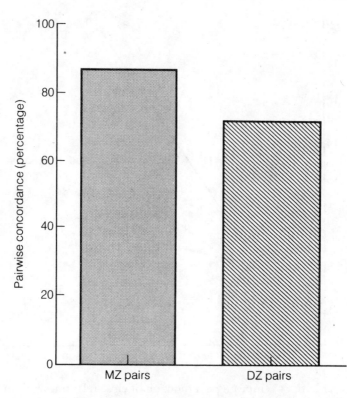

2.6 Pairwise twin concordancy rates for juvenile delinquency.
Data reviewed by McGuffin and Gottesman.[417]

associated with parental criminality, family discord, poor supervision of the children, weak parent–child relationships, social disadvantage and large family size.[416] The implication is that these family-wide variables are important in the causation of delinquency and that, to a large extent, the effects are environmentally mediated.

The next qualification is that many variables are *both* shared and non-shared in varying degrees. That is obviously the case with the family features just listed. In many cases, there will be a general family tendency to quarrel, to have poor relationships with one another and to supervise the children ineffectively. This will affect all children to some degree but it will impinge on some much more than on others. An example is provided in

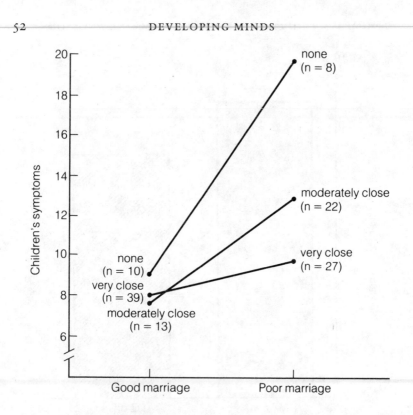

2.7 Children's symptoms as a function of close relationship with an adult in good and poor parental marriages.
Data from Jenkins and Smith.[229]

Figure 2.7, showing the results of Jenkins and Smith's[229] study of nine-year-old children. The children were more likely to show psychological problems when there was marital discord between the parents and also when there was a poor mother–child relationship. The lesson is that attention needs to be paid both to the presence of these family-wide qualities *and* to the ways in which they impinge differentially on the children.

The third qualification is that the evidence on the relative lack of importance of the shared environment derives from studies of samples that are largely middle-class, or at least not seriously disadvantaged. The evidence is convincing that within these non-deprived groups, differences between families do not make much of an impact on most psychological characteristics. How-

2.8 IQ of adopted children according to social level of biological and adoptive parents

Social level of biological parents	Mean IQ		All children
	Social level of adoptive parents		
	high	low	
high	120	108	114
low	104	92	98
All children	112	100	

Data from Capron and Duyme.[77]

ever, it does not follow that the same will apply to family influences when extremes are considered. Figure 2.8 shows the findings from Capron and Duyme's[77] study of the effects on IQ of the social status of biological and adoptive parents, contrasting privileged and disadvantaged homes. It is clear that there is an IQ difference of some dozen points according to the social circumstances of the family of upbringing (as well as a similar, biologically – probably genetically – mediated, difference according to the biological family of origin). Other evidence is entirely in keeping with the inference that family-wide influences on IQ are quite marked when extremes are considered.[401]

A related point is that the genetic data necessarily apply strictly to the populations studied and to the environmental variations that occurred within that population. It follows that if circumstances change, the effects found may also vary. The findings on height illustrate this point. Dunn and Plomin[128] summarized the genetic evidence and concluded that 80 per cent of the variance in height was genetically determined and that shared environmental influences had no effect whatsoever on individual differences. Figure 2.9 portrays Tizard's[479] analysis of the very considerable increase (some 12 cm) in the height of London schoolboys over the first half of this century. The explanation almost certainly lies in the marked improvement in

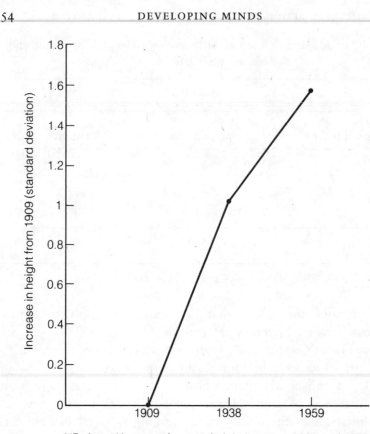

NB. Actual increase in mean height between 1909 and 1959 was 10.2 cm.

2.9 Increase in mean height of boys aged 7½ to 12½ years (in standard deviations).

Data from Tizard.[479]

nutrition that took place over those years. Because this improvement applied across the population as a whole it would not be reflected in the findings on the partitioning of genetic and environmental influences at any one point in time. Nevertheless, the data strongly point to the major effect of a shared environmental influence (albeit one shared between, as well as within, families).

A fifth qualification is that, as well as influences impinging *on* siblings, the relationship *among* siblings may also play a part in reducing or accentuating differences between them – so-called equalizing or polarizing (or de-identification) effects (see Goodman[301]). We know remarkably little about such effects but there are suggestive pointers to their likely operation. For example, there are several examples where, in relation to the other genetic evidence, the correlation between DZ twins for temperamental attributes has been found to be unexpectedly low.[71] There are also a few instances where the correlation between MZ twins living apart has been as great, or even slightly greater than that for MZ twins living together (see Plomin[350] and Shields[438]). Both findings suggest that the interaction between brothers and sisters living together may sometimes lead to contrast effects in which one becomes a leader and the other a follower, or one the naughty and the other the good one, one the bookworm and the other the sporty one. The opposite may also take place. Siblings may sometimes engage in the same activities to such an extent that they come closer together in their styles of behaviour.

It should be added that these identification and de-identification – or equalizing and polarizing – effects are not features that have to be confined to siblings. Family therapists point to the possible importance of somewhat similar mechanisms in families in which the members interact in ways that accentuate the particular role of one of them – with someone taking a sick role, someone the spokesman role and so forth. Examples of this kind undoubtedly occur but it has to be said that there is scarcely any systematic evidence on their frequency or importance.

Protective and Vulnerability Mechanisms

In our discussion of environmental influences so far, we have concentrated on direct effects of one kind or another. However, it is important also to recognize the role of catalytic mechanisms that either enhance resistance to risk factors (protection) or reduce it (vulnerability), without necessarily having any direct effect on psychological functioning.[293,376,494] These are pervasive in biology and medicine. For example, we all appreciate that we are more likely to catch infections when we are 'run down'. Our poor physical or psychological status does not cause the infection, but it does reduce our resistance to the infective agent (the bacterium or virus). That constitutes an example of one sort of negative influence increasing the effect of another different type. However, as we have noted already, there are many instances in which exposure to the risk factor is necessary in order to build up resistance to it. This is obviously the case with infections, but the effect applies much more widely than that. For example, animal studies some years ago showed that the experience of stress in early life had measurable effects on the body's neuroendocrine system and enhanced resistance to later stress.[201] The experience of becoming accustomed to stress experiences may also alter the *pattern* of bodily responses to stress, as well as the level of reaction. Thus, with adaptation to stress, the main endocrine response comes to take place in the anticipation phase rather than after the event.[378] Because these protective or vulnerability mechanisms operate catalytically, it follows that their effects will be evident only in circumstances of risk. Two further features need to be noted. First, it is necessary to refer to *mechanisms* and not to *factors*, because the same variable may provide risks in some circumstances but protection in others. For example, the sickle-cell gene leads to sickle-cell disease but it also protects against malaria. Similarly, adoption may be protective for children subjected to extreme abuse and neglect in their biological families but the experience of adoption carries with it stresses of its own (albeit usually small ones). Second, quite often the protective effects are not linear; that is, more and more of the protective agent may carry no additional benefits. Thus, exposure to infections builds up immunity but, having acquired immunity, further exposure to the infectious agents does not make much difference. In a somewhat comparable fashion, people are better able to deal with psychosocial stress when they experience social support, but having a very great deal of support is not necessarily better than a moderate amount; indeed, too much support can create its own stresses.[28]

With these considerations in mind, psychosocial protective and vulnerability mechanisms may be examined. Figure 2.10, from the Jenkins and Smith[229] study, shows that, in the presence of marital discord, a close relationship between children and an adult outside the family was protective, whereas it had little

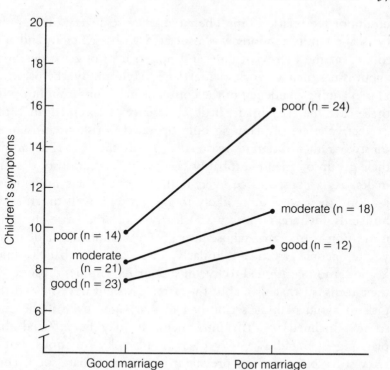

2.10 Children's symptoms as a function of the mother–child relationship in good and poor parental marriages.
Data from Jenkins and Smith.[229]

effect when the parental marriage was a good one. A good relationship exerted a beneficial effect when the family situation was a troubled and difficult one for the child.

Figure 2.11 (see Rutter[376]) summarizes findings from Quinton and Rutter's[361] follow-up into adult life of women who spent most of their childhood years in a group foster home because their parents could not cope with bringing them up. These women were contrasted with a comparable group of women from a similar social background in inner London but who had been reared by their own parents. The institution-reared women had a worse outcome in adult life but it turned out that this was, in substantial part, a consequence of their marrying deviant men, often during their teens, with whom they had a discordant, unsupportive relationship. Their tendency to marry on impulse to escape family tensions was associated with a general tendency to feel 'at the mercy of fate' and not to take positive decisions about issues such as work or marriage. Interestingly, the presence of a 'planning' tendency in the comparison group brought up by their own parents made little difference. It seemed that the protective effect of planning only operated in risk circumstances for two rather different reasons. First, in the low-risk sample their group of friends probably contained few seriously deviant males. As a consequence even if they picked their husband at random, they were quite likely to end up with well-functioning husbands, whereas this was clearly not the case for the institution-reared girls whose peer group was mainly made up of young people from a similarly disadvantaged background. Second, most continued to live in supportive families throughout their teens, so that probably the parents would have helped the girls to avoid making seriously bad marriages, even if the girls seemed inclined to drift into them. It may be inferred that planning operated as a way of avoiding risky situations, but if risky situations were less prevalent in the immediate social context, this was less necessary.

Figure 2.12, from the same study, takes the protective process back one stage further by asking why it was that some institution-reared girls showed planning whereas many did not. The findings showed that part of the answer lay in positive school experiences. These could be academic or non-academic (such as with sports, drama, arts and crafts) but in the institution-reared group it involved exam success only rarely. Probably the experiences of pleasure, success and accomplishment at school helped the girls acquire a sense of their own worth, with feelings of self-efficacy, and hence a feeling that they were able to control what happened to them. It is notable, again, that the protective effect was not evident in the low-risk group. Probably, this was because most of the girls had ample sources of reward in their families, so that the additional experiences of success at school merely reinforced self-esteem rather than creating it.

The next set of findings, summarized in Figure 2.13, from a study of toddlers by Lee and Bates,[265] focuses on temperamental

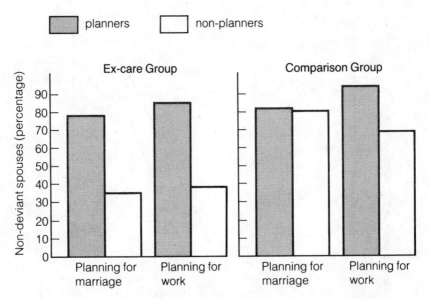

2.11 Proportions of planning and non-planning women marrying non-deviant spouses.
From Quinton and Rutter.[361]

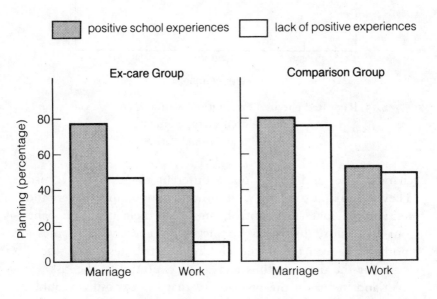

2.12 Positive school experiences and planning.
From Quinton and Rutter.[361]

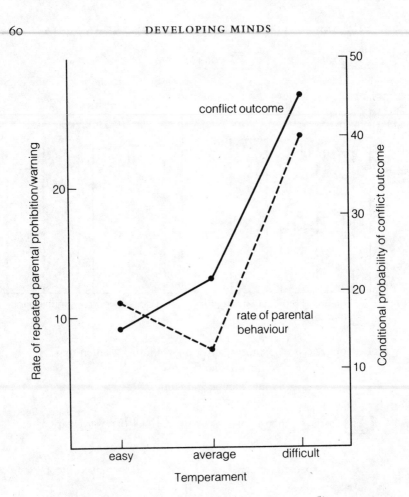

2.13 Repeated parental prohibition/warning, conflict outcome
and children's temperament.
Adapted from Lee and Bates.[265]

characteristics and brings out a different range of mechanisms.
They found that toddlers with difficult temperaments were more
resistant to maternal control, and that their negative behaviour was more likely to be met with coercive responses by
mothers. It seems that the children's attributes made them a
focus for the discord (thus increasing exposure to the risk variable) and increased the probability that the exposure would set
in motion a train of adverse interactions that prolonged the risk.

Rutter[376] has used these and other research findings to try to draw some general lessons on possible mediating mechanisms in psychosocial protective processes. He suggested that four stood out as the main contenders: (i) reduction of risk impact; (ii) reduction of negative chain reactions; (iii) establishment and maintenance of self-esteem and self-efficacy; and (iv) an opening up of opportunities. The first mechanism, reduction of risk impact, seems likely to arise in two different ways: (a) by alteration of the meaning or riskiness of the variable and (b) by alteration of the child's exposure to intimate involvement in the risk situation. It reflects the fact that most risk factors do not represent absolutes that are independent of the person's involvement in the appraisal of the experiences and thinking about them. It constitutes, of course, a facet of the importance of non-shared experiences and one of the reasons which explains why they are so influential. The second mechanism emphasizes that most risk processes and most protective mechanisms do not happen at just one moment in time; rather they involve a series of chain reactions that may extend over quite lengthy time periods. The third mechanism underlines the importance in development of people's concepts and feelings about themselves, about their social environment, and about their ability to deal with life's challenges and to control what happens to them. The evidence suggests that both secure and harmonious love relationships and also success in accomplishing tasks that are central to their interests play key roles in establishing a positive self-concept. The final mechanism points to the importance of life experiences as determinants of later experiences. For example, continuing in education is likely to extend career opportunities; a new friendship or love relationship will bring social support; and a move of home will change the social network (in ways that may be beneficial or deleterious). All four mechanisms show the crucial relevance of a developmental perspective on risk and protective mechanisms; in the next chapter we focus more directly on some of the processes involved in development itself.

Chapter 3

Change and Continuity:
Some Developmental Processes

As we mentioned earlier, it is not sensible to think of development only in terms of a progressive increase in the level of structure and function up to the point when maturity, and therefore stabilization, is reached (see Rutter[417]). Of course, that is part of the story and for some aspects of development it constitutes a fair enough approximation to what happens. Thus, physical growth continues until adult height and bone structure are achieved. After maturity, people can gain or lose tissue bulk, but height and skeletal structure are more or less fixed thereafter in ordinary conditions of health and environmental circumstances. As we argue in Chapter 9, this still leaves open the question of what maintains the structure, but it is not unreasonable to view physical growth largely in terms of maturation to a relatively fixed end-point reached in early adult life. It is not too difficult either to extend this concept to the growth of intelligence (although, as we argue in Chapter 6, even this extension is rather misleading). It is not so self-evident, however, that this view can encompass socio-emotional development. Of course, this involves the acquisition of various skills and capacities that have clear parallels with the growth of intelligence and physique. But, there are two major problems intrinsic to any attempt to view socio-emotional development as simply the attainment of a final mature level. First, it seems artificial to confine development to capacities with no attention to the *content* and quality of behaviour. Any such constraint would rule out many of the phenomena that have most interested developmentalists over the years. For example, it would seem to rule out the finding that the imprinting of the following response in birds in infancy influences later sexual preferences, and that rhesus monkeys' social isolation in infancy affects their parenting behaviour at maturity.[396] It would seem absurd to exclude those features from concepts of the developmental process. But, if the content of behaviour, as well as its complexity, is to be included, how is it possible to define developmental progression? Which behaviours are to be regarded as the most mature, and why? Also, how should one deal with loss of, or regression in, supposedly mature behaviours? If, following a series of personal losses or humiliations, an adult loses his sense of self-esteem, has he regressed developmentally? The parallel with physical growth and cognitive development is lost at this point. The second problem concerns definition of the end-point. Physical growth stops when a person's height and physique reach an adult level and no longer change to a marked degree; to some extent the same applies to IQ. But when is a person's personality development fully mature and what characterizes maturity? It is evident that a rather different approach to the concept of development is needed.

Yet it would make no sense to view development as change of any kind. The feeling of satiety after a good meal clearly involves change, but no one would see that as developmental. Catching influenza undoubtedly brings about temporary change of a most unpleasant kind but there is nothing developmental about it. Reference to *lasting* change does not provide a satisfactory solution, because some alterations that are obviously developmental may have no long-term consequences; they serve their purpose at the time but they leave no lasting imprint. That would be true, for example, of the stage of babbling that precedes language. On the other hand, *some* degree of carry-forward would seem to be necessary for most aspects of development. A related point is that, although environmental influences may be crucial, nevertheless some degree of change *within* the individual is necessary if the change is to be viewed as developmental. The other criterion usually invoked is that the change should be part of a universal, or at least very common, age-related progression. To specify that it should be universal would rule out some transitions that are clearly developmental from any other viewpoint. For example, most children crawl before they walk, but not all do so, and those who shuffle or scoot on their bottoms rarely crawl at all (as was the case with all three of our children). Also, too close a tie with age cannot be required because, as we shall see, some transitions are related as much to particular experiences as to chronological age as such.

We are left with recourse to some rather fuzzy definition that conveys the general notion without providing an unambiguous set of rules to allow a clear-cut differentiation between changes that are, and those that are not, developmental. Such a fuzzy definition would probably view development as systematic, organized, intra-individual change that is clearly associated with generally expectable age-related progressions and which is carried forward in some way that has implications for a person's pattern or level of functioning at some later time. That is the general concept to which we shall adhere, but, in doing so, our focus throughout will be on *how* the changes come about, *how* they are maintained or fade or alter over time, and *how* the course of development comes to vary between individuals.

Some Developmental Issues

Before proceeding to consider some of the possible processes underlying change and continuity in development, some overarching developmental questions need to be addressed.

Does Development Comprise Cumulative Accretion?

Many people have tended to assume that development proceeds through cumulative accretion in which each advance grows out of, and builds upon, the one preceding it. It is thought that development is based on slow, continuous growth, involving a strong connectedness between the past and the present and a preservation of earlier structures. Kagan[236] expressed this view as likening 'development to a journey in which the mind absorbs each new experience, never discarding any of its acquired treasures' (p. xiv) – a notion that he went on to criticize strongly. In particular, he challenged the idea that each stage is necessarily derivative and dependent upon the preceding one. Instead, he proposed that 'many instances of developmental change can be characterized by replacement of an old structure or process by a new one, with little or no connectedness between the two hypothetical structures. This suggestion implies that some structures and processes vanish' (p. 68[234]). He urged that many maturational changes involve a reorganization of behaviour or cognition that is not dependent on either earlier neural structures or earlier experiences and that, in essence, the new developments wipe clean the tape of previous development.

Several rather different issues are involved in the concept that Kagan criticized. To begin with, there is the view of development as a process moving steadily forward through progressive building, with change involving psychological advance at each point. As we have seen, that is not how the brain itself grows; a major part of the developmental process involves *loss* of neurones, a loss that enables function to be improved through selectivity and not just by more of the same. It is clear that the same applies to psychological functioning. As we grow older, we *lose* many reflexes, skills and sensitivities that were well established at an earlier age.[100] In some respects, the capacities of the young exceed those of the adult. The skills fade, or are lost, because they have served their purpose and are needed no longer. Development involves *qualitative* change, as well as quantitative accretion, and some of the changes include losses as well as gains.

A corollary of this point is that the basis of psychological functions may change with age. For example, infants from a wide diversity of language backgrounds show similar skills in speech perception, involving high levels of discrimination; it appears that responsiveness to speech is innately determined and not reliant on exposure to specific types of early linguistic experience (see Aslin *et al.*[190]). By contrast, there *are* differences between adults according to their native language; phonetic discriminations become much more difficult if they are not present in the language used. It seems that the *maintenance* of perceptual skills after the first few months is dependent on experience, at least in part. Much the same applies to the production of sounds. The vocalizations of deaf infants are closely similar to those of hearing infants in the first few months of life but become obviously different thereafter, as auditory input becomes increasingly crucial. The fact that the site for the

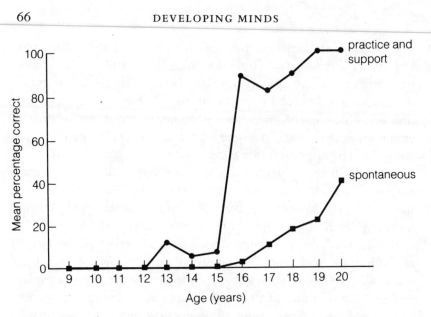

3.1 Developmental changes in the understanding of problems
involving abstract mappings.

From Fischer, Pipp and Bullock, in Emde and Harmon, eds., *Continuities
and Discontinuities in Development*, Plenum, 1984.

neural basis of some psychological functions alters over the
course of development has been noted clearly.

The second issue concerns the extent to which development
includes rapid, abrupt transitions as well as gradual change.
There are many examples of marked change over short time
periods. Figure 3.1 provides an example from the field of cognition, dealing with the understanding of abstract relationships.
Optimal performance jumped from near zero correct at fourteen
to fifteen years to over 80 per cent correct at sixteen. However,
the graph also brings out a further point that although there was
a stage-like spurt in performance under optimal conditions, the
improvement in spontaneous performance was much more
gradual, indicating that it takes time to make regular use of skills
acquired.[153]

Kagan[236] used the acquisition of reproductive fertility at
puberty as an even more vivid example of abrupt change. There
can be no doubting that the changes of puberty are dramatic

and, equally, it is obvious that the ability to conceive introduces a radically new element into life. However, although the capacity to reproduce emerges over a brief period of time, the physiological changes that underlie that transition extend over a much greater period – some four to four and a half years as a rule.[393] It seems unhelpful to link the speed of change with the extent to which the change creates a fundamental transformation.

The impression of gradual or abrupt change is highly dependent on the index of change used. The eruption of teeth occurs very rapidly but the preceding growth of the teeth within the gums went on for years before the act of eruption took place. It seems more important to focus attention on the extent to which developmental changes, whether gradual or sudden, transform functioning. Clearly, many do. Puberty obviously does so but there are many other examples that could be given. Locomotion markedly increases children's ability to explore and control their environment and the development of language opens up new vistas in relation to social communication. These are very apparent to all parents and it is no exaggeration to say that they represent a radical transformation both in what children can accomplish and in the quality of their interactions with other people.

The transforming quality of the acquisition of locomotion and language, and the onset of puberty are obvious to all, but there are other changes that alter the child's psychological situation to a similar degree. Those occurring in the latter half of the second year of life have received particular attention from a range of psychologists who have emphasized their far-reaching implications. Kagan[234] drew attention to what he called the 'emergence of self' in terms of the development of a capacity to make inferences about causes of events and of an ability to appreciate the psychological state of other people. He saw the accompanying self-awareness, recognition of standards and ability to set goals as constituting the basis for a sense of morality – a sense not possible before that age. Dunn,[126] in her vivid account of *The Beginnings of Social Understanding*, emphasized the emergence of an understanding of other's feelings, of other's goals, of social rules and of other's minds. She pointed to the emotional and social significance of this growth in understanding. Cognitive psychologists have used the term 'theory of mind' to describe children's understanding of other people's desires, emotional states and intentions.[499] Like Dunn, they have underlined the importance of these skills for socio-emotional relationships and it has been hypothesized that a lack of these skills constitutes the basis of the syndrome of autism.[20,162,268] It is very apparent that development includes many examples of changes that are so radical that they transform psychological functioning.

However, it is one thing to accept the crucial nature of the transformation and it is quite another to suppose that it has no connection with what has gone before and that it wipes clean the tape of past skills and experiences. So far as the lack of connection with prior phases of development is concerned, the mere fact that a new skill creates a transformation does not necessarily mean that its development has nothing to do with earlier functions. As we have just noted, the emergence of a theory of mind (and other related functions) at about the age of two or three transforms social understanding, but it may well be that mind-reading develops on the basis of a precursor skill of joint attention.[499] On the other hand, it must be accepted that later skills sometimes have little or no connection with earlier ones. For example, although voluntary radial grasping replaces the primitive palmar grasp response, there is no consistent relationship between the emergence of the former and the loss of the latter; indeed they may co-exist for some time. This is not an uncommon situation in early motor development.[100]

Somewhat similar issues apply with respect to the suggestion that new developments erase the effects of earlier ones. The fact that early behaviours are no longer manifest does not necessarily mean that the basic skills have been irrevocably lost. There are many examples of the re-emergence of lost behaviours as a result of later brain injury or changed environmental circumstances.[100] Hinde and Bateson[210] and Rutter[334] have pointed to the methodological issues involved in testing the notion of total behavioural reorganization as well as to examples of continuity even across the most major reorganizations. Thus, even metamorphosis does not necessarily erase previous memories – as shown by findings with insects and amphibians. Learning of sensory preferences in the larval stage may persist into adult life after metamorphosis. As Hinde[190] suggested, Kagan's vigorous attack on concepts of continuity and connectedness overstated the discontinuities in development but was, nevertheless, a needed and helpful corrective to the misleading prior assumption of a lack of radical reorganizations in development.

Are There Sensitive Periods for Learning?

The concept of sensitive periods in development caught the public's imagination through Lorenz's demonstration in the 1930s that during a brief period of hours after birth, and only then, young goslings would follow any object presented to them and would thereafter continue to follow it as they would a parent. Films of a string of young birds forming a close line behind Lorenz as he swam across the lake created what was undoubtedly a startling picture. To begin with, this was regarded as instantaneous, irreversible learning that was confined to a narrow, maturationally determined 'window' of sensitivity in early life. Research findings soon showed that this extreme view was untenable; the limits of the period are not irrevocably fixed by intrinsic processes and the learning is not irreversible.[22,23] An appreciation that imprinting was not quite so special as was at first thought led to an excessive rejection of the whole notion of sensitive periods in some quarters.

We need to separate several different aspects of the sensitive-period concept. First, there is the notion of irreversible learning. That has to be rejected (although some forms of learning are less easily reversible than others). On the other hand, as we argue later, there are plenty of examples (extending well beyond imprinting) of quite long-lasting effects of early experience.[42,334] The issue then becomes the broader one of determining the range of factors that influence the extent to which the sequelae of experiences persist.

Second, there is the notion that certain types of learning take place much more readily during particular phases of development than during others and/or that the consequences of specific experiences will vary in pattern or character according to when they take place. There is extensive support for this suggestion and, indeed, it would be very surprising if susceptibilities to environmental influences did not change as development proceeds. We have noted the sensitive period for visual experiences organizing the visual cortex as a particularly striking example. However, there are many others (see Hinde[190] and Rutter[334]). For example, children are more vulnerable to stressful separation experiences during the preschool years, but after the early months of infancy; environmental effects on cognitive development are less during the first eighteen months of life than between the ages of two and five years; and a lack of opportunity to form selective attachments in the first few years of life probably has a more enduring effect on the quality of social relationship than does a similar lack when older. We lack adequate knowledge on the extent of such sensitive periods but there is no doubt that there are some age-related differences in susceptibility to particular environmental influences.

The third facet of the sensitive-period concept is that the timing and limits are maturationally determined. Clearly, some are, to a very large extent, but equally clearly maturation does not account for all. Even the sensitive period for imprinting is influenced by experiences and the other examples given here probably reflect much weaker and more indirect connections with maturation. Thus, the age variations in environmental effects on cognitive development probably reflect a combination of a greater effect on verbal than visuospatial skills and age-linked variations in the qualities of parent/child interactions. It is important that we recognize the reality of sensitive periods but, equally, it is necessary that we seek to find out the mechanisms that they reflect and not assume automatically that they have to be due to neural maturation. Even if that were so, of course, it would not explain the mechanism, as maturational determinants could operate in several different ways.

Greenough et al.[186] have suggested that there are two rather different types of sensitive-period effects. In the first type (which they termed experience-expectant) environmental input is necessary to 'drive' neural development. In these cases, the input will be of a type that may be expected to be present in any ordinary environment. The effect of visual experiences as determinants of the pattern of neural connections in the visual cortex (through their influence on the selective pruning of neurones that takes place) is an example of this type. In the second type (which they called *experience-dependent*) neural development proceeds without the need for any particular environmental input, but the specific information that is stored (or coded) is crucially determined by experience. In these cases, the experiences are specific to the individual. Imprinting constitutes an example of this kind. The neural structure provides the propensity but the experience gives the specifics. In this type, the processes involve some kind of incorporation into the neural structures of specific information derived from experience. This may involve the formation of new synaptic connections, as well as intracellular changes.[220] The learning of language may comprise another example of this second type. The organism is, as it were, pre-programmed to learn language in any ordinary environment but the specific language learned will be dependent on the particular language used in that environment.

Biological Preparedness

One important aspect of the biological basis of behaviour concerns the organism's preparedness for certain forms of learning. That is, we need to ask whether species-specific biological features influence *what* we learn, as well as how and when learning takes place. For example, it is clear that learning plays an important role in the development of fears but it is obvious that it does not explain why some objects are frequently feared whereas others rarely are. Thus, city children are very much more likely to be afraid of snakes than of lambs, although in all probability they will not have encountered either. The differences cannot be explained by real danger, because the risk of being killed by a car vastly outweighs the risk from snakes, but fears of cars are decidedly uncommon. Hinde[209] has drawn attention to the interesting monkey data. He summarized the results as follows:

(a) wild-reared rhesus monkeys tested in the laboratory are almost always afraid of snakes; but, (b) laboratory-reared rhesus monkeys show little fear of snakes; (c) laboratory-reared rhesus monkeys shown a videotape of a wild-reared monkey showing fear of a snake are likely to be afraid of snakes thereafter; but (d) laboratory-reared rhesus monkeys shown the same videotape with the snake erased and a flower substituted do not become afraid of flowers. (p. 224).

Both monkey and human data indicate an initial biologically determined (but individually variable) propensity to fear snakes, but a propensity that is affected by the behaviour of others of the same species. In other words, biological factors create a predisposition that shapes the content of our fears. For some objects (such as flowers and pyjamas), it would require quite unusual experiences for us to become afraid of them; for others (such as snakes), almost any experience (even a vicarious one) is enough to induce fears; and for others (such as dogs) moderate levels of experience may induce fear. Hinde went on to note that it is not irrelevant in the case of humans that snakes play a very important (usually frightening) role in our mythology. Biology and culture interact.

Self-regulating Mechanisms

Sometimes it is assumed that very severely adverse experiences 'must' leave deficits because, although later good experiences may allow normal development to proceed thereafter, they are unlikely to allow catch-up unless the later experiences are super-normal. In fact, that is a wrong assumption. There are many examples of catch-up in quite ordinary environments. Figure 3.2 shows what happens to growth after a period of severe malnutrition; the restoration of a normal diet leads to very substantial gains that go a long way to making good the earlier losses. That is not to say that there may not be scars or subtle sequelae (in some circumstances these may be marked) but it does show that, through a rather diverse range of mechanisms, biology provides the means to use good, but unexceptional, circumstances to make up for earlier deficiencies.

The same catch-up has been shown for cognitive development in many (but not all) cases of children suffering appalling degrees of neglect.[443] There are well-documented instances of children

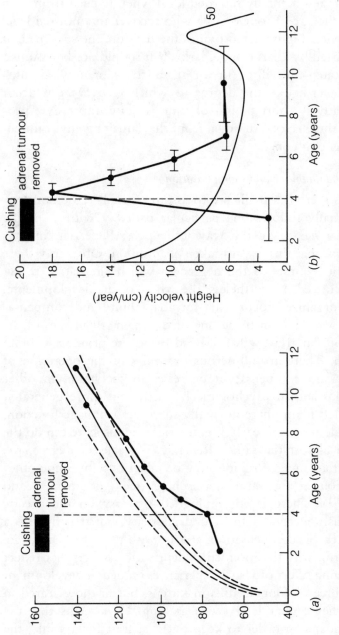

3.2 Catch-up growth following removal of the adenoidal gland in a patient with Cushing's syndrome showing (a) height and (b) height velocity. (The dark solid line shows the patient's growth; the lighter solid line shows average growth. In graph (a), the broken line shows the normal range.)

From Tanner.[470]

functioning at a mentally retarded level when rescued from such neglect at the age of four or five who recover to a normal level of intelligence. Figure 3.3 provides the data on one such pair of twins reported by Clarke and Clarke.[93] It should not be assumed that such catch-up will occur for all functions or in all circumstances. Nevertheless, the degree to which recovery can occur over a relatively short period of time is quite impressive, provided that there is total removal from the damaging environment to a good enough one.

Biological Adaptability and Compensation

Sometimes there is a tendency to assume that, because development normally follows one particular pathway with a specific timing, that *has* to be the way it happens. Research findings clearly show that this is a mistaken assumption. Obviously there are substantial limits to the degree to which alternative routes may be followed. Nevertheless, the whole of the developmental process is organized to provide for adaptability and compensation. That would seem to be one of the main advantages of the sequence of neural growth followed by severe pruning in brain maturation. There are numerous examples of the operation of adaptation and compensation processes in the brain, in other body organs and in psychological functioning more generally. Thus, the left hemisphere normally subserves language function, but if it is destroyed in early life, the right hemisphere can do the same with almost the same efficiency. To a lesser degree, the function of a damaged region may be taken over by some other intact region in the same hemisphere (see Goodman[506] and Witelson[501]). There is continuing controversy on the precise mechanisms underlying this neural plasticity, but that there *is* a most remarkable compensation, at least with respect to language, is clear. Ordinarily the monocular deprivation effects that reflect the organizing effect of visual experiences on neural development last only three or four months in kittens, but in those reared in the dark they last at least twice as long.[186] It seems that the organism adapts in order to keep open, at least for a while, the chance of making use of visual input. Norepinepherine has been shown experimentally to regulate this neural sensitivity, and this

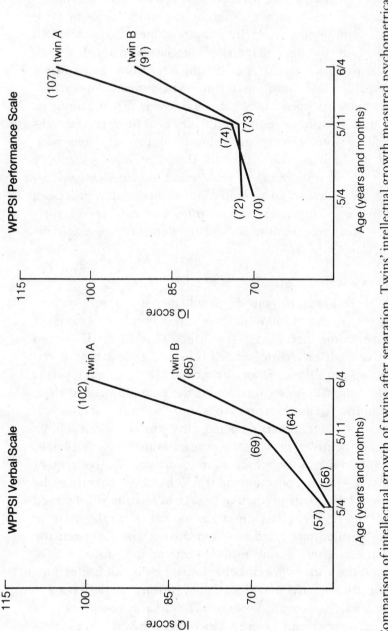

3.3 Comparison of intellectual growth of twins after separation. Twins' intellectual growth measured psychometrically with the Wechsler Preschool and Primary Scale of Intelligence (WPPSI) before separation, after separation with no training and after separation with language training. The test permits separate presentation of tasks that are primarily verbal in nature and those that involve visuo–motor performance.

Data from Clarke and Clarke.[93]

may be why plasticity may perhaps be renewed under conditions of extreme stress. A rather different example of plasticity is afforded by the evidence on human attachment (considered in greater detail in the next chapter). There has been much discussion of the particular qualities of dyadic interaction (particularly between parent and child) that foster attachment. The matter remains somewhat open but what is evident is that it cannot be dependent on any simple sensory modality because normal attachments (albeit sometimes slowed in development) have been observed in children who are blind, deaf, limbless or mentally retarded.[39] It is important to understand the mechanisms involved in these various adaptability and compensation processes, and we need to appreciate their limits, but the fact of their existence constitutes a most important element in what is involved in development.

Personality Growth as a Stabilization of Traits

The last general issue to consider is whether it is appropriate to think of personality development as the shaping of personality traits that become increasingly stabilized. That adults do indeed tend to have characteristic ways of behaving and that to an important extent, these generalize across situations and persist over time cannot be in serious doubt; the establishment of these stable patterns (traits do come to show increasing stability as children grow older) is part of personality growth and it will be necessary to consider how that comes about.[405] Nevertheless, there are several reasons for dissatisfaction with the concept of personality as just a collection of traits, however they may be determined. First, their predictive power in relation to observed behaviour in different circumstances is rather weak, even in adult life. Second, they provide no explanation for the systematic changes in behaviour during different age periods; for example, the marked drop in antisocial behaviour in early adult life[416] or the major rise in affective disturbance during adolescence.[166] Third, predictive strength does not always lie in consistency. In later chapters, we consider the evidence that coherence in psychological functioning is often to be found in complementarity or reciprocity in relationships rather than generalization of behaviour. Fourth, there may be consistencies over time in certain specific situational reactions without any consistency in patterns of behaviour in non-stressful and non-challenging situations. That is so, for example, with the temperamental trait of behavioural inhibition. Finally, adverse childhood experiences may predispose to an increased risk of social maladaptation without that risk necessarily being mediated through behavioural characteristics manifest in childhood. Clearly, there is more to personality development than just the stabilization of personality traits, and it is most unlikely that either neural maturation or the effects of experiences operate only through effects on such traits, although the stabilization of traits must be part of the story of development.

Change and Continuity

Before turning to a discussion of possible developmental processes, a few words are necessary on the facts to be explained. The details of specific aspects of different facets of development are considered in later chapters, but at this point it may be helpful to sketch out something of the broad patterns. Turning first to change, several different types will have to be accounted for. That which involves increasing skills and capacities constitutes the type traditionally associated with growth and development. In many cases, key transitions tend to occur at much the same time in most people, although substantial individual variation is always present (as, for example, with age of walking, language acquisition or puberty). However, for some characteristics the spread is so great that questions have to be raised about the possibility that different mechanisms may be operative at different points on the curve. Figure 3.4 presents the findings on the acquisition of bladder control from the study by Oppel et al.[332] The majority of children acquired control during the first five years, but some lost it between five and seven years. By twelve years, some 8 per cent still wet occasionally, although far fewer did so regularly. Even more strikingly, the likelihood of gaining control during the next twelve months (in those still enuretic at the beginning) does not alter appreciably during the middle years of childhood.

Then there are psychological characteristics in which different

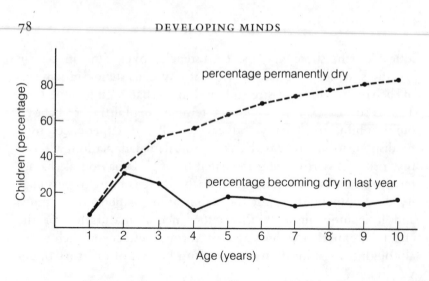

3.4 Age trends in acquisition of nocturnal bladder control.
Data from Oppel *et al.*[332]

subtypes follow quite different age trends. For example, although negative mood can occur at any age, depressive feelings and disorders increase markedly in frequency during adolescence. Attempted suicide peaks in early adult life but completed suicide goes on rising in frequency right into old age. Fears, too, show contrasting patterns, with animal phobias at a peak in early childhood but fears of open or closed spaces not peaking until adult life. Other examples could be given but the general point is that there are quite varied and complex age trends that require explanation.

So far as continuity is concerned, the general message for behavioural traits is that a person's qualities in the first two or three years of life show only a very weak relationship with qualities in adolescence or adult life. During the middle years of childhood, there is a moderate degree of consistency over time in the extent to which individuals remain high or low on a given characteristic (such as activity level or emotionality), but even so, many people change in their behaviour to a considerable extent (see Moss and Susman[55]). However, some traits, such as aggressivity, show a rather greater continuity over time. Figure 3.5 shows the findings from several studies brought together by Olweus.[329] The correlations are quite low (extreme left of

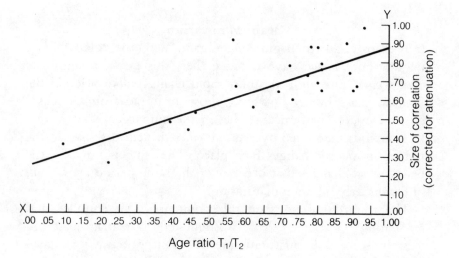

3.5 Behavioural traits: relationship between correlations over time (corrected for unreliability) and age ratio (time 1/time 2). A very low ratio means that the children were very young when first tested and quite old when tested for the second time.

Data from Olweus.[329]

graph) when the continuities extend from infancy to adult life but increase markedly when the first testing is at a slightly older age, even when continuities over quite long time spans are considered. Also, a variety of investigations have shown that continuities for psychological disturbance or problem behaviour tend to be particularly strong. Even from age three, psychological disturbance is associated with a three-fold increase in the risk of disorder at age eight,[369] and continuities from middle childhood into adult life are even stronger, although marked change still occurs in some individuals.

Thus both marked change and marked continuity are present. We need now to consider some of the influences that shape both change and continuity in developmental processes. Not surprisingly, these parallel those that we discussed in relation to individual differences, but here we focus on their role in changes over time, rather than individual differences at any one time.

Brain Maturation

It is appropriate to begin, once again, with the role of brain maturation. As we have noted earlier, this goes on until late adolescence, although the most rapid changes take place in the first few years. Figure 3.6 a and b shows examples from Conel's[99] classical micro-anatomical studies of the human cerebral cortex. It is obvious that, even over the six-month period shown in the figure, immense changes take place. The issue is how far the behavioural changes that occur over the same period are a *result* of the underlying brain maturation.[100]

The research findings on this point are both complex and fascinating. Gottlieb[178,190] has suggested four main patterns. First, for some skills, maturation seems all-important, with experience playing little or no role. This has been shown in three main ways. During the 1930s, Gesell, McGraw and others undertook various studies of the effects of training in human infants. They showed that many motor skills, such as walking, occurred without the need for any form of teaching. Below a certain age, no amount of training could induce the skill. At a particular point, training marginally speeded up skill acquisition, but the effects soon washed out and made no difference in the end. Fantz *et al.* used a different strategy to show that a preference for patterned stimuli in full-term and premature infants was a function of their gestational age (i.e. time since conception) rather than their postnatal age (i.e. time since birth). The much longer period of postnatal experience of the premature infants carried no benefits; the overall duration of brain growth seemed to be the crucial factor. Experimental approaches in animals have tested what happens to development when normal experiences are prevented. Thus Carmichael,[78] in a classical study in the 1920s, showed that amphibians still became capable of swimming even after prior muscle movements had been prevented by paralysing drugs. More recently, Crain and colleagues[104] showed that foetal rodent cerebral cortex differentiated normally even after electrical activity had been deliberately blocked. Although, even with these skills, experiences make some impact, their effect is marginal, with maturation providing the main driving force in development.

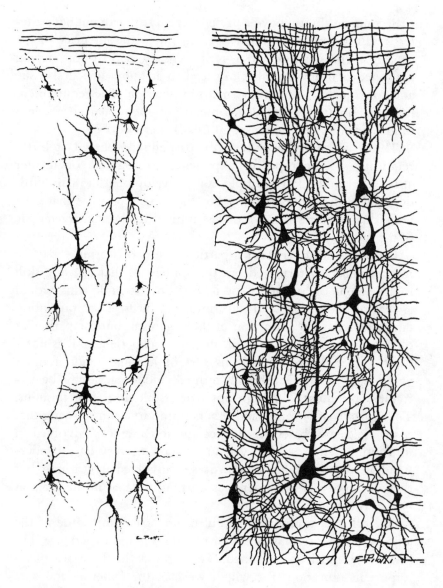

3.6 Micro-anatomical studies of the human cerebral cortex. Area PG.
Crown of gyrus angularis.
Left, Newborn infant; camera lucida drawings from Golgi-Cox
preparations (1939); *right*, Infant six months old; drawings from Golgi-
Cox preparations (1951).
From Conel.[99]

Second, an ability may be present already at birth but nevertheless requires certain experiences to maintain the integrity of the capacity. For example, long-term sensory deprivation during early neonatal development can lead to atrophy of neural tissue and consequent lasting impairment in function. The requirement of visual input for the development of the visual cortex and binocular vision is a case in point (see Blakemore).[42]

Third, an ability may be only partially developed at birth, requiring specific types of experience to facilitate or further attune the ability. For example, song development in many birds depends on imitative learning but the song repertoire that each individual acquires is more or less limited to those characteristic of the species.

Fourth, a propensity for a particular sort of learning may be maturationally determined but the content of that learning skill is dependent on specific experiences. For example, this would appear to be the case with imprinting in birds. That imprinting takes place at all is a function of the organism, but the particular object imprinted is a function of specific experiences. It is noteworthy that the results of this sort of learning (and of other varieties of what Gottlieb[190] termed 'induction') may be extremely persistent, although not irreversible as at first thought. The research of Horn[220] and others is important in showing that there are neural bases for the recognition memory involved in imprinting. The results as yet do not take us very far in understanding the multiplicity of processes involved in learning but they do serve as a reminder that learning is based in the brain as well as the mind.

These four patterns are helpful in understanding some of the aspects of the interplay between maturation and experience, but they leave much unexplained. To begin with, there are many important transitions for which we lack the experimental data that could tell us which pattern is applicable. There is a tendency to assume that if transitions occur in all cultures, and do so at roughly the same time, this implies an underlying neural basis – especially if the behavioural transitions coincide in time with some known neural change. That was the argument used, for example, by Kagan[234] in postulating a neural basis for the

development of self-awareness in the second year of life. Figure
3.7 presents an example of the sort of evidence used by Kagan[235]
to show universality of the phenomenon. While the overall
pattern is indeed similar in the three groups studied, the curve
for the Fiji children is several months later in its peak than that
for the Cambridge, USA, children. Why? Let us take a different
example to see how experimental manipulation may alter the
impression of the role of experience. It has long been known
that all infants avoid heights between the ages of seven and nine
months (as shown by some cliff experiments in which the infant
is on a flat transparent surface with a table underneath at one end
but not at the other, so that it appears as if there is a marked
drop). It was assumed for a long time that this avoidance of
heights was due entirely to maturational factors. However,
giving babies enriched locomotor experience (through the use of
baby-walkers) accelerates the appearance of the reaction to
heights, whereas deprivation of locomotor experience (as in a
baby in a heavy plaster cast for an orthopaedic problem) retards
it.[35] Obviously, the phenomenon has a maturational basis but its
timing is influenced to some extent by experiences. Probably that
applies to many developmental transitions. It should be added
that experiential factors may predominate for some transitions,
as we argue in later chapters.

A second largely unresolved question concerns the extent to
which neural changes carry forward the effects of social experiences or types outside the range of those known to have structural
neural effects. For example, there is an abundance of experimental
evidence that rhesus monkeys reared in total social isolation in
infancy show serious behavioural sequelae, including abnormalities in sexual behaviour and parenting, that extend into adult life
and continue for years after returning to a more normal social
environment.[388,396] What constitutes the basis for this continuity? Could it lie in some subtle neural or other biological
alteration? It is possible that social isolation could have neural
effects, but the evidence to date has been negative,[156] and
although a range of types of environmental enrichment and
impoverishment have been shown to affect brain chemistry and
histology,[381] they have largely involved sensory input or physical

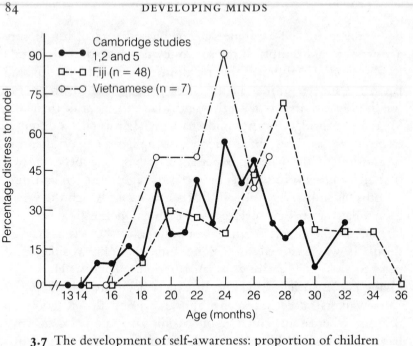

3.7 The development of self-awareness: proportion of children showing distress to the model.
Data from Kagan.[235]

experiences of one kind or another. The matter remains unresolved.

The third issue is whether the neural changes serve to prevent or limit later recovery of functions. Clearly, they do in some instances – of which binocular vision is the best example. On the other hand, the limitations are often far less than might be expected. Children who have been reared in dark attics, cellars and cupboards, and are without speech and function at a mentally retarded level at the time of rescue,[443] may well have had neural changes which would have been detectable if their brains could have been examined. Nevertheless, as noted already, their cognitive recovery has usually brought them up to levels of IQ well within the normal range.

This brief discussion of the ways in which maturation and experience interact serves as a further reminder that maturation has to take place in some experiential context. It is seriously misleading to attempt to dichotomize nature and nurture, pitting one against the other. On the other hand, it is necessary to seek to delineate the various ways in which the two interact and to differentiate processes in which one takes a predominant role for particular purposes. It is apparent that we have a lot still to learn on this matter.

Genetic Influences

Most people tend to think about genetic effects in terms of individual differences; of factors that determine in part why one person is more intelligent, taller or more emotional than someone else. However, genetic factors also operate as influences on development, shaping both change and continuity.[350,353] This may be evident in several different ways.

To begin with, it is necessary to account for the consistent finding that, on the whole, characteristics in infancy show only a weak predictive association for characteristics in later life (see Rutter[334]). In part this is so because development is shaped by many influences that impinge only in the years after infancy. But, in part, it is a consequence of the fact that the *pattern* of influences on behaviour changes with increasing age. Figure 3.8 portrays Plomin's[350] summary of the genetic findings, which indicate an increasing genetic contribution with age and a decreasing effect of shared environmental influences. In this way, genetic factors bring about both increasing stabilization and also change from the infant period.

There are some behaviours in which this shift in pattern of influences may be particularly important. For example, conduct problems involving either minor delinquent acts or aggressive defiant behaviour are extremely common in childhood, especially in boys. As already noted, genetic factors probably play only a minor role in such problems. However, genetic influences are rather more important in the case of adult criminality and personality disorders, and hence may well play a big role in the *persistence* of conduct problems into adult life, as when they persist they tend to lead to criminality or personality disorder.

Depressive disorders provide another possible illustration of this mode of action. Such disorders are much less common in childhood than in adult life but when they occur they are

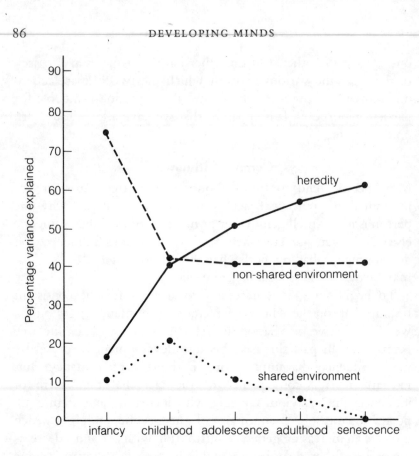

3.8 The pattern of influences on behaviour: life-span profiles of non–normative genetic and environmental influences on individual differences in mental development.
Data from Plomin.[350]

followed by a greatly increased risk of some form of depressive condition during the adult years.[195] In this case, the risk is for *episodes* of depression, and not for an enduring behavioural characteristic. Doubtless, many factors underlie this increased risk of a tendency to depression that extends from childhood to adult life, but one of them seems to be a family history of depressive disorders. It is likely that this reflects genetic factors in part, at least in the case of the most severe forms of depressive disorder.

Some changes over time, however, are more idiosyncratic and

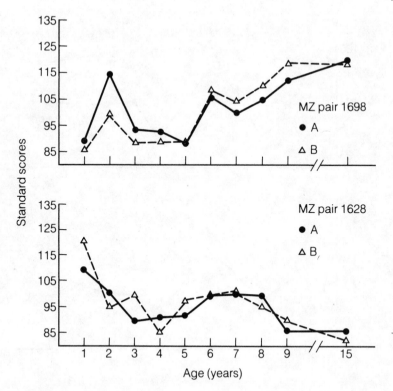

3.9 Trends in standardized scores from mental tests given from one to fifteen years of age in two monozygotic twin pairs. Data from Matheny.[295]

less consistent from individual to individual. Figure 3.9 shows the age trends in the IQ scores for two pairs of identical twins in the Louisville twin study and Figure 3.10 does the same for two pairs of fraternal twins.[295] The pattern of ups and downs after infancy is more similar in the identical pairs than in the fraternal pairs, indicating a genetic contribution. Interestingly, genetic factors have a negligible impact on developmental trends in infancy but, from about three years onwards, they account for approximately 40 per cent of the variance, the within-pair correlations being in the mid 80s for MZ and mid 60s for DZ pairs. A similar but rather stronger genetic influence on developmental pattern has been found for the temperamental trait of behavioural inhibition.[295]

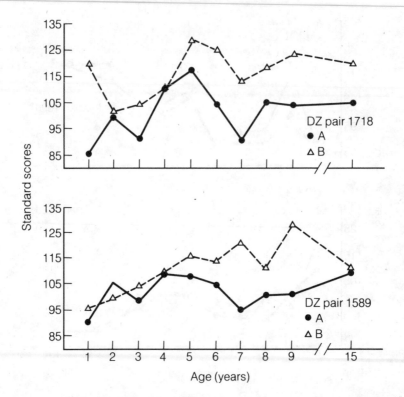

3.10 Trends in standardized scores from mental tests given from one to fifteen years of age in two dizygotic twin pairs.
Data from Matheny.[295]

A third way in which genetic factors influence development is through their effect on the children's environment.[351] Both twin and adoptee data indicate that the qualities of family relationships and interactions experienced by children as they grow up are in part shaped by genetic factors. This seems to be much more so in the case of affectional qualities than of disciplinary control. Of course, these findings do *not* mean that environmental factors are without effect.[411] On the contrary, as we have noted, genetic designs have served to confirm the importance of environmental influences. However, the evidence alerts us to the fact that because a measure is labelled 'environmental' and serves to describe the environment, this does not mean that the effects are entirely, or even mainly, environmentally mediated. But, in addition, we are making a further point. Some environmental features that truly have an environmentally mediated effect on development may, nevertheless, have been shaped in part by genetic factors – a little-studied but possibly important indirect genetic effect.

Genetic factors may also operate much more directly in the case of those few disorders that show both a very strong persistence over time and a very strong heritability. Autism is the most striking example of this kind. The vast majority of autistic children continue to show autistic characteristics in adult life[390] and genetic factors largely account for its causation (see Rutter[301]). In this case, the persistence of the disorder across the life span seems to be relatively independent of specific environmental experiences; that is, it is a function of the intrinsic qualities of a genetically determined condition.

With autism, although there are some changes in behavioural patterns with increasing age, the overall similarities in clinical picture between childhood and adult life are obvious. Nevertheless, this need not be so with genetically influenced continuity. For example, it is known that, about half the time, schizophrenia in adult life is preceded by social oddities and attentional difficulties in childhood. Because genetic factors play a major role in schizophrenia, it may be inferred that they also play a role in this continuity over time that involves a change in the form of the behaviour. However, because the behavioural pattern in childhood is not easily recognizable at the time as pre-schizophrenic (see Erlenmeyer-Kimling et al.[375]), it has not been possible as yet to quantify the genetic contribution to the continuity. Also, it remains uncertain whether the genetic effect is on the disorder as such, or on some susceptibility to environmental influences, or both (see Cannon et al.[375]).

It is apparent that the role of genetic influences on developmental processes has been much less investigated than genetic influences on individual differences. Such evidence as there is suggests their importance, although the strength of the effect varies according to the psychological characteristic in question. With but a few exceptions, however, environmental factors account for about half of the variance and it is necessary to consider *how* they influence the course of development. As with other influences, both pattern of change and persistence of traits or disorder have to be explained.

Environmental Influences

Before discussing some of the possible mediating mechanisms, we should first set the scene in terms of the overall pattern of research findings that has to be explained. Nine main features stand out. First, environmental factors have been shown to have an effect on people's behaviour at all ages, from infancy to old age. Thus, even infants respond to parental depression (see Field[152,334]), and bereavement constitutes an important stress factor right into old age.[365] Second, there are important age differences in the specific ways in which people process and respond to experiences. Thus, very young infants do not show anticipatory fear in relation to previously experienced stresses, such as the inoculation needle,[271] and do not show the distress reactions to hospital admission or other separation experiences that are characteristic of toddlers (see Rutter[395,398]). Third, although brief severe stress experiences may sometimes have enduring effects, enduring consequences are, for the most part, much more likely with long-lasting than with short experiences.[334] Fourth, in general, experiences during early infancy are less likely to have substantial long-term effects on cognition and behaviour than are similar experiences from the toddler period onwards.[236,334] Fifth, there are many examples of effects from experiences in childhood that have persisted long after the environment changed radically (see Rutter[334,408]). For example, this has been shown for early institutional rearing[215,216] and for preschool educational interventions of various types.[165,264]

Sixth, there is a general tendency for effects to fade with increasing time, but the extent to which effects persist or fade is much influenced by subsequent experiences.[93,334,396] Seventh, the tendency for effects to persist in spite of marked changes in the environment seems to vary according to the psychological characteristic being considered. For example, antisocial behaviour and emotional disturbance in Hodges and Tizard's[215,216] follow-up of children who spent their first few years in a residential nursery was much more a function of their current environment in adolescence than of their early experiences. But the reverse applied to the quality of peer relationships. Eighth, many of the findings in humans are paralleled by broadly similar findings in animals, although there are species differences that also have to be taken into account. For example, both apply to the results, short-term and long-term, of separation and social isolation experiences.[396] In so far as similar effects are found in animals with far less developed intellects, there needs to be caution in invoking complex mental processes as mediating mechanisms. Finally, the factors that *initiate* change may, or may not, be synonymous with the factors that promote the *persistence* of that change. For example, the weight changes associated with puberty are the key initiating factors for dieting in adolescent girls, but emotional disturbance is more important as a predictor of whether or not this continues in the form of anorexic-like problems.[8] Similar differences apply to some treatment responses. For example, the short-term response to appetite-suppressant drugs is superior to the effects of behavioural methods, but the reverse applies with respect to long-term effects.[103] The question, then, is how these diverse findings may be accounted for in terms of underlying processes. It is obvious, of course, that it is most unlikely that one mechanism will explain all the phenomena.

We need to consider five main alternatives: alterations in the biological substrate; establishment of some underlying psychological structure; the learning of some specific skill or behaviour; the development of a set of values or expectations that then serves to regulate behaviour; and alterations in patterns of social interaction that influence later behaviour.

The first possibility, that experiences make a lasting change in some aspect of the biological substrate, which will then have consequent implications for later behaviour, is known to apply to some effects. As we have seen, that *does* apply to the effects of sensory input (especially visual) on brain structure and function; to the effects of prenatal androgens as contributory organizing influences on certain aspects of brain development; and to the effects of acute stress experiences on the neuroendocrine system. Similar effects could apply to psychosocial experiences but, if they exist, they have yet to be demonstrated.

A somewhat related construct is the suggestion that experiences play a key role in the development of some basic organizing psychological structure, and that subsequent behaviour is dependent on the integrity of those hypothesized structures. In most instances, this concept applies to strongly biological, species-specific functions. Thus, development of language may be viewed in this way. Once language is acquired it is never lost (unless there is serious damage to the brain) and it is generally supposed that the capacity to develop language is an inbuilt human characteristic. The development of the capacity is not dependent on particular experiences but it does require language input and it will not develop in prolonged very severely depriving circumstances.[443,506] Although the evidence is not decisive, it is also probable that language input must be experienced during the first half of childhood if normal language capacity is to be acquired. Imprinting is another phenomenon that tends to be seen in terms of psychological structure; in this case requiring a much more specific experience during a much narrower time 'window'. Quite what the language-capacity psychological structure means in neural terms is not clear but some form of biological substrate is usually assumed, and in the case of imprinting it has been demonstrated.[220] While it is difficult to define psychological structures in unambiguous terms, there is little doubt that the concept has some validity; the problem, as we shall see, is how widely it is applicable.

At the other extreme, environmental effects may be viewed as learned skills or reactions of some kind. Thus, children may learn to speak English or French. The distinction from a psychological structure of a language capacity is that the skill applies to a *specific* language and not to a general ability to speak. Thus, one of us was born in the Middle East and learned to speak Arabic and English. However, following a move to the UK just before the age of three, the ability to speak Arabic was lost and never regained; his overall language capacity, of course, remained and it would be quite possible to relearn Arabic if the effort was made.

The fourth concept concerns the acquisition, or 'internaliza-tion', of a set of standards or attitudes that serve to shape specific behaviours in new circumstances. The need to invoke some such concept arose because of the evidence that children not only learned specific behaviours from their parents and from other adults, but also acquired values and internal controls that regu-lated new behaviours in new situations (see Maccoby and Martin[204] and Hartup[204]). Thus, it seems that children initially comply with parental requests, then identify with particular parental attributes and behaviours, and finally internalize some of their values. In this way, children come to develop internal controls that operate even when their parents are not present to provide surveillance and external control. It seems that the parental styles that foster such internalization are not identical with those that bring about immediate compliance. The exercise of strong power is effective in immediate control but mild pressure, responsiveness to children's reasonable demands and needs for independence, attribution of positive qualities to the child and approaches that involve understanding of other people's feelings are more likely to foster self-control. Baumrind[24] summar-ized the difference in terms of a distinction between 'authoritar-ian' and 'authoritative' parenting.

Similar findings have stemmed from studies of school classes and other social groups of children. Thus, Lippitt and White's[275] classic study showed that so-called 'democratic' leadership was more effective than authoritarian power assertion in producing positive behaviour when the children were left on their own. While there is continuing uncertainty on precisely which ele-ments are crucial in fostering internal controls, it is clear that these do develop and that the process is not synonymous with the direct learning of specific behaviours. It is necessary to invoke some kind of cognitive/emotional set of internal values and attributions that serve to regulate children's behaviour in new circumstances.

Finally, environmental influences may produce prolonged ef-fects, not because of any lasting change in the child, but rather because the initial behavioural effects channel the child into particular environments and patterns of social interaction that serve to perpetuate the initial consequences through their structuring of later environments (see Caspi,[42] Caspi and Elder[211] and Rutter[408]).

Biological Substrate or Psychological Structure

The suggestion that children's experiences often have an effect because they influence some psychological structure with a biological substrate has been applied widely in both the socioemotional and intellectual domains. Thus, Bowlby[48] argued that a person's ability to develop affectional relationships in later life was dependent on the development of selective attachments in the first few years of life. Somewhat similarly, the Headstart Compensatory Education programme[264] was influenced by the view that if there could be a boost to intelligence during the early years, this would have a lasting beneficial effect on later scholastic attainments. Let us consider the evidence on these two examples, starting with intelligence.

In spite of a long history of extensive and intensive research, there is continuing controversy and uncertainty on quite what intelligence means and how it 'works'. There is no doubt, of course, that IQ tests provide a most useful rough and ready measure of a person's general level of intellectual abilities, and that seems to provide a reasonable indication of the individual's likelihood of succeeding at a wide range of specific cognitive tasks, whether assessed by test or by performance in real-life situations (see Madge and Tizard[395]). What is less agreed, however, is whether intelligence is just an aggregate of a mixed bag of special skills, or whether (at least in part) it comprises a more basic organizing capacity that provides the basis for learning of most types. According to the latter view, intelligence represents a set of coping with novelty and information-processing capacities that allows problem-solving skills to be applied to all sorts of situations (see Sternberg[44]). Because there are neurophysiological correlates of these skills and capacities,[232] some sort of neural basis for intelligence has been inferred. Evidence on the nature of intelligence is discussed more fully in Chapter 6; suffice it to say here that there is a good deal of support for an information-processing concept as an important part of what intelligence is all about. However, research findings show only a moderate association between IQ and most scholastic attainments, with correlations in the order of .5 to .6, thus accounting for substantially less than half the variation between individuals in the general population. Accordingly the issue with respect to environmental influences is not whether IQ represents information-processing capacities, but rather whether the enduring environmental effects on attainments are mediated by changes in this psychological function or structure.

Three main sets of findings are relevant. First, as we have seen from adoption and cross-fostering studies, marked lasting improvements in environmental circumstances can result in appreciable rises in IQ scores, in the order of a dozen points.[411] Second, such rises tend to be less evident if adoption, and hence the change in environment, takes place after the first few years of life. There are several reasons why this might be so, including selective placement and the fact that the nature of parent–child interaction is less intense and different in pattern later in childhood,[401] but the finding is compatible with the suggestion of an environmental effect on some basic psychological structure. Third, however, the environmental effects on IQ and on scholastic attainments do not run at all closely in parallel. For example, the intensive interventions with socially disadvantaged families over the first six years in the Milwaukee project led to lasting gains in IQ but much more modest effects on scholastic attainment.[165] Conversely, Headstart effects on IQ washed out after a few years but scholastic benefits showed greater persistence.[264]

If we put these findings together, perhaps some tentative conclusions may be drawn. Environmental influences *can* have a lasting effect on IQ, and therefore perhaps on some basic set of information-processing capacities. However, these effects are most evident with influences that begin early in life *and* which persist through childhood and adolescence. On the other hand, there are still some effects on IQ as a result of environments in adolescence (for example, the IQ benefits from continuing education[419]), which can be dramatic in the case of children rescued from extreme neglect.[443] The very fact that placement in a normal environment at the age of four, five or six can lead to a rise in IQ from mentally retarded to normal levels in itself argues against the 'hard' version of a psychological structure hypothesis which supposes that this can only be established in the preschool years. However, it does not *negate* the suggestion that amongst other things, intelligence does comprise a basic information-processing capacity. The second main conclusion is that the lack of close connection between effects on IQ and effects on attainment means that the effects cannot be entirely, and perhaps not even mainly, explained in terms of some influence on a basic underlying psychological structure of intelligence.

The findings on social relationships are much more sparse because the hypothesis applies to a rather unusual set of circumstances – namely an early rearing environment that severely constrains the development of selective attachments. This is rare because such attachments develop even under quite severely adverse conditions of rearing.[363] However, the lack of any consistency in caregiving, such that it is provided by a large changing roster of adults, the situation in many residential nurseries, does impede the development of attachments.[396] The follow-up at age sixteen by Hodges and Tizard[215,216] of children who spent their first four years or so in such an environment is therefore instructive in its finding of social sequelae, in the form of effects on the quality of peer relationships, in spite of later adoption and hence good rearing conditions. We do not know whether these effects will persist into adulthood, and their meaning is open to several rather different interpretations. However, the results are compatible with the hypothesis of some sort of underlying psychological structure that influences the development of relationships. It is important to note, though, that the findings on the *quality* of selective attachments (as distinct from their presence or absence) are quite different; as we discuss later, and require a different explanation.

It is not possible to draw any firm overall conclusions on psychological structures. The notion seems to have some limited validity but it is difficult to translate the concept into something testable, and an effect on structure does not seem likely to constitute the main mechanism for enduring environmental consequences.

Learned Skills or Reactions

The notion that behaviours are learned directly is straightforward enough in essence but it incorporates a range of different processes spanning 'habituation' (learning through repeated exposure), 'classical conditioning' (learning through association), 'instrumental conditioning' (loosely thought of in terms of learning through rewards and punishments) and various forms of 'concept learning' (meaning the learning of rules or acquisition of ideas) (see Rovee-Collier[334]). All these learning capacities are present early in life, although the last becomes well developed only in the latter half of the second year. There is no doubt that the processes that they reflect take place but they are rather uninformative on the key issue of why some things that are learned persist indefinitely even if the skill is not used, whereas others fade rather quickly. Thus, once you have learned to ride a bicycle, the ability is not lost. It is possible to take up bicycle-riding again after a gap of forty or fifty years and still ride successfully (albeit less skilfully). By contrast, particular personal computer software routines get forgotten very quickly if not used regularly! Interest has turned, therefore, to processes of rehearsal, transfer, remembering and understanding (see Brown et al.[155]) in order to tackle the topic of how and why learning persists or fades.

It cannot be claimed that the issues are well understood. For example, it might be thought that children's fears and phobias constitute a clear example of learned reactions.[246] There are undoubted examples of fears directly learned in response to acute, severely frightening events (see Garmezy and Rutter[417] and Yule et al.[507]). However, learning constitutes an inadequate basis for any general explanation of fear acquisition and retention.[362] That is partly because many fears do not have any history of a recognizable traumatic precipitant and because people frequently fail to acquire fears in what are theoretically fear-provoking situations. But the main difficulty lies in explaining why fears do not fade fairly quickly. Sometimes they do, of course, but some are remarkably persistent. Part of the explanation lies in people's avoidance of the subject they fear (hence not allowing them to learn that in reality the objects are harmless). That is a feature of practical importance because most successful treatments of phobias involve some form of exposure to the feared object.[288] Nevertheless, learning theories of their own provide a rather unsatisfactory explanation for the persistence of fears.

Most examples of learning as a result of experiences do not, however, consist of mere persistence of specific behaviours or responses and it is necessary to consider other mechanisms to explain persistence. Thus, if a young child learns the elements of reading or multiplication tables, it is not self-evident why the results should be evident in, say, superior exam performance at age sixteen in English and mathematics, let alone history and chemistry. That is because the specific items learned at six constitute such a trivial element in what is required at sixteen. Similarly, 'learning' patterns of even severe misbehaviour at five has no obvious strong direct connection with stealing at fifteen or housebreaking at twenty-five, yet there are connections. Why? Part of the answer lies in the value of some skills for further learning – reading constitutes an obvious example of that kind. Part, too, may be found in the rewarding nature of some forms of learning, so encouraging people to put themselves in positions in which further learning opportunities arise. Learning to cope with responsibility, or social problem solving, or social skills may all involve this element. If persistence of learned responses is viewed in this fashion, attention shifts to issues such as the qualities of learning that encourage transfer, generalization and use of skills, and to the qualities of later environments that strengthen or weaken earlier learning. It is apparent that these are indeed important matters.

As well as the learning of specific skills or behaviours, we need to consider the possibility that some environmental influences operate through their effect in impeding, or at least not fostering, the acquisition of certain key skills. This possibility arises most strongly with aggressive behaviour because of the extensive evidence that aggressive children deal ineptly with social situations.[6,346] They fail to recognize obstacles, they do not show planning, they react inappropriately to social cues and they tend to respond adversely to failure. Dodge[346] has argued that their lack of social competence is a consequence of poor processing of social information. To an important extent that seems to be the case. However, it is necessary to add the crucial qualifier that their social deficits seem to be evident mainly in stressful or threatening situations; it is not a general processing deficit. Three issues need to be considered, however, in postulating that a lack of social skills (albeit situationally influenced) provides a mechanism for the persistence of environmental influences on behaviour. First, what are the determinants (environmental or otherwise) of poor social competence and poor social information processing? It is certainly plausible to consider that inept parenting in disorganized families might well fail to foster good social coping and encourage aggressive behaviour.[343] However, we lack an adequate understanding of the origins of social skills.[6] The second query is whether poor social skills constitute the mediating variable between the pathogenic environmental influences and behavioural disturbance. Dodge et al.'s[49,119] findings indicated that they do play a role whereas Downey and Walker's[124] findings suggested that they may not do so, there being more direct influences on aggressive behaviour. Clearly, more evidence is needed to decide on the extent to which social cognitive variables mediate the association between family adversity and child aggression.

The third issue is whether, regardless of its possible mediating role in the *initiation* of aggressive behaviour, social-processing deficits or biases play a role in its *persistence* over time. That it might do so is indicated by the evidence that poor peer relations constitute a predictor of continuing psychological disturbance of various kinds, but especially conduct disorders.[6,338] Once again, however, we have to ask why the children persist with socially unrewarding behaviour, and why should peer rejection increase the likelihood of psychological disturbance developing and persisting? Several possibilities have been suggested.[6] Rejected children tend to receive worse treatment from their peers, being the recipients as well as the instigators of aggression. Rejection thereby increases feelings of stress, loneliness and stigmatization.

In addition, their exclusion from social groups means that they lack opportunity to develop social skills and they lack social support. This, in turn, may lower their self-esteem. We may conclude that a lack of social skills may well play a role in the perpetuation of behavioural difficulties but its influence lies in its consequent chain or 'knock-on' effects rather than because a pervasive learning impairment is stopping the development of adaptive social behaviour.

Cognitive Sets and Models

The discussion of the possible role of social cognitive deficits in aggressive behaviour highlights the need to look at broader aspects of cognition.[404] It is not just that aggressive children are *impaired* in their social information processing; to a major extent they are also *biased* in their mental processing of social cues.[121] In particular, they are more likely than other children to attribute hostile intent when presented with ambiguous cues. As humans, we are thinking beings and, whether we like it or not, the way we think influences both our appraisal of our experiences at the time they occur and the ways in which we remember what happened afterwards.[207,241] When cues are ambiguous, as they often are, we tend to perceive what we expect to see. We are influenced by the other person's reputation, gender and social standing, and by our overall view of the situation. If we feel generally ill done by, innocent remarks and actions are more likely to be seen as hostile, mocking or rebuffing. Also, however, negative experiences are likely to leave behind feelings of self-blame, inadequacy, helplessness and low self-esteem. An important aspect of personality comprises the development of a set of cognitions about ourselves, our relationships and our interactions with the environment (see Harter[204]). Our concepts and ideas about ourselves then influence our behaviour. People tend to live up (or down) to their reputations (see Maccoby and Martin[204]) and the extent to which they struggle to achieve or cope with difficulties is influenced by whether or not they view themselves as socially effective.[15,16] The suggestion is that environmental factors influence these self-concepts and that the cognitive sets then serve to perpetuate the environmental effects because they influence how people deal with future social situations.

The developmental interest in the hypothesis derives from three main facets. First, it simultaneously provides a mechanism for continuity and for change. In so far as the cognitive set influences people's future reactions and interactions, it will promote continuity. However, inasmuch as the set is shaped by experiences, if later circumstances are very different from earlier ones, this will lead to changes in people's concepts of themselves and their environment, with consequent alterations in behaviour. Attachment theorists have used the concept of *internal working models* in this way to explain how earlier relationships influence later ones but also how the qualities of relationships may change over time (see Bowlby[49,50,51] and Bretherton).[53,334] Stern's[459] concept of *R.I.G.s* (Representations of Interactions that have been Generalized) is rather similar.

The second attraction lies in the potential for explaining why experiences in early infancy tend to have less enduring effects than experiences from eighteen months or so onwards. Kagan[55,236] has argued that for experiences to have a high likelihood of effects that are carried forward it is necessary that they be cognitively processed, with influences on self-concept. In other words, if maternal rejection is to have lasting effects it is necessary that the child translate the negative experiences into a self-concept of 'I am an unlovable person'. Kagan suggests that because the sense of self-awareness does not develop until near the age of two years, infantile experiences rarely have lasting sequelae.

The third potential strength of cognitive mediation mechanisms is that they provide a possible means of explaining long-term indirect effects, such as those postulated in the concept of vulnerability mechanisms. Thus, Brown and Harris[61,63] have argued that poor parental care in childhood, sometimes resulting from parental loss, leads to a negative self-concept. This, in itself, does not cause depression in their view, but rather it creates a psychological vulnerability that makes the person less likely to be able to cope with negative events in later life. They argue that the combination of this environmentally induced vulnerability and the negative life event leads to depression.

For clinicians, there is a fourth advantage – namely the implications for therapeutic interventions.[404] Cognitive concepts have played a key role in recent ideas on the genesis and perpetuation of anxiety disorders[18] and depression.[54] The hypothesis is that negative cognitions of various types make it more likely that people will develop an emotional disorder, perhaps because it impairs their coping with stress situations, and that these cognitions serve to perpetuate the disorder by predisposing to vicious cycles of negative thoughts and actions. Cognitive therapies have been designed to diminish dysfunctional cognitions and have proved reasonably effective, perhaps being especially useful in preventing relapses.[91,92]

So much for the attraction of cognitive mediating concepts; but do the research findings support these ideas? To a considerable extent they do, but some key issues remain unresolved. Certainly, it is obvious from young children's talk and play that they are seeking actively to make sense of their experiences, and in so doing, they derive concepts and schemes of various kinds.[126,459] Their awareness increases markedly at about the age of eighteen to twenty-four months and it is likely that their ability to form unifying concepts is quite limited below that age.[234] There is every reason to suppose that from the second year on, experiences are internalized in some way and incorporated into organizing self-concepts. It is also evident that, with increasing age, these concepts grow in complexity, abstractness and ability to include ambivalent or conflicting feelings (see Harter[204] and Saarni and Harris[427]). It is not known, however, whether this cognitive and affective transduction and internalization of experiences influences the persistence of environmental effects. It seems plausible that it would do so but the relevant comparisons have yet to be undertaken.

It is also evident that qualities become transformed over time and that some form of internal processing needs to be involved to account for what happens. For example, secure selective attachments in infancy have been found to lead to greater independence in early childhood[454] and positive responses to potential task failure.[280] The implication is that secure attachments foster a sense of confidence in both cognitively challenging and social situations. The main uncertainty in this inference concerns the possibility that both the earlier insecure attachments and the later independence and positive task performance stemmed from continuing environmental influences.

The crucial tests to examine that possibility regarding the transformation of attachments have yet to be undertaken. However, there are data on the broader question of whether personal qualities carried forward from earlier experiences influence people's reactions to later environments. Thus Brown and his colleagues[60] showed that low self-esteem, which was associated with reports of early inadequate parenting, served as a risk factor for depression in working-class women. The risk was particularly high when low self-esteem was associated with negative factors in the current environment. Similarly, Hammen[258] found that children of depressed mothers who were the target of maternal criticism were particularly likely to develop a negative self-concept. This negative concept increased the risk that they would become depressed over the next few years, and in part, the increased risk lay in a greater vulnerability to current stressors. Grych and Fincham[189] have suggested, too, that the impact of marital conflict is mediated by children's understanding of what is happening in the family.

We may conclude that self-concepts are influenced by adverse experiences and that negative self-concepts play a role in the risk that disorder will persist or recur. However, several basic issues have yet to be resolved. First, Brown and Harris's[61] original model postulated that early adverse experiences operated almost entirely through a latent vulnerability (reflected in a negative self-concept) with very little direct effect on depression. Subsequent work suggests that there are probably both direct and indirect effects, the former being rather more important in the case of chronic depression (see Rodgers[375]). Also, the indirect route involves both the *creation* of acute stresses (through maladaptive interpersonal interactions) and a greater *susceptibility* to these stresses (see Brown et al.[60] and Hammen[258]).

The second issue concerns the nature of the predisposing negative self-concept. Does it consist just of low levels of depressive symptoms, or a generalized negative self-image, or low self-efficacy, or specific cognitions (such as learned helplessness), or inadequate specific coping or social-problem-solving skills? Although many theorists have placed emphasis on specific cognitions, the evidence suggests that the negative self-concept that creates the psychiatric risk is often rather general, with both affective and cognitive components.[60] On the other hand, there are some pointers to a degree of specificity. Thus, it seems that negative views of personal worth tend to be particularly associated with depression, whereas cognitions about future danger and threat are more associated with anxiety.[63] Also, there is some indication that depression is more likely to be provoked when stress events and vulnerability factors involve similar issues (see Brown and Harris[63] and Hammen[258]).

A third uncertainty concerns the interconnections between cognitions, affect and overall disorder. Although some theories have suggested that the negative cognitions are basic, the evidence indicates a more complex set of two-way relationships. Thus, affective states influence cognitive processing (when you are depressed you are much more likely to remember negative events), as well as the other way round.[47] Also, although cognitive therapies relieve depressed mood, so also antidepressant drugs diminish dysfunctional cognitions.[314] We may conclude that cognitive/affective sets do indeed play a part in the perpetuation of environmental effects but they do not constitute the whole story and there is a lot still to be learned about the underlying processes.

Interpersonal Interactions and Indirect Chain Effects

As we have noted already, one key mechanism in the perpetuation of disorder is that people behave in ways that shape their later environments, so prolonging high-risk or low-risk experiences. One very useful way of investigating this possibility has been the setting up of contrived peer groups.[96,118] Children who have been observed to be popular or rejected, aggressive or non-aggressive, in their natural settings are brought together with other children whom they do not know. The results have shown that, over the course of just a few play sessions, social situations closely similar to those in their natural situations are recreated. However, the effects stem from reputations, as well as from the children's actual behaviour. This has been shown by noting children's responses to vignettes or actual situations with actors labelled as popular or unpopular. Ambiguous behaviour tends to be interpreted positively if children think the person is popular and negatively if thought unpopular.[6]

Similar processes, involving series of indirect connections, appear to account for many of the long-term effects of experiences in childhood. For example, Pedersen et al.[345] investigated the effects on children of one outstanding first-grade teacher. The findings showed that the teacher had a major effect on children's academic achievement, work effort and initiative during the following year, but that there were negligible *direct* effects thereafter. On the other hand, the *indirect* effects over the longer term were substantial. It was postulated that this was because the children had acquired styles of work and behaviour that brought success, which in turn reinforced their efforts. Similarly, it seemed that their behaviour in class probably made them more rewarding students for the teachers of later classes, who then responded to them in ways that facilitated their continuing success. The most systematic attempt to examine the long-term benefits of high-quality preschool education is provided by the Perry preschool project.[34] IQ benefits did not persist beyond the early years of schooling but other benefits were evident up to the age of nineteen – in terms of improved scholastic achievement, a lower rate of delinquency and a higher rate of employment. Analyses suggested that the initial effect of preschool on intellectual performance generated long-term effects through intermediate direct effects on scholastic achievement and its indirect effects on social maturity and commitment to the educational process. Long-term success was found to be dependent on parental and family support for education, the presence of positive role models (particularly those who demonstrated the value of schooling), a sense of responsibility that extended to other people, and an active goal-oriented approach to life. An effective mutually supportive 'mesh' between home and school was important in fostering positive chain effects leading to long-term benefits.

Two examples of long-term chain effects may serve to illus-

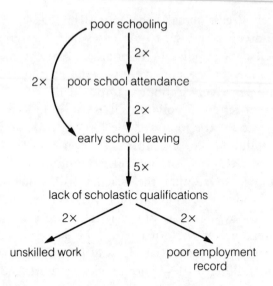

3.11 Simplified diagram showing pathway from poor schooling to poor job success. (2 × and 5 × indicate a twofold or fivefold increase in risk.)

From Gray *et al.*[182]

trate these processes. The first consists of a long-term follow-up of inner London children from the age of ten to one year after leaving school.[182] There was a strong immediate effect of the quality of the school attended[420] but no long-term effect of schooling that was independent of later circumstances. However, indirect continuities were quite strong (see Figure 3.11). The children who went to less effective schools were twice as likely as other children to show poor school attendance; poor attenders were twice as likely to leave school early without sitting national examinations; those without qualifications were twice as likely to go into unskilled work and were twice as likely to have a poor employment record, as shown by their getting dismissed from jobs. These continuities were still evident after controlling for other variables such as the individual's measured intelligence and social circumstances.

The second example comes from a follow-up by Quinton and Rutter[361] of girls reared in group foster homes; the findings showed a chain by which parenting breakdown in one generation

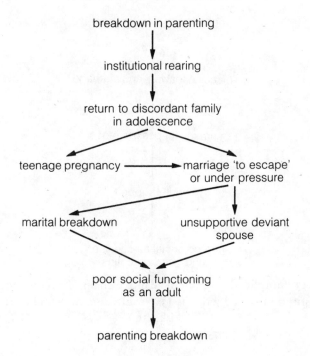

breakdown in parenting

institutional rearing

return to discordant family
in adolescence

teenage pregnancy ———————► marriage 'to escape'
or under pressure

marital breakdown

unsupportive deviant
spouse

poor social functioning
as an adult

parenting breakdown

3.12 Simplified model of intergenerational transmission of
parenting breakdown.
From Quinton and Rutter.[361]

sometimes led to parenting breakdown in the next (Figure 3.12).
The story began with a variety of psychosocial problems shown
by the girls' parents; these were associated with parenting difficulties and lack of social support, which in turn led to the girls'
admission to group homes where they remained off and on, or
continuously, until adolescence. On leaving the institution, many
of the girls either had no family to which they could go, or they
returned to the same discordant families from which they had
been 'rescued' when young. Faced with these stressful circumstances, many married hastily to 'escape' or under pressure as a
result of a teenage pregnancy. The institutional upbringing led
many of the girls to feel that they could not control their lives
and they tended not to plan ahead with either work or
marriage. As one might have expected, these impulsive marriages

positive school experiences

|3×
▼

planning for work and marriage

|12×
▼

marriage for positive reasons

|5×
▼

marital support

|3×
▼

good social functioning
and good parenting

3.13 Simplified diagram of adaptive chain of circumstances
in institution-reared women. (3 × indicates a threefold increase in
risk, etc.)
From Quinton and Rutter.[361]

undertaken for negative reasons were often to deviant men from
similarly disadvantaged backgrounds and many of the marriages
broke down. Alternatively, the women were left unsupported in
a complicated, unrewarding marital relationship. Those adult
circumstances were then associated with a markedly increased
risk of poor social functioning in adult life which, in its turn,
was accompanied by an increased risk of parenting breakdown.

Of course, this chain of negative circumstances applied to only
a minority of the women. That was because each link in the
chain involved a series of contingencies which, if met, were
likely to result in different consequences. Figure 3.13 provides an
example of how a particularly good set of experiences at school
for this same group of institution-reared girls could turn the life
trajectory on to a more adaptive path, resulting in a good
outcome in adult life.

In concluding this selective overview of the connections between childhood and adult life, it is apparent that there are
continuities and discontinuities. These rely on a complicated

mixture of direct and indirect effects, with a multiplicity of straight and devious pathways across the life span and a diversity of end-points.[375,408] Life-span transitions have a crucial role in the processes involved, strengthening emerging patterns of behaviour or providing a means by which life trajectories may change pattern. At all ages, people's psychological functioning tends to be most strongly influenced by factors operating at that time – be they maturational, genetic or environmental. However, the point that comes over repeatedly in longitudinal studies is that the outcome of transitions, and the ways in which they are dealt with, is partially determined by people's past behaviour and experiences. In the chapters that follow we consider these processes in greater detail with respect to some of the key features that apply to particular psychological characteristics or to particular age periods.

Chapter 4

The Growth
of Social Relationships

Social relationships constitute a vital part of people's lives at all ages and much attention has therefore been paid to their development. At one time, traditional psychoanalytic theory postulated an initial asocial, autistic or narcissistic phase. It was thought that infants had to learn to be social and that this learning took place through the rewards of feeding. Bowlby,[49,52] Stern[459] and others have argued persuasively, on the basis of extensive research findings, that this view is mistaken on both counts. Infants are social beings from a very early stage of development; the propensity to be social is part of the human biological heritage and it is not learned as such. Also, babies do not acquire social ties through the satisfaction of feeding needs. Socialization is primary and not secondary. Moreover, in so far as rewards play a part, they derive more from the reduction of anxiety provided by social contact than from satiety after feeding.

Selective Attachments

The focus of attention in the first two years of life has shifted from feeding and toileting to the acquisition of selective attachments. These develop through a series of overlapping phases (see Bowlby,[49] Lewis,[334] Stern,[459] Wolkind and Rutter[417] and Rutter[395]). In the first month or so, infants are perhaps not obviously social. Yet even very young babies show preferences for faces over other visual stimuli and by six weeks they tend to look more closely at faces that speak. Furthermore, from the outset, infants explore their environment and seek to make sense of what they see, hear and feel. Of course, their capacity to understand their experiences is rudimentary compared with what it is like later, but a degree of cognitive processing is evident from surprisingly early in life. At first sight, it seems implausible that we could know this, in that babies cannot tell us what they are thinking. However, researchers have been able to infer a good deal by studying babies' responses to different stimuli. By using looking or sucking (in which speed of sucking determines what is seen or heard from audiovisual equipment), it is possible to determine whether infants can differentiate two stimuli, and which they prefer. By using series of stimuli it is also possible to find out if babies can develop concepts or classes – such as 'a smiling face'. That is, for example, the experimenter checks whether babies continue to show the same response when the smiling face of one person is replaced by the smiling face of someone else. Concepts may also be evaluated by checking whether babies show the facial expression of surprise when presented with a discrepant stimulus – such as a dwarf who has the height of a child but the appearance of an adult (see Lewis[334]).

Initially babies smile and vocalize in an indiscriminate social manner. A positive response from anyone is enough to encourage these behaviours. At about eight weeks they begin to make more direct eye to eye contact, to smile more frequently and responsively to social cues, and to coo as they smile. Over the next month or so their social interactions become more integrated and organized.

By two to three months, babies begin to recognize their parents and respond preferentially to them. They are least likely to respond when presented with an expressionless face and most likely to do so when the mother or father laughs or talks back in a reciprocal responsive fashion. Typically during this period of increasingly intense sociability during the first six months, parents tend to provide exaggerated and somewhat stereotypic overtures and responses. They tend to lean over and put their faces close to the baby, with marked facial expressiveness, and use 'baby talk' with raised pitch and pitch contours as well as simplified syntax and increased repetition. Babies are most responsive to sounds within the register of human speech. At first, vocal and social interchanges are pseudo-dialogues, with parents timing their responses to fit in with their baby's smiles and vocalizations.

Then, over the two-to-five-month period, infants come to show increasing initiative and gradually take greater control over their interactions.

At about six to eight months of age, selective attachments first form. Infants begin to protest and become upset if the person to whom they are attached leaves them. Similarly, they seek closeness to that person when frightened, upset or in a strange situation. At about the same time, a wariness of strangers develops. It is not really a fear, in spite of sometimes being termed such. Rather, it is a cautious interest, circumspection and curiosity. But it does represent a marked change from the unalloyed positive response to strangers that most babies show in the early months of life. Fear as such does not develop until two or three months later and it is much more dependent on the situation. It is least likely to occur if the infant is with a parent, if there is a familiarization period and if the stranger's approach is linked with a toy or game. Conversely, fear is most frequent when a stranger approaches rapidly and seeks to pick up the infant.

It is noteworthy that wariness of strangers develops at about the same time that infants begin to show anticipatory responses based on earlier experiences. Thus, up to about nine to twelve months, infants may cry when given an inoculation but they do not usually cry when the nurse approaches with the syringe, even though they have had previous experiences of inoculation.[271] Cued recall can be demonstrated at earlier ages,[459] but it is in the second six months that memories come to play an increasing role in shaping children's reactions to experiences.

The period from one to three years constitutes the clinging 'I want Mummy' phase familiar to all parents. If toddlers are separated from the persons to whom they are attached, they tend to show characteristic emotional distress/protest reactions. Similarly, they seek closeness when they are tired, ill or upset, or if they are in a strange or frightening situation. The presence of a parent seems to provide a secure base from which children can explore. If parents sit down in a park, their toddlers tend at first to play close to them. Then they make forays further afield, returning every now and then as if to reassure themselves by contact with their parents that all is well. With increasing age, these forays extend further and further afield and 'checking back' occurs less frequently.

Although this is usually regarded as a 'Mummyish' phase, it would be wrong to suppose that children have only one selective attachment, that being with their mother. Most children have multiple selective attachments – perhaps three or four in number. These are likely to include the father, older siblings and other family members such as grandparents. Each of these attachments seems to serve similar functions in providing comfort and security.[396] However, there is usually a marked hierarchy among them, and, more often than not, that with the mother tends to be the most powerful in its anxiety-reducing qualities.

Over the preschool years children come to gain an increasing sense of security without the need for the parent to be physically close. At first the parent (or other attachment figure) needs to be in the vicinity, although less close at hand than was necessary at a year. One-year-olds tend to be very upset if left with an adult whom they don't know, even if they are well used to having babysitters. But, by the age of three years, most children are able to accept comfort from strangers. Also, by the age of three or four, children become less dependent on the actual presence of attachment figures. They become able to understand and accept the reasons for parents being away for short periods and hence less likely to show distress at separation. Nevertheless, if the parent's departure seems capricious, unexplained, unacceptable or frightening in context, separation anxiety will be manifest.

It is sometimes said that these changes reflect a weakening of selective attachments but that is a most misleading way of putting things. If anything, the reverse is true (see Wolkind and Rutter[417]). Thus, older children and adolescents are more likely to show prolonged grief reactions following bereavement and probably, too, they are less able to transfer affections when there is parental remarriage following divorce. It is not that attachments become weaker but rather that children become more able to maintain relationships during periods when they are away from the attachment figure. This is likely to be a consequence of their greater cognitive capacity allowing them to conceptualize the attachment figure as a person who has a life away from them and to appreciate that relationships can persist over time and space.

Bowlby's trilogy on attachment[49,50,51] revolutionized concepts on what is involved in the development of social relationships, and his ethological-based perspective now dominates the field.[53] It has proved to be most useful in a host of different ways[30] and it accounts for the phenomena of children's *early* social behaviour better than other theories.[363] Two main features warrant emphasis. First, attachment still develops in the face of maltreatment and severe punishment. Indeed, young children or young animals are *most* likely to cling when they are frightened and upset. If no one else is available they will cling even to the person maltreating them. Ethological concepts, on which Bowlby relied, suggest that attachment is an inbuilt tendency in social animals, that it has a biological function in providing security and that it does not need external rewards for it to develop; indeed the attachment tendency is evident in the most unpropitious circumstances and this tendency is extremely resistant to extinction in the absence of organic brain dysfunction. The one condition in which selective attachment seems to be seriously impaired, namely autism, is largely genetic in origin[412] and even autistic children do exhibit attachment, albeit not normal in quality.[439,440] Second, attachment is *not* the same as a dependency trait. Indeed, infants with secure attachments at twelve to eighteen months are *less* likely than other infants to show high dependency at four to five years of age.[454] Secure attachments tend to foster autonomy rather than dependency.

There is every reason to consider attachment as a crucially important feature of young children's social relationships. However, it is *not* equivalent to the whole of their relationships. Thus, in many circumstances children *prefer* to play with a peer or a stranger (perhaps because they have novelty value) but, nevertheless, when anxious or upset they will go to a parent for comfort. Four main features differentiate attachment from play. First, anxiety *inhibits* play but *intensifies* attachment behaviour in the form of proximity-seeking. That is, if children become frightened or upset, they tend to stop their games and leave those with whom they are playing in order to seek the comfort of their parents. Second, as already noted, the presence of an attachment figure promotes exploration. This secure-base effect is not seen with strangers. Third, the presence of the attachment figure reduces anxiety in stressful situations. The degree to which this occurs is related to the strength and security of attachment as shown in other ways. Fourth, there is protest and distress at the time of separation if the child is left by an individual to whom he is attached. It is clear that playful interactions differ from attachment interactions in many key respects. However, these are not the only form of non-attachment relationships in childhood. For example, even very young children exhibit strong nurturant qualities towards others, as evident in their doll play as well as in interactions with other children. It is also evident that attachment does not describe the totality of any one relationship. Most relationships involve a mixture of attachment, play and other qualities. In seeking to understand the development of social relationships it will be necessary to determine the connections between these various relationship qualities – a point to which we will return.

In thinking about attachment, it is also necessary to appreciate that, unfortunately, the same term is used to describe several rather different facets of social behaviour. To begin with it describes a set of various proximity-seeking *acts*, such as clinging. The specific set of acts that make up attachment behaviour are likely to vary according to age and circumstances; what they have in common is serving the function of proximity-seeking. These acts are applied to inanimate objects as well as people. Thus many young children have 'cuddlies' (usually a blanket, sheet or soft toy) that they like to hold close when they are tired or upset. Experimental studies show that these objects have much the same (although weaker) anxiety-reducing function as do people to whom the child feels close. However, the long-term consequences are quite different.[396] Young monkeys reared in social isolation cling to cuddly objects in much the same way that they would to their mother. But they grow up with gross social and sexual handicaps. The presence of a cuddly inanimate object is of no use in facilitating the later development of social relationships. In sharp contrast, young monkeys reared without their mother, but with peers, develop surprisingly normally in the long term. They treat their peers as if they were a mother by clinging close in a way that is not at all usual in play with other monkeys of their own age. It seems that normal social relationships at maturity require some form of early relationship that has attachment qualities but it is of no great moment whether or not that relationship is with the mother. In ordinary circumstances, it is formed with a caregiver but, in the absence of a caregiver, it will be formed with any other monkey, young or old, who happens to be available. Studies of humans suggest that much the same takes place.[396]

We need, therefore, to consider how specific attachment *interactions* lead on to selective attachment *relationships*. In doing so, it is necessary to recognize that the attachment features of such relationships will vary in quality, as well as strength. In that connection, Ainsworth's[4] concept of attachment 'security', together with the experimental paradigm (the 'strange situation') designed to assess these qualities has been most influential. The 'strange situation' involves eight episodes of three minutes or less in which the infant is alone, with the mother or with a stranger – a procedure designed to assess the child's reactions to separation and reunion. It works best with twelve-to-eighteen-month-olds and traditionally it has given rise to a three-fold classification. Behaviour indicative of security (type B) is shown by a tendency to seek proximity and contact with attachment figures, especially during reunion, together with a clear preference for the caregiver over the stranger, and no more than a little distress before the separation and after the reunion. Avoidant insecurity (type A) is shown by a failure to cling when held, avoidance of the caregiver during the reunion and a tendency to react to the stranger and the caregiver in similar fashion; as with type B, there is little distress. Resistant insecurity (type C) is shown by resistance to interaction and contact with the caregiver, associated with contact and proximity-seeking behaviour; there tends to be relatively high distress after reunion, and sometimes pre-separation.

Although not free of problems,[260] this classification has proved both reliable and predictive in ordinary populations (see Sroufe[30,452]) but studies of the interactions of infants with very severely depressed or physically abusing mothers have shown that some of these children behave in ways not readily encompassed by the usual A-B-C classification. Main, Radke-Yarrow and Crittenden have each come up with modifications to cover A/C or D patterns, variously termed 'disorganized' or 'avoidant-resistant'.[30,184,341] These are characterized by contradictory behaviour patterns (such as gazing away while held, or approaching with averted gaze), a combination of resistance and avoidance, and unusual expressions of negative emotion.

It is important to note that, initially, this security/insecurity quality refers to the child's side of a particular *dyadic* relationship with one individual. This is indicated by the repeated finding that the qualities shown in interaction with the mother are only weakly related to the qualities shown in interaction with the father (see Campos *et al.*[190]), although there is some association between the two.[158]

Nevertheless, several studies have shown quite substantial associations between security/insecurity in the infant–mother relationship at twelve to eighteen months of age and social relationships with peers and other adults one to four years later (see Campos *et al.*[190] and Sroufe[30,211,452]). The general finding is that securely attached infants are more sociable with adults, show greater competence with peers, more positive affect and higher self-esteem. In addition, there is limited evidence that insecure attachment may somewhat increase the risk for later emotional/behavioural problems,[30,211,452] although findings are somewhat contradictory on this point.[141] It seems that, somehow, what starts as a dyadic feature becomes a characteristic of the individual that, to a moderate extent, predicts across a range of social relationships. The finding raises several queries. The first issue is whether the continuity truly reflects some quality of the individual child rather than persistence of those environmental features that influence social behaviour. There is very little evidence to test these alternatives but it seems that both may apply to some extent.[453] In so far as the qualities of early attachment predict later peer relationships, we need to ask *which* dyadic relationship predicts (because children may show a secure relationship with one parent but an insecure one with the other, and because the qualities of any one relationship may change over time as social circumstances alter). Again, knowledge on this point is limited but it seems likely that the importance and duration of relationships, as well as the consistency in quality across dyads, will be influential.

The third query is how a dyadic quality becomes transformed over time into a characteristic of the individual. Actually, that is rather a misleading way of putting things as the evidence clearly shows that relationship qualities do not distil down to a single behavioural trait. Of course, to some extent, individuals may show a somewhat general tendency to be open or guarded, warm or cold, trusting or suspicious in their relationships. However, not only do these qualities alter over time if people's experiences with relationships change, but it is also necessary to account for complementarity, rivalry and jealousy in relationships. The general assumption is that relationships are modulated and controlled by some sort of internalized set of social styles and expectations which includes both cognitive and emotional components. As we noted earlier, following Bowlby, Bretherton[334] termed this an 'internal working model' of relationships; Stern[459] referred to R.I.G.s (Representations of Interactions that have been Generalized) and Lewis[334] to self-concepts. In essence these terms simply mean that as we accumulate more relationships, our expectations about new relationships and our behaviour in those relationships are shaped by those we have had in the past. However, the terms also emphasize the cognitive element in the internal concepts that shape our social behaviour. There is no doubt that something of this kind takes place but, so far, the notions remain at too general a level to have much predictive power.

Factors Influencing Attachment

In considering influences on attachment, a sharp distinction needs to be made between attachment behaviour, attachment relationships and the security qualities of those relationships. As we have seen, attachment behaviours develop in nearly all circumstances. The propensity to show such behaviours seems to be biologically inbuilt and related to some aspect of maturation in that, regardless of experiences, they do not appear until about halfway through the first year. However, once they have developed, the *circumstances* of their manifestation are much influenced by situation and state – being increased at times of tiredness, distress or anxiety.

The development of a relationship with attachment qualities differs in that it requires a responsive partner in the dyad and, moreover, it requires one who is regularly available over time. The practical consequence of this latter consideration is that an ever-changing roster of warm, responsive, interactive caregivers is *not* enough. It has been found that a lack of continuity in caregiving, as unfortunately is the situation in most residential nurseries, is accompanied by impaired selectivity in attachment relationships (see Rutter[396] and Wolkind and Rutter[417]). Thus Tizard and her colleagues undertook a prospective study of a group of infants placed in residential nurseries.[476,478] In most respects the nurseries provided a high-quality environment, but staff turnover was high. During the first four and a half years the children experienced on average some fifty different caregivers. At two years of age, the children were found to be more clinging and diffuse in their attachments than children brought up in ordinary families. Note that they were not impaired in the *amount* of attachment behaviour; on the contrary, they were *more* clinging. The difference lay in the reduced selectivity. At four years they were still less likely than controls to show deep attachments to their caregivers, but also they had become attention-seeking and unusually friendly with strangers. At eight, these qualities continued but, in addition, they tended to be restless, disobedient and unpopular at school. Altogether, it seemed that these institution-reared children were impaired in the selectivity of their attachment relationships.

The factors influencing the *security* of such relationships are somewhat different. Other things being equal, security is more likely when parents interact actively with the baby and are responsive to the baby's cues. Insecurity becomes more probable with parents who are stressed and unsupported, who are irritable and critical with the children, who have a strained marital relationship and when there is a poor 'mesh' between the parent and the infant. This 'mesh' will, of course, be influenced by the child's characteristics as they impinge on and are perceived by the parents, as well as by the parents' own personal qualities. In that connection, the child's temperamental qualities are likely to be influential,[474] although uncertainty remains on the connections between temperament and attachment security. The type of insecurity generally thought to be most deviant, the D or disorganized type, is most frequently found with infants reared by severely depressed, abusive or neglecting parents. Because the development of secure attachments seems to be fostered by continuity in sensitive care-giving by the same person, it used to be assumed that care-giving outside the family was to be avoided and that group day care was especially likely to be damaging. Of course, the notion that the normal form of care-giving is exclusive care by the mother is quite wrong. As the title of Werner's book[492] on the topic, *Kith, Kin and Hired Hands*, makes clear, it has always been usual for care-giving to be shared – with grandparents, neighbours, older siblings, au pairs and nannies participating in this role. So far as we know, children cope perfectly well with shared care-giving of this kind. Of course, group day care is somewhat different in that it involves a different kind of sharing – namely between infants of about the same age being looked after together by the same adult – as well as between the mother and the group-care worker. Even so, it is evident that most young children who experience good-quality day care with continuity in care-giving show no detectable ill-effects and, in particular, are just as likely as other children to show secure attachments.[508] Regrettably, much day care lacks continuity and provides less personalized care than is desirable. In these circumstances, there are some risks, albeit not as great as originally claimed. For the most part, such risks as there are derive from the poor quality of the care rather than from the fact that it has been provided on a group basis.[298] Nevertheless, it has been suggested that group day care may itself be difficult for babies under a year old when it is on a full-time basis while both parents are working.[29] There is too little evidence for firm conclusions. It is developmentally plausible that group care *might* have different effects when infants are developing their first selective attachments, but it is not yet clear whether in fact this is so. Clearly the risks were greatly overstated in the past; also, even when under a year, most infants develop attachments with normal qualities. However, it is possible that young infants may be somewhat more vulnerable than older preschool children. Whether or not that is the case, it is evident that the *quality* of day care and of children's relationships with their caregivers, parental and non-parental, does have implications for their social development.

Attachment Qualities across the Life Span

Until the last few years, almost all research into attachment concerned very young children. However, it is obvious that selective attachment is not something that applies just to infants. If it is conceptualized in terms of those aspects of relationships that reduce anxiety and provide emotional protection in circumstances of stress, it is evident that these apply across the life span right into extreme old age. This is apparent in the extensive body of evidence showing that bereavement or loss of a love relationship constitutes a potent stressor throughout life (after early infancy) and that the presence of a close, confiding relationship is protective against stress in adults of all ages, as well as in children.

The difficulty comes in measuring the qualities of selective attachment in the years after infancy. It is all very well viewing attachment in these security-providing terms but how is this quality shown? It is relatively straightforward in the infancy period because separation followed by reunion is such a universal eliciting stimulus and because the seeking of physical proximity is such a widespread manifestation of attachment. It has proved possible to extend the concept to early and middle childhood through the use of modified observational methods and parental ratings,[184] but the ground is much more uncertain in older age groups.

It may be suggested that confiding and the perception of closeness are reasonable indicators in adolescence and adult life. The suggestion arises on the basis of the finding that it is this sort of relationship that protects against stress.[61,63] If that were the

case, impairments in these qualities should be evident in adolescence in those children who were reared in institutions and who
lacked selective attachments when young. The Hodges and
Tizard[215,216] findings from the sixteen-year follow-up of the
residential nursery children they had studied in infancy are most
informative. By the age of sixteen, scarcely any of the children
were still in the institutions. Accordingly, the main comparisons
were among the ex-residential nursery children who had been
adopted – mostly after the age of three or four years – the
ex-residential nursery children who had been restored to their
biological parents and the comparison group of children reared
in ordinary circumstances. For most aspects of outcome, the
young people's behaviour was largely a function of their later
family environment. The restored group, most of whose families
were stressed, disadvantaged and disorganized, not surprisingly
had a generally poor outcome. The great majority were involved
with the police or had received psychiatric care for conduct
problems. The adopted children, whose families were rather
above average, fared much better. However, compared with the
general-population control groups, they showed an increase in
anxiety symptoms and emotional problems. This difference had
not been evident at age eight, and it probably reflected the
greater insecurity felt by adopted children as they pass through
adolescence. These between-group differences are what might be
expected on the basis of the children's ongoing experiences,
which were mostly good in the adoptees and mostly poor in the
restored group. The same applied to the children's relationships
with their parents; the great majority of the adoptees developed
close attachments to their adopting parents, in spite of late
adoption, whereas only half the restored children formed close
attachments to their biological parents.

The one important exception to this general pattern concerned
the young people's peer relations. These were strikingly *similar*
in the adopted and restored groups and, in both cases, very
different from controls. The children who spent their first few
years in residential nurseries, regardless of their later experiences,
tended to be more adult-oriented in their relationships; more
likely to have difficulties in peer relationships; less likely to have

4.1 Social relationships in ex-institutional adolescents

	Number of given characteristics shown *			
	0–1	2	3	4–5
Ex-institutional adolescents	19	12	19	50
Matched comparisons	58	21	16	4

* The characteristics investigated were: adult-oriented attitude; difficulties in peer relations; lack of special friend; lack of use of peers for support; lack of selectivity in choosing friends.

From Hodges and Tizard.[216]

a special friend; less likely to turn to peers for emotional support when anxious; and less likely to be selective in choosing friends. Half of the ex-institutional children showed at least four out of these five characteristics compared with only 4 per cent of the comparison group (see Figure 4.1). Adolescents with these characteristics were significantly more likely to show psychological problems, but what stood out was, not any general disorder, but rather an unusual pattern of peer relationships that seemed to lack depth and selectivity. The strong inference is that this pattern was a consequence of some aspect of their earlier institutional experiences and the likelihood is that the lack of selective attachments in the first few years of life constituted the key feature.

The finding is striking and provocative in its implications that the presence of selective attachments in the first three or four years of life may be important for the development of close friendship in adolescence. Some sort of sensitive-period effect is suggested by the finding that attachments to adoptive parents in middle childhood did not seem to have an equivalent effect. There are several reasons for caution in drawing these conclusions: data are lacking on the quality of attachments to the adopting parents, the findings derive from just one study of a small sample and we do not know whether the pattern of relationships in adolescence will persist into adult life. We need to turn to other investigations for support or refutation. Unfortunately the relevant findings are few in number.

What is probably best documented is the occurrence of indiscriminate friendliness and lack of social inhibition in children reared in institutions from the early years of life onwards.[503] The evidence on the long-term sequelae of these features is much less secure. However, Quinton and Rutter[361] found that women who spent most of their childhood in group foster homes tended to have marked difficulties in their social relationships in adult life. This was especially the case for those who were admitted to institutions in infancy and who remained there at least until the age of sixteen. The social difficulties included the domains of close friendships, sexual love relationships and parenting. There were no measures of the girls' selective attachments when young but the considerable turnover in caregivers in group foster homes in that era means that impairments in attachment are likely to have been present in many of the girls. Again, it seems that a lack of early selective attachments may predispose to difficulties in all kinds of very close relationships in adult life. Four caveats must be made, however. First, the women experienced adverse environments in late adolescence as well as early childhood. Second, the social difficulties were usually accompanied by a range of other psychological problems. Third, the women's social functioning was very much better if they succeeded in making a harmonious marital relationship. Fourth, there was some indication that the women's parenting of second and later-born children may have been better than the parenting of their first-born.

Animal studies are also informative. Harlow and his colleagues showed that rhesus monkeys reared in social isolation had severe abnormalities in sexual and parenting behaviour in adult life.[194,388] Again, the suggestion is that a lack of opportunity to form selective attachments is often followed by serious impairments in close relationships of all kinds in adult life. However, it should be noted that the isolation-reared monkeys were often better mothers of their second offspring and that experiences in adult life with young monkeys had an important reparative effect.[319,320]

Although the data are sparse, there is at least the start of a consistent story (see Rutter[395,412]). To begin with, it seems quite clear that attachment qualities in relationships are evident throughout life. This is shown by the consistent evidence that close relationships are psychologically supportive at all ages, and that their loss constitutes a severe stressor from infancy onwards. Moreover, it appears that confiding and emotional exchange may index attachment relationships during adolescence and adult life in a way that they do not in early childhood. Also, it seems that the experience of selective attachments may in some fashion underlie the development of a range of close relationships in adult life (friendships, sexual love relationships and parent–child relationships) even though the security-providing qualities that characterize attachment in infancy are lacking. Thus, parents do not usually feel more secure when their young children are with them. They *provide* security but do not *receive* it. Nevertheless, their early *experience* of selective attachments seems to improve their capacity to be well-functioning parents. The link seems important but it is by no means inevitable. Research findings suggest that, to an important extent, close relationships later may compensate for earlier lacks.

The findings discussed so far concern the consequences of a severe lack of selective attachments. We need to consider next the sequelae of marked *insecurity* in early attachments. There are no prospective studies that include measurement of attachment qualities in childhood to provide solid findings but some tentative leads are available. Thus, the Franz *et al.*[160] thirty-six-year prospective study showed that the experience of warm and affectionate parenting in early childhood was associated with having a long happy marriage and close friendships at forty-one years of age. The finding certainly demonstrates an important continuity over time in relationships but it does not test whether the key quality lay in attachment features. Retrospective studies also imply continuities. It seems that adults who experienced markedly poor parenting themselves when young tend to be somewhat less able to provide sensitive care-giving that leads to attachment security in their children.[53,184,341] Again, however, the connections are by no means inevitable. There are many examples of people who are excellent parents in spite of a severely stressed upbringing. It seems that good relationships later make this good outcome more likely. Main[53] has suggested that, in addition, it may be important for people to accept the reality of the negative aspects of their own rearing but also to achieve a balanced perspective in which their later good relationships allow them to have a positive view of themselves. It seems plausible that how we think about our experiences of relationships may be important but we lack any firm knowledge on the role of such thought processes.

Disorders Associated with Attachment

Over the years, several psychological patterns have been conceptualized as having a specific association with one or other aspect of attachment. It is appropriate to begin with the pattern of behaviour shown by many toddlers admitted to hospital or to a residential nursery. This has been vividly portrayed in the moving films made by James and Joyce Robertson and amply documented in numerous studies.[396]

Reactions of Young Children to Hospital Admission

Bowlby[49] has summarized the pattern in terms of three phases: protest, followed by despair, followed by detachment. Initially, children tend to show acute distress following admission to hospital or to a residential nursery. They cry and search for their parents, fretting and being resistant to comfort and other ministrations by nurses and doctors, appearing generally restless and irritable. Often this is associated with a return or regression to more babyish behaviours, such as loss of bladder control. There may also be intense clinging to comfort objects (such as cuddly blankets), much sucking of the thumb, and perhaps rocking.

After some days, children tend to become less acutely distressed but remain miserable and apathetic with little apparent interest in what is going on. Frequently this is accompanied by aggression to other children or to adults, together with destructive behaviour.

After a period of some days or weeks, the children 'settle down'. Having previously been distressed by parental visits, they are no longer so. When parents visit, they seem not to be very interested. Their interest in play activities renews and they become attached to new people, such as nurses, with whom they have a lot of contact.

When children return home, they often show unsettled behaviour for some time, perhaps weeks or months. There is considerable variability in how children respond to their parents but often there is an initial phase of ignoring, avoiding or rejecting them, followed by extreme clinging in which the parents are followed everywhere, with anticipatory distress at the prospect of any separation. Quite often, too, this is accompanied by anger and hostility to parents, so that the children hit out and behave in a generally difficult, oppositional manner. Many parents find this phase more difficult than that shown in hospital because, understandably, they feel that the children *ought* to be glad to be back home, instead of 'taking it out' on their parents.

This sequence of behaviour is well recognized by most people who deal with preschool children in these circumstances. However, the pattern is far from inevitable and is shown by only some children. Several factors are known to be influential. The first point is that the reaction tends to be at a peak in the toddler age period. Very young infants and school-age children are much less likely to show it. In other words, it is most marked after children first develop selective attachments but before they are old enough to maintain relationships well during a period of separation. Secondly, these 'protest' reactions are greatly reduced if the child is accompanied in hospital by a parent, or a sibling, or some other familiar family figure. Regular prolonged visits by the family also help. Thirdly, the reactions are much less marked if, during the period away from the family, just one or two adults continue to provide personalized parenting. This was shown, for example, by the Robertsons' interesting experimental study in which they took young children into their home while their mothers were in hospital for the birth of a younger sibling.[371] In these circumstances, the children readily developed attachments to their foster caregivers, and overall seemed generally less distressed. Taken in combination, these three sets of findings indicate that the main causal factors are: (i) separation from a key attachment figure, together with (ii) a lack of personalized caregiving during the separation. The implications for prevention are obvious.[398]

In addition, there are several other factors that help. Thus, preparing children and their parents for admission has been shown to be beneficial with children over the age of three, with a key element being the reduction in parental anxiety. Ample play activities during the hospital stay, plus a reduction in unpleasant medical or surgical procedures, are also helpful. Probably the children's temperamental qualities also make a difference, and children who have experienced previous happy separations (such as by staying with grandparents or with friends) are likely to respond better.

This pattern of reaction to hospital admission is one that may develop in children who have experienced a normal pattern of family care, as well as in those suffering adversities or deprivation. However, it is important to note that, in the great majority of cases, the emotional difficulties associated with a single hospital admission are short-lived and of little long-term significance. By contrast, *repeated* hospital admissions do carry some persistent psychiatric risk if at least one of the admissions has been during the preschool years, especially if the admissions have been accompanied by more prolonged family adversities. Probably the risk is diminished if the hospital experiences have been well dealt with, so that there has been minimal distress. The exact mechanisms involved in these modest long-term risks associated with repeated admissions are not well understood, but the way the reunion is dealt with by the parents is probably important. Clinical experience suggests that the risks may be greatest when children's normal clinging responses and unsettled behaviour are viewed as 'naughtiness' and punished, so creating an escalating pattern of insecurity.

Unusual Patterns of Attachment Insecurity

Because in American studies about two thirds of infants tend to show secure attachment, it has sometimes been implicitly assumed that this is the biological norm and that insecure attachments are therefore 'abnormal'. As Hinde[341] has pointed out, it is clear that this is an unwarranted assumption. In other cultures, insecure attachments have sometimes been found to be more common than secure ones. Also, it is clear that infants' responses to the 'strange situation' procedure are bound to be influenced by their prior experiences. For these, and other reasons, 'insecurity' as measured by the 'strange situation' *cannot* be regarded as indicating any sort of psychological 'problem' or need for treatment.[30] On the other hand, the much less frequent D, A/C or disorganized patterns, described above, may come much closer to such an indication.

These unusual patterns have the following features. First, the infants' behaviour with their caregiver appears contradictory, so that they may approach with averted gaze or, when held close, they may look away. Second, the sequence of their responses to separation and reunion contains contradictory elements; like secure infants, they show a strong tendency to seek proximity but also, on reunion, they tend to show both avoidance and resistance, with persistent crankiness and spontaneous aggression that seems out of context. Third, their body posture and movements seem odd, often with stereotyped features such as head-cocking or huddling on the floor. Fourth, all of this is associated with a generally depressed, apathetic or sad demeanour.

There has been too little research into this pattern of behaviour to know whether or not it constitutes a meaningful distinct psychiatric syndrome, but these elements do appear to be connected with rather extreme problems in parenting.

As we have noted already, Tizard's studies,[476,478] have shown that an institutional rearing is also associated with somewhat distinctive patterns of social behaviour. At the age of two years, institutional children tend to show a clinging attachment to their favourite caregiver but more diffuse attachments than would be the case ordinarily. Sometimes this is accompanied by marked shyness but sometimes by indiscriminate friendliness with strangers. By the age of four or five there is usually a similar picture of a lack of intensive selective attachments combined with very clinging behaviour and indiscriminate friendly reactions to all strange adults. Anyone who has visited traditional institutions for children will be very aware of this characteristic pattern. In addition, temper tantrums tend to be frequent and poor concentration is striking. By this age, poor peer relationships are beginning to stand out as a further problem. By the age of eight, overactivity, restlessness and poor peer relationships are coming to dominate the picture. Children who have been reared in institutions tend to be quarrelsome and not much liked by other children. With adults, both familiar and unfamiliar, they continue to be attention-seeking and over-friendly, demanding of attention but resentful and aggressive if corrected. When they reach adolescence, such children continue to show difficulties in getting on with their peers, with quarrels, bullying and generally being not much liked as prominent features. They tend to lack a special friend and, even among those who have such friends, there is a tendency not to confide, exchange confidences and share feelings. Also, there is a lack of selectivity in friendships with, still, some tendency to seek adult attention and approval.

As we have noted, the Hodges and Tizard[216] findings indicate that this seems to be a meaningful pattern. However, it is important to emphasize that these particular relationship features were usually combined with quite a heterogeneous mixture of other symptoms so that the syndrome does not stand out unless looked for especially.

Grief Reactions

For the next example of a psychological pattern that has been linked with attachment, we need to move up the age span to the experience of bereavement: the loss through death of a loved one. In this case, the trauma does not lie in the *development* of relationships but rather in the *loss* of an important relationship. The course of grief in adults has been well documented.[339,365] Often, but not always, there is a brief period of *numbing*, lasting for days, in which the person has difficulty realizing that the death has actually occurred. There is then a phase characterized by the *pain of loss*. Typically there is a pining and yearning for the loved one who has died, often accompanied by an intense preoccupation with their image, sometimes with momentary feelings of having heard or seen them. Usually, there is also a restlessness, agitation and high arousal, sometimes leading to a frenzy of activity at work or at home. Insomnia is frequent and usually there is a feeling of great sadness or emptiness. Typically this goes along with feelings of anger – often at those who 'let it happen' (doctors or family), sometimes directed at the person who died, and sometimes remorse over what the grieving person *could* have done (although marked guilt is *not* usual). Frequently, people both seek comfort from others but reject it when it is offered, so that carers frequently find it quite difficult to know how to help.

This period of pain may go on for months or even years, but usually this is followed by a period of reorganization (sometimes preceded by despair and overt depression). Life then gets re-established and the pain recedes, although it may resurface at times – often at anniversaries, which can occasionally lead to a marked resurgence of grief or even a clinical depressive reaction.

In order to understand the effects of loss and to develop effective modes of intervention, we need to look at factors that serve to modify grief reactions.[339,365] Although some are better documented than others, four main features seem likely to make things worse: (i) an ambivalent or unduly dependent relationship with the person who died (so that the complexity of negative and positive emotions complicates the grieving process); (ii) an unexpected or untimely death (as with the death of a child); (iii) the coincidence of the death with other stresses or crises (such as a family row or the loss of a job); and (iv) previous losses, especially when they have been incompletely resolved.

A clinical example may illustrate the point. She was a middle-aged woman with no previous emotional difficulties and a well-organized ebullient personality. She had a very close happy marriage but in mid-life her husband died after a long, painful illness with cancer of the stomach. She was very distressed by this, but coped well and recovered her usual vivacity and vigour. Her youngest son, a racing-car driver, and a bachelor whom she knew to be homosexual (but she could not quite face up to the fact and denied it), was a great support to her, and her relationship with him, which had always been good, became much closer. Both of them led very independent lives but the relationship was emotionally very important to her. All went well for some years but then he died in a tragic racing accident in circumstances that suggested that perhaps he had taken more risks than he should have done. His death coincided with strains over her daughter's divorce. Her grief was intense and prolonged and although it is now a decade later, her preoccupation with her dead son remains very great indeed. His death at a young age was untimely and unexpected; the blow was much intensified by the fact that she had already lost her husband and by the coincidence with the stresses of her daughter's divorce; also the grief was complicated by the uncertainties in the relationship with her son as a result of his homosexuality – an aspect of him that she had never been able to accept fully. This example well portrays the life-span issues. Here was a well-put-together person with no previous emotional difficulties, who had coped well with previous crises, including the loss of her husband. This was so despite the fact that she had grown up with a severely depressed stepmother whose moods had impinged greatly on the family. However, the timing and personal meaning of the second bereavement were sufficient to lead to a very marked and prolonged grief reaction, albeit one that did not include overt clinical depression.

There are four features that seem to be associated with *less* disturbing grief reactions: (i) the availability and effective use of social support from family, friends and others; (ii) the re-establishment of life patterns; (iii) the development of new intimate relationships; and (iv) the provision of crisis intervention (which several studies have shown to be helpful). A consideration of these influences brings out the fact that grief involves two separate, but interlinked components: the *loss* of a loved one and the *lack* of a love relationship. The pain of the former is intensified by the fact that it leads to the latter. Both the presence of one or more close, confiding relationships and the development of a new love relationship help mitigate the grief.

A developmental perspective involves asking whether grief reactions vary with age. There have been surprisingly few studies of bereavement in childhood but the few research findings that are available suggest some tentative inferences.[389] It seems that, on the whole, the *immediate* grief reaction in children may be less intense and less prolonged than that in adults, but the longer-term effects may be *worse*. Clearly, children *do* grieve, and the characteristics of their grief are generally similar to those seen in adults, but the reactions tend to be briefer and less marked. Probably this is because children tend not to project their thinking forwards and backwards in the way that adults do.[166,418] That is, adults tend to ruminate over what might have been, and on the implications for the future; this tendency to experience guilt and hopelessness is less a feature of childhood. The young tend to be more creatures of the present, and less inclined to dwell on the failings of the past or their fears for the future.

Grief is sometimes made more difficult for children because they are 'protected' from the rituals and rites of bereavement – the viewing of the body, the funeral and the talking about the loss. This well-meaning keeping children away from the external manifestations of death may make it more difficult for children to work through their grief because there is little overt recognition by adults that they have grief to work through. Children may be more resilient after the death of siblings or friends, compared with similar situations in adult life, because they are likely to find it easier to make new intimate relationships. As people grow older, that tends to be less easy because of both the social context (making it necessary to take active steps to have opportunities for new relationships) and because personality features and lifestyles tend to be less flexible. This protection, however, mainly applies to the loss of siblings or friends. The situation with the loss of a parent is more complex. Thus, children are exposed to the grief of the surviving parent as well as having to cope with their own. That is likely to make immediate grief a more difficult matter. Also, the loss of a parent not infrequently has adverse effects on the quality of subsequent parental care (see Brown et al.[418]). When this is so, this tends to put long-term adjustment at risk. In this case, the risks stem, not from the loss per se but from the parenting difficulties to which it sometimes gives rise.

Parental Divorce and Remarriage

The last circumstance to mention in relation to attachment is that of parental divorce and remarriage. Often it has been grouped with parental death as a cause of loss and hence of grief.

Nevertheless, research findings show that this is only one element in the processes involved and *not* usually the most important one.

The mechanisms may be inferred through the empirical findings from longitudinal studies of divorcing families such as those by Hetherington,[102,205,211] Wallerstein[485,486] and the Blocks,[41] as well as from broader-based epidemiological studies[142] and Rutter.[391] Five main points stand out. First, long-term psychological disturbance is more likely following parental divorce than parental death. Second, such disturbance frequently *precedes* the divorce, suggesting that the risks stem as much from the discord and tensions that lead to the divorce as from the marriage break-up as such. Third, psychological disturbance is as common in discordant *non*-divorced families as in those that split up, leading to the same inference. Fourth, the disorders tend to be of a conduct-disorder type – with aggression, poor impulse control, non-compliance and disturbed peer relationships, rather than depression. This suggests that the parallel is with the active stresses of family discord rather than the grief of loss. Fifth, the children's disorders that follow divorce are more likely to arise if parental conflict continues, if the resulting parenting is inept or if the custodial parent is depressed and not coping. It seems, too, that these effects may impact particularly on temperamentally difficult boys (see Hetherington[102]).

The clear inference is that the main risk factor stems from the discord and disturbed parenting that sometimes accompanies divorce rather than from the loss *per se*. Of course, loss may constitute an important element in children's reactions, but it is *not* the main element and the disorders do not take the form of loss reactions. They reflect long-standing problems in family *relationships*, but attachment is only one aspect of such relationships. As in other stress situations, however, children's successful adaptation is facilitated by the presence of social supports.[229] Psychological disturbances in association with divorce tend to be more marked in boys than in girls and, on the whole, they are transient, albeit quite long lasting. It seems that, on average, children's adjustment two years after parental divorce is as good as it was before the break-up of the parental marriage.

Fewer data are available on children's reactions to their parents' remarriage but such findings as there are are most informative. Hetherington[205] has followed children of divorced parents over a period of six years and has examined their reactions to remarriage. She found that the mothers' mental state usually improved following remarriage; the study was confined to the children who remained with their mothers. Other research has also shown that remarriage is almost always associated with a marked improvement in the economic status and living conditions of the mother and the children who live with her. This provides psychological benefits for the mothers but it seems to be less important for the children.

By contrast with mothers, children's adjustment following parental remarriage is much more variable; sometimes it improves but sometimes it gets worse. Hetherington[205] found that, on the whole, boys tended to benefit more from their mother's remarriage whereas girls tended to show more psychological difficulties. Also, younger children were more likely to benefit whereas adolescents did not. It appeared that the teenagers were not at a stage when they were prepared to take on a new parental relationship.

One important reason for this pattern can be inferred from the finding that girls who had a warm, close relationship with their mother *before* the remarriage were more likely to have a conflicted one afterwards. This observation parallels the finding from Dunn and Kendrick's[127] study of siblings. They found that girls with a close relationship with their mother before the birth of a sibling were more likely to be hostile to their younger brother or sister afterwards – some kind of jealousy or rivalry reaction. The same seems to apply to parental remarriage. From the girls' point of view they had not gained a father; rather they had lost a mother!

It was also found that when stepfathers attempted to exert control over the children's difficult behaviour early on, this was associated with poor stepfather–child relationships. It seemed that stepfathers had to build up a positive emotional 'currency' that earned them the right to act as disciplinarian.

We called this section of the chapter 'disorders associated with attachment', but it has been apparent that although attachment does indeed play a part in psychological disturbances associated with loss of, or problems in, relationships, the issues involved extend well beyond attachment.

Social Cognition and Social Relationships

Up to this point, we have considered relationships in terms of their attachment qualities and we have mainly focused on environmental circumstances that influence the development of secure attachments. We need to turn now to other aspects of relationships and to the role of child characteristics. In that connection, we focus first on the role of social cognition and of the psychiatric syndrome of autism. Two basic points need to be made in order to set the scene for what follows. First, attachment qualities are evident in the behaviour of animals such as dogs that lack the complex cognitive capacities of human beings. Also, attachments develop at an age (six to twelve months) when infants' cognitive skills are quite limited. Second, the ability to develop reciprocal, responsive, sensitive relationships would seem to require some ability to appreciate what the other person is thinking and feeling.

With these propositions in mind, we turn to the findings on what has been called 'everyday mind-reading'. Prelinguistic one-year-olds and subhuman primates have some understanding that an individual's behaviour is dependent on what he is attending to. During the second year there is an increasing understanding of other people's psychological states. Naturalistic studies show a steady growth in teasing, comforting and concerned behaviours.[126] At the same time, both helping behaviours and joking become more common. All these actions presuppose some understanding of people's desires and emotions, and research findings indeed indicate that these skills are present and growing at this age.[499] Towards the end of the second year, children's ability to pretend and make-believe begins to emerge. During the third year, the ability to understand other people's beliefs grows and children's pretend play comes to include many more examples of an appreciation of people's mental states, with references to remembering and forgetting, as well as feeling sad, happy or angry. It is striking that evidence of these cognitive capacities emerges earlier in naturalistic situations, especially those that are emotionally charged in some way, than they do in artificial experimental tasks. What stands out in observations of children's behaviour at home is their great interest in other people, together with their practical knowledge and curiosity about what other people are thinking and feeling. At first, this interest is constrained by their difficulty in dealing with ambiguities. Thus, two-year-olds tend to be 'thrown' when adults present a serious face when they are pretending something during teasing. By contrast, three-year-olds are quick to appreciate the difference between reality and make-believe and greatly enjoy the shared joke. Of course, this enjoyment is present at a much earlier age but young children are less able to appreciate jokes because of their more limited ability to understand the contrast between what is real and what is pretended.

Numerous studies have shown that autistic children are decidedly lacking in these mind-reading skills and it has been argued that this lack is the cause of their serious impairment in reciprocal social relationships involving both selectivity and sharing of interests.[19,162] The following provides an interesting example of one of the many ways in which studies of normal development may have important implications for clinical disorders. Wimmer and Perner[500] argued that an important step in social understanding was the ability to appreciate that another person's mental perspective might be different from one's own. They devised an ingenious experiment, using a false belief model, to test this notion; their findings showed that this step occurred at about the age of four years when tested in this way. Baron-Cohen, Leslie and Frith[20] used the same general method, outlined in Figure 4.2, to compare autistic, normal and mentally retarded children. The essence of the design is that a marble is placed in a basket in front of Sally, who then goes into another room. While Sally is out, Anne moves the marble to her own box. The test question is 'where will Sally look for the marble?' (in the basket where she thinks that it is because she saw it put there or in the box where it actually is but Sally has no way of knowing that). Normal and retarded children with a mental age above about four years were quick to appreciate that Sally would look in the wrong place and

4.2 The Sally-Anne experiment.
From Frith.[162]

were amused by the 'tease' that was involved. By contrast, the autistic children tended to say that Sally would look in the box; they seemed unable to understand that Sally's thoughts and expectations were bound to be different from their own because they had seen the marble moved, whereas she had not. Numerous further experiments, employing a variety of different test procedures, have confirmed that this ordinary 'mind-reading' still seems to be lacking, or at least seriously impaired, in autism. On the basis of these findings, it has been proposed that social relationships require some degree of appreciation of the other person's point of view and, hence, that the 'mind-reading' impairment might constitute the basis of the social deficit in autism.

A contrary view suggests that the basic deficit lies in the lack of an empathic appreciation of other people's emotions.[89] The matter is of considerable importance in terms of the basis of both autism and of the normal growth of social relationships. It cannot be claimed that resolution has been achieved, in that both emotional and mind-reading deficits have been found in autistic individuals. Nevertheless, it is clear that much of the fun and playfulness in early relationships require some appreciation of what the other person is thinking as well as feeling. Also, the deficit in mind-reading skills has been found to be more robust than the emotional deficit in autism. Autistic children do have some understanding of whether other people's emotions are negative or positive but they are much more at sea in differentiating emotions such as embarrassment, guilt or surprise that rely on an appreciation of mental states. We may conclude that, although we lack knowledge about the precise connections between mind-reading and emotional recognition, social cognitive skills play an important role in the development of close reciprocal relationships. In that connection, it is relevant to note, as we did earlier, that autistic children often show some elements of attachment even though they lack reciprocity in their social relationships. Clearly, attachment is not all!

Rivalry, Jealousy and Compensatory Relationships

Up to now, we have discussed relationships mainly in terms of their pervasive features. However, it is obvious that people's relationships are *not* all similar in their qualities and we need to consider the variety of ways in which one relationship affects others.[211] Research findings show both immediate and longer-lasting effects. Within families, the ways in which one individual behaves in a dyadic situation tend to be rather different from how they behave when a third party is present (see Lewis[334]). Thus mothers tend to be less involved with their children when fathers are also there. Conversely, the presence of one of the children tends to lead adults to be less involved and less intimate with one another. Because we are social beings, we are influenced in our behaviour by the social situations in which we find ourselves. However, this effect is not just a matter of environmental circumstances; relationships also involve mutual influences of various kinds. For example, as we have noted, Dunn and Kendrick[127] found that first-born girls who had a particularly close relationship with their mothers tended to have a more hostile relationship with their second-born sibling. Conversely, girls who had a rather confrontational relationship with their mothers were more likely to have a friendly relationship with their younger siblings. Two processes seem to be operating here. First, there is a jealousy response when the second child to some extent displaces the first child in their relationship with the mother – a hostile reaction to a usurper. Second, there is a compensatory response whereby a close warm inter-sibling relationship makes up, as it were, for a more distant or negative parent–child relationship.

A further process is probably also involved; this concerns the ways in which parents 'manage' sibling relationships.[126] Thus, Dunn and Kendrick found that in those families in which mothers discussed with their two-year-old first-born children in the early weeks after birth, the needs, wants and feelings of the second baby, the first-born was more likely to be friendly to the baby. It seemed that children, even as young as two years of age, pay attention to the feelings and actions of other family members. Similar processes emerge from Engfer's[211] longitudinal study, from birth to forty-three months, of the connections between marital and mother–child relationships. She found evidence for four different types of link. First, there was a 'spill-over' effect, whereby mothers who described their marital relationship as communicative and affectionate were more likely to show empathetic enjoyment of their child. Second, there was support for 'compensatory' mechanisms; mothers in distressed marital relationships tended to feel anxiously overprotective of their babies (a finding also reported almost half a century earlier in Levy's[270] classical study of overprotected children). Third, when the child showed 'difficult' temperamental characteristics, mothers felt irritable and overloaded; these maternal feelings were in turn associated with marital conflict. Fourth, there was also evidence that to some extent mothers' personality qualities coloured all their relationships in similar ways. However, other research makes clear that it is not just a matter of negative personal qualities leading to negative social relationships. Thus, it has been found that some depressed mothers tend to use their daughters as a kind of security blanket (see Radke-Yarrow[211]). On the face of it, this constitutes an affectionate interaction but, in the context of maternal depression, it may serve to enmesh the daughters in the mother's negative emotional state.

We may conclude that human relationships develop within a social milieu. Most people have both positive and negative relationships with other people. Intense relationships (whether between close friends, lovers or parents and children) tend to have exclusive qualities. When this exclusiveness is threatened by the other person's relationship with someone else, feelings of rivalry and jealousy readily arise. Similarly, it is important for all children to feel valued by their parents, and this means that they are very sensitive to any indication that another child in the family is being more favoured or that they are being less well treated in any way.[128] Also, the desire for close relationships is an important part of most people's biological make-up, so that when one relationship is failing, compensation may be sought in some other relationship.

Qualities of Social Relationships

As we have discussed different aspects of social relationships, it has become evident that they are multifaceted. For good reasons, attachment qualities have been the prime focus of much research. At one time these were seen as synonymous with the mother–child relationship but it is now clear that this is seriously misleading.

Attachment features are evident in many different types of relationship. Although, in our society, children's strongest attachments are most often with the mother, it is usual for attachment qualities to be evident in varying degrees in children's relationships with fathers, brothers and sisters, grandparents, regular babysitters, and other people with whom they interact on a regular basis over time. It *is* important that the children have a secure attachment relationship with someone but the particular person to whom they are attached is much less important. Also, it is clear that attachment is *not* just a feature of infancy and early childhood – it remains an important quality of relationships throughout life. Furthermore, in ways that remain ill-understood, attachment qualities seem to play a key role in the development of a wide range of close relationships – with friends, lovers and children.

There has been a tendency sometimes to view the presence of secure attachments as the key to good relationships of all types. Certainly, secure attachments do seem to predispose to positive qualities in a range of relationships with other people.[452] Conversely, insecure attachments predispose to negative qualities of varied types, including victimization of other children, a tendency to be victimized by others, seductiveness and exploitation (see Sroufe and Fleeson[211]). However, the overall pattern of social relationships will influence how these negative features are shown in different interactions. Thus, for example, Sroufe *et al.*[455] reported that mothers who reported having been emotionally exploited by their own fathers tended to be seductive with their sons but derisive towards their daughters. The tendency for compensatory reactions to occur might also be seen in attachment terms. That is, the need to have a close relationship is sufficiently powerful for people to turn to others when one relationship is inadequate. Hence the tendency for mothers in an unrewarding marriage to develop overprotective relationships with their children.

Nevertheless, attachment constitutes an insufficient explanatory concept on its own. It is clear, for example, that attention needs to be paid to the pervasive tendency for people to make comparisons. Even in the context of generally good relationships children are acutely sensitive to differences in the ways in which they are treated compared with their brothers and sisters. Also, the desire for exclusivity makes an important impact in relation to jealousy and rivalry between siblings. One might have thought that sibling rivalry would constitute an evanescent feature, if only because children change so much as they grow up. It would not seem likely that a two-year-old's relationship with a baby brother would show the same qualities four years later when the children are six and four years old respectively. Yet sibling relationships show surprising continuity over time;[463] it seems that the relationships develop mutually reinforcing qualities. Of course, children differ considerably in the styles of their relationships. Thus, adolescent girls (and perhaps younger girls, too) tend to have rather intense exclusive relationships, whereas boys are more likely to form looser groups of friendship (see Hendrick[125]). Also, whereas adult females usually exchange emotional confidences with their friends, this is less a feature of male –male friendships. It is interesting that even in early childhood, mothers are more likely to refer to feeling states when talking to girls than to boys.[126] However, it seems that males can show this behaviour in heterosexual relationships. Thus, the dyadic qualities to some extent influence individual behaviours, as well as the other way round.

But, even taken in conjunction, attachment and social-systems considerations do not account for the totality of relationships. This is evident in the fact that most people have a mixture of good and less good relationships, that people with the most secure of upbringings can go on to make disastrous marriages and that all sorts of factors influence people's relationships. For example, it seems that warmth and humour greatly facilitate good relationships. This is as obvious in the qualities that make for a good chairperson of committees as it is in the interactions of young children. Perhaps it is partly because these qualities tend to be seriously impaired when someone is depressed that depression tends to be associated with a deterioration in marital relationships (see Gotlib and Hooley[125]). Sensitivity to social cues is also important. Observations of children who are rejected by their peers show that they tend to be quite inept in their social interactions.[6,338,358] The timing and quality of their over-tures when seeking to join a group of other children tend to be all wrong, so that they elicit negative responses from their peers. It is not clear how far social skills lie in cognitive know-how and how far in being appropriately emotionally attuned to others, but both qualities seem to be important. A recognition of the importance of social skills in social relationships has led to various forms of therapeutic intervention designed to help soci-ally inept children learn how to interact more successfully.[6,358]

Lastly, it is important to emphasize the role of social under-standing in relationships. This is shown in its starkest form in the case of children suffering from autism. They are strikingly lacking in the ability to form friendships involving sharing and reciprocity, and in adult life they rarely form love relationships. This is the case even when the individuals show a normal level of intelligence. Conversely, many non-autistic mentally handi-capped individuals *do* form close relationships, so the problem does not lie in general intelligence. Rather, as we have discussed, it appears that it is a lack of an ability to appreciate other people's thoughts and feelings that constitutes the problem. In that this ability does not develop to any marked extent until the second year of life in normal children, it is necessary to ask why relationships are abnormal before that age in autism. The prob-able answer is a twofold one. First, many autistic children show a much broader range of cognitive handicaps that could well include a lack of qualities necessary for very early social relation-ships. Second, it seems that some autistic children, perhaps especially those of normal intelligence, do not seem socially abnormal until some time in the second or even the third year. At first sight, it might appear that something new was beginning to go wrong in development at that age. However, that need not be the case. As we saw in earlier chapters, there are many examples of psychological functions that rely on different qual-ities at different stages in development. Thus, early babbling is *not* dependent on auditory input whereas later babble is. It is highly likely that social relationships in early infancy do not require social understanding whereas later on they do. Also, it is known that the same psychological feature may be subserved by a different part of the brain at different ages. Again, this will mean that when only that part needed later in development is damaged, early performance will appear normal. It is not yet known whether either of these explanations applies in the case of autism but an understanding of how development works means that both possibilities need to be addressed.

In the case of autism, the evidence points strongly to the likelihood that a cognitive lack underlies the impairment in social relationships. However, in other circumstances, it is less obvious that this is the mechanism. Dodge[346] has suggested that it may be so with socially rejected, aggressive children who seem to lack important social skills and indeed that could constitute a part of the explanation. However, research findings suggest that such children show appropriate skills in some circumstances. The problem lies as much in the deviance of their interactions (as reflected, for example, by their tendency to read hostile intent into innocent actions by others) as in any general impairment in social cognition. Dunn[126] has argued that there is a two-way relationship between social understanding and social relationships. Sociocognitive capacities are *used* differently in different relationships according to their quality and, to an important extent, differences in relationships may foster the development of individual differences in social understanding.

Friends and Acquaintances

Sometimes, children's relationships with other children have been viewed as a later development than their attachment relationships, and derivative of them. However, that is not really so. As we have seen, impairment in early attachment does have implications for the quality of later peer relationships. But an interest in other children is evident from early infancy and, in many respects, peer relationships and parent–child relationships develop in parallel (see Hartup[204] and Nash[125]). As early as two months of age, infants orient to other babies; by three months they reach out and touch them; and by six months their interactions involve smiles and vocalizations (although touching still remains very important). Over the six-to-twelve-month period, there are increasingly frequent social actions but less than half of overtures to other babies are responded to. The form of social interactions tends to follow a predictable sequence, with looking first, then touching and reaching, followed by coordinated social interchanges. Year-old infants have a style of interaction with other infants that differs somewhat in pattern from their interactions with parents, touching playing a greater role in the latter. Babies' interest in peer interactions is obvious from early in development but they lack social skills and show limited patterned reciprocity in the first twelve months. During the second year, there is increasing social interaction, which comes to include a progressively greater emotional colouring. Although most of the interaction is positive, negative social acts are possibly becoming more frequent at this time.

Over the preschool years social participation continues to increase, with the interactions involving positive attention and approval, affection and personal acceptance, submission and the giving of objects to the other child. Sharing and sympathy as such do not increase greatly; both are clearly evident by two years of age (see Radke-Yarrow et al.[204]). Children's *styles* of prosocial behaviour alter in pattern as they grow older but empathy and altruism are part of children's make-up from early on. Positive social interactions tend to increase over the first five years or so, but competition and rivalry with other children also become more prominent. Talking, of course, also comes to play a much greater role in social interactions.

It used to be said, based on Parten's studies,[342] that solitary play was characteristic of the young child; then parallel play developed; both being replaced by cooperative play. Certainly, cooperation with other children does increase with age, both in frequency and complexity. However, children continue to engage in much the same amount of solitary play as they grow older. What changes is its *quality*. Such play comes to involve greater functional and constructive activities; make-believe drama also increases markedly (see Harter[204]).

Over the middle years of childhood, interactions with other children become more synchronous and better coordinated. Children also become more skilled in appreciating other people's perspectives, points of view and social circumstances. Aggressive acts in order to obtain other objects drop in frequency but hostile aggression to other children (in the form of insults, derogation and threats to their self-esteem) become more frequent (see Harter[204]).

These points all refer to moment-to-moment interactions between children but it is crucial to appreciate that, from infancy onwards, interactions tend to proceed to relationships (Hinde[208]). At first, this is evident only in a familiarity effect. Thus, babies and toddlers tend to show greater proximity-seeking with others whom they know from previous encounters. As children grow older, familiarity tends to be associated with interactions that are better meshed, more complex and which involve more fantasy. Acquaintanceship then comes to form the basis of friendship, meaning social relationships that are preferentially sought out. In young children these are largely based on common activities; then sharing comes to occupy a more prominent role and by middle or later childhood, empathic understanding and the exchange of emotional self-disclosures become increasingly important. Children's concepts of friendship show a parallel development, with an emphasis on intimacy and loyalty evident in older children, but not younger ones. Personal support is especially strong in adolescence. However, the presence of a friend brings a degree of security at times of stress at all ages. Friends show a higher level of cooperation with one another than do acquaintances or children who do not know one another. Their style of communication also tends to be different, being more telescoped and dependent on in-group knowledge and familiarity – what Bernstein[33] termed a 'restricted' code. At a formal level, it provides a less explicit message but it is the fact that it is not necessary to spell out what is meant that shows the shared assumptions and experiences of friendship. In-group jokes and allusions similarly act as markers of friendship.

It is obvious that children vary greatly in the ability to make friendships.[6] Those who are good at making friends tend to be outgoing, friendly in style, helpful and generally more socially adept. The differences between popular and unpopular children are particularly evident in terms of how they behave when trying to enter a social group of other children.[358] Unpopular

children are more likely to disagree, to ask informational questions and say something about themselves, asserting their feelings
and opinions. It seems as if they are seeking to exert control and
divert the group's attention to themselves rather than attempt to
integrate themselves into the ongoing conversation of the group.
By contrast, popular children are more likely to hover strategic-
ally at first in order to assess the activities and goals of the
group, and then establish themselves as sharing this frame of
reference. Interestingly, they do not necessarily conform with
the group's activities. The two important features seem to be
that they behave in a manner consistent with the ongoing
activity or frame of reference and that they are positive and
agreeable in their interactional style. The latter characteristic
involves a set of tactics for avoiding escalation of conflict and for
working towards harmony by provision of alternative courses of
action or by compromise.

In recent years there has been much interest in the role of
ineffective social processing as a possible determinant of peer-
relationship difficulties.[6,346] It has been found that unpopular
children tend to be less skilful in interpreting social cues, especially in peer-conflict situations; to be biased in their social attributions (being more likely to perceive hostile intent when it is not
there); to be less likely to perceive the probable consequences of
their actions; and to be more likely to use inept and aggressive
social-problem-solving strategies. However, it does *not* appear
that unpopular children have any general social-processing deficit, because their deficits and biases seem to be rather specific to
particular situations. In planning therapeutic interventions, it
appears important to take account of the abnormalities in social
processing shown by rejected children, but the mechanisms that
are involved are not yet clear. Children who are popular with
others tend to be more intelligent than average and physically
attractive (the latter seems to matter more with girls than boys).
An odd or peculiar name, a physical handicap and a tendency to
respond negatively to others' overtures are all associated with a
tendency to be less socially successful. In very young children,
social popularity, isolation or rejection are not very stable over
time, but the temporal stability becomes considerable as children

grow older. Children's friendships tend to be with others of the same age, gender and ethnicity; there is also a lesser tendency to choose friends with similar behavioural characteristics.

It is a striking feature of people that they tend to form social groups whenever they are brought together; this is as true of children as of adults. One of the classic studies of group formation is the so-called 'Robber's Cave' experiment undertaken by Sherif et al.[437] Boys who did not previously know one another were recruited for a summer camp and divided into two groups who lived together at separate camp-sites. Over the course of a week or two, these two groups adopted names, 'Rattlers' and 'Eagles', and developed distinctive styles and group norms. The evidence from this study and others shows that such groups form surprisingly rapidly, interactions within the group come to provide a rich source of satisfaction, and rivalry and competition with other groups is both characteristic and sustaining of within-group cohesion. Interestingly, bringing rival groups together to engage in pleasant non-competitive activities does *not* diminish between-group conflict. On the other hand, coming together in joint activities that require cooperation *does* do much to break down between-group barriers. In the Robber's Cave experiment the first feature was shown by the squabbling and fighting between the Rattlers and Eagles associated with coming together for meals, films and fireworks; the second was demonstrated by the cross-group friendliness and friendships that developed when a 'breakdown' in the truck bringing food was engineered, requiring the two groups to work together to get the engine restarted (the same happened with an engineered breakdown in the water supply).

In children's social groups, dominance hierarchies soon become evident, although the qualities associated with leadership change somewhat with age. Among younger children, the ability to use possessions brings social power; in older age groups the ability to direct play and games effectively is more important; and in adolescence both social skills and athletic prowess (in boys) are important in leadership.

It is striking that throughout childhood, from the preschool years onwards, children tend to prefer playing with those of their own sex.[281] This is especially so in free play situations that are *not* organized by adults. The tendency to form sex-segregated groups increases in middle childhood but it is already clearly evident by the age of three. There has been much debate on why this should be so. The fact that it is especially marked when children are left to their own devices suggests that adult shaping of children's social behaviour is unlikely to be the main determinant, although doubtless it often reinforces the tendency. Also, the sex segregation does not appear to be primarily a function of feminine or masculine play characteristics. These characteristics show little association with a tendency to seek same-sex playmates when assessed at an individual level. The segregation seems to be more of a group phenomenon than a reflection of the tastes and preferences of individual children. Maccoby[281] has argued that sex segregation seems to be largely brought about by children's concepts of themselves as boys or girls.

However, it should be noted that boys and girls tend to have rather different social styles (see Hendrick[125] and Maccoby[282]), there are also important differences between male and female childhood social cultures (see Maccoby[331]). Boys tend to play in larger groups, girls in clusters of two or three. Boys are more likely to engage in friendly rough-and-tumble play; there is also more fighting, both friendly and 'real'. Social encounters among boys tend to be oriented around issues of dominance and the formation of a pecking order; by contrast, in girls' groups there tends to be a strong convention of turn-taking. Both sexes tend to seek to exert influence over others but girls are more likely to do so by complimenting other girls, asking advice, asking favours or imitating, whereas boys are more likely to use hitting, pushing and other physical means. Boys' activities tend to centre on group activities whereas girls' are more likely to have one or two specific 'best friends' (with, however, shifting alliances). Girls' friendships tend to be more exclusive of others than those of boys, and styles of conversation also differ. Girls use talking as a means of cooperation and have difficulty in dealing with conflict. Boys, on the other hand, are more combative in their verbal interactions, with threats, boasts and the telling of jokes as a means of establishing power. Females (both child and adult) are more likely than males to disclose their personal feelings and to share emotions when talking with friends (see Hendrick[125]). However, although self-disclosure is much less characteristic of conversations between two male friends, males tend to show more emotional sharing when with a female friend. Thus, it is not that the quality is missing from the male repertoire; rather it is something about male–male interactions that makes it less likely for emotional sharing to take place. Perhaps as a consequence, females tend to be rather better at providing emotional support. By the same token they also tend to be called upon more often to provide support for others, which can bring its own stresses.[28]

The Importance of Peer Relationships

It is well established that problems in peer relationships are frequently present in a wide range of psychiatric disorders. Indeed, of all individual items of behaviour, it shows one of the strongest and most consistent associations with disorder.[424] However, the association is not just with *current* disorder. Poor peer relations show a substantial predictive association with the later development of a wide range of psychosocial problems.[6,338] The long-term effects are most evident in the case of peer *rejection* and least evident with shyness and social isolation. Several rather different issues need emphasis in any consideration of these findings, as it is clear that a number of different mechanisms are involved.

Peer Relationships as an Index of Emotional Disturbance

The first point is that peer relationships may serve as an index of emotional disturbance. At all ages, our social relationships are likely to be affected by our mental state. It is well recognized that when people are depressed they tend to become irritable and less easy to live with (see Gotlib and Hooley[125]). The effects are most obvious in family relationships, but interactions with friends are also affected. Thus, depressed children and adolescents have been found to have a range of difficulties in their social relationships.[357] To some extent these improve as they become less depressed but some difficulties continue, suggesting that, in part, the difficulties may have predisposed to depression rather than the other way round. Similarly, Hetherington[206] found that when children became distressed following parental divorce this was associated with effects on their play and interactions with other children.

Peer Relationships as an Influence on Personal Behaviour

The influences also operate in the reverse direction. Because, on the whole, people *choose* the social groups they enter, it is quite difficult to separate the effects of the peer group *on* the person from the effects of the person in choice of friends. However, to some extent, the two may be separated by focusing on instances when the social pressures derive from factors independent of the person's behavioural characteristics or when the peer group was influenced by factors outside the individual. An example of the former is provided by Stattin and Magnusson's[458] Swedish longitudinal study, to which we have referred already, in which girls who reached puberty unusually early were more likely than other girls to engage in heavy drinking and the taking of illicit drugs. However, interestingly, this effect was mediated via the peer group. Early-maturing girls tended to mix with older teenagers and hence became part of a social group with a different set of mores. But not all girls joined an older peer group and those who did not do so did not differ from their age group in patterns of drinking or drug-taking. Because the stimulus to mix with older girls and boys arose from early puberty, rather than prior deviance, we may infer that the association truly represented a peer-group influence on personal behaviour.

An example of an external effect on choice of peer group is provided by the finding, noted in Chapter 2, that delinquent boys who moved out of inner London showed a drop in their delinquent activities.[495] The same study provided an illustration of how social deficits may occasionally be protective. Farrington *et al.*[149] found that extremely shy or socially isolated individuals were less likely to become criminal. It did *not* foster good social functioning in adult life but very isolated boys were substantially less likely than other boys to become involved in antisocial activities. Presumably this was because so many antisocial activities are group behaviours and very solitary boys were less likely to be part of the groups that instigate delinquent acts.

Peer relationships may also constitute the origin of negative experiences – as with the experience of bullying or tormenting at school or serious rebuffs from friends. Curiously, apart from Olweus's important studies,[330] there has been rather little systematic research into bullying. However, it is clear that it can constitute a major stress. In that connection it is important that Olweus found, in a large-scale Norwegian intervention study, that appropriate ways of dealing with bullying in schools can have a substantial effect in reducing its frequency.

Peer Relationships as a Mediator of Social Difficulties

We have already noted that difficulties in peer relationships are a prominent aspect of the sequelae of earlier impairments in parent–child attachments. It seems that peer relationships in adolescence may constitute one of the main mediators of attachment qualities. The chief sequelae of an institutional rearing in environments known to impair selective attachments are to be found in a lack of intensity, selectivity and emotional sharing in peer relationships. The findings suggest the value of looking at these aspects of friendship when studying peer relationships, as well as the need to consider such relationships over time and not just with respect to interactions of the moment. Unfortunately, such research is distinctly thin on the ground. Accordingly, we lack knowledge of the mechanisms by which early attachments affect later friendship qualities and we do not know how such qualities predict love relationships and parenting qualities in adult life. The issue is part of the broader question of how one relationship affects other relationships.[211] In tackling that question, it is important to note the frequency with which findings in one sex differ from those in the other. For example, LaFreniere and Sroufe[256] found that attachment security and affiliative qualities in peer relationships were strongly associated in girls but not in boys. Also Stevenson-Hinde[211] found that shyness in girls tended to be associated with positive qualities in interpersonal relationships whereas in boys the association tended to be with negative qualities. Radke-Yarrow *et al.*[211] and Engfer[383] found much the same. The reasons for these gender differences are not known. It may be that shyness has different origins or involves different behavioural qualities in girls and boys. Alternatively, the answer may lie in people's expectations of males and females, with shyness regarded as an acceptable feminine trait, but not a masculine one. Either way, it is clear that the meaning of particular patterns of peer relationships needs to be viewed in its sociocultural context.

Poor Peer Relationships as a Predictor of Psychiatric Problems

As already noted, peer rejection (and, to a lesser extent, peer isolation) is associated with a substantially increased risk for a range of later psychosocial and psychiatric problems.[6,338] The risk may arise through several different mechanisms. First, peer rejection operates as a stressor. Rejected children tend to be the targets of others' aggression; over time their lack of social success leaves them on the outskirts of social activities, struggling to hook up with less socially acceptable peers; they are more likely than other children to feel lonely, unhappy and stigmatized. Second, because they are outside of social groups, rejected children are likely to lack social support and hence be less buffered against other stresses. Third, the lack of involvement in social activities means that rejected children are likely to miss out on important social learning experiences. Fourth, rejected children lack appropriate self-esteem and self-efficacy. Finally, the risk may stem more from the deviant behaviours closely associated with peer rejection than from the rejection *per se*. Thus, rejection and aggression are frequently associated and, on the whole, the long-term risks associated with high aggression may be greater than those associated with rejection. However, probably the risks are greatest when there is a combination of the two. It may be that we need to think of the problems in terms of multiple facets of a broader disorder characterized by social incompetence, rather than risks from separate psychological attributes. As Dodge et al.[346] put it, 'Aggression is a form of social incompetence.' Magnusson and Bergman[375] showed that both poor peer relations and aggression at age thirteen mainly predicted adult problems when they occurred as part of a composite of multiple difficulties (also including hyperactivity and inattention). Psychia-

THE GROWTH OF SOCIAL RELATIONSHIPS

trists have tended to classify personality disorders in adult life in terms of particular traits or behaviour (such as antisocial behaviour) but it may be that the unifying features lie in the pervasive social incompetence, rather than an exaggeration of any individual trait.[405]

However, it would be a mistake to think of peer rejection or social incompetence as a unitary phenomenon. For example, Rubin[6] has suggested that rejection associated with hostile aggressive behaviour ought to be differentiated from rejection associated with anxious, insecure, withdrawn behaviour, and argued that the former may be more likely to predispose to delinquency and antisocial disorders and the latter to anxiety and depressive disorders. That may turn out to be so, but the two pathways may not be so distinct as is sometimes thought. That is because poor interpersonal relationships and antisocial behaviour both tend to generate life stressors that carry an increased risk for depression. Thus, Robins's[372] follow-up of antisocial boys showed that, as adults, they experienced more rebuffs, rejections and broken love relationships than other men, and also lost more jobs, possibly as a result of quarrels at work. Similarly, Cadoret et al.[375] showed that antisocial personality disorders carried an increased, environmentally mediated, risk for depressive problems in adult life. On the other hand, the follow-up of depressed children by Harrington and his colleagues[195] showed that depression carried *no* increase in risk for adult criminality. So, it is *not* that depression and antisocial behaviour are part of the same risk predisposition. Rather, it seems that social incompetence and aggression create stresses that increase the risk for some forms of depression. Similarly, personality difficulties make it more likely that depressive disorders in adult life will persist (see Gotlib and Hooley[125]).

It is clear that problems in social relationships are intertwined with a wide range of psychiatric problems and there is a considerable need to understand the mechanisms involved better than we do at present. However, if the underlying processes are to be identified, it will be helpful to adopt a developmental perspective in the research to be undertaken.

Chapter 5

Anxiety and Aggression:
Fears and Delinquency

Apart from the dementias of old age, disorders involving disturbances of emotions (such as fear, anxiety or depression) or of
socially disapproved conduct (such as aggression or stealing or
child abuse) constitute the most frequent reasons for psychiatric
referral. In both groups of disorders, it is clear that the defining
behaviours are extremely common in the general population and
there is no obvious demarcation between normal variations and
clinical disorders. Thus, the great majority of ordinary children
experience several specific fears at some time in their development; fears of the dark, of animals, of ghosts or monsters and of
strange situations are all very common in childhood.[171,289]
Similarly, most boys engage in delinquent acts at some time.[416]
Often these are relatively minor crimes, such as travelling on
public transport without paying or breaking the windows of
empty houses. Nevertheless, in the cities, about a quarter to a
third of boys appear in the courts and acquire a criminal record,
so that the authorities have regarded many of these acts as of
sufficient gravity to take official action. It is obvious, therefore,
that with both fears and antisocial behaviour it is necessary to
consider continuities and discontinuities between normality and
disorder. By the same token, it is important to approach the
issues with a developmental perspective, asking how these behaviours develop and what features determine individual differences
in frequency and course. That is the aim for this chapter; comparable issues regarding depression are considered in Chapter 7.

Emotional Expression and Understanding

Before discussing anxiety and fears, we need to say a few words
on the broader question of how emotions, as a whole, develop.

At one time, it used to be thought that newborns exhibit only undifferentiated emotions and that, with increasing age (as a result of learning and maturation), specific emotions such as anger, fear and happiness gradually emerge. It is now clear from the work of Izard[334,418] and others that a range of different discrete emotions are already present in early infancy (see Campos et al.[204]). Of course changes take place as children grow older, and adolescents are capable of complex emotions, such as envy, guilt and embarrassment, that are quite outside the repertoire of babies. The question is what 'drives' these changes. Clearly, increasing cognitive skills play an important role. This is most obvious with the complex emotions. Thus, guilt requires an appreciation of what is meant by standards and of people's expectations that these be met. This awareness does not develop until shortly before the second birthday and it is its development that makes possible the acquisition of morality although it does not, of course, determine the specific content of moral standards.[234] Similarly, the experience of embarrassment requires an awareness of what other people are likely to be thinking about one's behaviour – an imaginative understanding. This, too, emerges during the preschool years.[126,499]

However, it is not just complex emotions that are influenced by children's cognitive capacity. Thus, anger may be elicited at any age but the circumstances that provoke anger will alter over the course of development (see Campos et al.[204]). A newborn may show anger if its movements are impeded; an eight-month-old when she appreciates that someone's moving of a desired object means that she won't be able to reach it; a two-year-old by a verbal prohibition of some desired activity; and a ten-year-old by an insult. Cognitive awareness may also change the predominant context of an emotion. For example, when given an injection, young babies mainly exhibit distress, whereas older toddlers predominantly show anger.[227] Comparable changes are evident with positive emotions, such as laughter.[456] This usually arises about the age of four months and is elicited first by vigorous stimulation associated with a steep gradient of building tension followed by rapid recovery. Then, cognitive incongruity (as with father putting on a funny walk or pretending to suck the baby's bottle) becomes increasingly important. Towards the end of the first year, infants will also laugh in anticipation when the parent makes the first premonitory movement of a familiar laughter game. As parents soon realize, social context also influences the infant's response. Crying and laughter are not far apart and games that begin one way may end the other way.

Similarly, even babies respond to the crying of other babies; emotional resonance or contagion is present from the outset (see Eisenberg and Strayer[132] and Radke-Yarrow et al.[204]). This has been regarded as the precursor of empathy. However, empathy is usually understood as involving both vicarious emotional arousal (for which emotional contagion does seem to constitute a variety) and understanding of the other person's feelings, which requires cognitive capabilities beyond those of young infants. During the first six months, infants develop the capacity to discriminate between different facial expressions but these probably become imbued with emotional meaning only in the second half of the first year. About the time of their first birthday, or shortly before, babies begin to show social referencing when confronted with ambiguous situations.[247] That is, when they do not know whether a situation should be viewed positively or negatively, they will scrutinize their mother's face for emotional cues (if she is not present, they will do the same with other adults).

During the second year, infants begin to respond vicariously to other people's situations, and helping behaviours begin to manifest. Over the preschool years, as role-taking abilities increase, children's prosocial behaviours grow in subtlety and complexity. Toddlers tend to share the emotion of the other person, crying when they cry, but older preschoolers become better able to differentiate their own emotions from those of the other person – showing concern and helpfulness without necessarily exhibiting distress themselves. It is not that prosocial tendencies as such increase, but rather that children's styles of responding become more complex. Also they become more likely to respond to emotion-eliciting *contexts*, as well as to facial or vocal expressions of emotions by other people. To that extent, empathic responsiveness probably increases up to the early years of schooling. However, whether or not prosocial acts increase or decrease depends also on other considerations.[76] As children become more aware of who is supposed to be dealing with particular situations they may become less inclined to intervene themselves. Of course, an appreciation of other people's feelings can also lead to negative acts. Thus, it may also give rise to teasing and tormenting – behaviours that increase over the same age period.[126]

The experience of empathy and the social implementation of that emotion in prosocial behaviour do not have a one-to-one relationship. After the preschool years empathic responsiveness *per se* probably remains about the same level. It should be added that there are substantial individual differences in children's propensity to show empathy and in their tendency to exhibit prosocial behaviour; both remain moderately stable over time. A variety of factors probably play a part in determining such individual differences, but one influence is the way in which the children themselves have been treated.[126,196] Those whose parents tend to talk about other children's feelings and reactions are more likely to show comforting behaviour to others. Abused children tend to respond aggressively to other people's distress. Children exposed to family conflict, but not abused, tend to be more responsive than other children to adults' angry behaviour, but tend to exhibit distress and concern.[108,109] It is important that even toddlers show responses to background anger.[107] It is clearly *not* true that it does not matter if parents quarrel in front of young children. Interestingly, children are sensitive to whether or not conflicts are resolved; this is more so with young school-age children than preschoolers.

The social impact of emotions will necessarily be influenced by children's understanding of their own and others' feeling states and that, too, changes with age.[126,196] By about two or three years of age, children can conjure up and pretend emotional states, desires and beliefs, and do so in their doll play. They can appreciate that different people will experience different emotions in the same situation if their desires are not the same. That is, they can identify the mental perspective that someone brings to various situations. They see people as agents pursuing particular goals and as feeling happy or sad depending on whether these goals are realized. Over the next half-dozen years a further important shift takes place as increasingly they come to understand that people's feelings are regulated not only by the consequences of their own actions but also by the emotions and the feelings of approval or disapproval that these engender in other people. Pride, shame and guilt come to be highly influential; at first as influences by evaluation from others and then by their own internal feelings of responsibility and sets of standards.

Quite young children express mixed feelings, but it takes longer for them to gain insight into their own emotional lives and realize that emotional ambivalence occurs and to recognize when this is present. Harris[196] suggested that this is because children's analysis of the links between situations and emotions requires a cognitive maturity that is not reached until a few years after starting school. To begin with, they understand that successive events may provoke one feeling and then another, and then they come to appreciate that the same ambivalence may derive from one situation having both positive and negative facets. By the age of six or thereabouts they have also learned how to hide emotions and are beginning to understand how this can be protective in certain circumstances. At the same time they are learning a range of techniques to control or regulate emotion.[166] Younger children tend to switch situations so that they experience something more enjoyable in order to counter distress. Older children do the same but also appreciate that emotions wane in intensity because one gradually ceases to *think* about the events that generated the emotion in the first place. They realize that painful feelings may prevent concentration but also that concentration on other things can block out painful feelings. Harris[196] made the important point that although these developments are dependent on cognitive maturity, they are also influenced by circumstance. Thus, he found the children experiencing distress in hospital were less able than other children of the same age to appreciate mixed feelings. The observation serves as a reminder that emotions regulate cognitions, as well as the other way round. Bower[47] found that induced mood states influenced memories. Clinicians are familiar with the fact that when people are miserable, not only do they tend to focus on negative experiences, but also they are more likely to remember such experiences than happy ones.

Fears and Anxiety

Fears and anxiety are usually considered together as if they were two facets of the same basic emotional state. However, that is probably a rather misleading oversimplification. Anxiety consists of an unpleasant state of tension associated with an anticipation that something unpleasant may be about to happen. Fear involves a feeling of alarm or dread that is invoked by some specific object or situation, or by an anticipation or thought of that object/situation. Clearly, the two are linked. The sensations of anxiety and of fear are somewhat similar and individuals who are especially prone to develop fears and phobias are often unduly anxious even outside the fear-provoking situation. However, anxiety also overlaps greatly with depression and, indeed, the two emotions may sometimes be quite difficult to tell apart in an individual instance. The dilemma over the interpretation of anxiety arises because, as we shall see, fears and depression seem to run a rather different developmental course and have a somewhat different set of correlates or associated features. Also, questionnaire studies indicate that although anxiety is associated with both fears and depressive feelings, there is only a weak link between fearfulness and depression.[327] Accordingly, in so far as anxiety is 'part of' both fears and depression, its pooling with fears may tend to confuse the picture somewhat.

Research findings on age trends for fears are somewhat limited (and mostly based on cross-sectional studies) but they are reasonably consistent in what they show (see Gittelman,[171] Marks[289] and Rutter and Garmezy[204]). Parental reports, teacher reports and observations of children's responses to experimental situations all show that the peak prevalence of fears is about the age of three years, with a progressive fall thereafter. However, against this background of a general diminution in fearfulness as children grow older, we need to differentiate at least four different groups of fears that differ in their age trends. First, there are those fears that are most characteristic of infancy and which are so common that they are most appropriately viewed as being part of normal development. These include separation anxiety, fears of noises, of falling, of strange objects and of strange persons. These peak by two years and decline rapidly during the preschool years. Although almost universal in their occurrence, there is very considerable individual variation in their intensity as well as a marked influence of social context. For example, the manifestation of fear is less likely if the infant is able to exert control over the situation.

The second group of fears comprises those that are rare in infancy but rise rapidly in frequency during the preschool period only to fall again during middle childhood. Thus, fears of animals peak at about three years, fears of the dark at four or five, and fears of imaginary creatures slightly later than that. Again, these are so common that they should be regarded as 'normal' when shown in mild degree. But, in some children they can be intense and socially incapacitating (and in that sense abnormal). Also, although transient in most instances, they can sometimes persist into adult life. On the other hand, it is very unusual for such fears to begin for the first time in adult life, and when this happens it usually follows some obvious stress event such as a dog bite. By contrast, these fears generally appear out of the blue in childhood without any marked provoking stimulus. There is one other fear, namely of blood injury, that might be considered to fall within this group in terms of its usual onset in early childhood. However, it differs from all other fears in terms of its association with a fall, rather than a rise, in pulse rate. As a consequence, affected individuals often faint at the sight of blood.

Thirdly, there is a group of fears that show no particular consistent age trend. These include both specific fears that generally arise in childhood but which remain common at all ages. A fear of snakes is the most striking example of this kind, but a fear of storms follows a somewhat similar pattern. This third group of fears also includes some, such as a fear of meeting people, that are perhaps associated particularly closely with temperamental features involving anxiety and timidity.

Finally, there are some fears, such as fears of sex or of open spaces, that are not part of normal development and which tend to arise later in childhood or adolescence or even in adult life. These more obviously abnormal fears are often associated with widespread emotional disturbance (unlike fears of early childhood, which frequently occur as isolated phenomena). This would be true, for example, of the state of fear that takes the form of school refusal arising in adolescence. The syndrome is complex, involving a variable admixture of separation anxiety, fear of school, depression and generalized anxiety. Although superficially it may seem to resemble the apprehension of school that is common among young children at the time they first start school, it differs from it in numerous respects. The early childhood variety, unlike that arising in adolescence, tends to clear up rapidly and has a good prognosis. Agoraphobia, a fear of open or closed spaces, also usually begins in adolescence and, again, it tends to be accompanied by more widespread anxiety and other forms of emotional disturbance. Indeed, many now consider that it represents the manifestation or consequence of panic, rather than the cause of it.[18] In other words, it is thought not to be truly a focused fear of a particular situation, but rather to represent, as it were, a rationalization of a panic attack (at least sometimes).

A key question in relation to these age trends concerns continuities over time. Do the markedly different age trends for, say, a fear of the dark and agoraphobia mean that they represent radically different phenomena, with little or no tendency for them to arise in the same individuals? Alternatively, do they both reflect the same latent predisposition but with the manifestations markedly modified by developmental phase, in which case the one should tend to precede the other, with both tending to occur in the same persons? Also, should a distinction be drawn between those that represent an exaggeration of normal developmental features (such as animal phobias) and those that are not part of normal development and which tend to be accompanied by more general emotional disturbance (as with adolescent school refusal or agoraphobia)? This is a distinction that is present, for example, in the World Health Organization's psychiatric classification.[410] The data needed to provide a satisfactory answer to these questions are largely lacking. However, some tentative inferences may be drawn.

Retrospective and prospective studies show that there is some tendency for anxiety disorders (including fears) in childhood to lead to emotional disorders (including phobic states) in adult life.[171] However, most of the studies have combined generalized anxiety with specific fears, and scarcely any have differentiated fears according to their type or age of onset. We are left with the very unsatisfactory conclusion that most children with fears develop into perfectly normal adults, but some turn out to have recurrent emotional disorders of some type, there being a paucity of evidence to tell which is which. The good outcome for most childhood fears is bound to be the case simply because the vast majority of the population suffer from them; nevertheless, probably even those severe enough to lead to clinic referral usually clear up without sequelae if the fears truly occur in isolation. By contrast, the outcome for phobic states arising in later childhood or adolescence seems to be rather worse.

The research findings on generalized anxiety are decidedly thin but, so far as can be judged, there are no marked age trends of the kind so striking with fears (see Rutter and Garmezy[204]). There is a moderate degree of persistence over time, with about a third of children with an emotional disorder at one age still showing a disorder four or five years later. Also, viewed dimensionally, it is clear that children who are extreme in terms of high anxiety at one age rarely move to the opposite extreme of very low anxiety as they grow older. A further important point, to which we return, is that children with anxiety disorders when young rarely go on to show conduct disorders when older and vice versa. There is a tendency for children with conduct disorders to show depression,[195,424] but this tendency does not seem to extend to specific fears.

The findings on sex differences also suggest a differentiation between generalized anxiety and isolated specific fears and phobias. Neither shows much sex difference in the preschool years, and during middle childhood *generalized* anxiety continues to occur in boys and girls with about the same frequency (although slightly commoner in girls). However, *specific* fears tend to be more frequent in girls at all ages from the time of starting school onwards, with sex differences increasing somewhat during the transition from childhood to adult life.

The explanation for these sex differences remains obscure. The animal evidence shows different patterns in different species; in rodents, males show greater anxiety whereas in primates, females do so. Gray[183] has argued that this is explicable in terms of the different effects of social pressures in different species. In humans, the most striking physiological sex difference is that women show *less* response to achievement demands in the laboratory; but that they show a somewhat *greater* response in the very different stressful situation of taking their child to hospital for a check-up.[159] We may conclude that men and women probably do not differ greatly in terms of any general characteristic of responsivity to stress but that they do differ somewhat in the situations that stress them and in their style of emotional and behavioural expression of stress.

In seeking to understand the meaning of anxiety and fears, it is helpful to consider the role of temperamental features and of autonomic reactivity. Kagan and his colleagues[251] have found that about one in six toddlers have a marked propensity to show behavioural inhibition – meaning shy, timid, withdrawn behaviour, in strange situations. This behavioural characteristic showed a moderate association with heightened physiological reactivity, and the combination of the two features was particularly likely to persist over time. Suomi[42] has shown the same in rhesus monkeys. This hyperreactivity is evident only in stress and challenge situations but it is fairly stable over time. The monkey data indicate both genetic and rearing influences on the characteristic, and human twin data[295] show the same. What remains rather uncertain is how far the characteristic of behavioural inhibition predisposes to anxiety or fear reactions and disorders. The available findings suggest that there is some predisposition, but its strength is not known. At the time of school entry, the inhibited children in Kagan's sample had more fears than other

children, especially unusual fears. Also, the offspring of parents
with depression or a panic disorder include a higher proportion
with the characteristic of behavioural inhibition.[380] It seems
likely that this temperamental feature increases the likelihood of
fears, perhaps especially those that are less strongly a part of
normal development.

Surprisingly, little is known about the environmental factors
that influence either anxiety or fears.[171] Bowlby[50] suggested
that insecure attachments in early childhood create a predisposition to later anxiety and phobic disorders. There is some indirect
support for this suggestion in the case of school refusal, where
separation anxiety is often involved (see Hersov[417]). However, it
is more dubious whether the same applies to other anxiety and
phobic disorders. Nevertheless, rhesus monkey studies suggest
that monkeys reared only with peers are more anxiety-prone
than other monkeys and it has been suggested that this may
reflect insecure attachments (see Higley and Suomi[251]). It is well
demonstrated that anxiety and fears (with respect to normal
variations and clinical disorders) tend to run in families (see
Silverman et al.[257] and Rutter et al.[414]), but there is continuing
uncertainty on the mechanisms involved. It is likely that genetic
factors play some role but both modelling of anxious, fearful
reactions and an anxiously overprotective style may also be involved.

What lessons for the clinician derive from these developmental
considerations? Because systematic research in this domain of
development has been so limited, only tentative conclusions are
possible, but the findings do provide some leads. First, there are
different age and sex trends for generalized anxiety, focused fears
and depression. Anxiety shows little change in rate with age and
only a trivial tendency to be more common in girls. Focused
fears diminish in frequency as children grow older and are more
frequent in females after the preschool years. Depression becomes
more prevalent in adolescence, as discussed in Chapter 7, and
shows a marked female preponderance only at and after adolescence. The findings suggest that the disorders that represent
extremes of these behaviours may also need to be differentiated.
Second, although clinical practice has tended to group all fears

and phobias together, this may be misleading. It is important to investigate the possibility that those arising in early childhood, which occur almost universally to some degree and which usually arise in the *absence* of generalized emotional disturbance, may need to be differentiated from those with an onset in adolescence, which are not an expectable feature of normal development and which are much more likely to be associated with generalized anxiety, depression and social difficulties. Third, attention needs to be paid to the predisposing role of the temperamental feature of behavioural inhibition, a feature that has both physiological and behavioural components. It is first manifest early in childhood, with a substantial tendency for individual differences to persist. This feature seems to cut across the distinction between neuroticism and introversion that has been thought to be important in studies of personality characteristics in adult life. We need to determine how the temperamental feature of behavioural inhibition in early childhood links up with later personality characteristics and how the link might be associated with increased risk for some sorts of emotional disorder at all age periods.

Anger, Aggression and Conduct Disturbance

The basic dilemma in tackling the possible developmental origins of conduct disorders and delinquency is that there is no consensus on the nature of the disorder. Of course, there is agreement that it is characterized by a failure to conform to society's rules and expectations, but which psychological process underlies the propensity to engage in socially disapproved behaviours? Traditional psychoanalytic views portray such behaviour as 'acting-out', meaning that the child has dealt with internal conflict by engaging in disruptive behaviour.[502] Modern psychometric approaches, although not accepting psychoanalytic views on aetiology, have perpetuated the concept through their basic subdivision of disorders into internalizing (i.e. emotional) and externalizing (i.e. disruptive) types.[1] The implication is that the focus needs to be on the styles of coping with, or reactions to, internal conflict or external stress.

Perhaps, most of all, there is now a tendency to see the roots in an increased predisposition to behave aggressively. It has been found that aggressivity is a behavioural characteristic that is rather strongly persistent over time (see Olweus[329] and Eron and Huesmann[273]) and it is a very common precursor of later delinquency.[416] However, there are alternative views on the underlying personality quality that leads to conduct disorder and delinquency. Quay[359] has suggested that it consists of a sensation-seeking propensity. Others have argued for a lack of empathy,[141] or an impaired moral development (see Smetana[273]) or a failure to learn from experience.[146] Also, it has been suggested that a key feature is an inadequate impulse control (see Pulkkinen[331]), or a reduced capacity to experience fear (see Venables[303]), or a behavioural trait or constellation of hyperactivity–impulsivity–attention deficit (see Farrington *et al.*[258]), or a deficit in social competence and in interpersonal relationship skills.[338,346]

Finally, social–learning theorists have focused on the peak of disruptive behaviour in very early childhood and the strong associations between conduct disorder/delinquency and family problems of various kinds,[277,402] and have postulated that anti-social behaviour represents a failure in socialization[343] or maladaptive socialization.[120]

All of this sounds very confusing. It might seem that, if we are to adopt a developmental perspective, we should review what is known about the developmental course of each of the many features that has been postulated to underlie conduct disorders. However, that would run the very considerable risk that we would fail to see the forest for the trees, and we are not following that course. Instead, we start with a broadly painted backcloth of the developmental course of some of the main behaviours that seem to characterize conduct disturbances as they occur in the general population. We then focus on the sorts of questions that necessarily stem from a developmental perspective as applied to psychopathology. Thus, we pay attention to factors involved in the persistence of aggressive or antisocial behaviour, to the correlates of age of onset of socially disruptive behaviours, to differences in correlates according to age of manifestation or persistence across age periods, to features that differentiate children showing aggressive/disruptive behaviours from those show-ing other behavioural characteristics, and to the extent to which extremes (which might be conceptualized as disorders) function as if they were extensions of variations within the normal range. We begin by noting the evidence on anger outbursts and temper tantrums as they have usually been viewed as the earliest manifes-tation of aggression and of socially disapproved behaviour.

Age Trends and Continuities

Ever since the classical study by Goodenough[174] some sixty years ago, it has been clear that anger outbursts are very common in infancy, with tempers reaching a peak in the second year (see Parke and Slaby[204]). Not for nothing is this age period often called 'the terrible twos'! Physical manifestations, such as stamp-ing and hitting, are particularly characteristic at this age. Clearly, in some sense this is physical aggression but it reflects both the manifestations of distress (toddlers may have a tantrum when afraid, and are also more likely to have one when tired, hungry or unwell) and of an attempt to gain something (such as parental attention or getting their own way over something they want). The latter is usually termed instrumental aggression and it is particularly common in the first few years, becoming progres-sively less common thereafter.

At the same age that instrumental physical aggression is decreas-ing (i.e. approximately three to seven years), there is an increase in person-directed retaliatory aggression (often verbal) and hostile outbursts (see Parke and Slaby[204]). Preschool children only sometimes reciprocate in kind when another child taunts, ridi-cules, threatens or insults them. School-age children, by contrast, usually do reciprocate and from then onwards people show a marked tendency to retaliate to coercive behaviour by some form of hostile response which, in turn, further increases the likelihood of a coercive cycle developing.[343] During the school years, a further shift takes place. At first, children do not differentiate in their response between accidental and intentional provocation, but by the age of nine years they do. During the next few years there is a further differentiation, so that aggressive children come to respond less aggressively to intentional verbal than to intentional physical provocations. In addition, over the early school years, children become more likely to attribute stable individual dispositions to other people and hence to assess their intentions according to their reputations, and to respond accordingly. Although these changes in the patterns of aggression over the early school years have not been assessed directly in relation to the parallel changes in the relevant social cognition skills (i.e. the ability to interpret other people's intentions), it seems clear that they are likely to be linked.

The main change in the overall level of aggressive behaviour occurs during the preschool years, when there is a drop from the peak at two to three years. There is a paucity of data on age changes during the school years but it seems that there is little overall alteration in the level of hostile aggressive behaviour or of conduct disorder as broadly defined. On the other hand, there is a change in the overall pattern of socially disapproved behaviour.[416] Tantrums, fighting and childish forms of destructiveness diminish as children grow older, but stealing, truanting and vandalism increase in frequency up to the early or mid teenage years. Within delinquent activities, shoplifting and minor theft are most characteristic of middle childhood, violent crime does not usually begin until the middle teenage years and drug abuse is more a feature of the later teens (see LeBlanc,[375] Loeber[257] and Robins and McEvoy[375]).

As is well known, criminal activities fall off markedly in early adult life. However, what is less appreciated is that this diminution does *not* apply to those individuals who persist in these activities; they continue to commit delinquent acts at much the same rate as they did when younger.[148]

Numerous studies have shown that both aggressive behaviour as a dimensional attribute and conduct disorder as a more extreme group characterized by a wider range of socially disapproved behaviours tend to be quite persistent over time. This is so regardless of which age period in childhood or adolescence is being considered. However, it is much less clear whether the continuity spans different types of behaviour. For example, does instrumental aggression in the preschool years predict hostile aggression in middle childhood? There *is* evidence that conduct disorders in the preschool period predict similar disorders in middle childhood.[369] Campbell's[90] important longitudinal study showed that persistence from age three into middle childhood was most likely when the problems at three involved a combination of hyperactivity, inattention, impulsivity and aggression, and when this constellation was associated with family stress and discord. Uncertainty remains, however, on whether the same continuity over time applies to specific behaviours manifest in the early years of childhood. Loeber et al.[278] found that fighting at age six (which is relatively common) did show some persistence over time but it was not until a year later that it had much predictive power. Coie et al.[257] also showed that instrumental dominance-oriented aggression in younger children was not associated with rejection by peers, whereas it was so in middle childhood; hostile aggression was accompanied by social rejection at all ages. However, rejected aggressive children differed somewhat from other aggressive children in *how* they were aggressive. Rejected aggressive children tended to escalate coercive exchanges to get their way or to humiliate the other child without regard for the other child's feelings, whereas non-rejected aggressive children were more likely to seek to end the episode on a positive note, as if appreciating that it is desirable for harmonious relationships to be restored in spite of the aggressive interchange. In the short term, this means that rejected children are more 'successful' in their aggression because other children tend to ignore their aggression or back away, rather than get involved. The price, of course, for the aggressive child is increasing social rejection.

In seeking to make sense of this rather complicated set of findings we need to address several rather different issues. To begin with, we need to ask why aggression and socially disapproved behaviour more generally are so persistent? Three rather different answers could be suggested. First, it could be that the reason is to be found in some genetically based predisposing personal psychological characteristic of aggressive children. That is not very likely to constitute a general explanation, if only because genetic factors play such a minor role in delinquency during the years of childhood and adolescence,[116] and family influences such a major one.[402] On the other hand, adoptee and twin findings indicate a stronger genetic component for adult criminality and hence by extrapolation (because this usually has an onset in childhood) for antisocial behaviour that persists from childhood to adult life. Second, the persistence of antisocial behaviour could be a consequence of the continuation of the family risk factors with which it is associated – namely, parental criminality, family discord, weak family relationships and ineffective discipline.[402] Certainly this is likely to constitute part of the explanation. Third, self-perpetuation of the behaviours could come about because antisocial children act and think in ways that both create vicious spirals of coercive behaviour and establish a negative reputation for themselves that leads other children to respond to them in a hostile manner (see Coie *et al.*,[257] Dodge[117,119] and Patterson[343]). Aggressive children are more likely than other children to misinterpret ambiguous acts as hostile. Because they over-attribute hostile intentions, they tend to come to see the peer group as greatly against them and so treat them in a hostile, coercive manner. Because they tend to follow through regardless of the consequences, they receive a short-term payoff that is reinforcing. However, this also leads to their achieving a reputation as unpleasantly hostile, so that other children treat them aggressively and assume that all their overtures are hostile even when they are not. This in turn reinforces the aggressive children's view of the world as hostile and negative; and so the self-perpetuating spiral continues. Clearly, something of this sort does occur and it is probable that it plays some part in the perpetuation of aggressive behaviour, although we do not know how much.

A second question concerns the apparent, relatively strong, predictive power of aggression in early and middle childhood for later socially disruptive behaviour and delinquency. It is clear from the evidence that aggression predicts non-aggressive as well as violent delinquency. However, it is not so self-evident why it should do so. After all, many delinquent and antisocial acts are covert and not confrontational (this would be so, for example, with cheating, many types of stealing and truanting) so why should aggression be a predisposing factor? Before seeking an explanation we need to be sure that it is in fact aggression that predicts. Perhaps it only seems to predict because it is itself associated with some other behavioural feature that provides the mediating mechanism. One possibility is that rejection by peers, perhaps as a reflection of social incompetence, is the key predictor. However, although poor peer relationships are predictive of later disorder, it seems that aggression is more important.[255] A most likely contender as an underlying predisposing factor is hyperactive–impulsive–inattentive behaviour. Pope *et al.*[354] found that, among primary-school boys, this behaviour accounted for the association with peer rejection. Aggression was associated with rejection only when it was part of a complex of behaviours involving hyperactivity, impulsivity and/or inattention. Farrington *et al.*[375] showed that hyperactivity was particularly associated with early-onset delinquency that tended to persist into adult life. Magnusson and Bergman[406] found that a multi-problem constellation of aggression, hyperactivity, inattention and poor peer relations strongly predicted criminality and alcohol abuse in adult life. However, when this extreme multi-problem group was excluded from the analyses, aggression on its own no longer predicted criminality. Too few studies have undertaken the form of statistical analyses needed to determine the predictive power of aggression when it occurs in isolation for any firm conclusions to be drawn. However, such evidence as there is suggests that aggression on its own may *not* be a particularly strong predictor of later antisocial behaviour.

Age of Onset and Individual Differences

That tentative inference leads us to the third basic question, which concerns the factors associated with individual differences in conduct problems and to the related query of whether such problems are more appropriately considered as qualitatively distinct disorders or as extreme ends of normally distributed behavioural features that occur in all members of the general population to varying degrees. As we have seen, socially disapproved behaviour is extremely frequent in the general population, so that it is natural to start with the assumption that a dimensional approach is applicable. However, it is also relevant that only a minority of young people who engage in such behaviour go on to show either criminality or other forms of disorder in adult life. Moreover, as we noted, genetic factors appear more strongly influential in these less common persistent varieties than in the extremely frequent transient varieties.[116]

In seeking an explanation for individual differences in antisocial behaviour, a developmental perspective requires us to consider whether the factors that are involved vary according to age of onset. Unfortunately, most research has not examined the matter, but those that have are informative. Most conduct disorders and delinquency begin before adolescence, but those that have an unusually late onset stand out as different in several respects. Most strikingly, there is no association with reading difficulties, an association that is strikingly consistent with the more usual varieties beginning in middle childhood or earlier.[306,307,374,393,495] The association with family adversity is also weaker than with earlier onset delinquency.[250,393,495] The findings point to the possibility that late onset delinquency may have rather different origins from that beginning in middle childhood or earlier.

Delinquency of unusually *early* onset also stands out as different (see Farrington *et al.*[258]). In particular, it is the variety most likely to persist into adult life. This is especially impressive because, on the whole, predictions are weakest from behaviours furthest removed in time. However, two aspects of the findings require emphasis. First, it applies to an early onset of *offending* and not to aggression or fighting at an early age. That is important because early offending is atypical whereas early aggression is normative. In other words, the prediction of persistence is from an unusual, and not a common, behaviour. Second, it seems that an early onset is associated with a constellation of other characteristics that identify an atypical group or groups. Most obviously, early onset tends to be accompanied by hyperactivity–impulsivity–inattention and poor peer relationships. Adult criminality and psychopathy have long been known to be associated with *reduced* autonomic reactivity and the same seems to apply to persistent delinquency in childhood (see Venables[303]). It is noteworthy that this is the opposite of what has been found with anxiety, as already indicated. Interestingly, the Swedish longitudinal study showed that such reduced reactivity was associated with hyperactivity and inattention, but not with aggression in the absence of these behavioural features.[248] Hyperactivity is also associated with cognitive deficits and learning disabilities,[471] which are also correlates of delinquency.[416]

Putting these findings together, it seems that serious, persistent delinquency and conduct disturbance are most likely to occur in the case of boys (we know less about girls) with hyperactive–impulsive–inattentive behaviour who show reduced autonomic reactivity, poor peer relationships and learning difficulties, and whose delinquent activities begin early in childhood. It is noteworthy that the risk seems to arise from a constellation of behaviours that are only *indirectly* associated with antisocial behaviour. In so far as that is so, we may infer that the predisposition lies less in a predisposition to behave in antisocial ways and more in terms of a set of characteristics that impedes social learning in some way or which creates an enhanced vulnerability to psychosocial adversities. Accordingly, we would expect the risk to be activated mainly when these individual features are accompanied by an adverse rearing environment, and the evidence suggests that this is indeed the case. In the Dunedin longitudinal study, Moffitt[307] found that the hyperactive children who did not become delinquent had rather better than average family backgrounds, whereas those who developed delinquent behaviour experienced considerable family adversity. Farrington *et al.*[375] found the same in their longitudinal study of boys living in inner London.

A further issue is whether these individual and psychosocial factors serve to pick out a distinctive clinical syndrome or whether, instead, they reflect attributes found in varying degrees in the population as a whole. The first point to note is that the risk seems to stem from a *constellation* of characteristics and not from individual behavioural traits (see Magnusson and Bergman[406]). That is very important to appreciate because it has both theoretical and practical implications. Nevertheless, it does not necessarily mean that we have to think in terms of a qualitatively distinct disorder. It could be that it functions as a

dimensional risk factor but one that is characterized by a combination of features rather than a single isolated trait. The disorder
hypothesis would seem to pick out the hyperkinetic syndrome
which is known usually to involve antisocial behaviour and
which is treated in psychiatric classifications as a condition that is
separate and differentiable from conduct disorder.[410,425] The
evidence is strong that this is a useful differentiation to make, but
it remains quite uncertain whether it is a matter of degree or a
categorical distinction.

There is a very considerable body of evidence on the psychosocial influences associated with aggression, conduct disturbance
and delinquency[343,402,416] (see also Parke and Slaby[204]). The
most important features seem to be: family discord and disruption, weak family relationships, criminality in other members of
the family (parents and siblings) and ineffective supervision and
discipline. With respect to the last of these issues, Patterson[343]
plausibly suggested four aspects as particularly important: (i) a
lack of 'house rules', so that there are no clear expectations of
what children may and may not do; (ii) a lack of parental
monitoring of the children's behaviour, so that the parents are
not adequately informed about their acts or emotions and hence
are not in a good position to respond appropriately; (iii) a lack of
effective contingencies, so that parents nag and shout but do not
follow through with any disciplinary plan, and do not respond
with an adequate differentiation between praise for prosocial
activities and punishment for antisocial ones; and (iv) a lack of
techniques for dealing with family crises or problems, so that
conflicts lead to tension and dispute, but do not result in resolution. In the past, much attention used to be paid to the use of
particular parenting strategies and to the severity of discipline,
but it is clear that neither provides the most appropriate focus.
Parents of aggressive, antisocial children are often quite punitive,
but much of their punishment reflects their own irritability or a
high level of family conflict and tension rather than any consistent attempt to get the children to behave in particular ways.
Maccoby and Martin[204] argued that the most effective pattern
of parenting involves high parental demands and firm control
that is accompanied by parental affection, attentiveness and

responsiveness to the children's needs, and open communication with the child during family social problem solving. It seems that this approach is most likely to result in the children developing their own standards of behaviour, so that they are likely to behave in appropriate ways when there is no adult person to provide immediate control. However, coercive family interactions probably also provide models of aggressive behaviour as an acceptable means of dealing with interpersonal difficulties or social problems. It is also relevant that the experience of physical abuse predisposes to aggressive behaviour.[120] It is likely that similar mechanisms underlie the modest effect of violence seen on films and television as a potentiator of aggressive behaviour in vulnerable individuals (see Parke and Slaby[204] and Rutter and Giller[416]).

The same question about continuities/discontinuities between normality and disorder arises with respect to these psychosocial influences. Do they apply just to extreme groups of recidivist delinquents and children with a socially handicapping conduct disorder or do they apply similarly to variations in behaviour within the normal range? The evidence shows that the associations are substantially stronger in relation to the extremes but they apply more broadly than that.

Where does this leave us? A developmental perspective has been helpful in focusing attention on the importance of age of onset (with respect to both particularly early and unusually late onsets). Findings on the early-onset group have helped to identify a constellation of individual risk factors. These have led to a partial shift away from aggression as the unifying concept to the possibility that at least some of the cohesion is to be found in features influencing social learning, with problems in social relationships a prominent feature. The findings also suggest that the explanation for temper tantrums, aggression and isolated delinquent acts as they occur in most children to some degree may not be identical with that for this persistent, social-handicapping set of problems, although they overlap.

The emphasis on both an early onset and early-appearing behavioural characteristics such as hyperactivity does, however, raise queries about the progression from early risk factors to recidivist crime and serious social problems in adult life. Researchers have begun to ask questions about developmental progressions (see Loeber[257]), stepping-stones (see Farrington[331]) and delinquent careers (see Farrington et al.[258]). The important point has been made that the predictors (and causes) of onset are not necessarily the same as those of progression and, indeed, the few available empirical findings indicate that they do seem to differ. However, a developmental perspective demands that we also ask about desistence from or de-escalation in delinquent activities, and this requires us to extend study into adult life. However, because the two issues seem to have some connection, it is convenient to consider sex differences first.

Sex Differences

It has been a near universal finding that aggression, hyperactivity, conduct disorders and delinquency are more frequent in males than females[225,283,284,343,416] (see also Parke and Slaby[204]). This has been true across a range of cultures and the sex difference in aggression applies similarly to subhuman primates. However, in seeking to account for the higher rate in males, several other points need to be borne in mind. The sex difference is greater for hyperactivity than it is for aggression; it is present in the later preschool period but it is more marked in later childhood and adolescence; the extent of the sex difference varies somewhat by culture, so that in the UK it is greater in youths of Asian background than in whites and least in those from Caribbean background; the sex difference applies to almost all types of delinquency but it is greatest for violent crime; and although the sex difference in delinquency has always been present so far as we know, it has reduced in recent times (in the UK from an 11:1 ratio in 1957 to 5:1 in 1977).[393,416] Moreover, the sex difference for crime varies considerably by age, apart from violent crimes which are always much commoner in males.[148] The sex ratio rises in adolescence to reach a peak in early adult life, with a progressive and marked fall thereafter (see Figure 5.1). Also, the sex difference in aggression seems to apply mainly to retaliatory, rather than initiatory, aggression and to behaviour in male–male rather than mixed-sex dyads or groups.

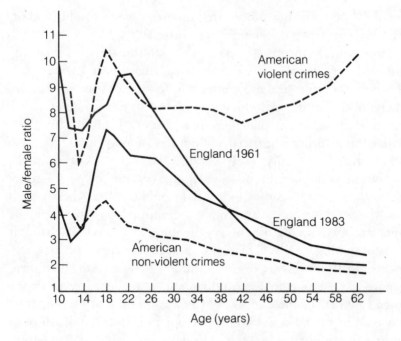

5.1 The sex difference in crime: male/female ratios at different ages.
Data from Farrington.[148]

The evidence, taken as a whole, suggests that *part* of the sex difference is likely to have biological roots. Its pervasiveness across cultures and species argues for such an influence. The organizing role of prenatal androgens on brain development probably plays a minor predisposing role. The factors (as yet unknown) that lead to the marked male preponderance in hyperactivity are likely to be more influential and the rising levels of testosterone during adolescence in males may also potentiate aggressive tendencies, although they do not seem to relate to delinquency (see Rubin[14]). But the variations in extent of the sex difference across behaviours and over time, as well as the increase with age, suggest that social factors are likely also to play a role. Condry and Condry's[98] 'baby X' study showed the importance of sex-differentiated expectations: the same emotional reaction tended to be labelled 'angry' when the rater thought the baby was male and 'fearful' when the baby was thought to be female. Also, of course, there are numerous ways in which adults treat boys and girls differently (see Huston[204]).

However, Maccoby[331] made the additional point that the rather different cultures of male and female peer groups may also be important. She drew attention to several features that are likely to be influential. First, boys' social groups tend to be larger and this means that there is a greater likelihood that they will contain other antisocial children who may influence each other; this is especially likely because the base rate of antisocial behaviour is higher in boys. Second, because boys are more likely than girls to gather together in public places, their play is less closely monitored and boys are more likely to have the opportunity of seeing other boys engaging in antisocial behaviour and not getting caught. Third, fighting, assertiveness and disagreements are all more part of the culture of boys' groups than girls' groups. The Dunedin longitudinal study has recently provided some support for these ideas.[81,82] It was found that early-maturing girls in mixed-sex schools, but not in girls' schools, showed an increase in norm-breaking behaviour and delinquency. Moreover, the increase was a function of their association with older delinquents.

Why, then, should the sex ratio fall so markedly after the mid-twenties? Part of the explanation may lie in the fact that men are less likely as they grow older to be part of all-male groups and hence less likely to be involved in a delinquent subgroup. In support of that suggestion, it has been found that marriage to a non-delinquent female is associated with a marked drop in men's delinquent activities, whereas this is not found if the wife is herself criminal.[249] There has been remarkably little research focus on the marked and well-established sex difference in antisocial activities, but the indications are that both biological and social influences are operative.

Diminution in Delinquent Activities in Adult Life

The last issue to consider with regard to developmental perspectives on conduct problems and delinquency is why there is such a dramatic fall in rates in early adult life. Figure 5.2 provides a summary of English crime statistics, which show the massive

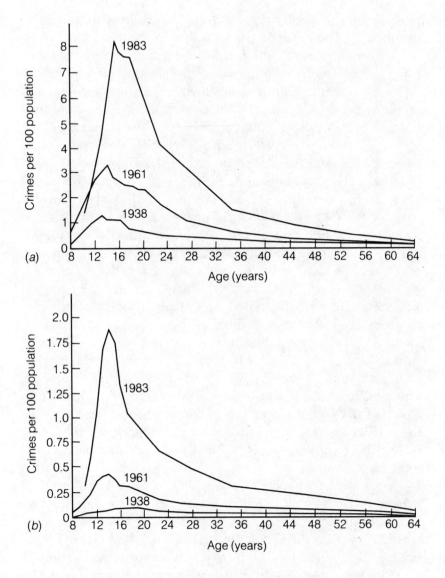

5.2 The relation between age and crime. (a) English males. (b) English females. Both graphs show the rate of findings of guilt and cautions per 100 population for indictable offences in the years 1938, 1961 and 1983. Source: Home Office statistics (1940, 1962, 1984).

From Farrington.[148]

peaking in late adolescence and the huge drop in the early twenties.[148] There has been a tendency to see this as an invariant relationship representing a direct effect of age on criminal behaviour,[212] with the implication that in some way it reflects a biological maturation process. However, a closer examination of the data suggests that this is a misleading over-simplification.[148] Several rather different points are pertinent. First, the age trends have varied substantially over time, with secular trends going in opposite directions in males and females. Thus, in England, the peak crime rate for males was at thirteen years in 1938, at fourteen in 1961 and at fifteen in 1983. American statistics for 1982 showed a later peak than that in England; at seventeen for non-violent crimes and at eighteen for violent crimes. The pattern suggests that the peak is more a function of the age at which compulsory schooling ceases than of chronological age as such. In keeping with that suggestion, Elliott and Voss[140] found that the period of leaving school to enter employment was associated with a drop in delinquent activities. However, the important feature is not just leaving school; it also involves getting a steady job. Those youths who remain unemployed are more likely to continue with their delinquent activities.[17] The life situation seems crucial, one important aspect of it being the peer group. However, the secular trends for females are not compatible with that suggestion. The peak was at nineteen years in 1938 but by 1983 it had dropped to fourteen.

The second point is the one to which we have already drawn attention: namely that whether or not men showed a reduction in delinquent activities in their early twenties was a function of whether or not their wife was criminal.[249] West and Farrington[496] also found that men who continued with criminal activities were more likely than those who gave up crime to be still going around in all-male groups. Other research has shown the same (see Farrington *et al.*[258]). Moreover, a person's own future convictions are predictable in part by the extent to which his friends and acquaintances are delinquent. Of course, it is difficult to sort out cause and effect, because people choose those with whom they associate, but the evidence is certainly compatible with the view that the peer group has some effect on whether or not people continue with delinquent activities.

Third, we need to draw a distinction between the number of *people* of any age who are delinquent and the rate of delinquent *acts* committed by those who are delinquent. Although the evidence is not as strong as one would like, the research findings show that the main drop in early adult life is in the number of delinquent persons, and not in the number of delinquent acts.[148] That is to say, a lot of young adults give up crime in their early twenties, but those who do not continue to commit delinquent acts at much the same rate as when they were younger. Either the age-related influences that bring about a reduction in delinquent activities only impinge on some people or some individuals are resistant to them. For example, if being part of a delinquent peer group was the key factor, no reduction would be expected for those who remained part of an all-male criminal set. Alternatively, it could be that those individuals who continue in crime are relatively resistant to positive influences. Perhaps they are the ones with the high-risk personal characteristics that we discussed earlier in this chapter – with hyperactivity–inattention–impulsivity, low physiological reactivity, etc. The probability is that both apply to some extent. Unfortunately, too few studies have made use of the powerful research tool of examining changes in behaviour over time, in individuals studied prospectively, according to alterations in their life circumstances (see Farrington[406]).

The fourth issue is whether increasing age is associated with an overall improvement in social functioning or just a change in the pattern of problem behaviour. Numerous studies have shown that conduct disturbances in childhood are associated with a greatly increased risk of pervasive social malfunction in adult (life see Robins[331,372,373,375] Zoccolillo et al.[509]). The common adult sequelae include drug and alcohol problems, dismissal from jobs and unemployment, lack of friendships, serious marital difficulties and depressive symptoms. Criminal activities, at least for a while, constitute part of the pattern in many cases but not invariably so, especially in females. Longitudinal studies show that well over half of young people with multiple conduct problems in childhood/adolescence show extensive and persistent social malfunction in their twenties and thirties (we know less about what happens when they are older). The findings make clear that a reduction in delinquent activities is far from synonymous with a general improvement in social functioning. This result also reaffirms our earlier inference that conduct problems may be most appropriately viewed as a reflection of serious social difficulties rather than a consequence of aggression. Aggression is a prominent part of the behavioural pattern, especially in young males, but it does not seem to constitute the basic underlying feature from which all else derives.

Because this progression from conduct disorder in childhood to pervasive social malfunction in adult life is such a consistent one, it has come to be viewed by many clinicians as an inevitable reflection of the 'natural history' of a qualitatively abnormal disorder conceptualized as sociopathy or personality disorder. As we have seen, some of the research findings point to the validity of a categorical distinction between normality and disorder and some to continuity between the two. The jury is still out on the matter and is urging the court to seek more evidence! However, whatever the final verdict on that issue, it would certainly be misleading to see the progression as pre-ordained and inevitable. To begin with, it is not known how far the progression is determined by the children's behaviour considered in isolation and how far by the *combination* of conduct disturbance and adverse psychosocial circumstances (meaning family discord and disorganization rather than social disadvantage; social level as such does not seem to make much difference). However, Quinton and Rutter's[361] longitudinal study of institution-reared children did show that those individuals, men and women, who made a harmonious marriage to a non-deviant spouse were much more likely to show generally adaptive social functioning (see Rutter et al.[375]). It might be thought that this was merely a consequence of a tendency of better-functioning adolescents to make better marriages, but detailed analyses showed that this was not a sufficient explanation. Rather, there seemed to be a truly protective effect stemming from a harmonious marriage relationship – an effect that went well beyond an impact on delinquent activities.

In later chapters, we consider in more detail the consequences of changes in life circumstances as they apply in adult life. However, these findings do point to the value of a life-span perspective when studying developmental continuities and discontinuities.

Temperamental Differences

In our discussion of anxiety states and conduct disorder, we noted that temperamental characteristics may act as predisposing features; behavioural inhibition with anxiety and hyperactivity–impulsivity with conduct disorders. It has been recognized for centuries that human beings are constitutionally different in ways that shape their personality style.[168,251] Thus, people may be described as melancholic, choleric, sanguine or phlegmatic in temperament – terms that derive from ancient concepts of vital body 'humours'. No one seriously questions the reality of basic differences in individual styles of behaviour; they are readily demonstrable at all ages from infancy onwards. Nevertheless, temperament has proved difficult to define in unambiguous terms and controversies continue on just how it should be conceptualized. Perhaps the key consideration is that temperamental qualities are abstractions and not directly observable discrete behaviours. As Rutter[251] argued, they may be thought of as those aspects of behaviour that reflect the intrinsic non-maturational, stylistic qualities that the individual brings to any particular situation. These intrinsic qualities will have a biological basis (including a genetic component) but, like other such biological features, they will also have been influenced by experiences. For this reason, as well as because of maturational effects, they will show changes with development, along with continuities over time, continuities that are likely to increase with age. The qualities have to be inferred, rather than observed directly, because all behaviour will be influenced by situational and relationship characteristics, as well as by personal attributes. Also, all behaviour will include cognitive and maturational components. The intensity of a person's emotional reactions, or activity level, or approach to new situations will be influenced by their cognitive processing of the situation and by their self-concept, as well as by stylistic temperamental features. In other words, temperament constitutes just one aspect of personality. Nevertheless, despite all the difficulties in conceptualization and measurement, temperamental qualities *can* be inferred and they *are* clinically useful. As we have noted, there are children who tend to be behaviourally inhibited in a wide range of stress or social-challenge situations and who continue to show this characteristic to a substantial degree over the course of development. Similarly, there are children who show a pervasive and persistent tendency to behave in an impulsive, overactive, inattentive fashion. Moreover, studies have shown that these (and certain other) temperamental qualities are associated with an increased vulnerability to psychiatric disorders of particular types.

That finding, deriving from a range of different investigations, speaks to the importance of temperamental differences. However, from both a developmental and a clinical perspective, it may be more useful to consider *how* a variety of children's characteristics may influence both their behaviour in the here-and-now and their psychological development over time, rather than focus on the niceties of which ones should be regarded as part of temperament. This broader approach is necessary because it is clear that a range of other 'person' variables are also influential. For example, physical appearance makes a difference. Attractive children are more likely to elicit positive responses from other people (see Patzer and Burke[257]) and those who have facial deformities or who are obese are more likely to be socially rejected (see Barden[258]). Accordingly, we need to consider the mechanisms that may be involved in the connections between personal characteristics and a vulnerability to psychiatric disorder (see Rutter[251]). The first alternative is that the characteristic creates a direct vulnerability. That is what has been suggested for the association between inhibition and anxiety states. In this case, it is argued that the strong tendency to show behavioural inhibition and high psychological arousal in stress situations is, in effect, the trait equivalent of the anxiety disorder, with the one leading to the other. Doubtless, this is part of the explanation but by no means all children with extreme behavioural inhibition develop anxiety disorders, and, in any case, the trait is only obviously evident in stress situations. Accordingly, the second mechanism lies in an increased susceptibility to psychosocial adversities and hazards. As we have already noted, it may be that hyperactivity –impulsivity operates in this fashion, at least in part. The main risk for later delinquency is seen when the behavioural attribute in the child coincides with problems in the family. Of course, it should not be assumed that any particular temperamental attribute creates an increased susceptibility to all psychosocial adversities, or that, conversely, some traits are universally adaptive. Obviously, some characteristics tend to be largely positive and others largely negative in their effects, but the consequences do depend on the 'goodness of fit' with the environment. For example, effects often vary with the sex of the child. Thus, several studies have shown that whereas shyness in boys tends to be associated with largely negative interpersonal interactions, in girls the correlates are largely positive.[383] Similarly, what is viewed by one parent as 'difficultness' may be seen by another parent as 'manliness' or 'independence'.

One crucial aspect of considering temperament in interactional terms is the appreciation that children's characteristics may shape other people's responses to them. Nearly a quarter of a century ago, both Bell[26] and Thomas, Chess and Birch[472] pointed out that some of the findings generally assumed to reflect an effect of parents on children might in reality reflect a causal influence in the opposite direction. Since then, evidence demonstrating that this is sometimes so has slowly accumulated.[27,222] It is clear that children with extreme characteristics of various kinds do elicit different reactions from other people.

A further way in which temperamental attributes operate is in children's *choice* of activities and environments. The friendly, outgoing child will seek more social encounters than will a timid, inhibited child and, as a result, will gain more experience in coping with social situations and with meeting and getting to know unfamiliar people. In this way, temperamental features may predispose children to, or protect them against, stress situations, but also the experiences so engendered may serve to strengthen or accentuate the characteristics themselves.

Finally, we need to consider the role of temperamental differences in personality development (see Rutter[251,405]). While it cannot be claimed that we understand fully the ways in which temperament plays a part in the growth of personality, the latter may be viewed as the end-result of how we react to, and what we make of, the qualities with which we have been endowed (by constitution and experience). Personality reflects the pattern that each person, as a thinking being, develops as a way of dealing with her temperamental traits, the social contexts that she encounters and the experiences she has undergone. Thus, it involves a set of cognitions about ourselves, our relationships and our interactions with the environment. These constitute the self-system that is made up of such qualities as self-esteem, self-efficacy and social-problem-solving skills (see Harter[151,204]). As we grow older, the initial temperamental traits remain a part of our make-up, but our behaviour in social situations will reflect the more complicated personality mix that represents how we have dealt with those traits in developing the style that is distinctive of ourselves as individuals. As we shall see in later chapters, this style influences our response to the situations we encounter as we grow older but it is, in turn, also modified by those experiences.

Chapter 6

The Growth of
Intelligence and of Language

No one doubts that intelligence develops as children grow older. Yet the concept of intelligence has proved both quite difficult to define in unambiguous terms and surprisingly controversial in some respects. Although, at one level, there seem to be almost as many definitions of intelligence as people who have tried to define it, there is broad agreement on two key features. That is, intelligence involves both the capacity to learn from experience and adaptation to one's environment (see Sternberg and Powell[155]). However, we cannot leave the concept there. Before turning to what is known about the development of intelligence, it is necessary to consider whether we are considering the growth of one or many skills. That question has been tackled in rather different ways by psychometricians (psychologists concerned with test construction and measurement) and by developmentalists.[44]

The former group has examined the issue by determining how children's abilities on a wide range of tasks intercorrelate, or go together. Statistical techniques, such as factor analysis, have been used to find out whether the patterns are best explained by one broad underlying capacity, general intelligence, or by a set of multiple, relatively discrete, special skills in domains such as verbal ability and visuospatial ability. While it cannot be claimed that everyone agrees on what the results mean, most people now accept that for practical purposes it is reasonable to suppose that both are operative. In brief, the evidence in favour of some general capacity is that people who are superior (or inferior) on one type of task tend also to be superior (or inferior) on others. Moreover, general measures of overall intelligence tend to have considerable powers to predict a person's performance on a wide range of special tasks. On the other hand, it is clear that this cannot account for other well-demonstrated phenomena. Thus, it is obvious that it is not at all uncommon for individuals to be very good at some sorts of tasks and yet quite poor at others. Furthermore, the influences (either in terms of brain damage or rearing experiences) that affect verbal skills are not quite the same as those that affect visuospatial skills. In general, in adults, the former are subserved by the left side of the brain, whereas the latter are subserved by the right side, as shown by evidence from both experimental studies and the effects of one-sided brain damage (see Goodman[506]).

This subdivision is based on the nature of the task involved, but studies of age-related changes show that this is not the only, or necessarily the most important, basis of subdivision. For example, just over a quarter of a century ago, Horn and Cattell[221] argued for a differentiation between what they termed 'fluid' and 'crystallized' intelligence. Fluid abilities are best assessed by tests that require mental manipulation of abstract symbols such as figural analogues, series completions and classification problems. Crystallized abilities, by contrast, reflect knowledge of the milieu in which we live and past experience of similar tasks; they may be assessed by tests of vocabulary, comprehension and information. It seems that fluid abilities peak in early adult life whereas crystallized abilities increase up to advanced old age. Developmental studies also show that the interconnections between different skills vary with age.[297] Thus in the first year an interest in perceptual patterns is a major contributor to cognitive abilities, whereas verbal abilities predominate later on.

These findings seemed to suggest a very substantial discontinuity in intellectual development between the infancy period and middle childhood. The same inference seemed to derive from three other sets of evidence. First, infants' scores on traditional developmental assessments designed to tap cognitive skills in the first two years of life show only a very weak association with IQ as measured in later childhood.[297] Second, genetic influences on these early cognitive measures are quite weak, whereas they are much stronger for intelligence as assessed when the children are older.[350] Third, the family environment between the ages of two and five years seems to have greater effect on IQ than does that in infancy.[401]

However, it is important to recognize that the apparent discontinuity is much influenced by the particular cognitive skills that are assessed in infancy. Research during the last decade has shown that that is a crucial consideration.[45] It has been found that tests of coping with novelty in infancy *do* predict later IQ. Babies who rapidly lose interest in a familiar stimulus, and who rapidly regain interest when presented with a novel stimulus, tend to be the ones who show higher IQ levels later. These two facets of attention, as assessed in the first six months of life, correlate about .5 with IQ at school entry, as compared with a near-zero correlation for the traditional developmental test scores. Of course, a correlation of .5 means that a lot of children go up or down in their cognitive abilities, but it also suggests a much stronger continuity in cognitive development from infancy to middle childhood than had hitherto been appreciated. These findings also reinforce the clinical view that young children's intellectual performance needs to be assessed from their interest in and curiosity about their environment, and the extent to which this curiosity is applied to new situations, as well as by standardized testing.

Stages of Cognitive Development

These psychometric approaches have focused on children's increase in cognitive skills as they grow older. Piaget brought about a revolution in the approach to cognitive development through his arguments (backed up by observations of children's problem-solving and by conversations with them on *how* they solved the problems) that the focus should be on *styles* of cognitive performance, rather than on *levels* of cognitive achievement (see Hobson[417]). Thus he suggested that during the first two years – which he called the 'sensorimotor' period – infants are constrained by the here and now and have no mental representation. This period is followed by the so-called phase of 'pre-operational thinking', in which the child is able to construct internalized representations (as reflected, for example, in language or make-believe play), but still cannot formulate rules or concepts. Around the age of five to seven years, this leads on to what Piaget thought of as the stage of 'concrete operations'. This is chiefly characterized by the ability to acquire rules that allow the making of deductive inferences. At the same time, children are supposed to become able to appreciate other people's point of view and appreciate the significance of rules in competitive games and social situations. This is followed by the 'formal-operations' period, roughly coinciding with adolescence, in which young people are supposed to become able for the first time to engage in abstract manipulation of propositions, to formulate hypotheses and make deductions, so allowing more scientific problem solving.

These ideas of Piaget gave rise to an immense body of research and it would be true to say that current thinking is heavily dependent on his genius in opening up new ways of thinking about cognitive development. Nevertheless, most of his concepts have had to be so radically revised, or rejected, that his theory no longer provides an appropriate basis for thinking about cognitive development. To appreciate why that is so, we need to focus on the several rather different concepts involved in Piaget's theorizing.

The first element, which *has* stood the test of time, is his view of the child as an *active* agent in learning and of the importance of this activity in cognitive development. Numerous studies have shown how infants actively scan their environment, preferring patterned to non-patterned stimuli, choose novel over familiar stimuli, and explore their environment as if to see how it works. Children's questions and comments vividly illustrate the ways in which they are constantly constructing schemes of what they know, trying out their ideas of how to fit new knowledge into those schemes (or deciding that the schemes need modification). Moreover, a variety of animal studies have shown that active experiences have a greater effect on learning than do directly comparable passive experiences.[224,396] For example, Held and Hein[200] showed that animals whose visual experiences were the result of their own active movements showed superior judgement of distance and space to those whose visual

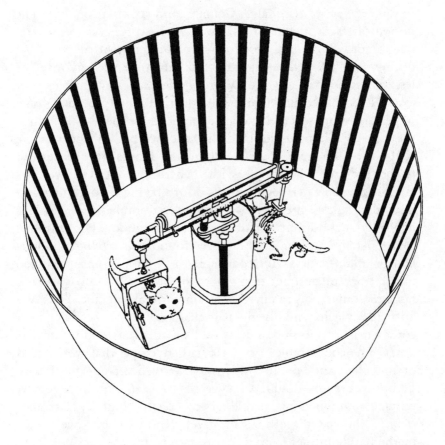

6.1 Active and passive kittens in the Held and Hein experiment.
From Held.[200]

experiences were a result of their being passively transported. A simple apparatus (see Figure 6.1) that allowed only progressive movements around a circular box controlled the visual experience in the two cases.

A second element concerns the notion that development proceeds through a series of discrete stages that have to be gone through in an invariant order in step-by-step fashion, each of which is characterized by a particular cognitive structure. That has turned out to be a rather misleading way of thinking about cognitive development, although it is not wholly wrong[114,123,154] (see also Gelman and Baillargeon[155]). The notion of stages, defined by cognitive structure, involves several related ideas. First, the cognitive-structure concept suggests that during each age period cognitive tasks are all tackled by more or less the same strategy (i.e. a strong horizontal structure). For example, young children in the sensorimotor and pre-operational stages are supposed to have an egocentric perspective in which they are unable to understand that another person's perspective will not be the same as theirs. However, that has turned out not to be the case. To begin with, whether a child appreciates another person's perspective turns out to be highly dependent on how the task is presented. It should be emphasized that this dependency is not just a characteristic of childhood. For example, Johnson-Laird and his colleagues[233] found that intelligent adults had great difficulty with conditional-rule tasks when presented in arbitrary or abstract terms but no difficulty at all when the same reasoning was required in a familiar real-life task. Thus, the 'difficult' version involved cards that had either a vowel or a consonant on one side and an odd or an even number on the other. The comparable 'easy' task had envelopes that were sealed or unsealed, and, on the other side a fivepenny or fourpenny stamp (in the good old days when that was enough to cover the postage, and when unsealed letters cost less!). Similarly, Carraher et al.[79] showed that Brazilian street vendors coped well with mathematics in their everyday commercial transactions but often could not do so when exactly the same problems were presented in conventional school style. However, it was also evident that they used computational strategies that differed from those taught in schools.

The second mistaken feature of the cognitive-structure/stage linkage is that in any particular stage, failure on a task necessarily means that the cognitive construct is missing. For example, Bryant,[68] Trabasso[481] and others showed that young children's difficulties with transitive inferences (e.g. understanding that if $A > B$ and $B > C$, then A must also exceed C) was more a matter of memory than lack of logical ability. In comparable fashion, Goswami[176] showed that children as young as three could solve analogies if they understand the relations on which they are based and, moreover, could defend their solutions. The finding is striking in that Piaget claimed that this skill does not develop until the formal-operations period beginning in early adolescence. A related notion is that, in any one stage, tasks are dealt with through only one cognitive route. Siegler,[114] and others, have shown that, on the contrary, children use diverse strategies on many familiar tasks. While it is certainly true that there are age differences in strategies (with some only shown by older children), quite a few are used by all age groups.

The stage concept also supposes that once children have acquired a particular cognitive structure, it has an enduring effect on reasoning. For example, one classic Piagetian concept concerns conservation – the idea that objects retain their weight or volume even if they look different (e.g. water poured from a short fat glass to a tall thin one or balls of plasticine kneaded into different shapes). It was supposed that once children had appreciated that that was so, it would be quite difficult to trick them into believing otherwise. An early study by Smedslund[445] suggested that that was the case, but later investigations have failed to confirm the finding.[192] It seems that resistance to unlearning is a feature of many 'overlearned' skills, such as bicycle riding; it is not particularly a function of acquiring a given cognitive structure. Finally, the stage concept expects quite a strong degree of vertical structure. In other words, it is expected that children do not progress to a supposedly more advanced stage until they have become well established in an earlier, less complex, stage. That, too, has not been borne out. Children can be at a higher stage on some tasks but a lower stage on others.

All of these findings might seem to leave the stage concept largely discredited. Clearly, Piaget's idea that all cognition develops through four successive stages, with each stage characterized by the emergence of qualitatively distinct structures, has to be rejected (see Gelman and Baillargeon[155]). However, it is not possible to throw out the idea of stages altogether. No amount of training will cause, say, a four-month-old to walk or talk, or a six-year-old to learn differential calculus. There is plenty of evidence that well-planned training can accelerate specific cognitive skills to a greater extent than was accepted by Piaget, but it is equally apparent that there are limits. Even so, it is necesary to recognize the importance of knowledge in the development of specific skills. For example, Siegler[114] instanced the advanced memory and metamemory skills in child chess experts and the superior spatial reasoning of Australian aboriginal children who spend their lives trekking great distances across deserts in search of new oases.

It is more difficult to know what to conclude about the role of cognitive structures in cognitive performance. The general idea is that specific cognitive processes underlie how children deal with cognitive problems and that these change qualitatively, as well as quantitatively, with increasing age. Although the specifics of the structures proposed by Piaget have not been supported by empirical research, most neo-Piagetian and other cognitive theorists accept the general notion of underlying, or deep, structures even though they may disagree on what form they take (see Demetriou,[114] Sternberg and Powell[155] and Gelman and Baillargeon[155]). Pascual-Leone's[114] model is based on units of mental attentional capacity, so that qualitative changes in styles of thought are entirely dependent on quantitative in-creases in these units. Case,[114] by contrast, although accepting that there is quantitative change that spans development, proposes several information processes that regulate cognitive perform-ance. Sternberg and Powell[155] have summarized what is known on information-processing in terms of the role of seven key features: (i) the knowledge base; (ii) the range of cognitive processes available (with metacognitive skills to comprehend second- and third-order relations not developing until early adoles-cence); (iii) memory capacity; (iv) the strategies employed (so that as children grow older they tend to use more of the information to hand); (v) efficiency of representations of informa-tion; (vi) process latencies and difficulties (e.g., what makes one sort of addition problem more difficult than another); and (vii) executive control (the ability to think about one's thinking in order to decide how to tackle a problem in a given task environment). Intellectual development, it appears, probably comprises the growth of more sophisticated executive control strategies, increasing thoroughness in information-processing, the

emergence of an ability to comprehend higher-order relationships and increased flexibility in the use of strategies and information utilization.

These views all assume the emergence of specific cognitive
skills and, in that sense, structures. Thus, metacognitive skills
undoubtedly serve to regulate cognitive performance; these are
not available to very young children. However, they do not
emerge as a qualitative leap of an all-or-none nature that spans
all cognitive domains. To an appreciable extent they are con-
tent-driven and context-specific so that children will vary in the
extent to which these skills are available according to the nature
of the task and of the context in which they have to deal with it.
On the other hand, the degree to which broadly similar cognitive
progressions are evident across widely divergent cultures indicates
that maturational influences are likely to play a key role.

Special Cognitive Strategies and Skills

Piagetian theory largely ignored cultural variations and individual differences (both within-individual and between individuals), two features that have to be accounted for in any adequate
conceptualization of cognitive development, as Desen and de
Ribaupierre[114] have emphasized. Although many key issues
remained unexplained, modern information-processing concepts
have the capacity to meet this challenge as a result of their
recognition that most cognitive tasks involve a combination of
cognitive operations that may be combined in a number of
different ways, some of which are more efficient than others.
The neglect of individual differences by Piaget stemmed from
his focus on what he called the 'epistemic' individual, a kind of
theoretical abstraction that deliberately ignored the fact that
children vary greatly, not just in the level of their cognitive
skills, but also in the ways in which they deal with cognitive
tasks. In this section, we focus on some of the clinical examples
of special cognitive strategies and skills to consider how these
may be accounted for.

A key issue is whether the lack of sensory input, in the form
of congenital deafness or blindness, affects styles of cognitive
processing.[322] The possibility arises from the commonplace

observation that it is much easier to reconstruct memories of sounds and sights (such as a familiar tune or face) than it is to recall the feel or smell of things. The implication is that different sensory modalities may be 'stored' in the brain in different ways. Experimental evidence is in keeping with this supposition; thus, people's ability to remember visual material is not affected by the intrusion of irrelevant auditory items, whereas there *is* interference from irrelevant visual stimuli. However, it has also been found that, in some circumstances, information received through one sensory modality is stored in another. Thus, words, even when presented visually, tend to be processed as if they had been heard. Also, it is clear that, from quite an early age, children are able to transfer information from one sensory modality to another. Thus, children presented with only the feel of an object can recognize that it is the same object that they have previously seen, but not felt. So the question arises whether people who cannot see or hear process information in different ways and, if they do, whether it matters. Because blindness and deafness may be associated with subtle handicaps of different kinds, an important control in studying the effects of lack of vision or hearing is the inclusion of groups of normal individuals who have been blindfolded or fitted with sound-occlusive ear muffs. However, there is the further question of whether *never* having had vision or hearing affects the way people interpret the world.

These issues have been tackled in a series of experiments by O'Connor and Hermelin[322] with a range of interesting findings. For example, they tested whether the dot patterns of Braille were perceived better by the right or left hand by congenitally blind children and by blindfolded seeing children. The point of the comparison is that, ordinarily, words are processed by the left side of the brain (controlling the right side of the body), but shapes by the right side of the brain. The results showed that both groups 'read' Braille better with their left hands; in other words, although Braille deals with words it is processed like other shapes and patterning, irrespective of whether children have the experience of sight.

Another test tackled the question of whether the mode of

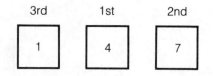

6.2 Testing sensory perceptions: incongruent temporal and spatial presentations.
Data from O'Connor and Hermelin.[322]

sensory presentation affects memory differently for temporally or spatially structured series. An example of the former would be a time series of long and short sounds or light flashes, in a sort of Morse code. An example of the latter would be a series based on whether the stimuli came from the right or left. It was found that sounds were better remembered in time-series terms, but, with visual stimuli, memory was better for a spatially organized series. This was so for individuals who had all their senses but who wore blindfolds or earmuffs as well as for those who had never had vision or sight. In other words, it was the sensory modality available at the time that seemed crucial and not the previous experience of seeing or hearing.

Another set of experiments pitted one sensory modality against another in an ingenious way. Numbers were simultaneously presented in temporal and spatial presentations. Thus, in the example illustrated in Figure 6.2, the 4 was presented first, in the middle, then with the 7 on the right, and finally with the 1 on the left as well. The question, then, is whether this is remembered according to the time order (i.e. 4 7 1) or the spatial order (1 4 7). The results portrayed in Figure 6.3, overleaf, clearly showed that normal children strongly tended to remember the numbers in the time order, whereas deaf children strongly tended to do so in the space order. Because O'Connor and Hermelin were interested in the cognitive processing of children with brain abnormalities, as well as the effects of sensory lack, the same experiment was undertaken with mentally retarded children (labelled subnormal in the figure according to the terminology of the 1970s) and with autistic children. The results clearly showed that autistic children, although they could hear, processed like deaf children. Retarded children were intermediate but

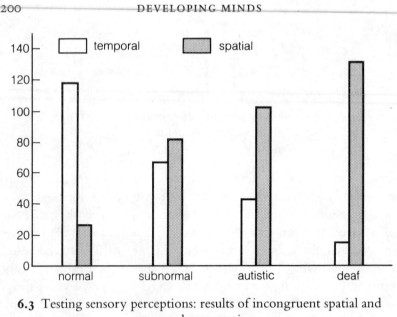

6.3 Testing sensory perceptions: results of incongruent spatial and
temporal presentations.
Data from O'Connor and Hermelin.[322]

those who also had very poor language (like the autistic group)
were similar to deaf children.

A broadly comparable design was used with visual stimuli,
but focusing on whether the stimuli could be thought of in
words (as with the ordinary Roman alphabet) or not (as with
Arabic letters). The results showed that normal children tended
to remember patterns as if they were auditory, provided that the
stimuli could be verbalized, whereas the deaf and language-
impaired autistic and retarded children did not. A further set of
experiments used tasks that could be solved either by using feel
(the most direct means in each task) or by employing some
visual image. For example, blindfolded children were presented
with right and left artificial hands that were placed in different
positions and had to say whether it was a right or left hand. In
these tasks, blindfolded normal children made fewer errors than
blind children, suggesting that although the task was presented
in 'feel' terms they were able to use visual strategies to help
them, whereas the blind who had never experienced sight could

not. Interestingly, the autistic group, although able to see normally, behaved much like the blind group (although the mentally retarded did not).

An opposite research strategy is afforded by the study of people who have been blind since birth but who have had their sight restored in later life.[187,188] The question is whether the fact that they could now see 'put everything right' in their cognitive processing or whether the fact that they had grown up without vision meant that some tasks were still difficult for them. The findings showed that, for many purposes, they could make immediate use of vision (implying that these skills do not have to be learned through visual experiences), but the results also showed that the normal appreciation of depth took some while to develop. At first sight, this finding seems to run counter to the evidence from studies of normal infants that depth perception requires very little experience. However, the explanation may be that this form of learning is much easier in early life than it is later – a sort of relative sensitive period for a specific form of learning (it is only relative because depth perception is acquired later; it is just that it takes rather longer). Other difficulties in using vision after restoration of sight are much more variable from individual to individual and they probably derive from the need to make a radical change in perceptual habits and strategies, and from the fact that many people recovering their sight experience depression. In part this seems to stem from a realization of what they have missed but in part, too, from the change from being an expert in the world of the blind to being someone who is handicapped in the world of sighted people.

These experiments are fascinating but sceptics may query whether the findings have any practical implications. We think that they do. First, it is clear that, for certain sorts of tasks, the sensory mode of presentation makes quite a difference to the ease of cognitive processing, irrespective of the children's sensory or other handicaps. Second, for other sorts of tasks, not having had the experience of vision or hearing makes them much more difficult. That is because, when faced with difficulties, it may be helpful to be able to turn to a different form of cognitive processing. The lack of sensory modality may cut people off from this flexible strategy. Third, for many tasks it is helpful to make use of language as a mediator, and both mentally retarded children with little speech and autistic children are impaired in this skill; a lack that makes many cognitive tasks more difficult for them.[202,321]

Fourth, certain sorts of cognitive handicaps may cause real-life impairment because they impede flexibility in cognitive processing. In this respect, autistic children act in many ways as if they were both blind and deaf, although in fact they are neither. The finding is important for two separate reasons. First, it reminds us that impairments in cognitive processing may lead to socio-emotional as well as intellectual difficulties. The ways in which we feel about other people are influenced by how we are able to think. In Chapter 4 we discussed this issue in terms of autistic children's relative lack of a 'theory of mind', an inability to appreciate what other people might be thinking in particular situations. Second, the breadth of these problems in autistic children's cognitive processing should make us question any suggestion that autism can be reduced to a single cognitive lack, such as 'theory of mind'.[162] Of course, the breadth of the cognitive problems could merely reflect the fact that many autistic children have multiple handicaps. Thus, most (but not all) of the autistic children studied by Hermelin and O'Connor also showed some degree of mental retardation. On the other hand, studies of autistic adolescents and adults with an IQ within the normal range have also shown a breadth of cognitive difficulties extending beyond a lack of 'theory of mind'.[335,336,386] In particular, autism seems to be associated with deficits in executive functions – meaning an appropriate problem-solving set to attain a future goal (comprising planning, search and flexibility of thought and action, amongst other things). In these psychological studies of autism, we have striking examples of how helpful it may be to adopt a developmental perspective, applying what is known about normal cognitive functioning to an abnormal group. The results also show how, sometimes, it may be useful to change from thinking about illnesses or symptoms to thinking about functions. In this case, the research evidence leads us to an appreciation of the role of cognitive processing in social interactions.

The findings also bring out another, quite different, point – namely, that sometimes a cognitive-processing handicap can lead to advantages. For example, deaf children are not as impaired as normal children in recalling lists of letters in the reverse order to which they were presented[322] and also they do not find irregular words (i.e. words like laugh or receipt, where there is a weak correspondence between letters and sounds) more difficult to spell than regular words, whereas hearing children do.[177] In both cases, this is probably because they do not have available a language-related strategy that helps in one task but is irrelevant for, or interferes with, performance in the other task. Another example is found with autism. Normal people find it extremely difficult to recognize faces upside down, but autistic individuals are *better* at this task.[214,263] It seems that, ordinarily, faces are recognized in terms of an overall holistic picture with personal meaning; this makes for great difficulties when the face is the wrong way up. Probably autistic individuals make less use of this strategy, treating the face instead as a perceptual pattern, an approach less affected by turning it upside down.

The individuals who stand out in terms of their unusually superior skills in spite of general mental retardation are the so-called '*idiots savants*', many of whom are autistic. Thus, there are well-investigated examples of individuals with an IQ below the normal range who are greatly superior to the general population in their ability to remember complex pieces of music on a first hearing or to undertake complex mental arithmetic (such as multiplying three- or four-figure numbers together), or to work out what day of the week some day in the future (e.g. 3 July 2006) will be, or to draw extremely detailed drawings to exact perspective.[482] The investigation of these extraordinary outstanding skills has been informative, but many questions still remain unanswered. Thus, it has been found that, to a limited extent, some of the particular cognitive strategies used are linked with general intelligence. For example, the calendrical calculators who use rules rather than rote memory tend to be of higher intelligence than those who do not.[203] On the other hand, both the calendrical and the artistic skills[323] stand out in terms of their relative independence from IQ. Two main questions await firm answers. First, do these *idiots savants* use cognitive strategies that differ from those employed by normal individuals or is it just that they have a most unusual isolated talent in the same strategies? The answer so far seems to be a bit of both. Second, why has the talent been able to develop in such an extraordinary fashion; is it perhaps because of the narrowing of vision that stems from the overall cognitive handicap when it is associated with obsessive-like preoccupations?[324] In relation to that query, it is relevant that very few *idiots savants* use their skills productively in everyday life and that, at least among autistic individuals, the extreme isolated talents seem to fade somewhat when the individuals improve in their overall social functioning and use their cognitive skills in a broader, more constructive fashion. From a clinical perspective, therefore, it is necessary to appreciate that it may well be beneficial to encourage special talents in so far as they enhance self-esteem and provide social opportunities, but in so far as the benefits enable the individuals to function better on a broader front, the price may be that the talent fades to some extent.

Reading and Spelling

In years gone by, some psychologists have seemed to assume that intelligence (as measured by intelligence tests) is the basic innate capacity and that scholastic attainments all derive from it, although of course influenced by specific teaching. As we argue later in this chapter, the notion that intelligence is innate is an absurd oversimplification (although genetic factors are indeed important). However, we need to consider first whether the cognitive basis of scholastic attainment (however determined) is synonymous with general intelligence. We take reading and spelling as our examples, but similar arguments apply to other attainments (although the underlying specific cognitive processes are almost certainly different; see Rourke and Strang[400]).

It is necessary to start with the general finding that there is a moderate, but only a moderate, association (a correlation of about .5 to .6) between IQ and reading. There are many, many children of normal intelligence who have very considerable difficulties in learning to read and spell. The question is why? Certain explanations can be quickly ruled out.[177,449] It cannot be limited to general intelligence because their overall intelligence is unimpaired. Also the problem does not usually lie in any impairment in visual perception. At first sight, that seems surprising, because reading necessarily involves shape recognition. Moreover, the perceptual task requires some unlearning. Young children quickly come to appreciate that a chair is still a chair whichever way it is turned around. Thus, schematically

expressed,   is equivalent to   .

However, b is not the same as d or p, although they are all the same shape. It is true that children who are just learning to read frequently confuse these letters. However, numerous studies have made it clear that most children who are poor readers do *not* have any unusual difficulty in making these or other, visual perceptual discriminations (such as those involving closure, O versus C, or line-to-curve transformations, U versus V). Of course, children who could not make these discriminations would indeed have difficulties in reading, but the point is that the great majority of poor readers do not have this problem.

One of the long-standing controversies in education concerns the merits and demerits of the 'look and say' method, by which children are taught whole words without spelling them out phonetically. The evidence is clear-cut that young, as well as older, children can and do read words that way. That is as true of English children who have to deal with an alphabetic script as it is with Japanese children who use a logographic script, in which each character symbolizes a whole word, and therefore which *has* to be read that way.[177] It is clear that much early reading does indeed rely on a global strategy and we may infer that, as that is so, this approach should presumably play some part in the teaching of reading at school.

However, it would be most unwise to place exclusive, or probably even main, emphasis on this approach, as it obviously does not work with spelling, and children need to learn to write as well as read. There is now abundant evidence that children depend on a phonological code (meaning some sort of sound-to-letter convention) when they are working out how to spell words. The question that follows is whether phonological skills are also important in reading, in spite of the fact children can and do read whole words. Research findings are conclusive in showing that they *are*, as Goswami and Bryant's[177] riveting and readable book on the topic makes clear. However, in drawing that conclusion we need to make an important distinction – that between grapheme–phoneme correspondences and the use of analogies, rhyme and alliterations. It used to be thought that children used grapheme–phoneme correspondences when they read; in other words, they worked out words on a letter-by-letter basis: c-a-t means cat. It is evident that for the most part, they do not. It is easy to appreciate intuitively why this strategy is most inefficient. The most obvious one is that English contains many irregular words (such as 'cough') where this correspond-ence does not exist. There is a tendency to assume that this mainly applies to longer words with particular letter combina-tions such as –ough or –eigh but it also applies to many short ones. Try sounding out 'one' on a letter-by-letter basis! Also, the position of a letter in a word affects its sound. Thus, y– is not much like –y, as it is easy to see by trying out the sounds that way.

The use of onsets and rhymes is, however, a different matter altogether, and it is clear both that children *do* use phonology in this way when reading, and that it is helpful that they do so. It has been found that children make analogies based on sounds, and that this helps with the reading of new words that share spelling sequences, but not those that do not, in spite of rhyming. For example, knowing how to read 'head' helps when presented with 'bread' but not 'said'; similarly, 'most' helps with 'post', but not with 'toast'. It is evident that a phonological strategy is being used but it is one that is based on onset and rhyme, and not a grapheme–phoneme correspondence.

That shows that there is an association, but how do we know that it truly plays a causal role in the development of reading skills? Several pieces of evidence build up to a convincing demonstration that the link is indeed causal.[177,436,449] First, it has been found that not only are poor readers worse in their rhyming skills than normal readers of the same age and IQ, they are also worse than *younger* normal children of the same reading age. The latter comparison is important because effectively it rules out the possibility that reading causes rhyming, rather than the other way round. The poor readers were worse at rhyming in spite of being older, presumably of higher mental age and at the same reading level. Second, this association holds even within a group of deaf people, where phonological processing would seem least likely to be helpful. Hanson[436] found that successful deaf readers appreciated the phonological structure of words and that they exploited this knowledge in reading, even when they used American Sign Language (which is not phonetic) to communicate. Third, a study by Olson and his colleagues[328] of twin pairs in which at least one twin was a markedly poor reader, showed that a heritable phonological-coding deficit was linked with reading disability. That is, the co-twins of the identical twins with a reading problem were almost equally bad at rhyming, whereas the co-twins of fraternal twins were much better. Fourth, longitudinal studies have shown that non-reading four- to five-year-olds with poor rhyming skills made less progress in reading and spelling over the next three or four years than good rhymers, even after controlling for initial IQ levels.[177] Moreover, the association was specific; rhyming did *not* predict mathematical skills. Fifth, training in phonological and rhyming skills improves those skills and this is associated with some parallel improvement in reading and spelling. The case for a causal relationship is a most impressive one and the combination of different research strategies provides an excellent illustration of how causal hypotheses may be put to the test.

Clinicians need to go several stages further, however. The first issue is whether the conclusions apply equally to the more severe reading difficulties (often diagnosed as dyslexia) seen in clinics. Almost certainly, to a major extent, they do with respect to the links between lack of phonological awareness and reading difficulties. However, there may be one key difference. In the general population, most children with phonological limitations do not have any general problem with language, whereas many children with severe reading difficulties do. This has been shown by the finding of a raised rate of later reading difficulties in children with a specific developmental disorder of language (see Rutter and Mawhood[415]), by the raised rate of language delay in children with severe reading difficulties[424] and by the finding that, within a group of young children who had a parent or older sibling with a reading problem, those with language difficulties tended to show later reading difficulties whereas those without such difficulties did not.[430]

Those findings could mean no more than that children attending clinics have a more severe variety of the same difficulty seen in a lesser degree as variations in reading skills within the general population. So, the second query is whether the difference is qualitative or quantitative. It is important to appreciate that this question is *not* the same as the first one. It is quite possible for there to be continuity between normality and pathology in terms of the psychological functions involved but yet *dis*continuity with respect to cause. For example, IQ functions in much the same way in severely retarded people, mildly retarded people and individuals of normal intelligence. But the causes and consequences are quite different (see Rutter and Gould[417]). Mildly retarded individuals have a normal life expectancy, have a normal capacity to have children and in most cases, the causes of their low IQ involve a somewhat similar mixture of polygenic and environmental factors to those that apply within the normal range of IQ. By sharp contrast, most severely retarded individuals die when relatively young and are unable to have children (or at least have a markedly reduced fecundity): single major genes, chromosomal abnormalities (such as with Down's syndrome) or obvious brain damage are the most frequent causes, although none of these play much of a role in normal variations in intelligence. In the case of mental retardation, then, there is strong continuity in psychological processes but strong *dis*continuity in causes and consequences. As we shall see later in this chapter, the likelihood of a degree of discontinuity between normality and disorder arises also in the case of language. Does the same apply with reading retardation? We do not know, but it may do so. The possibility is suggested by the finding that children with reading difficulties frequently continue to show reading, spelling and other cognitive problems in adult life.[65,66] However, further research is necessary before any firm conclusions are warranted.

The third query is whether reading disabilities constitute one condition or several different varieties. That seemingly straightforward question has proved extremely difficult to answer definitively.[177,450] No one doubts that poor readers vary somewhat in their cognitive pattern; what is less clear is whether these reflect qualitatively distinct routes to reading difficulties. It has been suggested, for example, that reading disabilities may arise from either phonological or visual perceptual difficulties. Also, detailed individual case reports indicate that some poor readers exhibit highly unusual types of spelling mistake, not seen in normal children. A further consideration is that marked reading difficulties occur quite commonly with Chinese and Japanese children who have to learn a logographic script, rather than an alphabetical one.[462] As, presumably, this requires a rather different set of cognitive skills, it may be inferred that Asian children's reading disabilities may show different patterns from those evident in English readers.

It is possible, even probable, that distinct types of reading disability exist, but it has to be admitted that, to date, we lack the clinical means to identify them reliably at the individual level and we do not know whether differences in cognitive pattern mean different causes. One controversy in the classification of reading disorders concerns the value or otherwise of differentiating between a reading difficulty that is out of line with expectations based on children's age and intelligence (specific reading retardation or dyslexia) and one that is part of more general cognitive difficulties (general reading backwardness) – a distinction proposed by Yule and Rutter.[417] As Snowling[450] noted, the evidence is not decisive one way or the other, but certainly it would be premature to abandon the distinction.

The fourth issue is what causes the cognitive deficits that underlie reading disabilities. No satisfactory answer is yet available. The Olson et al.[328] twin-study findings, to which reference has been made already, strongly suggest the importance of a specific genetic influence on phonological skills but the data also showed the importance of environmental factors. The influence of the environment is also suggested by the finding that specific reading difficulties were twice as common in inner London ten-year-olds as in comparable children living in the Isle of Wight,[32] a difference that is most unlikely to be due to genetic factors.

Influences on Intelligence and Scholastic Attainment

Because so little is known about specific influences on different cognitive processes or on specific causes of different types of cognitive or scholastic disability, we need to turn to the broader question of influences on intelligence and scholastic attainment. It should not be assumed that they will operate equally on both, but it is unclear how far the causal patterns are distinctive.

Genetic Factors

Over the years, an incredible amount of heat has been generated in controversies over the extent to which genetic factors influence intellectual development. To a substantial extent, as we noted in Chapter 2, this is because claims about the importance of heredity have been linked with attempts to cast doubt on the value of interventions to aid the development of disadvantaged children or to argue that racial differences in IQ are genetically based.[230] Neither issue is closely bound up with the extent of heritability of intelligence. It is quite possible for a major change in environmental circumstances to increase IQ substantially, even if IQ is strongly heritable.[411] Also, the factors that account for individual differences in IQ *within* a group may be quite different from those that account for differences *between* groups in average level of IQ.[479] Accordingly, we need to keep those issues rather separate from the question of whether genetic factors constitute important influences on intellectual development. The evidence is clear-cut that *both* genetic and environmental factors are strongly influential – to a roughly equal degree.[350,419]

Several different research strategies show the importance of genetic factors. None of these strategies is decisive on its own because each has significant limitations, but the limitations of each design are different and if they all point to roughly the same conclusion, which in the case of IQ they do, the genetic influence can be asserted with confidence.[414] Some of the main pieces of evidence are as follows: (i) monozygotic (identical) twins are much more alike in IQ than are dizygotic (fraternal) twins, and this is so even if they are reared apart; (ii) the IQs of adopted children show higher correlations with those of their biological parents than with those of their adoptive parents; (iii) the IQs of adopted children correlate less strongly with the characteristics of the homes in which they are reared than is the case with IQs of biological children; (iv) genetically related adoptees reared apart are more alike in IQ than genetically unrelated adoptees reared together; and (v) the risk of having a second mildly retarded child is twice as great when there is a retarded uncle or aunt than when there is not, even when both parents are of normal intelligence. Each of these findings reflects a 'pulling apart' of genetic and environmental effects and each points to the importance of genetic factors. However, as already noted, the results also show that environmental factors are influential.

Family Influences (Environmentally Mediated)

As with genetic effects, there is now substantial evidence regarding the impact of the family environment on cognitive functioning, and, as they have been reviewed previously,[401] the findings can be summarized quite briefly in terms of the key research strategies. As discussed in Chapter 2, perhaps the clearest evidence derives from adoption studies. We referred there to the Capron and Duyme[77] finding that, controlling for biological parents' social background, rearing in a socially advantaged adoptive home was associated with an IQ advantage of about 12 points compared with rearing in a socially disadvantaged home. Figure 6.4 presents the findings from another French study,[433] this time comparing the IQs of children from a disadvantaged background reared in advantaged adoptive/foster homes with those of their half-siblings reared by their biological parents. Again, the favourable environment of rearing was associated with a 12-point IQ advantage. In Chapter 2, we noted the importance of within-family factors with respect to variations within the normal range, but these findings show that between-family differences are also highly influential when dealing with extreme environments.

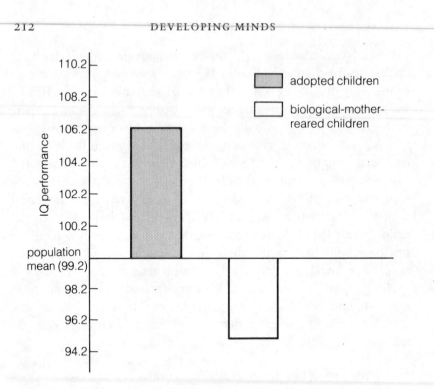

6.4 IQs of children of socially disadvantaged parents (adopted children reared in advantaged homes compared with half-siblings reared by biological mother).

From data reported by Schiff and Lewontin.[433]

The second set of evidence derives from intensive-intervention studies in which there has been a prolonged attempt to improve the conditions of rearing. The first and most prolonged was the Milwaukee project,[165] in which the mothers received remedial education, home management and job training, and the children participated in a structured education programme up to age six. All the mothers had an IQ of 75 or less and the families were markedly socially disadvantaged; twenty of the children entered the experimental programme and twenty served as controls. The initial findings were dramatic, with the experimental group greatly outperforming the controls during the preschool years. The follow-up results continued to show benefits but they diminished progressively over time, so that an IQ advantage of some 28 points at four years of age reduced to one of about 10

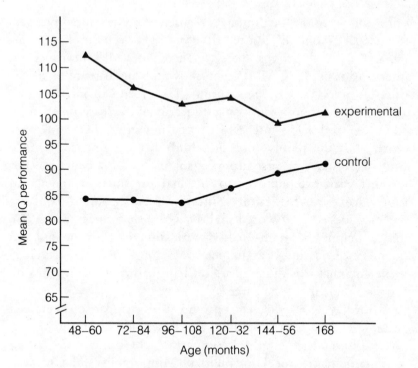

6.5 IQ performance with increasing age of severely disadvantaged children participating in a broad-ranging intensive intervention programme in the preschool years.
Data from Garber.[165]

points at fourteen. More disappointing still were the very modest benefits with respect to scholastic attainment; the experimental group did have somewhat better scores than the controls in reading (the difference after four years of schooling being equivalent to just over half a year's progress) but there was little difference in maths, in which both groups were performing poorly. The results (see Figure 6.5) do show that a vigorous and relatively prolonged intervention makes a substantial difference to the cognitive performance of severely disadvantaged children, but they also demonstrate that much of the gain is lost in the years after the programme came to an end (at the time of school entry).

The Carolina Abecedarian project[364] was somewhat similar,

with intervention beginning in infancy. The outcome data showed an 8-point difference at five years between the experimental and control groups (98 v. 90). Ramey's[489] more recent intervention study, CARE, again showed benefits from intervention, but added a sobering caution. Two forms of intervention, an intensive variety comprising educational day care plus family education and a less intensive variety in which there was only work with the family (not the child), were compared with a control group. The first group again showed IQ benefits, after the first year, extending up to the final assessment at the age of four. However, the family-education-only group showed *no* benefits; indeed they scored slightly worse than the controls. We may conclude that high-quality work directly with the children (in a day-care setting) can influence children's cognitive development, but that it is much more difficult to bring about gains by focusing on helping the parents.

A third type of evidence is provided by comparisons between nations. The largest-scale studies are those undertaken by Stevenson and his colleagues[460,461] comparing achievements in reading and mathematics for US children (Minneapolis and Chicago) and for Chinese children (Taipei and Beijing). The results clearly demonstrate the superior attainments, especially in maths, of the Chinese children, graphically portrayed in Figure 6.6. Interestingly, the Americans (parents and children) were quite pleased with their children's accomplishments. For this, and other reasons, Stevenson *et al.* concluded that the lower attainments in the US stemmed from setting lower standards (at home and at school), although of course it was not possible to rule out genetic effects.

School Influences

In Chapter 2, we noted the evidence from longitudinal studies that the quality of school attended makes a substantial difference to children's scholastic achievement and behaviour. The findings provide strong evidence for school effects, which we will not repeat here. Instead, we turn to some different research strategies, all of which again show school effects on children's cognitive performance. In each case, the strategy involves the identification

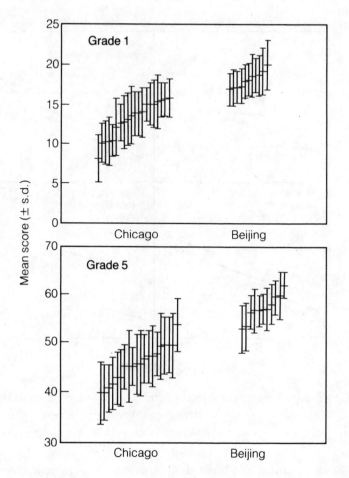

6.6 A comparison of achievements in mathematics, in Chicago and Beijing.
Data from Stevenson *et al.*[460,461]

of some 'experiment of nature' in which real-life circumstances happen to have brought about substantial differences in children's experience of schooling. For example, forced closure of schools as a result of war or political activities has been followed by IQ decrements of the order of 5 points or so, and continued schooling during late adolescence has been found to be associated with a mean IQ gain of approximately the same degree.[419] Figure 6.7 shows the results of yet another design, based on the recognition

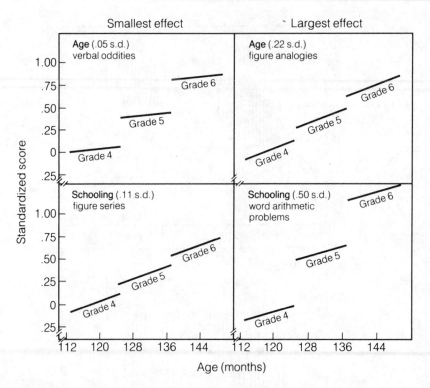

6.7 Comparisons of the effects of children's age and of schooling
on cognitive performance.
From Cahan and Cohen.[74]

that because children's birth dates span the whole year, any one
school year necessarily contains a year's span in ages.[74] The
consequence is that it is possible to contrast the effects of schooling (i.e. one school year with the previous one) and the effects of
age (i.e. age effects within any one school year). The graphic
presentation in Figure 6.7 includes both the smallest and largest
effects for each. The effects of age are evident in the steepness of
the slopes of the lines (the steeper the line the greater the effect
of age), whereas the effects of schooling are apparent in the
vertical distance between the lines for grades. Overall, the results
showed that the effects of schooling in this Israeli sample were
about twice as great as those for age.

Nutrition

The last influence on cognition to mention (although there are others that could have been discussed[400,415,419]) is malnutrition. Numerous studies in developing countries have shown the cognitive deficits associated with severe chronic malnutrition (see Cravioto and Arrieta[400] and Grantham McGregor[181]). Because the malnutrition arises in the context of severe social disadvantage, it is difficult to disentangle the effects of nutrition and of the families' social circumstances. Intervention studies providing nutritional supplements or social stimulation or both suggest that both factors play a part. However, less is known about the cognitive consequences of malnutrition in Western societies. On the whole, it seems that there are few effects.[419] However, recent research findings suggest that the adverse consequences may be significant if the malnutrition takes place in the first six months of life when brain growth is at a peak.[444] The finding needs to be confirmed in other investigations, but it serves as a reminder of the need to take developmental considerations into account when assessing the effect of any influence.

Behavioural Consequences of Cognitive Impairments

Clinicians are sometimes impatient with teaching on cognitive development, thinking that it does not have much relevance for them. That is a mistaken view for several rather different reasons.[404] To begin with, as we have seen, research findings strongly suggest that cognitive deficits constitute the basis, or at least part of the basis, of certain psychiatric disorders, of which autism stands out. But, in addition, there are quite strong associations between reading difficulties and conduct disorders/delinquency and somewhat weaker associations with other psychiatric disorders.[306,308,416] As a consequence, children attending psychiatric clinics include a relatively high proportion with poor scholastic attainment. The key issue is what this association means. Although reading and verbal skills stand out as particularly involved, it is clear that the connections involve a rather wider range of cognitive functions and of scholastic attainments. Moreover, the links are evident from the very start of schooling or earlier. On the other hand, they are not so apparent in disorders that do not begin until adolescence.

Reviews of the evidence suggest that it is most unlikely that a single unidirectional process accounts for the findings. The fact that the association is seen so early suggests that, in some way, the cognitive deficits may constitute risk factors for behavioural disturbance. Probably this represents the main explanation for the cognitive–behaviour connections. If so, the findings suggest that the risk is especially for early-onset hyperactivity–inattention disorders rather more than for conduct disorders or delinquency, which have attracted more attention in the literature. The ways in which cognitive deficits create a psychiatric risk remain ill understood but Moffitt and Henry[308] have suggested that it may be mediated through impulsivity.

A second possibility is that early antisocial behaviour predisposes to academic failure (through truancy and lack of commitment to schooling). It is plausible that this takes place, although this route could not account for the associations already present at the time of school entry. A third possibility is that the experience of school failure predisposes to emotional/behavioural disturbance. Again, this could not account for the association at school entry but there is some evidence that the link may operate this way in some individuals whose academic problems increase or emerge when they are older.

In that connection it is necessary to broaden the focus to consider whether cognitive factors play any part in children's resilience in the face of stress or adversity. The evidence suggests that probably they do. By and large, children of above-average abilities or superior scholastic attainments appear less vulnerable to psychiatric disorder, even when social background has been taken into account.[394] The apparent protective effect could come about in several different ways. To begin with, it might represent no more than an absence of the cognitive risk factors that we have just noted. Alternatively, it could reflect an association between above-average IQ and superior social problem-solving or coping skills (see Rutter[376].) However, the apparent protective effect might stem from the increased self esteem and self-efficacy brought about by successful task accomplishment.

This possibility is suggested by the evidence that positive experiences at school, outside the realm of academic achievements, are also protective.[413] In other words, in part, cognitive assets may be helpful, not just through the qualities that they represent, but also through the beneficial social experiences that they help to bring about.

Language

Finally, we need to discuss the development of language. In a sense, it may seem curious to introduce an early emerging skill so late in this account of cognitive development. However, we have left it until last because traditionally it has been considered a very separate skill with its own developmental course, which is independent of general intelligence. It will be necessary to consider the extent to which that assumption is justified. The literature on the normal and abnormal development of language is vast, with a host of technical and conceptual controversies that need not preoccupy us here. Instead, we shall focus on just a few key issues that have a particular importance in terms of their clinical implications[21,105,506] (see also Howlin[395]).

First, it is necessary briefly to outline the chronology of language development. Clearly, communication begins well before children say their first words and, equally, there are many skills that are related in some way to language but that do not involve words. In the early months of infancy infants orient to sounds and then differentially to *voices*. Around the age of three or four months babies begin to babble – producing varying combinations of vowel and consonant sounds. Over the next few months these increase in range and complexity, and by the age of seven or eight months the babble is used both in social interactions and in soliloquies for self-amusement. At first, babble is not influenced by sensory input (so that the early babble of deaf infants is essentially normal) but by six months or so it is affected by what is heard (so that the babble of deaf infants fades and becomes abnormal in quality). In the middle of the first year there is much reciprocal social and vocal interchange between parents and their children, at first regulated by the parents who time what they do to fit in with what the child does, but later directed and coordinated more by the children.

Often by the age of nine months or so the babble is beginning to acquire speech-like cadences with rising and falling intonations. There is no *direct* connection between the sounds used in babble and those used in speech, but children with language problems often exhibit delayed, impaired or unusual babble. About the same time, infants begin to show clear evidence that they understand a few words. Pointing tends to develop around the age of a year but it is not until some months later that it becomes integrated with vocalizations and with alternating gaze between the parent and the desired object. However, pointing is not only used to obtain things, it is also used to show objects of interest to parents. Longitudinal studies[21] show that this communicative use of pointing is a predictor of language development over the coming months.

There is huge individual variation in when children first begin to use single words with meaning; some time between twelve and eighteen months would be usual but a few normal children do not speak until two years (or occasionally later). Once meaningful words are used, vocabulary tends to develop quite rapidly, so that by the age of two the average child has a spoken vocabulary of about 200 words. There is considerable variation in what words make up early vocabulary, but usually names of familiar people and objects predominate at first. Word combinations soon follow and it would be most unusual for these not to have developed by the age of thirty-three months – however, as with first words, the range of timing is very wide.

As vocabulary increases, so grammar develops and meanings and concepts become better established. At first, underextensions of words may occur so that 'dog' is used only to refer to one particular dog; later overextensions become quite common, so that 'dog' may be applied to all manner of animals. Overlaps and mismatches of words also occur and sometimes the wrong usage may be so peculiar that it seems that a wholly new word has been invented. However, ordinarily, if the misuse is met with incomprehension, the child soon drops the word from his or her repertoire. It is not clear how these normal misuses of words and phrases relate to the abnormal language usage seen in autism, but perhaps autistic children's impaired social understanding means that they fail to regulate their language in accord with adult conventions and hence abnormal patterns persist as a result of the lack of response to other people's reactions. As language develops, different parts of speech appear; usually nouns first and then verbs, linking words (such as conjunctions and prepositions) and descriptors (adverbs and adjectives) following shortly afterwards. In English, grammatical constructions are evident in the addition of morphemes such as -ing ('jumping', etc.) or -ed ('looked'), the use of auxiliary verbs ('do', 'can', etc.) and by sentence embedding (e.g. 'I think he will come' – in which the last three words denote what is thought). Often these are acquired gradually with a phase of incorrect rule application ('sheeps', 'goed', etc.), but frequently without sudden transitions as a result of rule-guided insights.

Numerous queries arise with respect to the process of language development. One very basic question is whether it develops in modular fashion with different processes governing syntax (grammar), semantics (the meaning of words), phonology (organization of speech sounds) and pragmatics (the aspects of meaning controlled by ways in which language is used in relation to the perspectives of a speaker and listener). The longitudinal study of a normal group of young children undertaken by Bates and her colleagues[21] suggests that this form of modularity is not how language divides up developmentally. While it is certainly useful to describe these different aspects of language separately (because children with language disorders may differ somewhat in the extent to which each is affected), they seem to be closely interconnected in normal children. The strong continuity from first words to grammar suggests that both are paced by the same mechanism. On the other hand, there *is* a different form of modularity: that between comprehension, rote production and analysed production (i.e. involving concepts). This supports the value of the clinical distinction between developmental disorders that involve a major deficit in comprehension as well as production and those that do not (although they overlap considerably).

A further query is whether language develops independently of general intelligence. Opinions on this issue have swung both ways over the years[105] but it now seems to be agreed that they are fairly separate. This is shown by the evidence of rather weak associations between the course of development of the two within normal groups and by the occurrence of individuals who show precocity in language in spite of mental retardation. The evidence that mentally retarded individuals are often delayed in language does not necessarily indicate an IQ–language connection, because the impairments in both may stem from the same underlying brain pathology. However, it should be noted that the linguistic *savants* who have been studied have not shown their remarkable language abilities until they have achieved a mental age equivalent of somewhere between two and four years. Bates *et al.*[21] argued that perhaps a minimum level of cognitive skills is required but, once that is reached, the language system is able to break free of the cognitive yoke.

During the 1950s, intellectual battle raged between Skinner,[442] who argued that language is wholly learned step by step, and Chomsky,[86] who proposed that language was innate, being organized by a language-acquisition device. It soon became obvious that the Skinnerian position was untenable, if only because an essential feature of language is its extremely rich creativity. Some kind of abstract representation of linguistic knowledge must be involved. Equally, however, Chomsky's notion that the essence of language lay in a transformational grammar (that is, one grammatical pattern, such as 'the boy was mowing the lawn' can be translated into others, such as 'the lawn was being mowed by the boy'), although intuitively attractive, has proved to have too many inconsistencies for it to be supportable as an adequate explanation (see Maratsos[155]). It is now accepted that there is some type of inborn capacity for people to acquire language in the way in which they derive and apply language rules. However, it appears that, to some extent, grammatical skills need to be learned – they do not just develop entirely through autonomous maturation. Bates *et al.*[21] pointed to the fact that young children practise and play with language – the crib soliloquy, first described by Weir – and that when people learn a second language, to a considerable extent, automatic control over lexical and grammatical processing has to be reacquired.

That raises the issue of which aspects of the environment affect language development, and by which mechanisms. Four rather separate questions are involved here, as outlined by Puckering and Rutter.[506] First, can major environmental deprivation or disadvantage in early life retard language development to a substantial degree? The answer is an unequivocal 'yes'. There are well-documented accounts of individual children reared in cupboards, attics and cellars in conditions of quite appalling abuse, restraint and isolation.[443] When such children have been rescued at ages ranging from $2\frac{1}{2}$ to $13\frac{1}{2}$ years, they have usually been mute, as well as functioning at a severely retarded level more generally. However, when placed in a normal environment, it has been striking that the process of recovery usually begins rapidly (within a few weeks or months) and, some years later, most (but not all) of the children have been within the normal range for language and general intelligence. These are dramatic examples, indeed, of the devastating effects of a grossly abnormal environment, as well as of the remarkable resilience of many children when removed from the circumstances of severe abuse and neglect.

The second question is whether variations in environmental circumstances within the normal range can have an effect on language development. Again, the answer is 'yes' (see Puckering and Rutter[506]). This is shown, for example, by the slight retarding effect on language of being brought up in an unusually large family with diminished opportunities for parent–child interaction; of being reared as a twin, probably for similar reasons;[423] possibly, of maternal depression; and of being brought up in a socially disadvantaged (but not abusive) home. The effects are modest; and there is very considerable variation between children in whether, or how much, they are influenced; but the impact of the environment seems real enough. Some years ago, people tended to talk about the need for a 'stimulating' environment, but it is now clear that this creates a seriously misleading emphasis. The need is, not for noise and bombardment of talk directed *at* children, but rather for responsive, reciprocal interactions and communications *with* them.

The third point is whether the specific styles of parental

communication matter. Is it better, for example, to restate what children have said in order to demonstrate how it should have been said correctly? Or to focus on speaking simply so that children can understand? Or is the main need to encourage and reward communication without too much regard to the niceties of the language? No firm answer is available but the balance of the evidence suggests that, although certain forms of communication may have advantages, it is not likely that the fine-grained features of parental language make much difference to the process of language acquisition. A related point is that the features that are most beneficial for normal children are not necessarily the same ones that are most helpful for those with some form of language handicap. Thus, autistic children (because of their cognitive processing limitations) seem to need a more structured approach than is optimal for normal children; and deaf children may do better being reared by deaf parents (who cannot talk properly but who use gesture well to communicate) than hearing ones.[506]

A fourth, somewhat related, issue concerns the question of whether language-delayed or socially disadvantaged children receive language benefits from attending nursery schools. It is generally assumed that they may do so, and numerous studies in the USA have shown the cognitive gains made by many socially disadvantaged children when they go to nursery schools, although these do not necessarily persist (see Clarke-Stewart and Fein[190]). Whether or not the same applies to ordinary British nursery schools is less certain,[504] if only because the observed benefits are most obvious with schools of special quality and many nurseries provide less than optimal care.

The issue came to the fore again in the mid-eighties as a result of an important observational study by Tizard and Hughes.[477] This showed that there was more, and more varied, conversational interchange between parents and their children in working-class homes than the same children experienced at nursery schools; although, compared with middle-class mothers, those in the working-class group used fewer examples of complex language. The findings were used to cast doubt on the notion that nursery schools can compensate for language deficiencies at home. The results rightly caused us to question the naïve (and misguided) expectation that schools can provide the same language environment as that found in 'good homes'. They do not, and probably cannot. Equally, they emphasize that we should be wary of assuming that what children use at school is representative of what they can produce in optimal circumstances. However, in our view, it would be equally unwise to deny the potential benefits of *good* nursery schools for children from socially disadvantaged families. Three main points are relevant. First, the Tizard and Hughes sample contained few seriously socially disadvantaged families (it excluded single-parent and ethnic-minority families and there were few children from very large or indigent families). Second, the home conversations were deliberately recorded in circumstances when the mothers were relatively unpressured by competing demands (such conversational lacks as there are in disadvantaged homes are likely to stem as much from stressful situations as from parental limitations). Third, it would be unwarranted to assume that the only sort of linguistic experiences that are beneficial are those seen in 'good homes'. It may well be that children benefit from *both* the more didactic talk used for teaching at school *and* the open-ended exploratory conversations characteristic of linguistically rich homes. Perhaps the complementary environments meet different needs.

A fifth query is whether the pace of early language development matters. Most of the literature on early language development has been concerned with variations in the speed with which young normal children acquire particular linguistic skills during the preschool years. The clinician has to pose the further query whether it matters whether children acquire language early. An important recent study by Bishop and Adams[38] suggests that it may *not*. They undertook a longitudinal study of children who showed a marked language delay at the age of four years. Of those of normal intelligence, just over two fifths had more or less caught up in language by the age of $5\frac{1}{2}$ years. The crucial finding was that this 'good outcome' group were intellectually and educationally indistinguishable from the general population at the age of $8\frac{1}{2}$ years, whereas those with continuing language difficulties were substantially retarded in their reading and spelling, as well as showing continuing evidence of language difficulties. The implication is that even quite marked *transient* delays in language development may be of little significance in the long term, but that *persistent* delays carry with them many problems, an issue to which we return later in this chapter.

The sixth issue follows on naturally from that point; do persisting language delays represent the end of a continuum of normal variation in the pace of language acquisition or do they constitute qualitatively distinct disorders? The question may be tackled through several different research strategies, but here we focus on just two. As we noted earlier, it seems that, within the normal range, the development of language is relatively distinct from the development of general intelligence. Does that apply to extreme delays in language? The evidence shows that it does *not*, inasmuch as research with children with severe language disorders has shown them to have a broader range of cognitive abnormalities that include deficits in auditory processing, short-term memory and hierarchical planning.[105,467] The second strategy comprises a follow-up into adult life in which the question is whether deficits remain long after conversational language has been acquired. Rutter and Mawhood's[415] follow-up of boys of normal intelligence with specific developmental disorder of receptive language showed that substantial sequelae were present in the mid-twenties in the majority of men. There had been a drop of some 10 points of IQ on average; half were still below the ten-year level in scholastic attainments; and subtle language impairments (most obvious in writing) were common. At least with these severe developmental language disorders, it is clear that they do not 'catch up' and also that their problems extend well beyond language.

Psychosocial Sequelae of Language Disorders

The psychiatric sequelae of language disorders have been studied in a range of longitudinal studies, with findings summarized by Rutter and Mawhood.[415] As reading and spelling involves written language, it is not surprising that severe language delay is often followed by difficulties in these scholastic attainments. Bishop and Adams's[38] finding that this risk is largely confined to those whose language impairment is still present at school entry is important. It seems that the risks are low when the problems are purely phonological; that is, when they are confined to the production of speech sounds and do not include either the use or understanding of words. What is perhaps a bit more surprising is the high frequency with which language delay is associated with socio-emotional and behavioural problems. Moreover, the social deficits often persist into adult life. Rutter and Mawhood[415] found that a third of their group had never had either a close friendship or a love relationship by their mid-twenties and a further third had not had a love relationship (although they had experienced friendship). The majority, too, showed job difficulties and had limited leisure activities. The reasons for these persistent social difficulties are not well understood. It is possible that the explanation could lie in some common antecedent, such as neurodevelopmental impairment. Alternatively, it could be that children's difficulties in communication increase the risk of social isolation or rejection; or the risks could stem from the associated scholastic difficulties and the stresses of educational failure; or the origins of both the language delay and the social impairments could lie in some underlying specific cognitive deficit. Although the last possibility seems particularly likely because of the strong persistence of the deficits, a puzzle is evident in the lack of association between the cognitive/language features and the social deficits in the language-disordered men studied by Rutter and Mawhood.[415] A final point needs adding; that some instances of language delay and later psychopathology may represent different stages in a constitutionally determined disease state. The clearest example of this sort is to be found in the evidence showing that in about half the cases of adult schizophrenia there have been prior non-psychotic abnormalities in childhood, frequently including some form of developmental impairment (see Rutter and Garmezy[204]).

Brain Damage and Language

As we noted earlier, the left half of the brain specializes in the grammatical and semantic aspects of language; however, the right is concerned with prosodic features and with emotional gesturing (see Goodman[506]). As a consequence, in adults and older children or adolescents widespread disease of or damage to the left hemisphere usually results in aphasia, meaning a partial or complete loss of language that is associated with a distinctive pattern of language abnormalities during the recovery phase. There has been much interest in the somewhat different effects on language of brain lesions occurring in infancy or early childhood. Goodman[415,506] has succinctly summarized the main differences. When left-sided brain damage occurs *in utero*, or in infancy, language development is little affected. This is quite unlike the situation in adult life, and the sparing of the language functions seems to be due to the right hemisphere taking over language functions. This potential persists in diminishing degree throughout early and middle childhood so that, although left-sided damage *does* lead to language impairment in this age period, the degree of recovery seems to be somewhat greater than in adulthood. Also, however, there is a difference in the pattern of language abnormality. When very young children have a left–sided brain lesion, there is a consequent delay in language development but the aphasic-type abnormalities of language seen in adults are not much evident. Nevertheless, it should not be thought that all is benign with early brain lesions. Compared with similar lesions in later childhood or adult life, unilateral damage in early infancy is more likely to lead to some general intellectual impairment. Damage to a developing psychological function tends to have somewhat different effects from those seen with damage to a well-established function, but these differences cannot sensibly be reduced to single statements of whether it is better to have your brain damage early or late.[400]

One of the unavoidable dilemmas in any discussion of development is whether to focus on particular functions, as we chose to do in the last three chapters, or to concentrate on particular age periods. There are advantages and disadvantages to both and, in order to seek an appropriate balance, we switch strategy in the following three chapters, focusing first on adolescence.

Chapter 7

Adolescence:
Sexuality, Self-image and
Depression

More than most age periods, adolescence has been associated with various myths about its special qualities.[393] At the turn of this century, G. Stanley Hall argued that it was a time of 'storm and stress' and psychoanalysts[161] came to believe that it *necessarily* involved an interruption of peaceful growth, so that the maintenance of psychological equilibrium during the teenage years was *ipso facto* a sign of abnormality. Erikson[145] saw adolescence as a 'normative crisis' in which young people had to go through a disorienting process in order to achieve an identity involving commitment to adult roles. As has often been the case with stereotypes, these views were largely based on young people seeking help for psychological troubles, and epidemiological studies of the general population have been consistent in showing that the notion that all normal adolescents experience turmoil and alienation from their families is mistaken.[97,151,347,393] Nevertheless, the myths were not wholly wrong. It is obvious that puberty involves major bodily changes; the transition to adulthood requires a range of adaptations; and the teenage years are associated with a substantial rise in several different kinds of psychiatric disorder. Accordingly, in this chapter, we survey these changes and adaptations in terms of their psychological implications and their possible relevance to the increased prevalence of certain disorders in this age period. As in previous chapters, we pay special attention to individual differences and to the elucidation of the mechanisms that may be involved.

Puberty

It is appropriate to begin with puberty because in a real sense it does represent a degree of discontinuity in development. Not only does it involve a major change in physique but it makes possible the radical transition from child to parent. In both sexes, there is a rapid increase in the *tempo* of physical growth and a very substantial alteration in its *pattern*. Figure 7.1[469] brings out three further crucial points; the earlier maturation of girls compared with boys, the very long duration of the pubertal processes and the marked individual differences in their timing. In the UK, the typical girl begins her growth spurt at about $10\frac{1}{2}$ years, reaching peak height velocity at approximately twelve. Boys begin their growth spurt some two years later, with a greater peaking than that in girls, but with slower growth continuing for a few years after that. It is notable that the growth spurt in girls is an *early* manifestation of puberty, whereas in boys it is a *late* one. In both sexes there are huge individual variations in the timing of puberty – thus the onset of the growth spurt in boys ranges from ten to sixteen years.

This spectacular increase in height at puberty is accompanied by marked changes in physique, the pattern of changes differing between the sexes. Girls increase in hip width, with an accumulation of fat as they cease to gain height. Thus, it is sometimes said that the height spurt is closely followed by the fat spurt! Boys show a greater increase in shoulder breadth and a greater increase in muscle than girls; also boys tend to lose, rather than gain, fat during adolescence, although there may be some increase in fat as height growth slows. The net result of these sex differences is that most boys welcome and are pleased with the physical changes of adolescence, whereas most girls in our society are unhappy about the acquisition of fat, even though they may be glad about other aspects of sexual maturity.[97,151,347,393] By late adolescence, about half of all girls in the UK and USA have dieted – usually unsuccessfully! This is much less common in boys, whose main interest tends to be in the gaining of strength and physique, with exercise rather than diet being their response to these wishes.

Considerable changes in hormone secretion also occur during adolescence. The first event is an increased secretion of gonadotrophic hormones by the pituitary, which causes the follicles of the ovary and the tubules of the testis to develop. The production

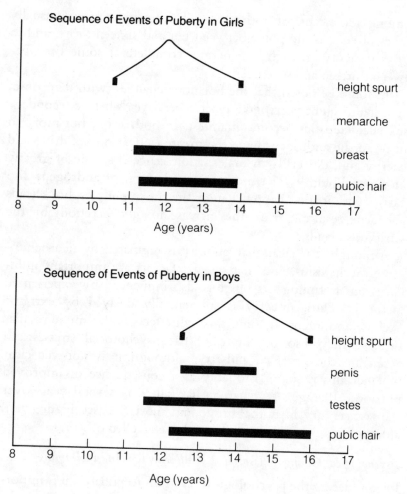

7.1 Sequence of events of puberty in girls and boys.
Data from Tanner.[469]

of adrenal androgens (male sex hormones) increases in both sexes at about eight to ten years, with a further much sharper increase a few years later, this being substantially greater in boys as a result of the addition of testicular androgens. The excretion of oestrogens also gradually rises from about seven years, with a secondary, very large, rapid rise in girls at the time of puberty, with accompanying cyclicity. Again, timing varies greatly among adolescents of both sexes. The menarche in girls usually takes place at some point between ten and sixteen years, and in boys testicular growth is generally complete at some time between thirteen and seventeen.

It should be noted that the hormone changes (with their onset at seven or eight years) take place several years before secondary sex characteristics become manifest. In both sexes, but more so in boys, the androgens have the greatest effect on sex drive and energy and, especially in males, adolescence is a time of greatly increased libido.[14] The increased production of androgens also carries with it a less happy change: the rise in pimples, blackheads and acne resulting from the increase in oily secretions by the sebaceous glands.

Although it is clear that puberty is regulated by neuroendocrine mechanisms, and that genetic factors are important influences on its timing, its onset is also influenced by experiential factors.[14] Thus, puberty is substantially delayed by extreme exercise and intense dieting, through effects on hormone regulation. It may also be the case that psychosocial stresses can accelerate the onset of puberty, although it is not yet clear whether this is so.[307] Probably as a consequence of improved nutrition, the age of menarche has fallen by several years over the last century in both Europe and the USA (see Figure 7.2), although it seems that the fall may have levelled off.

Psychological Changes Associated With Puberty And Its Timing

In considering the psychological reactions to puberty, it is important to recognize that puberty is not a single entity. Thus, the reactions may be to the reaching of some landmark (such as menarche or first ejaculation), to the variety of associated physical changes (such as muscularity, adiposity or acne), to other people's reactions (such as the increased responsibilities given to a youngster who now has the appearance of a man or the sexual attentions paid to a nubile girl) or to the timing of maturation (either ahead or behind peers); also, of course, there may be direct hormonal effects on behaviour.

Girls tend to have rather ambivalent attitudes to the menarche, but some are clearly positive and some clearly negative in their

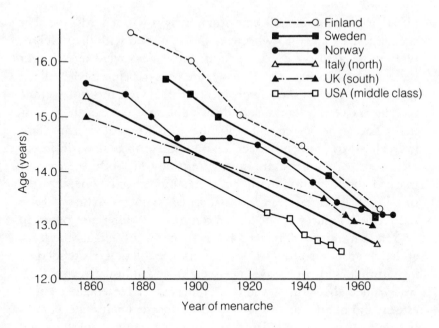

7.2 Age at menarche, 1860–1970.
Sources of data and method of plotting detailed in J.M. Tanner, *Foetus into Man*, 2nd edn, Castlemead Publications, 1989.

feelings. The colloquial terms for menstruation (e.g., the 'curse') reflect the negative side of the reactions, but surveys such as that by Ruble and Brooks-Gunn,[385] show that the traditional percept of the menarche as necessarily anxiety-provoking and distressing is misleading; this applies to only a minority of girls. The physical changes associated with puberty, and its timing relative to other girls, have proved to be more influential.

Being thin is seen as a desirable attribute by most girls today in our society. Accordingly, when puberty is associated with adiposity, as often it is, this may lead to both lowered self-esteem and attempts to reduce weight by dieting. Attie and Brooks-Gunn[8] found that it was weight gain, associated with negative feelings about their body image, rather than puberty *per se*, that led girls to engage in marked dieting. However, this course of events is much influenced by social attitudes. Figure 7.3 shows the sex difference found in an American study by Richards and her colleagues.[368] The girls who were most satisfied with their weight were those who were *under*weight, those who were overweight were very dissatisfied, those of average weight being intermediate. By contrast, the boys who were most satisfied were those of average weight; the overweight *and* underweight boys were both dissatisfied. The general tendency in the girls concealed important individual variations, however. The sample comprised two different communities, Northshore and Westside. In both, there was marked dissatisfaction with being fat but in only one, Northshore, was unusual leanness associated with particularly high satisfaction (Figure 7.4). It turned out that this difference between two communities was largely a function of engagement in athletic and other after-school activities. Athletic girls tended to be satisfied with both average weight and unusual leanness. It was argued that athletics and exercise may have enhanced self-esteem and bodily satisfaction by three different routes: its contribution to a firmer and trimmer body; the sense of mastery and competence engendered; and the satisfactions derived from positive team activities. An *increased* concern about being thin is found among ballet-dancers, a group who are expected to maintain a slim physique, and eating problems are particularly common in dancers.[466] The point is that reactions to the physical changes of puberty are not a 'given'; they vary according to the particular features that predominate in the individual and according to the prevailing social attitudes to what are valued physical features.

A further point needs emphasis: the factors that initiate a particular psychological reaction are not necessarily the same as those that lead to a *perpetuation* of that reaction. Eating problems illustrate this difference. As we have noted, a marked increase in fat is a key influence inducing dieting in adolescent girls. This dieting, when extreme and when associated with a profound dissatisfaction with body image (as is often the case), shows many parallels with the phenomena of the psychiatric condition of anorexia nervosa. However, only a small proportion of dieters go on to show the full picture of anorexia nervosa, a serious syndrome that causes a mortality of about 3 or 4 per cent.[367]

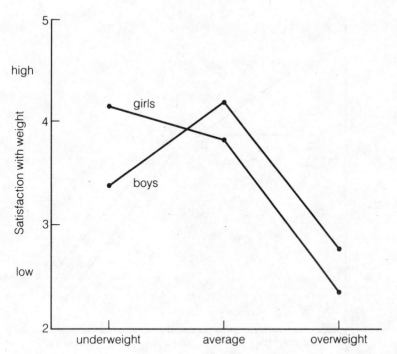

7.3 Satisfaction with weight by weight category and sex.
Data from Richards et al.[368]

Moreover, pubertal weight increase is not the main feature associated with this progression. Attie and Brooks–Gunn[8] found that the persistence of disturbed eating patterns (falling well short of anorexia nervosa) between fourteen and sixteen years was more associated with depressed mood and disturbed family relationships than with the weight gain that seems so important in the younger age group. Similarly, Szmukler et al.[466] found that anorexic-like dancers did not have the poor prognosis usually associated with anorexia nervosa. We may conclude that in our society, weight gain in adolescence that is perceived as excessive and undesirable may be sufficient to induce marked dieting and bodily dissatisfaction. However, its persistence into later adolescence and its progression into frank anorexia nervosa tends to occur largely when there are also associated emotional disturbances and/or family difficulties.

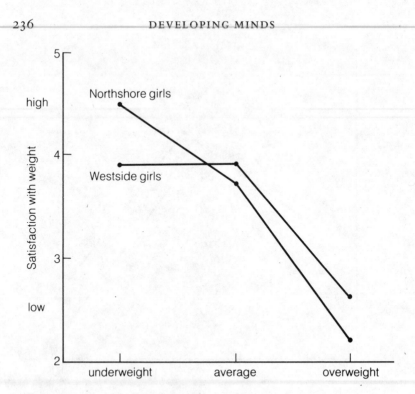

7.4 Weight satisfaction in girls in two communities according to weight category.

Data from Richards et al.[368]

Girls' and boys' reactions to unusually early puberty are somewhat different. Several American studies have shown that early maturing boys tend to have a slight advantage in personality (being more popular, more relaxed, good-natured and generally poised) and that these advantages may persist (see Brooks-Gunn and Petersen[58] and Graham and Rutter[417]). The measures used in these studies were not particularly satisfactory but the findings have been fairly consistent, so the tendency is likely to be real. The probable explanation is that most of the pubertal changes in males have a positive connotation and that early maturing boys tend to be more muscular, with the attendant social benefits in the peer group of being strong and good at sport.

Physical maturation in girls is not associated with the same unequivocal social response. On the whole, early maturity is associated with a poorer body image and an increased risk of eating problems – probably because early maturing girls tend to be somewhat heavier than average. There may also be other consequences. As we have noted earlier, Magnusson and his colleagues,[286] in a Swedish longitudinal study, found that girls who reached their menarche before the age of eleven were more likely than girls who matured at the average time, or later, to play truant, get drunk, take drugs and generally engage in rule-breaking behaviour. They were also more likely not to continue with their education after the end of compulsory schooling. However, these effects were found only in those girls who joined peer groups of older girls. By the time the girls reached adulthood, the early maturers no longer stood out from the remainder in terms of their behaviour. As their social groups changed, the effect was lost. Nevertheless, they landed up with lower academic qualifications. Clearly, this was *not* because the psychological effects of early puberty persisted but rather because, having opted out of education, it required a definite, and unusual, set of actions to re-enter.

Sometimes, it has been assumed that it is the fact that early puberty is not at the usual time that creates the stress. If that were the case, similar effects should be found with unusually late puberty in girls but that was not the case in the Magnusson study, nor was it in the Dunedin longitudinal study in New Zealand.[81,82] The latter, like the Swedish study, showed an increase in problem behaviour among early maturing girls, but not late maturing ones. The results also showed that this increase in behaviour problems was largely found in girls already exhibiting some behavioural difficulties before puberty. On the whole, times of stress accentuate personal characteristics that are already present in some degree. However, if the environmental circumstances are of a kind that are markedly discrepant from those operating earlier, there can be a turning-point that involves a change in life trajectory, and not just a strengthening of continuity; we discuss this point further in this chapter in relation to teenage pregnancy and also in Chapter 8 when discussing marriage.

As we noted in Chapter 5, the Dunedin study[81,82] also

brought out a further important point: namely that the effects of early puberty in increasing norm-breaking behaviour were found only among girls in mixed-sex schools. It seemed that the effects arose through peer-group influences, which were more likely to be antisocial in coeducational schools, because of the effects of delinquent boys.

Sexuality

Because adult sexuality is made possible by the physical changes of puberty, it is easy to assume that the latter brings about the former. Nevertheless, research findings show that it is not as simple as that. To begin with, it is necessary to draw a few distinctions – such as those between 'dating' the opposite sex, sexual drive and interests, and sexual behaviour.

Although dating often involves sexual attraction, and may involve sexual activities ranging from kissing and petting to intercourse, it is initially a sociocultural phenomenon with a different meaning in different societies. One large-scale American study showed only a weak connection between the timing of puberty and the timing of dating; there are considerable pressures to date once an adolescent has reached a certain age, regardless of pubertal status.[151] Exactly comparable data are not available for European adolescents, but it seems that there may be a stronger temporal association between dating and puberty; the cultural pressures are probably less and the role of puberty is correspondingly stronger. Similarly, the effects of puberty on dating vary among social and ethnic groups within the USA. Gargiulo *et al.*[167] found that prepubertal ballet-dancers were less likely to date than non-dancers, but that the menarche was associated with the onset of dating in dancers (who tended to be later in reaching puberty), whereas it was not in non-dancers. We may infer that prepubertal dancers experience less peer pressure to date because their peer group is different. The reason for their dating after puberty may stem either from the physiological 'presses' that arise from the hormonal changes, from the psychological 'presses' stemming from an awareness of their growing sexual maturity or from changing social 'presses' as post-menarcheal dancers move away from the dance world because of lack of goodness-of-fit between the requirements of the dance context and their physical characteristics.

Sexual interests and motivation rise markedly with puberty and this appears to be so regardless of culture. Moreover, within any one culture, hormone levels are associated with the strength of the sex drive, albeit more strongly so in males than females.[14] Such drive can be repressed, as it was for girls in Victorian England and is in many religious communities today. Also, the mode of its expression varies according to sociocultural mores. In days gone by, masturbation may have constituted the main sexual outlet, whereas today some form of heterosexual activity is more common and sexual intercourse is increasingly acceptable among unmarried teenagers. In the United States, nearly two thirds of boys and just less than half of girls have had sexual intercourse by the age of eighteen.

Overt sexual behaviour with a partner is also influenced by hormonal changes. Thus, early pubertal development is strongly associated with an early initiation of sexual activity.[198] But sexual behaviour is also affected by sociocultural factors. This is shown, for example, by the marked secular changes that have taken place during the last generation – shown graphically in Figure 7.5. Sexual intercourse by young teenagers has become much more common. There are also marked ethnic differences; black youths become sexually experienced at a much earlier age than their white counterparts in the USA.[218] Indeed, a sizeable minority of black boys report initiation of intercourse prior to puberty. Poverty, social disadvantage and family disorganization are all associated with earlier engagement in sexual activities. Also, there are important gender differences. Although girls reach puberty two years before boys, fifteen-year-old boys are nearly three times as likely as girls to have had sexual intercourse. In both sexes, the first intercourse is usually with older partners; in the case of girls some three years older and in boys about a year older.

There has been a tendency in some quarters to view the increase in sexual behaviour among young people as a growth in promiscuity and a loss of moral values. However, that seems to be a misleading oversimplification. Much premarital sexual activity takes place within a monogamous relationship and there is

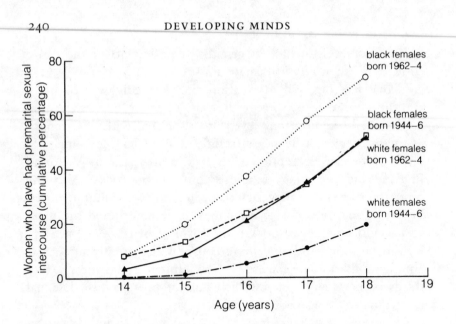

7.5 Cumulative percentage of US teenage women who have had premarital sexual intercourse, according to race and year of birth.
Data from Hofferth et al.[218]

little really indiscriminate activity: serial monogamy rather than promiscuity is the most usual pattern. However, there do seem to be differences (at least in emphasis) between the sexes in their approach to sexual relationships.[451] Boys tend to have more sexual partners (implying a small core of promiscuous girls), while the girls are more likely to have an enduring sexual association. Girls tend to look for a romantic relationship, remaining faithful to one partner at a time, whereas boys are more likely to seek sexual adventure in a variety of relationships.

It is evident that there are many influences on sexual behaviour, other than the hormonal changes of puberty.[198,217] The most important personal factors (other than those already mentioned) associated with an unusually early initiation of sexual activity include:

1. Low intellectual ability, low scholastic achievement and low interest in educational goals;

2. Poor parent–child communication and poor parent–child relationships;
3. A broken home or a single-parent family;
4. A mother who had unusually early sexual experiences;
5. An involvement in other adult-like activities that are socially disapproved of in the young – such as smoking, use of alcohol and delinquency;
6. Lack of religious commitment.

However, the initiation of sexual activity is also much affected by sociocultural influences, perhaps most especially peer-group mores. The earlier engagement in sexual intercourse by black (compared with white) teenagers in the United States stands out in that connection. The reasons for the large ethnic difference are not well understood but it is clear that they are not entirely explicable in terms of personal characteristics, and the pattern suggests the importance of social expectations and pressures.[5] In that connection, it is relevant that one study found that black students in racially isolated schools were several times more likely than those in racially integrated schools to be sexually active.[163a] Rowe et al.[382] have suggested that the combination of somewhat earlier puberty in black girls and social influences may together account for the ethnic difference in age of sexual initiation, by means of a kind of 'epidemic' effect.

Contraceptive Use, Teenage Pregnancy and Abortion

There is substantial variation among young people in the extent to which sexual activities are accompanied by the use of any form of contraception. To a substantial extent the same variables associated with unusually early initiation of sexual activities also apply to *non*-use of contraceptives. However, some other considerations also apply. Thus, girls who use contraceptives on a regular basis are more likely to have started sexual activities later; to be in a committed heterosexual relationship; to have accepted their own sexuality; and to have high self-esteem and a feeling of sense of control over their lives. Rather similar variables apply to the use of abortion for unwanted pregnancies, but it is also important to note that there are major differences between countries.[198] American teenagers stand out from the rest of the industrialized world in being less likely to use contraceptives; clearly the major factor here is the lack of accessibility and acceptability of family-planning services. The pregnancy rate in fifteen- to nineteen-year-olds in the USA, 96 per 1,000 a decade ago (165 in blacks and 83 in whites) is double that in Canada and the UK, the gap having widened in recent years (see Forrest[14]). This is not a function of national differences in sexual activity, which are very similar in the UK and USA, but rather it is due to a lower use of contraceptives. The advent of AIDS has also had an effect on contraceptive practice, with a recent increase in the use of condoms by young people in Britain.[326] The basic point here is that behaviour of all kinds is strongly influenced by sociocultural factors, even in an age period like adolescence when biological forces are strong.

Of course, individual psychological factors also play a major role and we need to consider these in relation to teenage pregnancy. As we have seen, public attitudes towards family planning and the ready availability of inexpensive, effective contraceptives are relevant. Knowledge about sexuality and contraception is another factor. Young adolescents, who are just beginning to engage in sexual activities, are those least likely to use contraceptives. Sex education can sometimes help in this connection[131] but, on its own, it may do little to change behaviour.[464] As one of our clients put it, 'When I'm having sex, all those school things go out of my head!'

One of the key issues is the need for foresight and planning. This has two rather different aspects. On the one hand, in many cases, a failure to plan in relation to sexual behaviour is part of young people's much more general failure to plan any aspect of their lives – often associated with a lack of self-esteem and a feeling of not being able to control what happens to them. On the other hand, perhaps especially among males, a lack of contraceptive use is associated with impulsive, risk-taking behaviour more generally. But there is also a third aspect of a lack of planning in sexual matters. Perhaps especially in younger girls, there may be a wish for sex to be truly 'spontaneous', a wish that seems to run counter to planning ahead to use contraceptives.

Probably this feature is more evident in girls who have not yet come fully to accept their own sexuality (where there is ambivalence about being in a sexual relationship), or in circumstances when sex is taking place outside an established relationship, or when there has been a lack of open discussion about sex in the young people's families.[70]

Finally, although most teenage pregnancies are unplanned and unwanted, there are some in which the girls have at least run the risk of pregnancy with some feelings that having a child might 'help'. In some cases this is done through a desire to 'save the relationship' (although it rarely does so). Sometimes it constitutes a form of escape from an intolerable family situation or a generally unrewarding life in socially disadvantaged circumstances. Sometimes, too, it represents a reaction to an unloving upbringing, so that a pregnancy is viewed as a way of having a child whom they can love and who will love them. This range of mechanisms was evident in the Quinton and Rutter[361] follow-up of girls reared in institutions (cottage-style group homes) many of whom married and/or became pregnant in their teens as a means of escape from a very stressful and unrewarding family situation, or as an impulsive act which was part of a more pervasive feeling of being at the mercy of fate.

Teenage Motherhood

It is clear, then, that there are identifiable developmental as well as social antecedents of teenage motherhood. From a policy and practice perspective, it is evident that successful family-planning services must do much more than distribute effective contraceptives; it is necessary to appreciate the variety of reasons why young people engage in sexual behaviour that leads to pregnancy, as well as the fact that a failure to use contraception may reflect a general lack of planning, or risk-taking behaviour, as much as anything to do with contraception as such.[393] However, a life-span developmental perspective also requires that we consider the consequences of the experience for the young people concerned. Most of the research literature has focused on the risk for the offspring that derives from having teenage parents, but there is now a growing set of studies of what it means for the teenagers who become pregnant;[163,198,217,299] very little is known about what the experience means for the young males concerned.

The first point is the one that we emphasized in Chapter 2; young people vary greatly in how they cope with this major life transition and the consequences are not uniform. Rather, they vary with the social circumstances and with the style and adaptive success of the coping process.

The first decision, of course, is whether or not to continue with the pregnancy or to terminate it. Clearly, this constitutes one of the turning-points[349] to which we drew attention in earlier chapters: times of decision or opportunity when life trajectories may be directed on to more adaptive or maladaptive paths. Studies of working-class London women,[61,62,63] of girls reared in group foster homes,[361] of black girls in Baltimore[163] and of other groups[198,217,299] have all shown that, in general, teenage motherhood tends to predispose to a negative trajectory. This comes about through several rather different mechanisms, the occurrence of each of which is dependent on the particular circumstances operative at the time. Thus, there is an increase in school drop-out, which leads to a lower than average level of educational attainment, which in turn predisposes to later low occupational status. While this is indeed an important consequence, it is not inevitable. Thus, in the Baltimore follow-up, nearly half completed high school and a significant minority returned to school some years later, with a few going on to college.

Secondly, marriage to the father of the child tends to mean marriage to someone in an unskilled job because that is their characteristic in the main. Among girls from a high-risk psychosocial background (such as those reared in institutions[361]), it is also probable that the husband will be someone from a similar disadvantaged background, often with substantial psychosocial problems. That is simply because, at that stage in their lives, these are the sort of youths whom the girls know.

Teenage marriage also carries a *much* increased risk of later marital discord and marital breakdown. This is so in the population as a whole,[69] but it is probably especially so among early marriages precipitated by pregnancy. In the Baltimore study, when the women were re-contacted seventeen years later in their mid-thirties, only 16 per cent had remained married to the father of the child who was born when they were a teenager and two thirds were without any marriage partner.[163]

Associated with these first three factors, teenage motherhood usually carries with it a substantial economic penalty, both in the years that immediately follow and in the long-term. About a quarter of the Baltimore women were on welfare at the seventeen-year follow-up. Whereas this is a much lower proportion than at the five-year follow-up (about 70 per cent had been on welfare at some time), it is much higher than that for comparable women who had not become teenage mothers.

Finally, teenage mothers tend to go on to have further unintended births during the next few years. However, the Baltimore study data are striking in showing that this tendency did *not* persist when they were older. The average fertility per year between the fifth and twelfth year follow-ups was only a third of that in the first five years. Doubtless, in part this reflected the increasing availability of abortion and sterilization over this time period, but also it seemed to stem from a greater tendency of the women to plan, to control their lives and to make use of the services available to them.

We need, in addition, to consider the consequences for the children born to teenage mothers. It is clear from a variety of studies that they experience an increased risk of educational difficulties, emotional and behavioural problems, and teenage parenthood themselves.[163,198,217] Equally, however, it is apparent that there is major heterogeneity in outcomes, with the children's prospects linked to what happens with their mothers, and some doing very well.

The life course following teenage motherhood is an instructive one that well illustrates some of the developmental principles that we outlined in earlier chapters. Several points require emphasis. First, it is evident that it did indeed constitute a turning-point with long-term negative consequences for many individuals, consequences that could not be accounted for by the girls' characteristics and circumstances before they became pregnant.

Second, however, the teenage pregnancy was not a chance event; to an important extent it was the result of the girl's own behaviour (not just in having sex but also in not using contraception and not having an abortion) which constituted part of a broader life pattern. Third, the sequelae of teenage motherhood are both varied and influenced by the individual's own actions. Some teenage mothers go on to advance their education, find employment, go off welfare, establish their own household and regulate their fertility. The outcome that was least easy to change was marriage; nevertheless a few go on to make harmonious, stable marriages, usually those who postponed marriage and completed schooling. Furstenberg et al.[163] summarized their findings in terms of four dimensions that predisposed to positive life trajectories following teenage motherhood: (i) good economic and social resources, including parental support and good role models; (ii) good personal competence and motivation combined with high educational aspirations; (iii) appropriate societal interventions aimed at postponing further births and completing schooling; and (iv) appropriate career decisions with the avoidance of further births and the making of a stable marriage particularly critical. The final developmental issue concerning turning-points is that the persistence of effects is at least as much a function of the relative permanence of 'external' sequelae as of 'internal' psychological changes. Thus, the birth of a child creates a lasting change to the parents' social life and responsibilities (unless the child is given up for adoption or fostering); dropping out of school means that a major step is required to re-enter education; and psychological consequences are much influenced by the economic effects of teenage motherhood.

Termination of Pregnancy

Teenage pregnancies may lead to a decision to seek termination, rather than to go on to give birth and keep the baby. In most countries, abortion has become much more of an available option to young people, as a result of changes in legislation and altered public attitudes. As with teenage motherhood, we need to consider both the antecedents and consequences. As we have noted, the features associated with the use of abortion are the flip side of those associated with teenage births. That is, abortion users tend to be more socially advantaged, better educated and more likely to have good self-esteem and a feeling of control over their lives.

Until fairly recently, many people were concerned that therapeutic abortion is likely to lead to psychiatric disturbance. However, research findings show that this is *not* the case.[170] The rate of mental disorder after termination of pregnancy is far lower overall than that after childbirth. Depressive reactions may possibly be somewhat more frequent in teenagers than adults (although the evidence on this point is inconclusive), but even in this age group disorders are not common. The key risk factors for psychiatric disorder following termination seem to be: (i) previous psychiatric disturbance; (ii) marked ambivalence over the decision to abort; (iii) failure to involve the male partner in the decision; (iv) high anxiety when the girl discovered that she was pregnant; and (v) late termination.

Although the psychiatric risks associated with termination of pregnancy are minor, it cannot be regarded as a trivial surgical procedure of little psychological consequence. Feelings of guilt and ambivalence about the decision are relatively common, because it is an unpleasant decision to have to take and because of the punitive responses from some professionals. Also, one British study[254] found that abortion was associated with a significantly increased risk of depression during the next pregnancy; a potentially important finding but one that needs to be tested in other groups. Counselling for girls seeking termination may help them cope better with their mixed feelings. Also, however, it is a time when they may be more receptive to advice on how to avoid future unwanted pregnancies. Evaluative studies have yet to be undertaken on whether counselling succeeds in this objective, but experience with other threatening situations indicates the importance of timing. Thus, for example, people are more likely to give up smoking, lose weight and exercise *after* they have had their first heart attack than before it, when the risk may seem sufficiently hypothetical for them to assume that it will not happen to them. Perhaps, in a similar fashion, the otherwise negative event of an abortion has the potential of being transformed into a positive learning time.

Social Experiences In Adolescence

Up to this point, we have discussed adolescence largely from the perspective of puberty and emerging sexuality, and their consequences. However, it is obvious that there is much more to adolescence than that. It is an age period when there are changing social experiences of significance and also there are important 'internal' psychological developments.

To begin with, there are the various changes associated with schooling. In the UK there is a major move from primary to secondary school at the age of about eleven or twelve years, and in the USA there is a somewhat comparable move from elementary to junior high school. Within the British system this may involve a radical change in peer group because the pupils from any one primary school may move on to a large number of different secondary schools. This would be usual in inner London, for example. The consequence is that children may lose contact with old friends and have to make new friendships. The children's position in the school also changes; in the primary school they were in the oldest age group and likely therefore to be viewed as responsible and respected seniors. In the secondary school, by contrast, they are in the youngest group and likely to be seen as immature and irresponsible juniors. In most schools there is also a shift from a more personalized school class with one main teacher in primary school to a secondary-school class with many different teachers for different subjects and a less individualized approach, if only because teachers are likely to know their pupils less well.

We have expressed these changes in terms that suggest stress but, of course, many children may view them as positive challenges to be welcomed. Evidence is lacking on the effects in Britain, where the changes may possibly be more likely to be stressful, and the findings in the USA are somewhat contradictory. Simmons and Blyth[441] found that the transition from elementary to secondary school was associated in some girls (but not in boys) with a drop in self-esteem. However, this was marked only when the school change coincided in time with other changes either of a normative type (such as puberty) or a non-normative variety (such as parental divorce). The finding is in keeping with Coleman and Hendry's[97] answer to their own query of why so many young people go through adolescence undisturbed when they have as many major, and potentially stressful, changes to deal with. Their response was that, in part, this may be because usually the changes do not all occur at the same time, but that when they do the psychological risks may be somewhat greater. Nottelman,[318] however, did not find a drop in self-esteem following school transition and it may well be that school qualities also play a role in determining whether the change is seen by most young people as positive or negative.

In the British system, there are other potentially negative educational events later in the teenage period. Thus, there are national exams at sixteen and eighteen years of age, which many teenagers experience as stressful because success in them is so important in providing a passport to higher education – an experience available to only a few. There is no exact equivalent in the USA, but the issue of college entry and the competition to get admitted to the college of choice provides an important set of challenges. However, for those not engaged in academic pursuits, the last year or so of schooling may constitute a turn-off, and in both the USA and UK absenteeism and drop-out rise markedly at this time.[393] As we noted earlier, this is not a function of age as such, as the pattern has followed changes in legislation on compulsory schooling. Whenever it ends, it tends to be preceded by a period of disenchantment among pupils who clearly feel they have had enough of schooling. However, the extent of absenteeism and drop-out varies markedly from school to school.[420]

We have noted already that the impact of changing life experiences may be influenced by the extent to which major changes coincide or occur in series. It is important also to appreciate the huge individual variations in timing, the national differences and the shifts over time. Figure 7.6 compares the trends in England and Wales and the USA between 1900 and 1980 (see Modell and Goodman[151]). At the turn of the century,

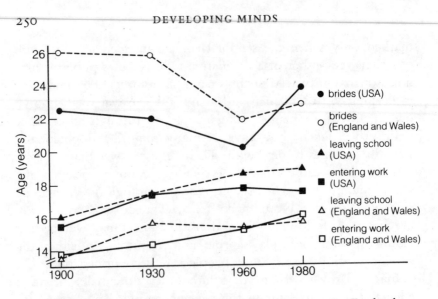

7.6 Trends in the median ages of transition, 1900–1980, England
and Wales and the United States.
Data from Modell and Goodman.[151]

young people in the UK left school and started work at fourteen
but did not marry until some twelve years later on average. By
contrast, young people in America in 1960 tended to start work
a year *before* leaving school at eighteen, with marriage following
only two years later on average for girls. Curiously, next to
nothing is known about the psychological consequences of these
variations in timing; an important task for future research.

These changes in experience are imposed by the social system
but there are many others brought about by the young people
themselves. As we have already seen, adolescence tends to be the
time when young people have their first love relationship. This
may well be a source of great pleasure but early loves tend to be
short-lived and the pains and stresses of broken love relationships
and of rebuffs and rivalries can be quite considerable.

It is not only love relationships that bring a complex mixture
of pain and happiness. Same-sex friendships also tend to become
more intense over the teenage years and change somewhat in
quality (see Savin-Williams and Berndt[151]). Whereas in childhood friendships tend to be focused on shared activities, during

adolescence there is a greater concern over reciprocity and loyalty, and over emotional sharing and exchange of confidences. On the whole, this emotional intimacy is more marked in girls than in boys. Girls also differ from boys in being more likely to have relatively exclusive same-sex friendships. As a result, tensions and rivalries are probably more common among teenage girls than boys. Boys are more likely to be part of loosely knit, larger peer groups.

In both sexes, there is probably some increase in the stability of friendships, although the findings on this point are somewhat contradictory. Certainly, with increasing age, there are greater concerns about the character, attitudes, beliefs and values of friends. It is no longer enough just to share the same leisure activities. It is clear that satisfying and harmonious friendships are associated with more adaptive psychosocial functioning, although the mechanisms remain somewhat uncertain; also it is not known whether the overall number of friends is of any importance. Although same-sex friendships remain important throughout the teenage years there is often a temporary decline with the growth of romantic relationships.

It is generally thought that peer influences increase during adolescence, and there is evidence that they do. However, the main influences come from *friends* rather than from the broader peer group. It should be added that it is also a misleading oversimplification to think of *one* peer group. There are varied adolescent peer cultures and many young people may be part of several 'crowds' or 'cliques'. The influences tend to be interactional, rather than normative. That is, teenagers are influenced by friends whom they choose and with whom they discuss ideas and exchange confidences, rather than by overall social pressures from their age group as a whole to conform to a particular pattern of behaviour.

The balance of time spent with family and friends also changes during adolescence. Increasingly, young people spend more leisure time with their friends and less with their parents. It used to be said that this shift in pattern went along with a distancing from parents, a diminution in parental influence on their children and the parent–child alienation typical of this age period. In fact, general population studies in both Britain and North America show that this stereotype is quite misleading.[151,347,393] What is true is that parent–child clashes over hairstyle, dress, time of getting in at night and the like increase, and that during the teens many young people, especially girls, become moody and difficult in ways that try their parents. However, in the majority of families, these stresses occur against a background of generally good parent–adolescent relationships and a continuing reliance by young people on their parents for advice and support on major issues in spite of a degree of rebelliousness and independence on all manner of minor matters. Indeed, as Steinberg[151] has pointed out, these disagreements may have positive effects. In most cases they are a reflection of psychological growth rather than discord.

Adolescents need to develop autonomy and their own styles of thinking and behaving, and it is, in a real sense, necessary to have some 'battles' with parents in order for this to happen. Probably, it is appropriate to see this as a more grown-up version of the 'terrible twos period', in which a similar psychological growth is occurring. Most teenagers maintain close ties with their parents while simultaneously gaining greater independence; it is inappropriate to view this as 'detachment' and there is no evidence that parent–child closeness is damaging.

Of course, some adolescents are seriously at odds with their families and mental-health professionals see many such young people. However, it is important to recognize that these constitute an atypical minority subgroup with psychiatric disorder, and also that in many cases the strained family relationships have *antedated* the adolescent age period.

Self-concepts and Identity

As we noted in Chapter 6, there are important developments during adolescence in young people's ability to conceptualize, to think about the meaning of their experiences and to establish concepts about themselves as distinctive individuals. Piaget expressed these changes in terms of the emergence of 'formal operational thinking' – meaning that, at about twelve years of age, there is the development for the first time of an ability to generate and explore hypotheses, to make deductions and to derive higher-order abstractions. As we have seen, research findings have not confirmed the idea that this constitutes a coherent distinctive phase with a qualitative shift in the nature of thinking. Some of these skills are manifest earlier in the right circumstances, and there is a more gradual increase in this type of conceptualization, with its operation highly dependent on task and context. Nevertheless, as Keating[151] noted in his summary of the evidence, during early adolescence, young people's thinking does tend to become more abstract, multidimensional, self-reflective and self-aware, with a greater use of relative, rather than absolute, concepts. The increase in their powers of thought arises, however, less from a qualitative jump deriving from the availability of a new cognitive process than from a greater automatizing of basic intellectual processes, from a greater familiarity with the context of knowledge and an increased capacity for working memory. As a result, they are better able to hold in mind several different dimensions of a topic at the same time, and so generate more alternatives in their decision-making. Metacognitive skills, too, increase. That is, young people become better able to monitor their own thinking for its inconsistency, for gaps in information and for the accuracy of its logic.

Obviously, this increase in intellectual powers carries with it many advantages. Nevertheless, there are unsettling aspects too. Especially to begin with, as thinking becomes more relative and abstract without yet becoming more systematic and principled, the calling into question of the concrete realities of knowledge of childhood may lead to a growth in idealism or to an increasing uncertainty, with an overgeneralization to a scepticism about any general 'truth'. Moreover, more skilled decision-making may not necessarily lead to 'better' decisions, as viewed from an adult perspective. Keating[151] gave the example of a mathematically talented ninth-grade girl giving up mathematics because continuation threatened her peer relationships at the time, which meant more to her than academic success. The use of drugs, similarly, may reflect a considered risk–benefit judgement in oppressive circumstances, rather than any failure to consider consequences. It is very obvious that many adult judgements are faulty in a host of respects and, as with those in adolescence, the problems may lie in the factors felt to be important at the time or in biased attitudes or prejudices, rather than in any limitations in the intellectual processes as such.

Individual differences are marked and these may stem from social as well as cognitive experiences. For example, Dweck and her colleagues (see Henderson and Dweck[151]) noted that children differ in the extent to which they see academic attainment as constrained by a fixed level of intelligence or as something that is much influenced by motivation and effort. The former concept is more characteristic of girls than of boys and it has been suggested that this plays some role in girls' relative fall-off in maths and science in the later years of schooling. The tendency of many adults to be more critical of boys ('you didn't study as you should' or 'if only you'd concentrated better on your work instead of fooling around') may encourage them to strive to do better next time, whereas the more 'understanding' approach to girls ('never mind, you did the best you could') may serve to deter them from greater efforts and foster a view of themselves as not quite bright enough to achieve really well.

The greater cognitive sophistication that comes during the teenage years is accompanied by a firmer establishment of self-concepts and of a sense of personal identity. There is a shift from relatively concrete percepts of the self and of other people to more abstract portraits that include not only behavioural traits but also attitudes, expectations and values that may be both complex and contradictory. In some respects, as Harter[151] noted, this greater abstraction constitutes a two-edged sword, because such concepts are more open to distortion, as well as representing greater subtlety. There is an increasing differentiation of self-concepts according to domains so that young people may see themselves as academically competent but athletically weak (or vice versa). At first, this may be a source of distress at a time when young people are still finding it difficult to compare abstractions and integrate inconsistencies, as well as to decide which personal qualities 'matter' to them. There is a greater appreciation of the ideal self that they would like to have, and possibly the discrepancies between the ideal and the actual may be greater in mid-adolescence. This goes along with a marked increase in emotional introspection and with a greater tendency to look back with regret and to look ahead with apprehension. In addition to domain-specific self-concepts, there is the development of a sense of global self-esteem – a sense that is not just an average of the specific self-concepts. Perceived physical attractiveness, especially in girls, is important for this global self-esteem, as is also social acceptance by peers.

Erikson[145] argued that the main psychosocial task of adolescence is the achievement of a stable identity or self-concept, and that to achieve this in a manner that allows for later healthy personality development it is necessary for young people to pass through a sort of 'identity crisis'. Like all Erikson's notions, the concept has considerable intuitive attraction. It is obvious that the process of establishing an identity will involve a degree of trial and error as young people gradually sort out for themselves what sort of person they are and want to be. A trivial, but obvious, example of this tendency is seen in the way adolescents often try out different ways of signing their name – varying from styles with flamboyance and flourish to those with greater dignity and gravitas.

However, the specifics of Erikson's concepts have been only partially supported by research. In particular, although on average there is some tendency for Erikson's stages to follow an age order, the progression does not hold at an individual level. Not only does the course vary by domain and according to the person's past and present circumstances, but also individuals may revert to supposedly earlier stages for a while as they grow older.

Changing Patterns of Psychiatric Disorder

Adolescence is associated with quite dramatic changes in the pattern of psychiatric disorder (see Rutter[14] and Feldman and Elliott[151]). It is not that the overall rate of disorder changes greatly, although it may rise slightly. Rather, it is that the particular mix of conditions alters. Thus, childhood disorders such as bedwetting continue their decline in frequency and the overall rate of fears and phobias also drops. However, substance abuse (including alcoholism) becomes much more common;

schizophrenic psychoses increase markedly in frequency and anorexia nervosa has its peak age of onset. Of course, the processes involved in these changing patterns are likely to be quite varied. Thus, the emergence of anorexia nervosa is probably related to the physical changes of puberty and the psychological reactions to them as shaped by societal attitudes. However, the explanation for the marked increase in schizophrenic psychoses in the late teens is almost certainly quite different. There is a strong genetic component to schizophrenia and also in about half the cases there have been non-psychotic behavioural precursors at an earlier age. These usually take the form of abnormalities in interpersonal relationships accompanied by neurodevelopmental immaturities (as reflected in clumsiness or verbal impairment) and attention deficits (see Murray[42,301] and Rutter and Garmezy[204]). It may be inferred that the predisposition to schizophrenia has been present from the outset; the question is why it does not usually become manifest in the form of a psychosis until late adolescence. As we noted earlier, there are many examples of changing clinical manifestations of fixed brain lesions. The effects of a lesion may remain relatively silent until the structure or system affected reaches a degree of maturity. Weinberger[491] has suggested that the emergence of schizophrenia may be related to the normal maturational aspects of dopaminergic neural systems, particularly those innervating the prefrontal cortex. This maturation may also render the vulnerable individual more susceptible to the effects of stress experiences. It is known that high levels of intrusive family criticism make schizophrenia more likely to remain manifest once it develops[173,266] and possibly they might play a role in its initial precipitation.

Depression

One of the most interesting and puzzling changes in psychiatric pattern during the teenage years is provided by the rise in the rate of depressive and depression-related disorders (see Rutter[166]). It is *not* that negative emotions as such become more frequent at this age period. Feelings of sadness, misery and unhappiness are shown by children of all ages, at least after the early months of babyhood. Rather it is that there is a dramatic rise in the rates of serious affective disorders; there is less certainty about the extent to which this is paralleled by similar changes in depressive feelings. The age trend in affective dysfunction is most obvious in the suicide statistics, which indicate a thousand-fold increase in rate over the decade between ten and twenty years of age. Indeed, suicide is almost unknown before the age of ten and the rate continues to rise throughout adult life. At-tempted suicide, or parasuicide, is also a relatively infrequent occurrence in childhood, but shows the same massive increase during middle and late adolescence. Unlike completed suicide, however, the peak rate is achieved in the late teenage years, with a progressive fall thereafter. Of course, although suicidal behavi-ours are quite strongly associated with depression, they are not a direct consequence of it and they are also associated with conduct disturbance, substance abuse and risk-taking behaviour.

However, epidemiological studies also indicate that overt de-pressive disorders become more frequent over the adolescent age period and clinic investigations indicate that, among young people presenting with a psychiatric problem, the proportion showing a depressive condition increases markedly over the teenage years, especially in girls. By contrast, anxiety disorders do not show this regular increase in frequency during the teens.

If depressive disorders are not synonymous with extremes of negative mood, and they are not, it is necessary to ask which features do characterize them. First, the negative mood of depres-sion, unlike that of fear or anxiety, is represented by a loss of pleasure and interest (a feeling of 'flatness' or 'emptiness') as much as by sadness or dysphoria. Second, depressive *disorders* involve three further features: (i) negative thoughts about the self, the world and the future (as reflected in feelings of self-blame, worthlessness and hopelessness); (ii) accompanying social impairment (a reduced capacity to work or engage in leisure activities or social relationships); (iii) often associated somatic symptoms such as insomnia, loss of appetite and psychomotor retardation or agitation. It should be added that depressive disorders at any age are not all of the same kind. The best-established distinction is between bipolar and unipolar disorders (with the former involving abnormal swings of mood upwards, as well as downwards). Also within unipolar disorders, there is a distinction between the more serious varieties leading to hospital admission (which show a strong genetic component) and the milder types seen in the community or at out-patient clinics (in which there is a much weaker genetic component).

A range of rather different possible explanations for the rise in adolescent affective disturbance has to be considered. Thus, it could be postulated that genetic factors predisposing to depression 'switch on' during this age period. There is some tentative evidence that depressive disorders of unusually early onset may be more strongly genetic but the findings are inconclusive so far. Alternatively, the rise could be a consequence of the hormonal changes associated with puberty. It is unlikely that sex hormones lead directly to depression, if only because the main rise follows puberty by several years. However, it could be that hormones provide a sensitizing vulnerability factor of some kind, even if they do not precipitate the onset of depression as such.

A third type of explanation suggests that the rise is a function of an increase in negative life events during the teenage years or of a relative loss of social support. However, we do not know whether either takes place. Because abnormal cognitions (such as self-blame and hopelessness) are such key elements in depressive disorders, it could be argued that children are less prone to depression because they lack the cognitive attributions. It does seem that young children are less likely to respond to failure with feelings of helplessness and they are less likely to project such feelings into the future in the form of hopelessness (see Rutter[166]). Accordingly, it may be that this serves to some extent to protect them against depression. On the other hand, it is evident that pre-adolescent children do sometimes become seriously depressed and, when they do, they may exhibit depressive cognitions. Finally, it could be argued that adolescents may be less good at coping with stress because their growing cognitive competence leaves them for a while too concerned with the uncertainties of life and with the range of alternative solutions open to them. Maybe life was simpler, and in some ways easier, when the choices seemed more limited!

It is all too apparent that a satisfactory explanation for the rise in depressive disorders during adolescence has not yet been found. A developmental perspective has been helpful in indicating the possibilities and it remains for future research to determine which are the ones that are most strongly operative.

Chapter 8

Adulthood:
Marriage, Careers and Parenting

Continuity and Change

To an even greater extent than with other age periods, theorists differ greatly in the extent to which they emphasize continuities or discontinuities, stability or change, in their concepts of personal development in adult life. To a large degree, these differences arise from variations in the ways in which these words are used, together with disagreements over the interpretations of findings. The findings themselves are, however, reasonably consistent in the picture they show.

To begin with, we need to be clear on whether we are considering continuities from adolescence into adult life, or continuities across different ages within adulthood. It is evident that both are substantial, but the latter tend to be stronger than the former.[55,267] However, a more important difference derives from the varying meanings of 'continuity', 'consistency' and 'stability' (see Kagan[55] and Rutter[334]). For our purposes, we need to differentiate between five main meanings: normative consistency (meaning that people tend to retain their *rank order* in the population); ipsative consistency (the tendency to show a similar *pattern* in behaviour over time); consistency in *meaning* (so that at all ages, behaviours reflect the same underlying function); stability of *level* (that is, on the whole, people neither increase nor decrease over time in the extent to which they show a particular characteristic); and population *homogeneity* in life-course consistency (meaning that age trends are universal in pattern and course across the whole population).

Most often, psychologists use the first meaning, making reference to correlations between different ages. These values (which range from -1 to $+1$) assess the degree to which individual differences remain 'normatively' similar over time. That is, they provide a quantitative measure of the extent to which the individuals who are most aggressive, or least sociable, or most shy at one age are still extreme on these characteristics at a later age. Research findings show that there is indeed substantial consistency in these individual differences across adult life. For example, Costa and McCrae[101] found ten-year correlations in the .50s for 'openness to experience', in the .60s for 'neuroticism' and in the .70s for 'extroversion'. Because all measures are imperfect (that is, they include error), the true correlations for consistency in individual differences are likely to be higher than that. Nevertheless, it is important to appreciate that these figures still indicate that quite a lot of change must be taking place. Thus, a correlation of .70 between two ages means that the individual differences at the first age account for about 50 per cent of the individual variation at the second age. The situation is the familiar 'half-full' or 'half-empty' difference. In other words, the research findings indicate that individual differences between people show a substantial degree of consistency over time, but also they demonstrate that changes take place, and we need to account for both.

Many of the findings showing moderately strong correlations over time apply to relatively crude questionnaire measures, but a broadly comparable degree of consistency has been found for more complex and subtle aspects of personal functioning; such as people's social styles or methods of coping with stress (see Block[40] and Vaillant[12,483]). We may conclude that most aspects of psychological functioning exhibit moderate 'normative' consistency over time. Of course, that does not mean that people behave in the same way in all circumstances; obviously they do not. Even with characteristics such as aggression or delinquent behaviour that show quite high consistency over time, situational factors play an important role in determining whether an individual predisposition to behave in a particular way leads to actual aggressive or delinquent behaviour at any one time.[416]

It should be added, however, that traits vary in the extent to which they show temporal consistency, and it may well be that it is greater for predispositions to disorder than for variations within the normal range.[408] In that connection, it is necessary to note again that the consistency applies to individual differences in a propensity for certain sorts of disorder rather than to unchanging behaviour. Thus, individuals who suffer from a depressive disorder when young continue to exhibit a greatly increased liability to depressive disorders in adult life,[195] but typically this increased risk is manifest only in occasional episodes of depressive disorder and not in a persistent unremitting depressive condition.

A second meaning, 'ipsative' consistency, refers to the overall *pattern* of behaviour, rather than to individual differences. For example, an individual may show a consistent tendency to be better at language-type tasks than puzzle-type tasks that require skills in the appreciation and manipulation of shapes. This tendency may vary in degree over time, so that there is a lack of consistency in whether he is most extreme on this tendency in his age group, but the pattern always remains the same. In the same fashion, we often think of temperamental characteristics in this way. Thus, we may think of a child as someone who always tends to withdraw from strangers on first acquaintance; meaning that this is his characteristic mode of response even though its degree may fluctuate over time or from situation to situation.

A third concept concerns stability or instability over time in the *level* of a skill or behaviour. Thus it is obvious that cognitive skills, or intelligence, increase markedly in level as children grow older. This change in level is so great that IQs are specially designed to take age into account to *remove* the lack of stability in level over time (so that mental ages go up with increasing chronological age, whereas IQs do not). Behavioural characteristics vary considerably in the extent to which they tend to retain the same level over the course of development. For example, children tend to become *less* fearful but *more* prone to be depressed as they grow older. It is important to appreciate that it is quite common to have normative and ipsative consistency, but not stability in level, or the reverse. Thus, the rate of depressive disorder increases markedly between childhood and adult life, and the rate of criminality falls substantially (i.e. a *lack* of stability in level). However, in both cases there is considerable

'normative' and 'ipsative' consistency; that is, people who tend
to respond depressively or behave in a delinquent way continue
to exhibit this pattern as they grow older, and moreover, there is
substantial consistency in the extent to which they remain extreme (or moderate or low) in this propensity. This means that,
while the overall risk of experiencing a particular form of
disorder is increasing or decreasing markedly with age, those
individuals who are relatively more (or less) at risk tend to be
the same.

A fourth concept of consistency concerns the extent to which
the meaning of a behaviour, and its basis in a particular underlying psychological or neural function, remains the same over
time. As we saw in Chapter 3, there are important examples of
changes of this type but, by and large, the evidence suggests that
most psychological features and most life circumstances do maintain their meaning. Thus, close, confiding relationships are emotionally protective at all ages and a loss of such relationships
constitutes an important stressor throughout life. There may be
some age-related shifts in emphasis, however. For example,
Lerner and Hultsch[267] reviewed studies that suggested that
people's attitudes towards death change as they grow older, that
marriages in old age may place more weight on the desire for
companionship and involve less strain from conflict, that sources
of stress alter in pattern with increasing age, and that there is a
reduction in risk-taking with age and a greater tendency to
adopt a passive style to life's challenges. However, the evidence
on all these changes is quite limited and it remains uncertain
whether they apply generally or only to certain social groups in
particular societal circumstances.

In order to understand the possible mechanisms underlying
these various types of stability and instability, or continuity and
discontinuity, we need to bring in a fifth, quite different, concept
of life-course consistency; namely that the age trends are universal
across populations and largely derive from internal psychological
qualities rather than life events and experiences. In that connection, research findings on life-course issues are distinctly limited
by the extent to which most stem from American studies of
heterosexual middle-class males. It is by no means self-evident

that either life events or age transitions have the same meaning for everyone. For example, an early study by Christensen[88] suggested that the effects of a premarital pregnancy on the timing of marriage were radically different in different communities according to the prevailing sexual attitudes. Also, the meaning of events may change over time. For example, there has been a huge rise in illegitimacy rates in the UK over recent years.[317] The tendency is to think of these as unwanted, unplanned births to unsupported women. Of course, some do have these qualities but very many do not. There has been a comparable rise in the number of illegitimate births registered in the names of *both* parents. It is clear that many are planned, wanted pregnancies in the context of a stable partnership, albeit one that has not involved a marriage ceremony. In addition, attitudes to ageing may have been affected by the major changes over time in life expectancy.[393] For example, the average British female had a life expectancy at birth of forty-two years in 1851, but one of seventy-five years in 1971.

In more recent times, we have seen a huge rise in the rate of divorce (see Figure 8.1 for the trends over time in England and Wales). We do not know whether this reflects a change in the prevalence of unhappy, quarrelsome marriages but it does mean a change in children's family-life experiences and probably, too, in their expectations with respect to marriage.[393]

There have also been major changes over time in the proportion of women working full time, the rise in both the UK and USA having been particularly great among those with children. Thus, the findings from an American survey in the 1970s (see Moen[134]) showed that less than a fifth of women aged between forty-five and fifty-four with school-age children had a full-time job but over two fifths of those aged between twenty-five and thirty-four were working full time. In the UK, there has also been a marked rise over the last few decades in the proportion of women among university students and the proportion expecting to combine a career with having a family.[393] In most industrialized nations, this century has seen a massive rise in the overall standard of living, but in recent times in both the UK and USA there has been an increase in socio-economic divisions, with the

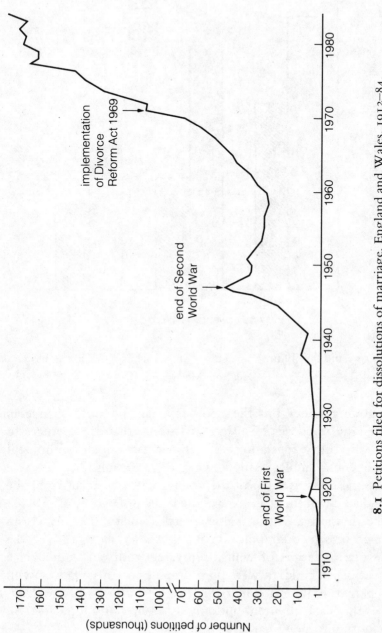

8.1 Petitions filed for dissolutions of marriage, England and Wales, 1912–84. Data from Burgoyne *et al.*[69]

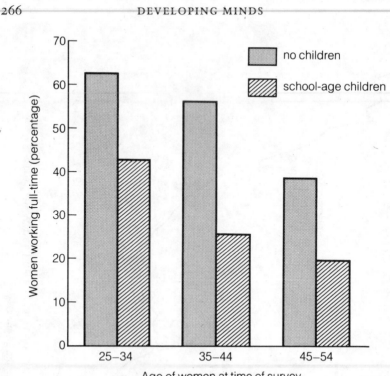

8.2 Age and family life-stage effects on women's work in the USA. Data from Moen.[134]

rich getting richer but the poor experiencing little change in their living standards.[317] We may assume that the attitudes to work and the expectations of job satisfaction and fulfilment among young adults without work or in an unskilled job will not be the same as those of the young business executive or the individual establishing a career in medicine or law.

The divisions in society also reflect ethnicity. The American findings presented graphically in Figure 8.3 show that in the 1970s three quarters of white, compared with only just over a third of black, children were born into a two-parent family with both parents in their first marriage (see Hofferth[134]). By contrast, half of the black children, but only 8 per cent of white children, were born into a one-parent family.

We have emphasized these contrasts because it makes no sense

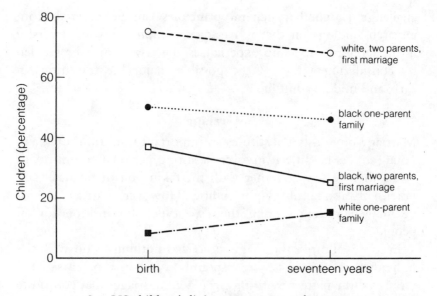

8.3 US children's living arrangements by race.
Data from Hofferth.[134]

to view life-course continuities and changes as given features that are independent of life circumstances. We have chosen a range of examples to indicate that life-course expectations vary substantially across different sociocultural groups, that they have changed markedly over time and that in some respects these changes have involved alterations in the meaning and implications of the life circumstances. Of course, there are many other contrasts that could have been mentioned – between homosexuals and heterosexuals, between housewives and career women, between the married and unmarried, and between rural and inner-city groups to mention but a few. Our purpose, however, is not to survey the many heterogeneous patterns in our society. Rather, the point that we wish to underline is that in considering personal development we need to view it in its social context within our own country, as well as within more diverse cultural groups. As various life-course researchers have emphasized,[137,193] not only do individuals at any one time vary in the synchronization and sequence of difference transitions, but also there has been major historical change in these patterns. The challenge is whether general principles can be derived from research findings on the psychological implications of diversity in life circumstances and experiences. The issues may be tackled by considering a few of the possible major life transitions in early and middle adult life.

Marriage

Marriage obviously constitutes an important transition for many young adults because it involves a lasting personal commitment to another person, together with the taking on of financial and potentially also family responsibilities. However, marriage cannot be viewed as representing the *same* type of transition for all people.

In some cultures, the main choice has nothing to do with the individual; rather it is the responsibility of the parents. That would be the pattern with the arranged marriages that constitute the tradition in many Asian cultures. These may take place in either childhood or early adult life but, either way, it is the parents who decide *when* the marriage will take place and *who* the marriage partner will be. Certainly, it constitutes a major life transition for the individual, but the transition involves little or no decision-making by the individuals themselves.

At the opposite extreme, there is the love marriage following a long engagement that used to be the normal expectation in our own culture. This was meant to be based on a personal love relationship but also it was supposed to involve a carefully weighed decision that both people were emotionally prepared for marriage and also that the man was financially equipped to take on the responsibilities and commitment involved. In some social groups, the magnitude of the step was indicated by the man having to ask the woman's father for permission to marry and by the woman bringing a dowry.

It is interesting that for some individuals, this major decision can prove very stressful. Several decades ago, in a clinical study, Davies[113] described the occurrence of psychiatric disorder arising *de novo* in those becoming engaged to be married, drawing attention to the literature on the topic going back to the nineteenth century. The usual symptoms were anxiety and depression, and it was characteristic that they often began in relation to some event on which the marriage date hinged, such as booking the room for the reception or finding a place in which to live. Davies described the scenario as follows. The symptoms were almost always displayed to the marriage partner, the patient's attitude being summarized in the words 'You can see how ill I am. It would not be fair to you to go on with the marriage.' The almost invariable response of the healthy partner could be summed up in the words, 'I love you and will stand by you.' At this point, the patient's symptoms became worse and usually this was the stage at which psychiatric help was sought. The subsequent course varied across patients but in most instances, *either* breaking the engagement or going ahead with the marriage was followed by improvement.

The pattern clearly indicated that the stress did not lie in *being* married, but rather in the *decision* to make the commitment. Also, it was evident that neither a sexual relationship nor cohabitation made much difference.

There were examples of couples who had lived together happily for some years but still the decision to marry led to stress and psychological disturbance. Curiously, this syndrome has received little attention in the psychiatric literature in recent years and we do not know how commonly it occurs. Nevertheless, it is clear from experiences with friends, colleagues and clients that the pattern, at least in degrees falling short of overt disorder, is not at all rare.

The growing tendency now in many Western societies is for many young people to live together, and often to have children, without any single point at which there is a clear decision to make a lifetime commitment. The pattern has been little studied so far and it is not at all clear how the balance of psychological pluses and minuses work out. Observations suggest that it can work very well but also that sometimes there may be stresses for one partner because the couple differ from one another in their degree of commitment, regardless of what may have been agreed beforehand about the openness and freedom of the relationship.

In addition to these forms of positive decision-making on

marriage by individuals or parents, it is important to recognize that many marriages do not take place like that at all. Rather, many represent impulsive ventures or drift,[287] and some reflect hasty steps taken as a means of escape or under external pressure. The Quinton and Rutter[361] follow-up of institution-reared boys and girls, to which we have referred several times, illustrates this last tendency well. Several points need to be made about the findings. First, marriages for such negative reasons usually arose through a combination of external circumstances and personal characteristics. The young people who married in haste to escape usually showed a general tendency not to plan their lives, associated with a feeling of helplessness about their life situation and a belief that there was little that they could do to affect what happened to them. But, also, most both lacked family support and experienced severe family discord, conflict and stress. The girls leaped into pregnancy and/or marriage in a forlorn attempt to make their situation better.

The second point is that this tendency was very much a female characteristic. The institution-reared boys showed a range of multiple responses to their stressful life circumstances but there was very little tendency to use marriage as a means of escape (see Rutter *et al.*[375]). The girls were *much* more likely than average to marry and have children in their teens but this was not so among institution-reared boys to other than a very minor extent.

Thirdly, this pattern among institution-reared girls to marry in their teens as a means of escape was associated with a much increased likelihood that the husband would be from a similarly disadvantaged background and would suffer from psychosocial problems himself (delinquency, drug abuse or psychiatric disorder). Again, this pattern of marrying someone with problems was not present in males, who showed no significant assortative mating (meaning non-random pairing such as like marrying like) with respect to behavioural deviance. At first sight, it is not obvious how this could apply to females and not males, because marriages involve both sexes! The main explanation lies in two features. The most important is that the tendency to marry someone with problems was strongly connected with teenage marriages. Because in the institution-reared groups these were much more frequent in the girls than the boys, the likelihood of their landing up with a deviant spouse was greater. However, it was also relevant that the main type of behavioural deviance evident in the husbands, namely delinquency, is several times more frequent in males than females. Accordingly, this meant that the chances of having a delinquent husband were much greater than of having a delinquent wife, just because the proportion of the former in the general population is much higher.

There is a general tendency (if only of moderate strength) for people to marry someone rather like themselves – in terms of physical attractiveness, intelligence and interests.[144,304,484] It is often supposed that this represents a predilection to want to marry someone similar to ourselves. To a substantial extent, undoubtedly this is the case in so far as we are likely to seek a partner who can share our interests, activities and values. Also, research has shown that assortative mating is evident even when account has been taken of opportunities; that is, there is some tendency to choose a partner of similar characteristics even within relatively homogenous social groups.[292,348] Nevertheless, it is likely that one major shaping influence is that we are bound to 'choose' a partner from among the people whom we meet. Almost certainly, the main reason why the institution-reared girls in the Quinton and Rutter[361] study frequently married deviant men is that most of their friends and acquaintances were socially disadvantaged individuals with psychosocial problems. It was the *limitations* in their choice of partner, rather than active *selection*, that meant they landed up with a husband experiencing similar problems to their own. That this was the case is indicated, for example, by the finding that the likelihood of having a deviant spouse was strongly associated with age of marriage, being greatest with teenage marriages and cohabitation.[349] The young people who, for whatever reason, were able to postpone marriage until they were older had usually broadened their horizons and experiences, and therefore had a much more varied (and less deviant) 'pool' of potential partners.

In summary, then, the evidence suggests that the timing of marriage and the characteristics of the marriage partner are to some extent predictable on the basis of personal characteristics, qualities of upbringing and social situation at the time.

The next question concerns the psychological effects of marriage itself. The evidence indicates that there is no sensible general answer that can be given. What is important is not so much being married *per se*, but rather the qualities and pattern of the marriage relationship, the characteristics of the marriage partner and the consequences of marriage with respect to the person's style of life and social group.

On the whole, it does seem that marriage provides a protective function for many men. This is shown, for example, by the findings from many studies that married men are physically and mentally healthier than single men, divorced men and widowers.[25,179,180,252] Of course, it is difficult to sort out which is cause and which effect. To an important extent, selection factors are likely to play a part, in that individuals with serious chronic mental disorders or physical ill-health are less likely to marry. However, the finding that divorce or death of a spouse is frequently followed by a deterioration in health and/or the development of (or increase in) psychological disturbance indicates that this cannot be the whole story. Loss of a marriage partner is a serious stress event for most people.

This is so for both men and women but there do seem to be important sex differences in the effects of marriage. Possibly women cope somewhat better than men with widowhood, although the evidence on this point is a bit contradictory.[370] Both men and women tend to experience divorce as stressful, but the sources of stress differ somewhat between the sexes.[169] For both sexes, the loss of social support is a stressor but this is more likely to occur for men following divorce. For women, divorce tends to be associated with both a loss of income and increased parental responsibilites; neither change applies so much for men. However, the more consistent difference lies in the contrast between the single and the married, where the pattern for females tends to be the reverse of that for males.[25,56,179] Whereas marriage seems to be on balance psychologically protective for many men, this is not so evident for women. This does *not* mean that a close, confiding, harmonious relationship is any less important for women; to the contrary, if anything, it is more important.[60,61] Rather, what it appears to indicate is that many marriages do not provide such a relationship and that there are other consequences for marriage that differ between the sexes.[302] Thus, in spite of major changes in attitudes to the education and work careers of women, women continue to bear the brunt of housework and child-care responsibilities. Accordingly, for females, the potential benefits of a harmonious marriage relationship may be counterbalanced by the stresses involved in giving up their job or being handicapped in career progression or promotion through having to combine a career and parenthood. Also, the physical and mental stresses of having to look after several preschool children (or adolescents!) can be substantial, particularly for women living in socially disadvantaged circumstances. In considering the effects of marriage it is necessary, therefore, to look at what it means for the particular individual rather than to treat it as a standard life transition.

In that connection, we have noted already the importance of the spouse's characteristics and the effect of marriage on the person's social group. It is often said that marriage helps delinquents to 'settle down' and to desist from criminal activities. The findings from the West and Farrington follow-up study showed that this was *not* particularly the case.[495] If the wife was also delinquent and part of the delinquent subculture, the men tended to continue their criminal activities; conversely, if the wife was law-abiding and not part of a delinquent peer group, marriage was associated with a significant diminution in the man's delinquent activities. The benefits of marriage to a non-delinquent wife were real and substantial but it is important not to overestimate their magnitude. Some writers on adult life transitions tend to describe 'transformations' of personality. Occasionally these may occur, but more modest changes are the rule. These may be quite sufficient to provide a shift from a delinquent to a non-delinquent life trajectory, a transition with major implications, but that does not mean that the men gave up all their activities and characteristics that had previously been associated with their delinquent lifestyle. West's[495] findings showed that that was unusual – at least in the short run.

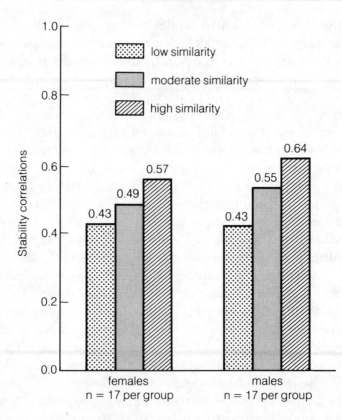

8.4 Individual stability (1970–81) as a function of the similarity of
the partners of a marriage in 1970 – Oakland growth study.
From Caspi and Herbener.[80]

It should be added that the effects of having a spouse with
similar psychological characteristics are not confined to delinquents. Caspi and Herbener[80] showed that people were more
likely to remain psychologically the same over time if they
married someone like themselves. Figure 8.4 shows their findings
from the Oakland study. Both women and men showed higher
correlations over time for personality characteristics when they
and their spouses were closely similar on the same measures. Our
behaviour is influenced by the social group in which we live and
one important social influence is that which comes from our
spouse.

The benefits of a harmonious marital relationship with a non-deviant spouse have also been evident in other studies. Thus, Sampson and Laub's[429] analysis of the Glueck's follow-up data showed that a strong marital attachment in adulthood inhibited criminal behaviour and Quinton and Rutter's[361] follow-up of institution-reared children showed the benefits of a harmonious marriage with respect to social functioning in adult life. Figure 8.5 (which gives the findings for those who had shown conduct disorder in childhood) and Figure 8.6 (which gives the comparable picture for those without conduct disorder) illustrate the effects. The first branching on the left shows the benefits for adult social functioning deriving from the characteristic of 'planning', to which we have referred already. The main benefit stemmed from the indirect effect deriving from the influence on choice of marriage partner, but there was also a lesser direct effect.[509] The second branching on the right shows the benefits deriving from having a non-deviant spouse. It is apparent that the effects were quite substantial for the individuals concerned and were likely to have major life-span implications. However, the figures, while showing the great power of the turning-point effect, do bring out two crucial qualifications, both of which emphasize the relatively small effect on the overall pattern of individual differences. First, as a comparison between the two figures reveals, conduct disorder in childhood had a strong effect on adult social functioning regardless of whom the person married. The deviance or non-deviance of the spouse did a good deal to amplify or reduce this effect but it did not come anywhere near to obliterating it. Second, there was a strong effect of the young person's characteristics (in terms of 'planning' and, to a lesser extent, of conduct disturbance) on choice of spouse. In other words, not many non-planning, conduct-disordered adolescents landed up with a non-deviant spouse. For the few who did, the benefits were substantial, but the overall effects in population terms were small simply because it was such a minority occurrence. The turning-point phenomenon was real and substantial but its impact on overall continuities was modest, in part because of the tendency for the psychologically disturbed who are most at risk to perpetuate their own adverse environments.

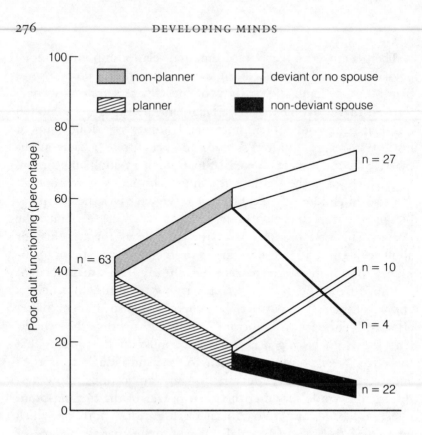

8.5 The effect of planning and having a non-deviant spouse on adult social functioning: children with conduct disorder.

Numerous studies have shown strong associations between marital discord and depression (see Gotlib and Hooley[125]) Detailed analyses of the findings indicate that this is likely to reflect a two-way causal process. That is, the presence of marital discord constitutes a major stress factor which substantially increases the risk of developing depression. In addition, however, the causal arrow runs in the reverse direction, with the presence of depression in one partner putting substantial strain on the marriage.

Because of the importance of the marriage relationship in relation to psychiatric risk, we need to consider what is known on the factors that influence the quality of the marital relationship and the likelihood of marital breakdown.[89,465,475,497] Of course, it is obvious from the high frequency of marital difficul-

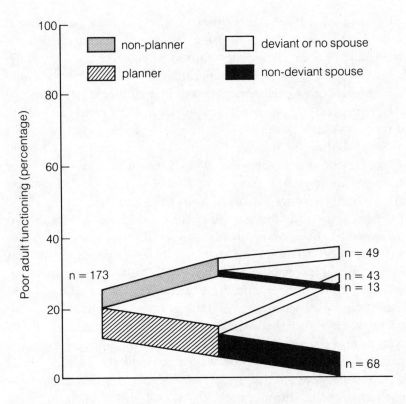

8.6 The effect of planning and having a non-deviant spouse on adult
social functioning: children without conduct disorder.

ties and the high rate of divorce that it is most unlikely that a
high predictive accuracy could be achieved. Also, it is not to be
expected that the same features would predispose to early marital
discord in successive marital relationships and to the later breakdown of a first marriage that has been harmoniously stable for
many years. Marriages may fail for a diversity of reasons.
However, several factors stand out as carrying a significant risk
for marital discord and marriage breakdown.

First, the presence of serious conduct disturbance in childhood
is associated with a much-increased risk for marital discord and
for recurrent marital breakdown. In Chapter 2, we referred to
Robins's[372] finding that 15 per cent of conduct-disordered boys
had had at least two marriage breakdowns by their early thirties

compared with 2 per cent of those without conduct disorders. It was apparent that, in most cases, the men's marital difficulties were part of a much broader pattern of disturbed interpersonal relationships and poor social functioning. Not surprisingly, those individuals with a general problem in maintaining close harmonious relationships with other people are more prone to conflict, disharmony and disruption in their marriage relationship.

Second, those people who have been brought up in seriously discordant homes themselves, or in an institution, or – to a lesser extent – those whose parents divorced during their childhood are more likely to have marital difficulties and to divorce.[351,419] In part, this modest degree of intergenerational continuity is mediated by the personal qualities (especially conduct disturbance and poor peer relationships) that may be engendered by such an upbringing. However, perhaps especially in relation to parental divorce, it may reflect attitudes towards marriage and a reduced expectation that persisting in trying to make the relationship work will preserve the marriage. Nevertheless, this is unlikely to constitute the main explanation in view of the findings from the British National Survey following into adult life all individuals born in one week in 1946.[253] These indicate that women whose parents divorced during their childhood showed an increased tendency to marry in their teens, to have emotional difficulties in adult life, to drink heavily and to have lower educational attainments, as well as to have been married more than once. The long-term effects of bereavement in childhood were much less marked.

Third, those people who experience a chronic or recurrent psychiatric disorder in adult life have a substantially increased risk of marital discord (see Gotlib and Hooley[125]). As follow-up studies of children and adolescents with depressive disorders show,[357] depression interferes with harmonious social interactions. When there is recovery from disorder, social relationships improve considerably, but they remain impaired in some instances, suggesting that to some extent the association may reflect a predisposition to depression stemming from poor interpersonal relationships, as well as the reverse direction of causation. The same applies in adult life.

Fourth, social disadvantage, poverty and poor living conditions make it more difficult to maintain harmonious marital relationships.[419] This is also reflected in a higher rate of divorce.[69] Inner-city life also seems to be associated with an increased rate of marital and other family difficulties.[422] This is only partially explicable by the greater economic and housing problems that tend to be found in inner cities.

Fifth, marriages that have been brought about through an unwanted pregnancy have a higher rate of breakdown.[198,217] To some extent, this is likely to reflect the lack of a pre-existing stable relationship that could form the basis of marriage and, in part, it may derive from resentment over the pressure to marry.

Sixth, the *timing* of marriage is also associated with the risk of its later breakdown. Numerous studies have shown that teenage marriages are much more likely to end in divorce.[198] There are many factors that are involved with this raised risk. As we have seen, girls who experience a discordant, disrupted upbringing, who grew up in social disadvantage and/or who show conduct disorder are more likely to marry in their teens; also many such marriages are brought about by pregnancy. Economic factors are also relevant. People who marry young are likely to be at an early stage in their careers and not earning much; if marriage is quickly followed by the birth of a child (as is often the case) there may be considerable economic strain. However, this does not seem to be the whole story. Probably it is important that considerable personality development takes place after the teenage years. This is likely to be influential in two different ways. On the one hand, many teenagers are emotionally immature and not yet prepared to cope well with the demands and challenges of a marital relationship. On the other hand, because there is ongoing psychological growth, with the development of new interests, ideas, and attitudes, very young husbands and wives are more likely to grow apart. Perhaps this is especially likely to be the case when the woman stops working to have children and the husband continues a career that takes him into social groups that differ markedly from those in which he and his wife grew up.

However, the increased divorce rate following a teenage marriage is also likely to be in part a consequence of the personal characteristics, however determined, or social circumstances of the young people who marry in their teens. This is shown by the evidence that the divorce rate following *second* marriages in the late twenties and thirties of women who were teenagers at the time of their *first* marriage is greater than that for other women.[291]

We have noted the consistent finding that marital discord and marital disruption (or breakdown in a non-marital love relationship) constitute important stress situations that may provoke the onset of a depressive disorder. However, research findings also show that people vary considerably in their vulnerability to stress circumstances in adult life[60,61,62,63] (see also Rodgers[375]). In part, this vulnerability is a function of current life circumstances, with those who are suffering social disadvantage being most at risk. However, it is also a function of experiences and behaviour in childhood. Figure 8.7 presents Rodgers's[375] findings from the British National Survey. Women who experienced stressful life experiences (such as divorce or work crises) were found to have an increased risk of acute emotional disturbance, including clinically significant depressive disorders, at the age of thirty-six (the graph excludes those with chronic disorders). However, this risk was substantially greater in those who had experienced family adversity as children or who had shown emotional difficulties when young. The evidence showed that these childhood adversities were associated with an increased psychiatric risk in adult life through two routes: a direct effect leading to chronic emotional disorder and an indirect effect via an increased susceptibility to stress circumstances in adult life.

Army Experience as a Potential Turning-point

We have noted the indirect chain effect whereby social disadvantage increases the likelihood of teenage marriage and pregnancy which, in turn, makes later marital breakdown more probable. It is necessary now to recognize that there are various experiences that can serve to break this vicious circle. A surprising example is provided by army experiences, which, in some circumstances,

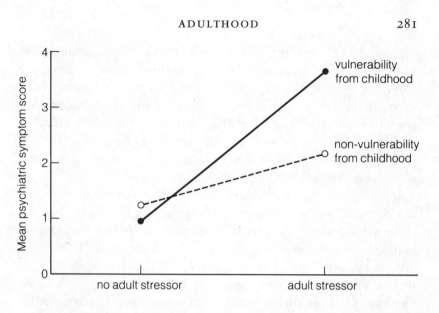

8.7 Acute emotional disturbance in women in relation to childhood
vulnerability and adult stressors. Chronic disorder excluded.
Data from Rodgers.[375]

can constitute a turning-point for some youths from disadvantaged backgrounds, as Elder's[135] interesting and informative re-
analysis of the Californian longitudinal studies showed. Socially
disadvantaged youths with a poor scholastic record and feelings
of self-inadequacy were particularly likely to enter the armed
forces at an early age. Follow-up showed that, compared with
non-veterans with similar characteristics, their adult functioning
was superior in terms of psychological features, occupational
level and marital stability. How did this remarkable turn-about
take place, despite the stresses and suffering that are inherent in
the evil of war (for those who are engaged in conflict)? Several
pathways seem to have been operative. One pathway involved
the situational imperatives that promoted independence, provided exposure to new ideas and models, and allowed a legitimate
'time out' for those unsure of the life course they wished to
follow. A second involved the educational benefits that came
with army service. Most of the young men had had their fill of
school, where they were not doing well, but the different ethos
of adult education led many to continue their schooling, with

the result that they finished up with higher qualifications than those who did not join the forces. A third pathway stemmed from the fact that early entry to the army tended to delay marriage and having children, thus avoiding the disadvantage attendant on a teenage marriage and widening the choice of marriage partners. A further route involved the importance of social ties, brought about by training and undergoing combat together, as an aid in coping with stress.

It is important to appreciate, however, that army service does not necessarily bring these gains, as evident in Elder's findings on those who entered the forces at a later age. Many had already married, started families and established a career, and for them joining the army was very disruptive, with such benefits as there were tending to be outweighed by the disadvantages. As with the other potential turning-point experiences that we have considered, the effects depend greatly on what the experience means to each individual.

Work

For both men and women, work constitutes both a powerful source of satisfaction and an important source of stress.[159,487] It is striking that these positive *and* negative aspects of work are more marked in those in professional and managerial jobs than in people in unskilled or semiskilled manual jobs. For example, Cherry[84,85] found that, among men, 55 per cent of professional workers reported job-related strain, compared with only 15 per cent of semi- and unskilled workers. The comparable findings for women were closely similar: 46 per cent versus 16 per cent. Warr and Payne[488] undertook a more focused study, examining work strain on a particular day. As would be expected, the absolute levels of strain were less than those reported over long time periods but the differences according to the type of job were the same: 15 per cent in professionals as compared with 4 per cent in unskilled and semiskilled workers. Adrenaline levels (a physiological reflection of stress) showed the same job difference. The stereotype of high-level jobs producing more strain seems to be correct; not all stereotypes are mistaken! However, there was a slight tendency for high-level jobs also to give rise to somewhat more satisfaction; 25 per cent as against 17 per cent in the Warr and Payne study.

Of course, the social status and skill level of particular jobs are by no means the only features that determine their psychological effects. The main work characteristics associated with both dissatisfaction and mental-health problems[487] are: (i) a lack of personal control over work demands and activities; (ii) a lack of opportunity for individuals to exercise their work skills appropriately; (iii) a lack of variety in the work tasks; (iv) unduly high job demands; (v) an unpleasant or uncongenial work environment; (vi) a lack of clarity about task expectations and a lack of feedback on work performance; and (vii) a lack of supportive and friendly personal relationships at work.

A variety of studies have shown that, on the whole, both men and women in regular employment are less likely to develop depression than those not in work. We may conclude that being in a paid job tends to be conducive to mental health, but the effects of employment are highly dependent on the nature of the job and working conditions, and some jobs have psychologically negative effects on the individuals in them.

These considerations are also relevant in relation to the effects of promotion and demotion at work. The research literature is rather sparse but several factors seem likely to be important in determining whether the overall psychological effects are positive or negative on balance.[487] As follows from what we have noted on work characteristics, a key issue is whether any change improves the job conditions and work qualities or makes them worse. A second issue is whether expectations have been disappointed; failure to get promotion when it is expected may be stressful because a lack of advancement is perceived as a rebuff and failure. A third feature is whether the change of job involves a social or geographical dislocation that carries with it other life changes which may be stressful. A fourth point, however, concerns the person's attitude to the change. What is a welcome challenge and opportunity for one person may be an oppressive demand for another. Finally, as with marriage, it is important to appreciate that people's own actions will have played an important role in shaping the type of job that they are in. Promotion, demotion and job characteristics cannot be regarded as purely external features that are outside an individual's control. In assessing the psychological impact of work features, and in seeking to help people find ways of improving their work circumstances and of coping better with them, it is necessary to understand how people have landed in the situation that they are in.

Although many of the findings on work apply similarly to men and women, there are some sex differences. In particular, women are more likely to experience role conflict between work and family responsibilities and, perhaps because of this, both physiological data and self-reports show that women are less likely to be able to 'wind down' in the evening on return home.[159]

Unemployment

In discussing the psychological effects of work, it is necessary also to consider the effects of unemployment. The current world economic recession has meant that this is a life experience for many people, particularly so in the UK where the recent years of Tory rule have seen the number of people out of work rise to levels unknown since the 1930s. Both cross-sectional and longitudinal studies are agreed in showing that involuntary unemployment is associated with a deterioration in mental health and, in young men, with an increase in delinquent activities. Longitudinal studies are particularly important in testing the causal hypothesis, because those who are out of work may include a disproportionate number already experiencing problems while still in employment. Thus, Farrington et al.[150] found that youths with at least three months' unemployment committed an average of 0.44 offences per year while in work compared with 0.16 in the total sample of young men. Nevertheless, the adverse effect of a period of unemployment was shown by the fact that the rate of offences increased (0.62) during periods of unemployment. The causal effect of unemployment on mental ill-health is indicated by the improvement usually seen following re-entry into work.[245] For example, Banks and Ullah[17] in their follow-up of unemployed young people found that those who

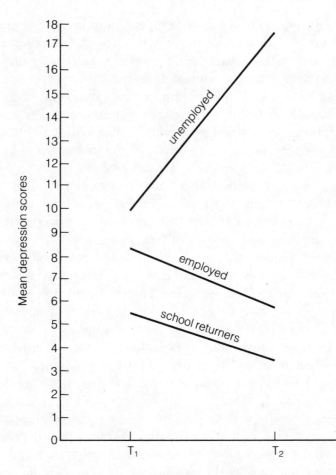

8.8 Effect of employment on depression scores.
Data from Patton and Noller.[344]

remained out of work continued to show much the same raised
score on questionnaires assessing anxiety and depression whereas
those who obtained jobs became much less anxious and depressed.
An earlier study by Patton and Noller[344] showed a very similar
picture, as shown in Figure 8.8.

The research evidence suggests that there are several somewhat
different features that are involved in the stress of involuntary
unemployment. Thus, most obviously, job loss is likely to lead
to a marked drop in income, with financial strains making a

major contribution to the adverse psychological effects of unemployment. In that connection, it is relevant that Farrington *et al.*[150] found that it was only crimes for material gain that increased during periods of unemployment. However, the loss of self-esteem associated with being made redundant, or being given the sack, is likely to be at least as important. The loss of the position in society that goes with having a job will be influential in a similar fashion. The effects of the jobless environment are likely also to be relevant, as are the losses of satisfaction that rewarding work provides. There may be strains associated with a lack of work routine together with the stresses on the family of having an extra person at home during the day when family life has been organized on the basis of their being at work.

Jahoda[228] argued that paid work had psychological value through both manifest and latent functions. These joint functions were summarized as follows: 'First, employment imposes a time structure on the working day; second, employment implies regular shared experiences and contacts with people outside the nuclear family; third, employment links people to goals and purposes that transcend their own; fourth, employment defines aspects of personal status and identity; and finally, employment enforces activity' (p.188).

In keeping with these suggestions, and of practical importance, it is relevant that Bolton and Oatley[43] found that depression following job loss was most likely when the person had few social contacts *outside* work, and was least likely when the person had good social support. The finding emphasizes that jobs are important as a source of social interaction that provides people with their sense of worth. In that connection, it is also pertinent that unemployment makes people more vulnerable to the effects of other stressful life events[244] and that the risk of depression is greatest when unemployment coincides with other stressors.

We noted earlier that stressful life experiences tended to accentuate pre-existing personal characteristics and to have their greatest effect on those already vulnerable for other reasons. Unemployment is no exception to this generalization. Thus, Farrington *et al.*[150] found that unemployment had an effect in increasing the crime rate only in youths with a high risk of delinquency as assessed from their adverse family background, disruptive behaviour and below average IQ. Similarly, Elder *et al.*[337] found that the economic depression in the 1930s had the greatest adverse effect on men who had shown earlier emotional instability.

In order to understand individual differences in people's responses to unemployment, it is necessary also to consider their style of coping with the experience. Banks and Ullah[17] found that several rather different sorts of features were influential. First, the ways in which unemployed people spent their time proved to be important. Those who sat at home most of the time, going through the same routines each day with long periods of inactivity, were most likely to be depressed. Conversely, the maintenance of psychological well-being was associated with a time structure to the day, shared experiences and contacts with people outside the immediate family, the existence of definite goals and purposes, and a degree of activity. Second, emotional disturbance was greater when unemployment led to severe financial strains – one of the important benefits of having a job is receiving pay – and usually finding a new job provided the only lasting solution. Third, however, as the period of unemployment continued, depression was more frequent among those continuing to make the greatest efforts to find work and who felt under the greatest pressure to get a job. To a degree, 'scaling down' job-seeking efforts seemed to protect the unemployed from the depression that stemmed from failure in those efforts; on the other hand, this did not appear to alleviate anxiety. Although counterproductive in relation to re-establishing a work career, the psychological acceptance of unemployment may reduce short-term stresses. Fourth, the availability of both emotional and financial support from other people reduced the risks of emotional disturbance.

These findings concern factors associated with success or failure in coping with unemployment. However, for most people successful coping must in the long-term result in their obtaining work. In that connection, a somewhat different set of variables appears important.[498] It has been found that jobs are most likely to be obtained by people with good educational or vocational

qualifications or attainments (especially those that are certifi-
cated); those with a driving licence (perhaps because it enables
them to consider jobs further afield); those with good sources of
information about possible jobs (either from friends and family
or from official sources); those with a relatively short period of
unemployment; and those with a white skin. White and
McRae's[498] survey of long-term unemployment among young
adults in the UK showed that young Asian men and young
Afro-Caribbean women had among the highest qualification
levels but among the lowest chances of getting jobs. Unfortunately, racial discrimination is still a factor that plays a part in unemployment.[59]

Life-span considerations are also important in work and in
responses to unemployment. As argued further in Chapter 9,
retirement at the expected age is *not* associated with the same ill-
effects on mental health. Also, unemployment in teenagers,
although leading to psychological impairment, tends to be somewhat less damaging than redundancy in middle life. Warr[487]
suggested that this might be because the financial penalty was less
and because most teenagers had relatively good opportunities for
interpersonal contact because they had carried on from school a
network of friends, together with established patterns of leisure
activities unconnected with work. Possibly, too, with unemployment so widespread among UK teenagers in recent years, personal responsibilities to work and the social stigma of being
unemployed may be liable to be felt less strongly. Even if that is
so, which remains uncertain, it is clear that unemployment does
have a significant negative effect upon teenagers' affective well-
being, as well as increasing the likelihood of their engaging in
delinquent activities. Also, it may well be that, in the long term,
the main harmful effect of teenage unemployment may not lie so
much on immediate mental health, but rather in terms of the
later psychiatric sequelae that may be associated with a failure to
acquire adequate autonomy and the self-esteem that derives from
it. Follow-up studies are needed to determine whether or not
that is so, but the data from the Berkeley longitudinal study
analysed by Elder *et al.*[337] are consistent with that suggestion.
They found that the economic depression in the 1930s tended to

lead to a loss of self-confidence and assertiveness in emotionally unstable men who lacked the support of a nurturant marriage, and that this left some of them less able to cope with the stresses and adaptations that accompanied old age many years later. Interestingly, the economic privations were more likely to lead to effective coping and subsequent resilience in women.

Parenthood

Parenthood and child-rearing constitute further key transitions for most people.[305] Even more than with some of the other transitions that we have discussed, parenthood varies greatly in its meaning and impact. It may take place at any time from early adolescence to incipient middle age; also it may be planned or unplanned, wanted or unwanted. The motives for wanting children are many and various, and the pregnancy may involve a single woman, a lesbian couple, a cohabiting couple or a marriage partnership, to mention just some of the permutations. In addition, of course, in the case of adoption or long-term fostering the taking on of the responsibilities of parenthood does not involve a pregnancy for the woman concerned.

It is something of a paradox that currently so many couples are seeking treatment for fertility and yet so many pregnancies are unplanned and unwanted. Among women under the age of twenty in the USA, the number of abortions is about the same as the number of live births – indicating that, in this group, over half the pregnancies are unwanted to the extent that they are terminated.[309] The UK figures are broadly similar. Presumably an even higher percentage of the pregnancies are unwanted, but for one reason or another, the woman decides to continue with it. However, the fact that a pregnancy is unwanted, even to the point of seeking termination, does not necessarily mean that the baby will be unwanted when it arrives. Follow-up studies of births following refusals to undertake abortion show that some four fifths of the women come to accept the pregnancy and want the child.[112] The women's attitude to becoming pregnant is one thing but the man's reaction is another. Difficulties arise when one partner very much wants a baby and the other does not. Of course, the positive and negative attitudes towards the pregnancy may be either way round. In male-dominated cultures, women may be expected to defer to their husband's wishes and sometimes they feel that they have played no role in the decision to become pregnant.

Having chosen to have a child, there is the further need to decide *when* to become pregnant. Over the last forty years or so there have been quite complex changes in the pattern of timing of first births.[393] On the one hand, the greater acceptance of sexuality among young people has been accompanied by a marked rise in teenage pregnancies, which is now falling off. On the other hand, the increasing importance of work careers for women has meant that more couples have postponed parenthood until their thirties so that the wives can be better established in their careers. Inevitably, this involves potential tension between the pull of parenthood and the pull of careers. In addition, there are the worries over the possible biological costs of delay – in terms of both diminishing fertility and increasing risks of foetal abnormality. Thus, the risk of a chromosomal abnormality (of which that associated with Down's syndrome is much the most common) rises from about 1 per 500 for women under the age of twenty to 1 in 20 at forty-five.[219] Because of this, prenatal screening is often undertaken as a routine in women who become pregnant over the age of thirty or thirty-five.

Several longitudinal studies have followed couples from early in the pregnancy and have charted the psychological adaptations that are entailed (see Osofsky and Osofsky[337] and Michaels and Goldberg[305]). It is evident that stresses, at least of mild degree, are not uncommon, especially in first pregnancies. Many women are concerned that their baby may be abnormal; they worry over the physical changes in their bodies, how they will cope with the pains of childbirth and how the process will change them. They may also feel concern about possible alterations in their relationship with their husbands and about changes in their own work and home patterns. Most men take longer than their wives to become emotionally involved in the pregnancy and a few feel decidedly left out. Although sociocultural expectations may play some role in this gender difference, the marked physiological changes associated with pregnancy are obviously important.

There are major hormonal alterations from early on and women tend to feel very different when pregnant. It has long been recognized that there may be alterations in appetite. For example, often there is a diminished interest in alcohol – a useful natural protection in view of the risks to the foetus from exposure to alcohol or other drugs.[355] On the whole pregnancy is a rather healthy time for most women, and they tend to feel good in themselves. Nevertheless, although major psychiatric problems are *un*common during pregnancy, longitudinal studies do show an overall slight rise in emotional difficulties during this period. Also, women who have relied on tranquillizers or sleeping pills to ease their problems previously may be troubled by the pressure to keep off medication for the sake of the baby.

Recent times have seen increasing medical interventions in pregnancies in the Western world, as indexed by the huge increase in the use of Caesarean section and induced labour. This is psychologically threatening to some women. One study found that preparation for parenthood was most valuable in increasing the mother's sense of control, with those who reported being in better control seeming to have better birth experiences.[143]

Concerns often focus on husband–wife relationships. Pregnancy undoubtedly brings many couples closer together and the shared anticipation and planning can be a great joy and pleasure. But for some, the woman's preoccupation with the baby, and the man's not wishing to share in this, pulls them further apart. The literature on pregnancy stresses is somewhat inconclusive but three sets of features seem to be important.[305] First, there are the individual characteristics that relate to previous 'competencies'. Difficulties in the transition to parenthood are more likely when the woman has experienced previous psychological difficulties; when there was pre-existing marital disharmony; and when there was a poor relationship between the woman and her mother. Rather less is known about the relevant features in men but probably similar individual characteristics apply. Second, the circumstances at the time of first becoming a parent are relevant. Difficulties are more likely when the person is either a teenager or unusually old; when there are career–parenthood tensions, when there is a lack of social support and when there is a sharp contrast between expectations and reality. Third, the transition may be more difficult when the infant is handicapped or when the neonatal period is marked by illness and medical interventions. Pregnancy constitutes another example of what Elder and Caspi[137] called the *accentuation principle*. By this they mean that challenges and stress situations tend to emphasize and accentuate pre-existing personal characteristics and interpersonal relationships, rather than change them.

The longitudinal study undertaken by Moss and his colleagues[313] in London showed just over a quarter of couples reported *gains* in their marriage consequent upon having a child. There were, however, rather more where there were negative effects, with about one in ten showing substantially weakened marriages (with adverse effects seen in both affection and sexual relationships). This worsening was most likely to occur in younger couples of lower social staus who had not been married long and who were having child-management problems.

It might be supposed that the transition to parenthood would be somewhat different when both partners have, and continue with, careers outside the home – a situation that is more frequent among those with higher status jobs. Lewis and Cooper's[274] longitudinal comparison of single earners and childless couples showed that major adaptations and some stresses occurred with most dual-earner couples, but major psychological problems arose in only a minority. Feelings of life satisfaction went down a little but not so much as in couples in which the wife gave up a valued career to become a full-time mother. Interestingly, although there was more sharing of child-care responsibility in dual-earner families, in all cases the mother took the major responsibility. (This has been the case in other studies, too.[159]) It appeared that good childcare arrangements merely served to relieve the husband rather than the wife! Not surprisingly, therefore, work–parenting conflicts and general pressures were much more evident in females than males. There are a few families in which the father stays at home to become the primary caregiver or has a particularly high involvement in childcare. Russell[259] has summarized the very limited evidence on this non-traditional pattern and it seems that there is a mixture of pluses and minuses. On the positive side, fathers tended to have better, closer relationships with the children and to develop enhanced self-esteem with regard to their own parenting role! However, like mothers, they tended to find the demands of care-giving heavier than they had expected. The effects on marital relationships have been quite mixed, with tensions stemming from rivalries between the two parents and from difficulties in sharing tasks and decision-making.

Obviously, there can be no one 'right' solution for all families. The birth of a first child necessarily involves a transition requiring change and adaptation, but whether the change is for the better or the worse − or just different − depends on both the prior circumstances and the parents' response to the challenges. Probably the transition is most likely to be positive in its consequences when the birth is wanted and occurs in the context of a sound, warm, reciprocal marital relationship; when the family tasks are shared (although not necessarily equally); when there is adequate social support and good housing conditions; and when both partners recognize that each has continuing emotional needs that must be met alongside those of the child.

In our discussion of the transition to parenthood we have focused on first births, but it is important to note that the birth of a second child also involves adaptations, albeit of a slightly different kind. As Daniels and Weingarten[111] succinctly put it, 'First children are born to couples; second children are born to families' (p. 222). One consequence, as we noted in Chapter 4, is the need for parents to distribute their attentions between two children and to deal with the relationship between the first-born and second-born.

Puerperium

The arrival of a child constitutes an important psychological transition for the couple, but the immediate postnatal period also has important psychological consequences for the mother, albeit ones in which physiological factors seem to play a key role. Two separate, but related, phenomena are involved. First, there are the so-called 'postnatal blues' in which, during the week after birth, many mothers have a transient period of dysphoria, manifested by crying, feelings of depression, confusion, anxiety and insomnia, often intermingled with times of feeling happy. Usually this does not develop until a few days after the birth, but it peaks rapidly on about the fifth day. There has been much discussion on the possible reasons for this puzzling response to what is usually a happy, much welcomed, event. It appears to be physiologically determined in large part, but there is continuing uncertainty about the precise nature of the metabolic change that is responsible. The reaction arises after Caesarean section just as it does after an ordinary vaginal delivery, and it does not seem to be related in any consistent fashion to the mother's psychosocial situation.

Comparisons with major surgery, such as hysterectomy, show an interesting pattern of similarities and differences.[243,272] Dysphoric reactions are about equally common after surgery and after childbirth, but their timing is different. Those after surgery peak immediately after the event and diminish progressively thereafter, whereas postpartum blues do not peak until some several days after birth. It has been suggested that these blues may be a function of the rapid drop in sex-hormone levels but this remains speculative at the moment.

The second phenomenon is the occurrence of a florid acute psychosis. The peak onset for puerperal psychoses is in the month after birth but the risk remains raised for two to three months, although in nearly all cases the true onset is in the first two weeks after delivery. Epidemiological data show that the risk for psychosis during this period is about twenty times that at other times, a particularly striking increase as the risk for psychosis is not particularly increased during the pregnancy (although, as we have noted, the overall psychiatric morbidity does increase slightly).

Most puerperal disorders, of both the psychotic and non-psychotic varieties, are affective in type, and the risk factors include those that apply to affective conditions generally; namely, a family history or a previous episode of affective disorder. In addition, however, there are risk factors that are specifically associated with puerperal disorders. Thus, they are more likely following a first pregnancy, with not having a partner at the time of childbirth, with perinatal death and with Caesarean section.[242] These findings suggest that, although metabolic factors probably create the time-specific vulnerability, psychosocial factors may often be important in transforming the vulnerability into overt psychiatric disorder. The postnatal period provides an interesting example of a life transition carrying a major psychiatric risk in which both physiological and psychological elements each play a part. The stress on the marriage of a major psychosis, especially one that coincides with the arrival of a child, can be considerable, but provided that the couple cope successfully with the crisis there are usually no lasting sequelae.

Child-rearing

In moving from the immediate postnatal period to the longer time span involved in child-rearing, we need again to consider which are the key elements in the transition, the factors that affect how people respond to it and how the transition affects their own psychological functioning both at the time and later. Parenting constitutes a quite complex task with several rather different elements (see Rutter[89]). First, it is a task that requires a set of skills for providing an environment conducive to the children's psychological development and adaptively responsive to the range of their needs and demands. These skills include sensitivity to children's cues; effective social problem solving; knowing how to play and talk with children; and the use of disciplinary techniques that meet the triple demands of bringing about the desired child behaviour, maintaining or restoring harmony and increasing the children's self-control.

Second, parenting incorporates the growth and maintenance of a positive parent–child relationship. This facet extends the parenting role from child-rearing skills to qualities in social relationships generally. Third, parenting reflects the psychosocial functioning of the mother and father, and hence it is likely to be affected by mental disorders, such as depression, in either parent. Fourth, parenting is an outcome of the learning involved in the very experience of bringing up previous children. Fifth, parenting at any one point will be influenced by experiences associated with earlier phases of interaction with the same child. Lastly, parenting constitutes a dyadic relationship that forms part of a broader nexus. That is, how a parent interacts with a child will be influenced by whether they are on their own, whether the other parent is also present and by whether other children are in the room.

The listing of these various elements in parenting highlights some of the possible influences that are likely to be important. In previous chapters, we drew attention to the role of a person's own upbringing in their functioning as a parent. People who have had an institutional upbringing, who have experienced abuse or neglect in their own childhoods or who grew up in a hostile, aversive environment are more likely to experience difficulties in parenting themselves.[89] It is important to note that these intergenerational links are *not* confined to parenting; rather, a seriously adverse upbringing is associated with an increased risk of pervasive difficulties in social relationships, which include but are not restricted to parenting.

These same studies, and others, have also shown that good parenting tends to be fostered by a good marital relationship and, conversely, that parenting problems are more likely when there are serious marital difficulties. A person's relationship in one domain affects their relationships in other domains (see Hinde and Stevenson-Hinde[211] and Dunn[125]). Several different mechanisms mediate this effect. Part of the explanation lies in the effect of a close, confiding harmonious relationship in fostering self-esteem and in buffering stress. In that connection, it is relevant that good parenting is also fostered by social supports outside the marriage. However, support does not reside only in emotional availability; practical help and the sharing of parental responsibilities are also important. Not surprisingly, living conditions are also important; poor housing and overcrowding make parenting more difficult.

Parenting may also be influenced by events in the postnatal period. At one time there were claims that for parents to 'bond' effectively with their babies there had to be skin-to-skin contact in the hours after birth. There is much evidence *against* this mechanical view of parent–child relationships.[172,215] The relationship does *not* develop suddenly as the result of any particular experience; rather it grows over time as the result of many different experiences. Nevertheless, there is evidence that when parents are denied contact with their babies or when infants are sickly, weak and requiring intensive care, parenting may have a more difficult start. That does *not* mean that it suffers lasting damage. Nevertheless, the postpartum period is physiologically and psychologically special, and events at that time are likely to have an impact. This is important in terms of implications for policy and practice in obstetric units and neonatal nurseries, and for the need for special help for parents with seriously ill or fragile babies. But parents need not be concerned merely because there were difficulties or a lack of contact with the baby during the early days of life.

In addition, parenting is affected by the experience of having brought up previous children.[396] Mothers and fathers respond differently to their first-born compared with the ways they deal with later children. Parents tend to have a more intensive relationship with their first child, interacting with them more and showing more social, affectionate and care-giving behaviours. Most families have more photographs of their first child than of their later children. It is not that they love them any more, but, rather, that the birth of a first child, like the first love affair, has a special intensity. Equally, however, parents tend to be more anxious and controlling with their first-born; it is not all good being the eldest child! As they become more confident with experience, parents become more relaxed and at ease with later children. In a real sense, the first child constitutes a practice run, or pilot study, for the rest of the children still to be born. In that connection, it would seem likely to be helpful for adolescents of both sexes to have more opportunities for looking after young children than is ordinarily the case in our society.

The last influence to mention is that of the characteristics of the children themselves. Parental behaviour is influenced by, for example, both the sex and temperamental qualities of the child.[27,222,251] (See also Huston.[204]) Difficult babies elicit different parental qualities from those brought out by easy infants. Girls elicit different styles of parent–child interaction than do boys. In part, this is because female babies behave differently from male babies, but in part it is a function of parental preconceptions. This was shown, for example, by the 'baby X' experimental studies that we mentioned in Chapter 3, in which infants of both sexes were dressed and named as either a boy or a girl, irrespective of their actual sex. The results showed that parental behaviour was influenced by *both* the actual sex of the infant and by the assigned sex – the sex the adult *thought* the baby was.

We have emphasized the range of influences in parenting because their diversity underlines the multiplicity of pathways to successful (or to maladaptive) parenting. Becoming a parent is a very different experience for different people. For some people it is an eagerly anticipated event, but for others it is yet another burden and stress. With that consideration in mind we need to consider the effects on the individual of becoming a parent.[305] Most of the research has been undertaken with women but in the last few years there has been an increasing number of studies of males.[259]

The most obvious change that comes with the transition to care-giving parenthood is that the parent, whether father or mother, loses his or her independence with the arrival of a child whose care and needs have to take priority. Most first-time, full-time parents of both sexes report initial difficulties in adjusting to the demands associated with childcare and housework. These stem from the unremitting quality of the childcare task, the boredom, the physical demands (including being up at night) and the lack of adult company. Of course, these qualities go along with many pleasures and rewards, but most parents admit that they had not quite realized beforehand just how tiring it would be. It is not just the physical demands, or even the psychological stresses, involved in being a parent. It is also the loss of autonomy, which means that it is no longer possible to go out whenever you want to or to engage in the same range of social activities.

Perhaps, not surprisingly, there is evidence that women who have several preschool children at home may have an increased risk for depression.[61] However, the research findings also show that this risk does not apply to all women; the limited data available suggest that it may mainly concern those living in socially disadvantaged circumstances and lacking adequate child-care arrangements.[62] The strain is less if the burden is shared and if the parent has other sources of interest and relaxation. It seems, too, that the main risk for depression arises when the task of caring for several small children coincides with other life stressors.

The next issue is what effect having a child has on the marriage relationship (see Cowan *et al.*[102]). Such evidence as there is indicates that difficulties are particularly likely to arise in the early years of marriage. Surveys indicate that marital satisfaction tends to fall over the first few years, and the arrival of a child may add to marital tensions in some circumstances. However, having a young child serves to protect against divorce in the early years of marriage.[465] Probably this does *not* mean that tensions are greater in childless marriage; rather it implies that, when there is severe tension, couples with children are more likely to stick together and try to solve their problems. Among couples who do have children, their arrival tends to be associated, on average, with some decrease in marital satisfaction. However, there is marked individual variation among couples; the shared responsibilities of parenthood enhance the marital relationship for many couples. As with other transitions, much depends on the prior relationship and on the way in which the couple deals with changes. On the whole, the transition accentuates previous characteristics (of the individual and of the couple); the reduction in marital satisfaction is most likely to take place in those showing psychological difficulties *before* the child's arrival. Nevertheless, it is clear that the transition to parenthood involves important adaptations. Usually, a drop in the family income is entailed; the time and interests of the care-giving parent have to be shared with the child and, if not much involved, the other spouse may feel left out; the couple's social life may be constrained; and the physical and emotional stresses inherent in childcare may detract from interest in love-making. These potentially negative effects, of course, have to be balanced against the real pleasures in having a child, in enjoying the child's love and attachment, and in the rewards of seeing the child develop, with new accomplishments of some kind coming every week.

Infertility

Not all couples have children. We have already discussed the issue of unwanted pregnancies and we shall now consider unwanted infertility. Of course, some couples choose not to have children. This may be because both husband and wife are strongly career-oriented and do not want either the distraction or responsibilities of children; or it may be because they had such negative experiences in their own upbringing that they do not want to repeat the experience. Also, of course, a substantial minority of men and women do not marry or cohabit. Relatively little is known about the life-span implications of these choices (or acceptances) of state. We should note that people's attitudes and expectations regarding marriage and parenthood are changing. Just as many more couples are deciding to live together and have children without marrying, and far fewer women are giving up their babies for adoption, so also more unmarried women (both heterosexual and homosexual) are choosing to become pregnant *outside* the context of marriage or even family life. Whether or not this has implications for attitudes towards infertility is not known, but it may have.

We have included infertility as one of our examples of important transitions in adult life because it is quite common.[457] About one in five couples take more than one year to conceive when trying to do so and probably about one in ten have more persistent infertility. The reasons for this are many and various; perhaps a third are due to some gynaecological disorder in the woman, about a fifth to low sperm counts in the male and another quarter to lack of sperm penetration of the mucus – an interactive feature in that couple.[223] Until relatively recently, emotional factors were thought to be a major causal factor in many cases of infertility; however, this view has not been supported by research findings. About four fifths of cases of infertility have been shown to be due to organic causes. Nevertheless, psychosexual difficulties play a substantial role in the minority of cases. It has been found that some 6 per cent of cases of infertility are a consequence of partial or complete failure to have sexual intercourse, and a few infertile couples have never

consummated their marriage. Sometimes the extent, or even presence, of psychosexual difficulties does not become apparent until
late in the course of physical investigations. The problem may
lie in the man's impotence or premature ejaculation, or in the
woman's lack of interest in sex, or she may suffer from vaginis-
mus (painful response to intercourse). Not infrequently, the
psychosexual difficulties in the two partners go together.
Whether this is a consequence of partner choice, or the effects of
mutual interaction, or a mixture of the two is not known. Such
psychosexual problems sometimes derive from deviant patterns
of upbringing or from negative sexual experiences such as rape
or incest. Sometimes, too, they derive from current emotional
problems or from the side-effects of drugs (such as beta blockers
or tricyclic antidepressants) or from medical conditions such as
diabetes. It should be added that some cases of infertility stem
from pelvic inflammatory disease, either as a result of complications following abortion, childbirth or the use of intrauterine
devices, or as a consequence of sexually transmitted disease. The
realization that this has been so, in the minority of cases where
that is the explanation, may lead to secondary psychological
sequelae. The research that has demonstrated the causal role of
organic factors in the great majority of cases of infertility has
been important in removing blame from the couple, but these
findings must not lead us to neglect the psychological factors
that, either as primary or secondary features, play a role in some
6–20 per cent of cases.

   Why should infertility matter any more than any other medical problem? It is not just that the couple are deprived of the
potential rewards of parenthood, although that is one consideration. The roots lie deep in history; in many cultures, for a
woman to be presumed to be barren was a sufficient ground for
divorce. Of course, society's attitudes have changed and, in any
case, that view has not been accepted within our own culture for
some time. Even so, for many men and women, not to have a
child is felt as being unfulfilled. For some, this not only reflects
their thwarted desire to bring up children but also involves the
failure to perpetuate themselves in the next generation ('handing
down the line') or a threat to their sexuality. Quite a number of

ing to be investigated for infertility for fear of
y are, as it were, 'at fault'. The question of who
not uncommonly leads to tensions between the
all these reasons, the recognition of infertility creates
a psychological challenge for many people. This is evident in the
incredible lengths to which many people will go in seeking a
solution to their infertility. There is now an impressive range of
new techniques to deal with infertility but their success rate
remains relatively low and they are very demanding of the
couple. In the infertility clinic where one of us works, it is
evident, too, that some couples continue – or even start – to seek
a pregnancy in spite of manifest marital difficulties. The desire to
have a baby and a considered decision that there is a harmonious
family suitable for rearing a child are far from synonymous.

To say that the experience of infertility constitutes a psychological challenge for most couples is not to say that it constitutes a
serious psychiatric risk factor. The available research findings are
somewhat inconclusive and contradictory, but it seems that the
rate of overt psychiatric disorder in infertile couples is *not*
appreciably raised,[457] although psychological distress is more
commonly experienced, perhaps especially by women. But individual differences in response are very large indeed. As with other
challenging life transitions, such as unemployment, adverse reactions are probably more likely in those individuals who have
experienced previous emotional difficulties, whose marriages are
unsatisfactory and who lack emotional support. Also, expectations
and the style of coping are relevant. It seems that the additional
risk factors for distress may include: (i) a strong expectation that
fertility is synonymous with high-level goals of happiness, fulfilment and maturity; (ii) a continuing search for causal explanations
for the infertility; (iii) low perceived personal control over their
situation; (iv) avoidance of the issues associated with infertility. As
with any other 'stress' situation, successful coping probably does
not lie in any one coping strategy or tactic. Rather, it derives
from an active means of dealing with the practical and emotional
issues involved. For some this will mean seeking suitable medical
or surgical interventions, for others it will mean seeking adoption
and for yet others it will mean a reappraisal of their life goal of

having a child. It is important to appreciate that, as with other life stresses and challenges, successful coping can be psychologically enhancing and can have positive effects on the marriage relationship. Many couples are able to readjust their goals, to appreciate that there may be benefits as well as disadvantages in infertility and plan their lives to capitalize on the positive aspects.

Infertility used to be seen as a stress deriving only from the loss of the child that might have been, with the task seen as working through the grief process in a manner that paralleled what was thought to be needed in relation to bereavement. However, it is evident that loss is not the only psychological element involved and it is an oversimplification to see the grief process as having to go through a series of universal stages. People deal successfully with loss through a variety of mechanisms. Denial of the situation tends to be unhelpful because it prevents any form of resolution, but there is no one 'right' way of coping and no predetermined series of stages to be gone through.

For those infertile couples who decide to seek medical or surgical remediation, a further set of psychological challenges has to be met. From then on, they become identified as *patients*, with the commitment to a search for a 'cure' that is implied and the threat of failure if this is not achieved. There can be many negative feelings that are intermingled with hope at this stage; a jealousy of friends who are pregnant, uncertainty and insecurity about their own feelings and those of their partner, and a sense of vulnerability. However, for many couples the greatest stress resides in their reliance on professionals and hence their loss of control over a crucial aspect of their lives. Elder and Caspi,[136] in writing about life transitions, argued that the loss, and restoration, of personal control was often a key element. It is an important part of human functioning to feel able to shape one's life and to direct the life trajectory – situations or events that take away that control tend to be felt as quite threatening.

The merry-go-round (unfortunately distinctly unmerry) of medical tests and procedures tends to add to this feeling of loss of control. In addition, there is the further stress of making sex into a mechanical procedure.[457] For men there is often the requirement to masturbate in hospital lavatories to produce sperm and for the couple there is the need to record their sex acts on a chart and to perform according to the calendar. The fact that many of the procedures rather leave out the husband, as he is often medically irrelevant, may increase the emotional disturbance between the couple. This focus on sex as a medically controlled mechanical act does not do great things for most marital relationships and it is not surprising that tensions are more evident in the marriage than they are in cases of personal emotional disturbance. Studies of infertile couples undergoing treatment indicate that marital and sexual difficulties increase in about half the cases, perhaps especially when the man is the infertile partner. Of course, all of this may bring couples closer together as they face a joint concern.

Until very recently, infertility has not featured in most discussions of life-span development – perhaps because it was wrongly thought to be an uncommon experience, but probably most of all because it was misleadingly viewed as a narrowly medical concern. As we have noted, contrary to these misconceptions, it is a relatively frequent experience and one with important psychological implications. Moreover, it well exemplifies some key life-span concepts. It underlines the importance of *unexpected*, as well as normative, life events. In most instances, infertility has no connection with past experiences or behaviour, but in a minority of cases it may be the consequence of complications of abortion, childbirth, intrauterine devices or sexually transmitted disease. However, irrespective of the cause, the personal meaning of the event is likely to affect the way it is negotiated. Like many stress experiences, it tends to accentuate pre-existing personal characteristics and relationship qualities, and it may have either positive or negative consequences according to the success or failure of coping. Its impact is as much on the couple as on the individual, and the life-span implications need to be considered in social as well as individual terms. Because the experience may require a reappraisal of life goals and expectations, it may constitute a turning-point. The transition, therefore, represents both an outcome of the past and a new determinant of the future. Some transitions have major psychopathological implications but some, of which infertility is an example, are mainly influential in terms of their effects on self-concepts and lifestyle rather than as precipitants of mental disorder *per se*. Most infertile couples who seek counselling do not have significant emotional disturbance, but they do have psychological challenges that may be better met with help.

Chapter 9

Mid-life Transitions and Old Age

No one doubts that adult life brings with it a host of stresses, rewards, challenges and transitions. However, there is a sharp contrast between those theorists who portray life-span development as a ladder-like progression through inevitable universal transitions and stages, and those who view the sequence as open to major individual variations, some of which stem from differences in self-concept, expectations and other aspects of intra-psychic functioning; some from vulnerabilities, adaptabilities or attitudes deriving from previous life experiences; and some from key external events arising in adult life that serve to close down or open up opportunities or which alter life circumstances in a lasting way.[102,135,137]

Concepts of Life Stages

Levinson's[269] concept of a 'mid-life crisis' exemplifies the first approach. He argued that the great majority of men experience a period of great struggle within the self and with the external world at about the age of forty. 'They question nearly every aspect of their lives and feel that they cannot go on as before. They will need several years to form a new path or modify the old one' (p. 66); 'it is not possible to get through middle adulthood without having at least a moderate crisis in either the Mid-life Transition or the Age Fifty Transition' (p. 62). He went on to argue that those men who do very little questioning or searching '. . . will pay the price in a later developmental crisis or in a progressive withering of the self and a life structure minimally connected to the self' (p. 199).

This picture of mid-life is a dramatic one and it is not surprising that it has so captured the public imagination that the term 'mid-life crisis' has entered our vocabulary. However, it is necessary to note that the concept involves three rather separate propositions, one of which is well supported by research, one of which receives only qualified support and one of which is not supported. The first postulate is that middle life is associated with a wide range of adaptations in life pattern. Some stem from major role changes that bring with them fairly drastic consequences for better or worse. Divorce, remarriage, a major job change, a block to promotion at work, redundancy or a serious crippling illness constitute a mixed bag of examples of this kind. Others are more subtle in that there is not such an obvious major personal experience but yet substantial psychological adaptations may be entailed. Thus, children growing up and leaving home will have implications for the marital relationship and for patterns of family life more generally. Similarly, the ageing of a man or woman's parents may mean a shift in roles so that an earlier dependence *on* them becomes replaced by a dependence *of* them on him or her. As offspring marry and have children of their own, adults have to take on the new role of grandparent. This first aspect of Levinson's concept is clearly correct and is accepted by theorists of all persuasions. Nevertheless, it is necessary to note that these adaptations may take place at any time from early adulthood to extreme old age; they are certainly not confined to the forties or fifties.

The second proposition is that middle age brings with it significant changes in the *internal* aspects of a person's life structure. That is, regardless of the presence or absence of external events or happenings, mid-life constitutes a time of reappraisal in which people question what they have achieved and what they want to accomplish. Such internal questioning may focus on work goals – asking whether the person should be content with where he has got to or whether he should strive for something more. Alternatively, it may be concerned with relationships – whether to be content with a boring but untroubled marriage or whether to seek a new partner. Or, yet again, the questioning may turn inwards to query the implications of a person's neglect of their family or ruthlessness towards colleagues to achieve work objectives. Again, few would doubt that many people do go through periods of doubt and self-questioning. Indeed, that is an intrinsic part of the human condition. We are *thinking* beings and, inevitably, that means that we will all ponder on what we are and what we want to be. What is controversial is the focus on issues that apply especially to the aspirant middle class in the Western world and the restriction of this self-questioning to the specific age period. It seems rather doubtful whether the issues will be the same for a beggar in Delhi, an alcoholic down-and-out in New York, a business executive in Chicago, a nomadic herdsman in Africa and a building-site labourer in London. However, we do not need to take such extremes to find variations in the way increasing age is associated with different trends in values and appraisals. For example, one study showed that top management executives placed an *increasing* importance on work as they grew older whereas lower level management gave a *reducing* importance to work.[432] Moreover, the issues *cannot* be confined to any one age, if only because external events will force self-questioning at other times. Thus, the French architect Eiffel seriously embarked on his scientific career only after most people retire, the transition being possible because the construction of the Eiffel Tower enabled him to use it for scientific observations. It is a curious feature of our political system, too, that so often we expect our leaders to be aged. Frequently this means that a person has to take on major new responsibilities at a relatively advanced age – an example is General Eisenhower, the army chief who became President.

But, for other people, similar major transitions arise very early in life. Top athletes, swimmers and tennis players (also most musicians) need to decide as children or adolescents whether to sacrifice all in the hope of becoming the world's best. By the time they are reaching early adulthood they may need to decide whether they are content to be just a local champion or whether their failure to make the Olympic squad or the Davis Cup team means that their whole life is a failure.

Levinson recognized this problem and commented on the fact that the tasks of mid-life individuation could arise at other ages, although he seemed to want to have it both ways in arguing that the transition at thirty is *different* from that at forty, even though it has many qualities in common. We need to appreciate that this type of internal questioning is part of many life transitions. In our society, for many men, it *may* be particularly prominent in mid-life, but there is wide variation in its timing and the extent of its occurrence. Moreover, self-questioning often takes place *several* times during a person's lifetime. Self-questioning about, say, marriage may not coincide with that about work, although sometimes self-searching about one domain of life may lead to similar re-evaluation of other domains.

Levinson's third proposition is the really controversial one; namely, that it is necessary to experience tumult and turmoil if one is to make the transition successfully. The parallels with outdated and discredited '*Sturm und Drang*' views on adolescence (see Chapter 7) are obvious. Thus, Anna Freud[161] maintained that '. . . the upholding of a steady equilibrium during the adolescent process is in itself abnormal'. We now know from epidemiological studies such as that on the Isle of Wight[393] and from longitudinal studies such as that undertaken by Offer,[325] to mention but two examples out of many, that many young people pass through adolescence in an essentially peaceful, untroubled fashion. Moreover, follow-up data show that this tends to be a *favourable*, and not a bad, prognostic indicator.

The available research findings on mid-life transitions are much more sparse, but the same pattern seems to apply. Vaillant's longitudinal study[12] indicated that a *lack* of emotional disturbance in mid-life predicted better psychological functioning in the sixties – in other words, the opposite of what Levinson proposed. Similarly, the limited data on the long-term outcome following bereavement, as reviewed by Wortman and Silver,[12] fail to support the view that intense distress at the time is a good thing. The few available findings are consistent with the view that a degree of self-questioning, as part of coping with the intrapsychic, as well as the external, tasks of transitions at any age (including mid-life) may well be adaptive and healthy. However, although there has been too little research for firm conclusions, the findings do not support the notion that the self-searching must be distressing and disturbing even when the transition is being managed well. In particular, it seems quite implausible that a lack of turmoil and turbulence implies a poor prognosis. After this preamble on the concepts, we may consider some of the key transitions that often occur in mid-life. As with other age periods, we have made no attempt to consider all major transitions. Rather, we have chosen a selection to illustrate some of the important issues.

The Empty Nest

At one time, much was made of the so-called 'empty-nest syndrome' in which mothers are supposed to become depressed when their children leave home. The idea was that women's emotional investment in child rearing was so great that when their offspring ceased to be dependent they experienced a great sense of loss. In fact, the limited empirical evidence runs rather consistently against this stereotype.[10] For example, Rubin[384] interviewed 160 women whose children were in various stages of leaving home, the mothers being in their mid-forties on average. The great majority viewed the impending or actual departure of their children with a sense of relief, albeit mixed with some ambivalence. One woman is quoted as saying, 'I can't tell you what a relief it was to find myself with an empty nest. Oh sure, when the last child went away to school, for the first day or so, there was a kind of throb but, believe me, it was only for a day or two' (p. 15). The ambivalence was expressed by another mother as follows: 'It's not that it's either good or bad, it's just that it's an era coming to an end and in many ways it was a nice era.' Other studies are in keeping with Rubin's finding that only a few women show the supposed 'empty-nest syndrome'. The stereotype is misleading and should be regarded as an unusual minority phenomenon.

Even so, that does not necessarily mean that the transition is of no importance. It may be just that it has been viewed from too restricted a perspective. Four rather separate issues need to be mentioned. First, it is scarcely likely that all parents will respond to the departure from home of their children in the same way. Presumably much is likely to depend on the quality of the parent–child relationship. If it has been bad, the departure may mean the relief of discord and tension, with consequent benefits for all parties. Perhaps, parents are most likely to respond with depression when they have used their children as an inappropriate solution for their own emotional needs – very much a maladaptive minority situation. We lack good data on the influences of such factors but it is clear that the event needs to be considered in terms of its personal meaning, rather than a universal one. This is, of course, the same point that has emerged from study of the other major life events, such as marriage or unemployment, where rather more data are available.

The second point is that a child's departure from home does not mean either their loss or an end of a relationship. The issue is closely similar to the changes in attachment that we discussed in Chapter 4. Because school-age children show their attachment in ways other than clinging, this does not mean that their relationships with their parents are any less close. Similarly, when children leave home, this is likely to signal a change in *pattern*, but not necessarily any weakening of the relationship. Probably the key difference is that parents and children will need to *choose* to come together rather than have their interactions *forced* on them through living together in the same house. Also, the departure may serve as a marker of the fact that the children are now adult and can make up their own minds on major decisions, as well as having to be economically independent. However, such independence may well precede, or follow, the physical departure by some years. Whether these changes in patterns mean an improvement, or worsening, in the relationship varies from family to family. When the basic parent–child relationship is good, but there have been tensions over specific issues, the child's departure from home may well bring about a restoration of harmony and an improved relationship on a new footing.[10] It should be added that there is now a growing awareness that a *failure* of adult children to leave home, the so-called 'full-nest syndrome', creates its own challenges and in some instances a crisis.[95]

Third, the departure of the children may provide the mother with an increased career independence. Of course, this opportunity may have been taken some years earlier when the children were old enough to look after themselves when they came home from school, or the mother may have decided from the outset to combine a career with parenting. Whether the career opportunity has mainly positive or negative effects is likely to be influenced by individual circumstances. For example, they may be negative if the mother finds that she has left it too late to return to the type of career responsibility she wanted. However, the point is that the departure of children needs to be considered in terms of its consequent or knock-on effects on other aspects of people's lives, and not just in terms of the parent–child relationship.

The fourth point brings in an ecological, or social-systems perspective in the need to view the empty nest in terms of its implications for the marriage relationship. The available evidence suggests that, although there are marked individual variations in pattern, overall satisfaction with the life stage, and to a lesser extent marital satisfaction, tend to decline during the period of child-rearing, with a sharp increase in satisfaction when the children leave home. Figure 9.1 shows the findings from Rollins and Feldman's[377] study. Most of the evidence stems from cross-sectional surveys of special groups, so that we need to be cautious in drawing conclusions. Also, necessarily, the findings apply to couples who have remained together throughout. Nevertheless, there does seem to be a tendency for many couples to come closer together when the children leave home. The greater opportunity to enjoy their time together free of the day-to-day concerns over the children may be rewarding. Of course, whether or not this is so will depend heavily on the quality of their pre-existing marital relationship. Some marriages may have been largely maintained through the children and, when the children depart, there may be little left to hold the couple together. Because the love or companionship relationship has long since gone, the departure of the children serves to highlight the fact that little remains of the marriage. In some instances, this leads to a divorce that occurs late in the marriage but had its roots much earlier. British figures show that nearly a fifth of divorces take place in marriages that have lasted twenty years or more.[69] The data are inconclusive on whether or not there is a peak in divorce that follows, or coincides with, the departure of the children, but it is evident that we do need to look to mid-life circumstances of some kind for an explanation for the end of relationships that have lasted for at least two decades.

Grandparenthood

In many cases the empty nest is followed by grandparenthood, so that it is appropriate to consider that topic next. As with the departure of the children, it is necessary to look beyond the grandparent–grandchild dyad in order to understand the implications of this transition.[31,448] Thus, for example, in most societies, it has the connotations of having moved into an older age group, an understandable expectation from having moved up a generation. Most pictures of grandparents in children's books portray a white-haired couple in rocking-chairs or with walking-sticks. However, the average age of becoming a grand-parent in Western societies is about fifty for women and a couple of years older for men – scarcely a time when most people are in their dotage! Moreover, the transition can be much earlier than fifty. For example, in one study a twenty-eight-year-old woman is quoted as saying: 'I could break my daughter's neck for having this baby. I've just got a new boyfriend. Now he will think I'm too old. It was bad enough being a mother so young – now a grandmother too!'[448] Similarly, a public figure has been quoted as saying that he was more than delighted to have become a grandfather but he wasn't so sure that he was yet ready for the idea of being married to a grandmother!

It seems that this ageing connotation is not a matter of great moment for most people, but it is a facet that may be important either when, for other reasons, the individuals are worried about the ageing process or when the transition occurs unusually early, so that it is discrepant with the normatively expectable time for the transition. It is necessary, too, to view grandparenthood in its sociocultural context. In many societies in years past it was assumed that grandparents would look after the children while their parents went out to work or just to enjoy themselves. This was possible when most grandmothers either did not have a job outside the home or had retired. Today, as more women have careers, as more children live far from their parents and as grandmothers tend to be younger (because of earlier marriages),

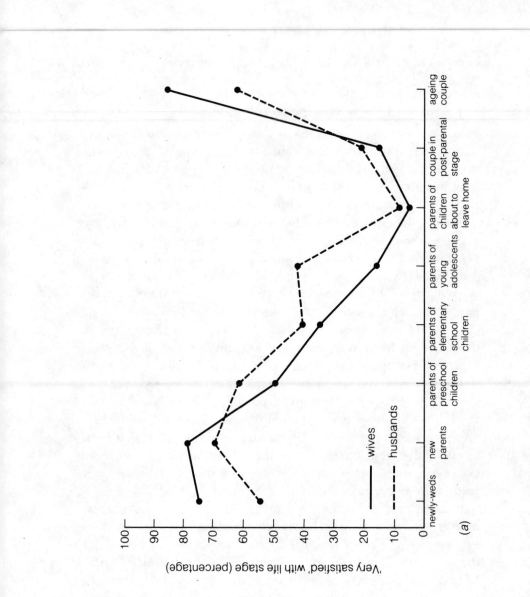

'Very satisfied' with life stage (percentage)

newly-weds · new parents · parents of preschool children · parents of elementary school children · parents of young adolescents · parents of children about to leave home · couple in post-parental stage · ageing couple

wives
husbands

(a)

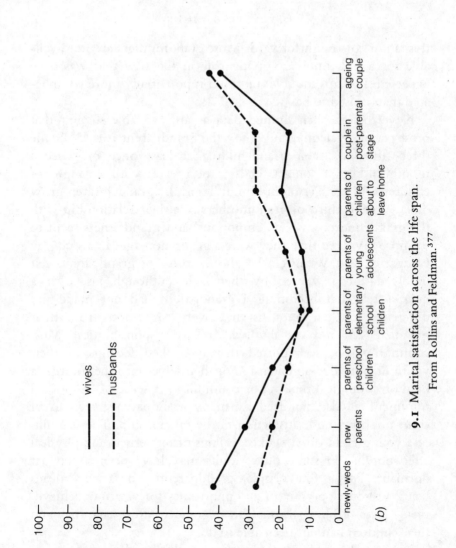

9.1 Marital satisfaction across the life span.
From Rollins and Feldman.[377]

this is not so straightforward. Most grandmothers are not available for a full-time care-giving role in the way that was once expected. Perhaps the role transition is potentially more complicated than it used to be.

Nevertheless, such limited data as are available suggest that most people welcome and enjoy the grandparent role.[448] Some three fifths see their grandchildren at least once or twice a month, although contact tends to be greater with a daughter's children and contact often diminishes as the grandchildren grow older. Over a third of grandmothers rate their relationship with the grandchildren as 'very important' and grandfathers seem to be more involved than they were a generation ago. In a study by Neugarten and Weinstein,[316] the majority of grandparents felt involved and rewarded by their role (although just over a quarter felt that becoming a grandparent had not made any difference to their lives, as they were so remote from their grandchildren and not involved in any responsibilities). Most commonly, people reported that it evoked feelings of their youth or provided an extension of themselves into the future – a kind of 'biological renewal or continuity'. A sense of 'emotional fulfilment' is also reported by many grandparents; feelings of companionship and satisfaction in the relationship. The stimulus of a young child often evokes feelings of tenderness and physical affection that in some older adults may have been somewhat dormant. For a few people, grandparenthood largely means being a resource person, or an opportunity for vicarious achievement, accomplishing through their grandchildren what they and their children had not been able to do.

In all studies, some people (up to a third or so) experienced some difficulties in the transition. It seems that in most cases these related either to feeling uncomfortable about the ageing implications or to conflicts with their children – the parents – over aspects of child-rearing. The reasons for these individual differences have been little explored up to now, but presumably the prior relationship between the grandparents and the parents, the grandparents' feelings about their own success or failure as parents and possible career–grandparenthood clashes over priorities will play a part. It seems important, as with other transitions, to view the transition in the context of both *prior* relationships and social context. However, for this to be possible, it will be necessary to undertake longitudinal studies in the second half of life of the kind that have been informative in earlier age periods. So far, there have been few systematic epidemiologically based longitudinal investigations of this type (other than with respect to cognition) and, as a result, we have had to be more tentative about conclusions in these last two chapters than we were when dealing with childhood.

Looking after Elderly Parents

An important role transition for many people, albeit a temporary one, is provided by the need to care for their own elderly, infirm or demanding parents. This issue has been a subject of study in the gerontological and psychogeriatric literature, but up to now it has received little attention from developmentalists. For example, when we visited China a few years ago we were struck by the fact that Chinese professionals were concerned over the implications for old people of their one-child-per-family policy. They pointed out that, when there are several children in the family, it is likely that at least one of them will have both practical circumstances and a sufficiently good relationship with the elderly parents to be willing to take on the responsibility of looking after them in their old age. This is not so likely when more people are living to a ripe old age and when there is only one child per family. Not only will each couple potentially have four old people to look after, but also they will need to have a good relationship with all of them. A tall order indeed! Of course, the US and the UK do not have a one-child policy but increasing longevity and a reducing average family size will involve similar issues for us.

Robinson and Thurnher[310] interviewed forty-nine people who had ageing parents and followed them up over the next five years. A third of the group viewed their parents in very positive terms and a few, mainly those with precarious marriages, still saw their parents as a source of emotional support in spite of their advanced age. Not surprisingly, positive and dependent views mainly referred to physically and mentally fit parents leading active lives. Another third described their parents in predominantly negative terms. Most of them had demanding parents whose difficult behaviour was seen as an accentuation of pre-existing negative personality traits. However, negative appraisals were also more common when the care-giving responsibilities were felt to be confining and stressful. One person commented: 'I think I've waited on people so much of my life and I wonder why I still have to do it.' Another comment was: 'The middle-aged are sandwiched between their ageing parents and their children; just as you've raised your family, you have to take care of your parents.' For most people, it was not the work involved as such that was stressful, it was the constraints. As one woman put it, 'The busy part of my mother does not bother me; it's the tied down part that gets me.' The follow-up over the next five years showed that tensions tended to get worse rather than better, although sometimes a shared bereavement brought an increasing sense of closeness. One woman described the situation in very positive terms initially; her mother was an 'angel'. Five years later there was only hostility and resentment as her mother's dependency had increased and her capacity to reciprocate emotionally had declined.

Research into the emotional well-being of those who have to care for old people suffering from dementia brings out several other relevant points.[311] It has been found that the care of the demented relative is associated with an increased risk of depression; this is most marked for spouses but it also applies to adult children looking after a parent. The strains tend to be less when the carers are able to avoid being too emotionally involved. Conversely, care-givers are more likely to become depressed if they feel unable to control what is happening and unable to cope with what is required of them. The effects of particular behaviours shown by the demented parent are somewhat variable but, on the whole, it seems that demanding behaviour and harassment of the care-giver tends to generate conflict and resentment, whereas apathy and withdrawal is more likely to result in an empty and increasingly unrewarding relationship. The demanding process is important as an influence because it destroys the personality of the parent and hence is likely to engender mourning and grief. The body is still there but the mind, and therefore the person, has been lost. As with other losses, social support is helpful in mitigating the grief.

The care of a demanding parent creates stress of some degree in most people. This may be quite marked but the extent to which it leads to emotional disturbance is influenced by the previous relationship with the parent; by the effects of old age and the demanding process on that relationship; by the extent to which the need to provide care disrupts other aspects of the person's life; and by the person's success in coping with the situation and their maintenance, or otherwise, of feelings of control.

Male Sexuality

Middle age is associated with physical change as well as with challenging events and experiences. These include alterations in male sexuality.[13,46,490] Surveys are agreed in showing that, on average, from mid-life onwards, there is a gradual diminution in sexual interest, arousal and activity. The frequency of orgasms tends to decrease, erections arise less readily and the length of the refractory period after orgasm increases. These changes are accompanied by falling levels of circulating testosterone and by a reduction in spermatogenic function. It would seem to follow that the hormonal changes cause the alterations in sexual function; as discussed earlier, testosterone is the prime hormonal determinant of sexual drive. Clearly, the two are connected but the relationship between testosterone and sex drive is a two-way one. Just as falling sex-hormone levels are likely to result in a diminution in sex drive, so also an increase in sexual activity will raise testosterone levels. In that connection, it is also relevant that there are huge individual variations in levels of sexual activity in old age. Many men remain sexually active well into the seventies and eighties, and may even father children then. Moreover, as in younger age groups, the development of a new, satisfying relationship may result in a renewed resurgence of sex drive and sexual activity. Although the physiological changes arise in part as a direct consequence of the ageing process and are an inevitable occurrence at some point, their timing and the degree of change

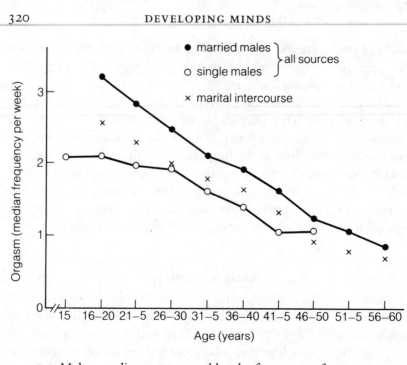

9.2 Male sexuality, as measured by the frequency of orgasms,
in relation to age.
From Botwinick.[46]

are much influenced by sexual experiences. It is a general biological principle that structures and their functions are maintained
through regular use. In Chapter 6 we noted that this applied to
intellectual functions, and the same operates with sexuality. As
Masters and Johnson[294] commented, 'the most important factor
in the maintenance of sexuality for the ageing is consistency of
active sexual expression' (p. 262). It also seems that individuals
who were more sexually active than average when young tend
to continue to be sexually active for longer when older.

Many of the factors that influence male sexuality in younger
age groups apply similarly in the second half of life, albeit with
some differences in emphasis. Thus, sexual inhibitions stemming
from a fear of failure are relevant. These may be brought about
either by a man's concern over what he considers to be his
failing performance (erections being more dependent on tactile
stimulation than they used to be, taking longer to develop, being

maintained for shorter periods and with a less powerful ejaculation); or by his partner's critical attitude. As ageing advances, sex may be less frenetic, but no less enjoyable for that. However, the expectations of both partners are crucial. If the man pines for what used to be, or if the woman's expectations are unrealistic, anxiety over failure may lead to sexual inhibition and a vicious circle of psyche–soma interactions. It is relevant that the average pattern of timing of sexual decline differs between men and women. Men tend to show a slow but steady decline from early adulthood onwards (although this may not be perceived until later), whereas women's interest in sex sometimes may actually increase slightly in mid-life. Overall, women's sexual interests decline to some extent with age but the decline starts later and is less marked than in men; the menopause sometimes bringing a slight increase in interest. Their level of sexual activity is, however, largely constrained by their male partners. Christenson and Gagnon[87] showed that women with younger husbands were more sexually active than those with older ones. Clearly, there is the potential for strain when the woman's sex drive is maintained, or even going up, while her partner's is going down. It should be added that the extent to which male sexuality declines with age is much influenced by whether or not there is disease, or the use of drugs that affect sexual function. Alcohol use, too, is relevant. As Shakespeare noted, alcohol 'provokes the desire but it takes away the performance'; this may be especially so with increasing age. Heavy drinking to reduce sexual anxiety does not provide a good solution!

Some men, like some women, feel concern over the physical effects of their ageing and the implications for their attractiveness, sexual or otherwise. Old age need not detract from attractiveness – as wonderfully portrayed in the film *On Golden Pond*. Of course, old people cannot be beautiful in the way that a young person can. The skin inevitably loses its elasticity and becomes wrinkled, and weakening muscles mean that the vigorous freshness of youth is lost. Men may worry over their physical changes and their self-esteem may become threatened. In some cases, this may lead to sexual 'flings' with younger partners as a way of seeking reassurance on their sexual selves. Usually, this is associated with a degree of guilt and anxiety, and may put a previously good marital relationship in jeopardy. However, sometimes, having received reassurance, the marital sexual relationship may be invigorated. That clinical observation serves as a reminder that sexuality in old age, as in earlier age periods, is strongly influenced by the quality of the relationship between the partners and by the social context more generally. In many instances, what seems to be an effect of ageing is in reality more a function of a deteriorating marital relationship or a lack of novelty or excitement.

The Menopause

More is known about the psychological and physical effects of the menopause in women than about age changes in male sexuality. Even so, factual evidence has a struggle competing with myths and stereotypes.[185] It is commonly assumed that the menopause necessarily means that sexuality will fade out and that the hormonal changes will lead directly to emotional disturbance. Neither preconception is correct. Oestrogen does not control sex drive, erotic thoughts, sexual sensations or the ability to experience orgasm. Testosterone is the sex hormone that mainly influences sex drive (in both sexes), but psychological factors are at least as important. After the menopause, when oestrogen levels fall, women are perfectly able to maintain interest and pleasure in sexual activity and most do so. Indeed, for some, sexual desire and satisfaction may be enhanced as the fear of pregnancy is lost. Nevertheless, there are physical changes that are part of the menopause that can, in some circumstances, have implications for sexual difficulties.

A woman's reproductive life usually ends between forty-five and fifty-five years, although the menopause can arise as soon as the early thirties.[13] The number of ova gradually decreases and hormone levels fall to about a fifth of their initial value. The menopause describes the *final* menstrual period whereas the climacteric describes the period of gradual transition, lasting about five years, when the ovarian production of oestrogen begins to falter. With this hormonal decline come symptoms that may be unpleasant. The vagina narrows and becomes more dry, giving rise to the possibility of soreness and an increased risk of infection. Hot flushes and flashes are common, with the skin temperature rising markedly. During this same period there is a loss of skin elasticity and muscle tone, together with osteoporosis (loss of mineral substance, mass and density in the bones); while somewhat comparable changes occur in men, they are both more rapid and more marked in women because of the fall in oestrogen levels.

Of these effects, osteoporosis is potentially the most serious because of the much increased risk of broken bones, especially the serious hip fractures that so often occur in old age. The loss of bone mass is worse if the menopause is very early, if the body weight is low, if the woman smokes or has high alcohol consumption, or if the nutritional status is poor. Nevertheless, osteoporosis occurs to a substantial degree after the menopause even if these factors are favourable. It is now widely recognized that bone loss can be arrested by hormone replacement therapy (HRT). It does not restore lost bone, however; hence the benefits are greater if it is started early and continued until at least age seventy.[360]

As with other biological events, there is considerable individual variation in the timing of the menopause.[9,505] Probably, the timing is under genetic control but the menopause also tends to be earlier in heavy smokers and in the malnourished. Clinicians have noted that severe psychological stress sometimes seems to cause a cessation of periods. This is plausible because it is known that autoimmune disorders are associated with a premature menopause and stress may have effects on the immune, as well as the neuroendocrine, system, but direct evidence on the role of psychological factors is lacking. It is curious that so much more attention has been paid to the physical and psychological consequences of the menopause than to the factors influencing its timing. It is important that life transitions are investigated to determine their origins as well as their sequelae.

Even when the menopause is expected, the psychological sequelae can be appreciable. There may be distress over the unpleasant physical symptoms, bewilderment over the widespread bodily changes and diminished self-esteem stemming from the loss of youth and the all-too-visible reminders of ageing. These several reactions reflect a variety of mechanisms and it is important to differentiate between the physical processes as reflected in symptoms such as hot flushes, the emotional response to the loss of fertility and all that that implies, and the mood changes that may occur during this period.

HRT is effective in relieving the first of these but makes no difference to the latter effects. It has no influence on libido but it will relieve vaginal dryness and hence help with several problems stemming from soreness due to a lack of lubricating mucus. Of course, it will also diminish hormonally influenced skin atrophy and breast shrinkage and that may aid self-esteem (although it would be wrong to expect it to keep women 'young'; it will not do that).

The situation with the depression that is supposed to accompany the menopause is more complicated.[13,185] Many people associate 'the change of life' with depression, weight gain, tiredness, headaches, palpitations, insomnia and digestive problems. Certainly, these do occur in some women but they are far from inevitable and studies show that they are *not* systematically associated with hormone levels and are not usually much helped by HRT. The explanation must be sought in non-hormonal factors, and the few available findings from cross-cultural studies are relevant.[185,197] In cultures where the postmenopausal role change is associated with either an increase in status or a decrease in burden (so that, as it were, the menopause is 'rewarded') it seems that there are no adverse psychological symptoms. The implication is that it is our youth-orientated society that increases the potential for psychological problems during the menopause. Also, other psychological life events at this time may induce mood changes. It seems that women are more likely to report depressive symptoms when the menopause coincides with life stresses such as illness or death of parents or close friends, a declining capacity for physical exertion and difficulties in defining a new role when the former ones of child-bearing and child-rearing have been superseded. Severne's[197] study in Belgium showed that housewives from a low socio-economic (SES) group were most likely (and high SES women with a job less

likely) to react adversely to the menopause; however this difference also reflected their psychological functioning before the
menopause. Other studies, too, have tended to show that psychological sequelae tend to be less marked in women with careers,
but the findings on social class are less consistent.[159] How
women adapt and adjust to these changes will be influenced by,
amongst other things, their view of their own sexuality, the
nature and quality of their relationships and their career commitment.

Female Sexuality and Fertility

Self-esteem and sexual body image are closely linked in many
women and, at the menopause, some become concerned that
they will lose their femininity and sexual attractiveness. On the
other hand, it is clear that there are marked individual differences
in reactions to physical changes involved in ageing,[290] differences
that stem from both societal context and personal features. Some
women feel relief in being less likely to be viewed socially as sex
objects and some feel that a more mature appearance helps in
being taken more seriously at work. Nevertheless, it is obvious
that some women invest a good deal in keeping themselves in
good physical shape, dyeing their hair, dieting and dressing
expensively to avoid losing their youthfulness. This may help to
maintain self-esteem, but surgical interventions (such as face-lifts)
have only a temporary effect and, although they can be useful,
there is some danger that they involve too much denial of
ageing. A supportive sexual partner can do much to reassure and
reaffirm other values of the love relationship. Unfortunately,
society's view of the menopause as meaning that women are
thereby 'past it' at that point does not help. For example, a
recent article quoted a gynaecologist's dismissal of hysterectomy
in a forty-four-year-old woman as a minor matter because 'you
don't need that any more', and another surgeon's comment to a
woman facing mastectomy that 'you've nothing there worth
saving'. Of course, in a narrow medical sense both comments
may have been correct, but their extreme insensitivity indicated
a lack of awareness of their emotional importance as symbols of
femininity. In that connection, it is relevant to note that hysterec-

tomy is associated with a much increased risk of an early menopause;[9] it is usually thought that this may be a consequence of the operation interfering with the blood supply to the ovary, but psychological factors cannot be entirely ruled out.

For some women, sexuality is so bound up with child-bearing that sexual intercourse is felt to be justifiable only for procreation. For them, the idea of a continuing sex life for its own sake may be difficult even when they have not wanted further children for many years. The fact that they are no longer *capable* of procreating may be felt to have diminished them as a sexual partner. This can also be a dilemma following sterilization, hysterectomy or removal of the ovaries.

For others, who have previously enjoyed their sexual lives, there may be a feeling that it is no longer 'proper' to enjoy sex. In the Well Woman Clinic where one of us works, it is surprising how many women are apologetic or embarrassed to acknowledge that they are still making love *and* enjoying it. The view that sex is not for grannies is all too common. Others may find that as their young reach adult sexuality, they somehow feel they are 'old enough to know better' and that it is the children's turn now.

Anticipation of the menopause can be a particularly stressful time for women who have delayed having children in order to pursue a career. A recognition that their fertility is reducing with every year that goes by may lead to fear that they may have left it too late. Until recently, it has been uncertain whether the reducing fertility was a direct function of an ageing ovary or whether it reflected either less frequent sexual intercourse or the effects of stress. However, a study[435] of *in vitro* fertilization with donor semen makes clear that there is a moderate direct effect of the age of the woman providing the eggs. This investigation provides a nice example of how it is possible to test whether age *per se* is responsible for age-related changes.

Some women have experienced ambivalence about whether or not to have a child and, by postponing a decision, have been able to enjoy both fulfilling sexual and work lives. For them, the incipient menopause may be an unwelcome reminder that a decision can be postponed no longer. At this point, some women become accidentally pregnant and come to the clinic for support and help in coming to a decision on whether or not to continue with the pregnancy.

The approaching menopause is often an upsetting time, too, for infertile couples still trying to conceive. After perhaps years of undergoing medical and surgical procedures to achieve a pregnancy, the menopause finally slams the door shut and they are forced to accept that it is the end of the road. Many women seek counselling at this time as they ruminate over all their 'wasted' efforts.

Yet, for other women, the menopause is viewed with relief. Sometimes this is because heavy bleeding or painful periods have provided monthly torment. They may be 'glad to get rid of all that', as one woman put it at the clinic. Others who have experienced unwanted childbearing or an unsatisfying sex life may be glad to feel that the menopause provides them with an acceptable reason for saying 'no' to further sexual activities.

As with male sexuality, women's responses to the menopause are to a large extent shaped by their previous psychosexual relationships, their attitudes to themselves and their current situation. For those with high self-esteem in a happy marriage, enjoying a satisfying sexual relationship, the menopause constitutes a relatively easy transition; but for others it is a time of stress and painful readjustment.

Age Trends in Psychiatric Disorder

Many people assume that psychiatric disorders become much more common with increasing age. However, the reality is rather more complicated than that. As Figure 9.3, from Adelstein et al.'s[3] case register data, together with other similar data,[240] shows, the most obvious and striking change is the marked increase in so-called 'organic disorders', of which Alzheimer's dementia is the most common. There is continuing uncertainty on the question of whether or not this constitutes an extreme of 'normal' ageing and, indeed, on what normal ageing involves and is due to.[36,434] Consideration of those very important issues would take us too far from our main theme. However, what is clear is that, although the rate of dementia rises very sharply in

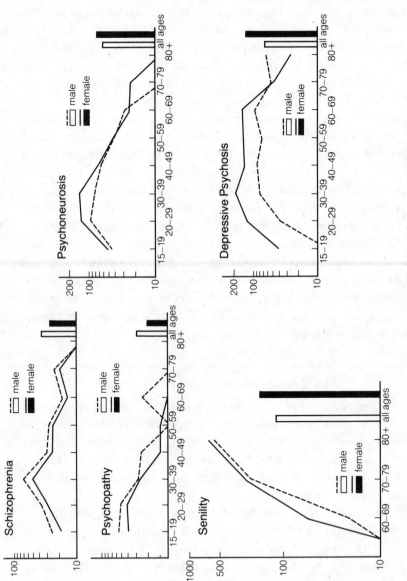

9.3 Age trends in psychiatric disorder: onsets by age and sex. Salford, England (1959–63). Average annual rate per 100,000.

Data from Adelstein et al.[3]

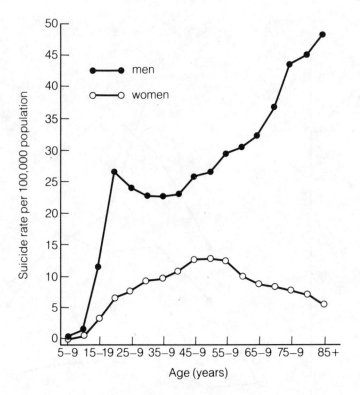

9.4 US suicide rate by age and sex among white people in 1976, based on US Census data.

From Botwinick.[46]

the eighth and ninth decades of life, there are still centenarians who remain intellectually alert and lively. The major mental disorders of earlier age periods, manic-depressive disorder and schizophrenia, diminish somewhat in frequency and the findings on ordinary varieties of depression are somewhat contradictory. Clinic data suggest a slight fall-off in frequency with age, whereas epidemiological general-population data suggest a possible slight increase. However, what is clear is that such changes as do take place are relatively small. The fact that different studies produce somewhat different pictures also suggests that particular circumstances (physical health and

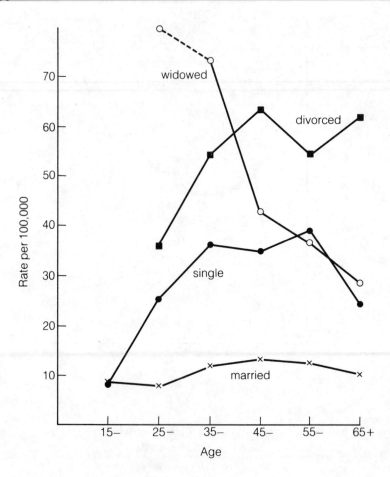

9.5 Males: suicide rates by marital status, Scotland, 1973–83.
From Kreitman.[252]

psychosocial stressors) may be more influential than chronological age *per se*.

It might be thought that suicide rates provide the exception to
this varied picture, in that it is well known that the rates increase
steadily with advancing age. So they do for US and UK white
males but, as Figure 9.4 shows, the age trends vary in startling and
marked fashion across gender and ethnicity groups.[46] Suicide rates
for white males peak in the mid eighties, but for white females
there is a much more gentle curve, peaking at fifty to fifty-five

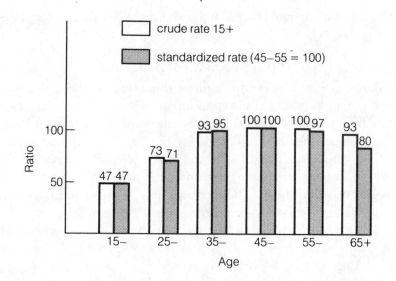

9.6 Male suicide rates: effects of marital status standardization
(Scotland, 1973–83).
From Kreitman.[252]

years of age and falling thereafter. Suicide rates in American
blacks peak in early adulthood rather than in old age and this
tendency is even more marked in native American-Indians. Also,
the suicide rate among old people in the United States has been
declining over the last few decades. It seems most unlikely,
therefore, that chronological age *per se* is the crucial factor.
Rather, we need to consider the possible role of physical illness
and decline, the loss of loved ones, interpersonal restrictions and
generally negative attitudes to what is involved in ageing.

The Scottish data analysed by Kreitman[252] well illustrate this
point. Figure 9.5 shows that the age trends in suicide among
men are dwarfed by the effects of marital status. The suicide
rates among married men are *much* lower than those for single,
widowed or divorced men and do not rise much with age.
When suicide rates are standardized for marital status, the age
trend after the thirties is abolished. The findings dramatically
demonstrate that even marked trends with increasing age may

be a result of changed social circumstances rather than chronological age as such.

Physical and Mental Decline

A key unifying theme throughout this book has been the need to consider key life transitions in terms of both the *new* challenges that they provide and also the ways in which the occurrence and their negotiation are influenced by the *past*. This theme applies to later life as much as it does to childhood and adolescence. At first sight, the claim that a developmental perspective is applicable to gerontology and psychogeriatrics may seem surprising, so let us look a little more closely at the issues.

The generally accepted popular stereotype of the second half of life is clear enough. It is a period of general decline and increasing illness. Mental powers diminish as people become forgetful and less able to deal with cognitive demands in their work and in their everyday life. Eventually, senile dementia is accompanied by a parallel run-down in physical body systems. The bones lose their mineral content, people become progressively stooped and fractured bones become increasingly likely. Similarly, sexual potency is lost and muscle power fades away. Retirement means that people lose their social status and may feel that they have been thrown on the scrap heap. Strokes and heart attacks take an increasing toll, cancer claims its victims and, for those who escape these fates, arthritis brings about progressive crippling. Psychiatric disorder becomes more common and suicide rates reach their peak in old age. Not a pretty picture! But how far is this accurate? To what extent are the changes uniform and inevitable? There is, of course, no doubt that increasing age brings with it a degree of functional decline.[36,46,434] For example, there is a progressive loss of hearing acuity, especially for the high-tone frequencies, as shown in Figure 9.7. It is also the case that some of these changes are likely to have psychological consequences. Thus, hearing impairment tends to foster social isolation.

Nevertheless, the same data show huge individual differences in the age-related patterns of decline and deterioration, and it is clear that a variety of experiences in both early life and old age

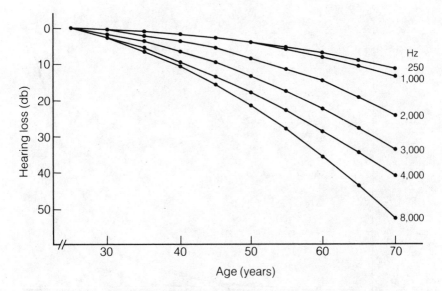

9.7 Hearing loss for different tone pitches in relation to age of men. Age twenty-five years is taken as the base line, i.e. no hearing loss.
From Botwinick.[46]

influence what happens. For example, for a long time, it was thought that osteoporosis was an inevitable aspect of ageing; that weakening and loss of substance in bones was an unavoidable part of the wearing-out process and hence that the only way for the elderly to avoid the huge rise in risk of osteoporotic fractures (see Figure 9.8) was to walk gently with extreme care. As we have noted already, a major influence on the osteoporotic process in postmenopausal women is the falling level of oestrogen (which can be substantially countered by hormone replacement therapy). However, very vigorous exercise also does much to prevent the loss of bone density. This has been shown by experimental studies in animals, and in humans by comparing runners with controls. Lane et al.[261,262] compared 500 runners and a similar number of carefully matched controls aged fifty-four and seventy-six years. Bone density was some 40 per cent greater in the runners and musculoskeletal disabilities showed little increase with age, whereas age changes in the controls were marked. Much the same beneficial effect of exercise is seen also with the

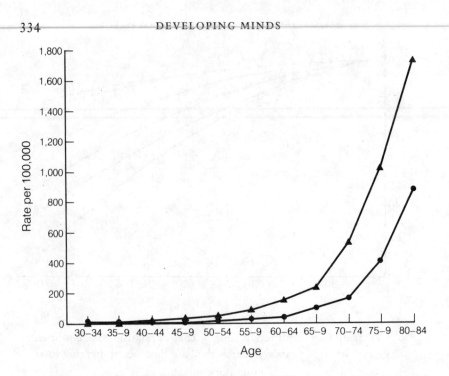

9.8 Age specific hip-fracture incidence rates for white women (●)
and black women (▲) by five-year age intervals. Source:
National Center for Health Statistics, National Hospital Discharge
Survey, 1974–9.
From Brock *et al.*[434]

efficiency of cardiac performance (see Fries[12]). Rather surprisingly, perhaps, what has seemed to be an intrinsic part of ageing,
has turned out to be in part a result of lack of exercise.

What about athletic prowess? Surely it is obvious at the local
sports club, as well as in the international arena, that performances decline with age. Top tournaments are won by the young,
not the old. That is indeed so; nevertheless, longitudinal studies
of top athletes who continue in active training show that their
decline with age is surprisingly slight. Figure 9.9 shows the best
10,000-metre race times for Paavo Nurmi over nearly two
decades. Although his peak performance was at twenty-seven
years of age, it was only about 5 per cent slower ten years later.
Figure 9.10 shows the longest hammer throw each year for the

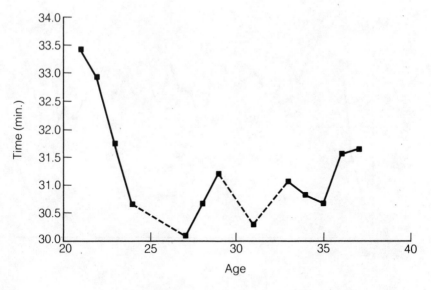

9.9 The best 10,000 m race time each year for Paavo Nurmi
as a function of age.
From Ericsson.[12]

German athlete, Karl Hein. He reached his peak at thirty, but his
throws at fifty-six were still substantially greater than they had
been at twenty-six – good enough to participate in national
championships! Of course, these two men were remarkable
by any standard but, as Ericsson[12] has shown, there is extensive
evidence that vigorous exercise makes a remarkable difference to
the athletic performance of even quite ordinary mortals. It may
be that the greatest benefits are dependent on beginning vigorous
exercise at a particularly early age, as well as continuing it into
the latter half of life, but even starting exercise in mid-life brings
substantial benefits.

In adopting a life-span perspective on the topic of ageing, it is
necessary to consider the possible effects of childhood circumstances, as well as factors operating in adult life. Their importance
is evident in the findings from studies by Barker and his colleagues[42] on the associations between infants' weight at birth
and at one year and the risk of death from ischaemic heart
disease in middle life. Figure 9.11 shows that the largest babies

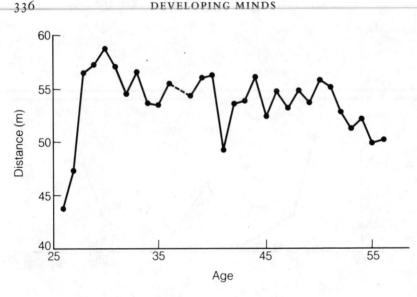

9.10 The longest hammer throw each year for Karl Hein as a function of age.
From Ericsson.[12]

had a risk only half the average (a relative risk of 45, as shown at the top right of the figure), and the smallest babies had a risk three times as great, over 50 per cent above average (a relative risk of 155, as shown at the bottom left of the figure). The finding is particularly striking because, of course, excess weight is a *risk*, not a protective factor, for heart disease in middle age. The implication is that poor nutrition in early life may increase susceptibility to the ill-effects of an over-rich diet in middle age and later. This may provide an explanation for the curious change in disease pattern in the UK over this century. Ischaemic heart disease used to be most frequent in the socially privileged whereas now it is most prevalent in the socially disadvantaged. The rate has risen overall with rising prosperity but the rise has affected the poor most of all. Other research provides numerous other examples of ways in which nutrition, infection and patterns of rearing in early life programme patterns of response in adulthood.[42]

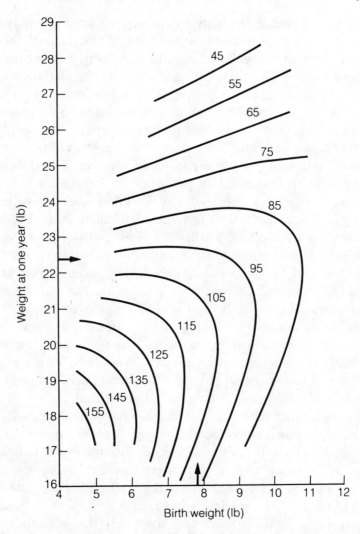

9.11 Relative risk for ischaemic heart disease in men who were breast-fed, according to birth weight and weight at one year. Lines join points with equal risk. Arrows indicate mean weights.
From D.J.P. Barker.[42]

Research findings on changes in cognitive functioning with age bring out some other important points.[12] As with most other biological functions, there is an overall trend for a decline with age but the decrements are quite small until age sixty and then there is huge individual variation. Thus, Schaie[12] found that a third of individuals, initially aged between twenty-five and fifty-three, showed no significant intellectual decrement over a twenty-eight-year period. Also, it was usual, even when there was a loss of skills, for this to apply to some cognitive functions but not others (the particular pattern varying from individual to individual). Declines were most evident in those who started with the highest levels of intellectual performance (suggesting that outstanding performance becomes increasingly less likely with advancing age), but also losses tended to be less in individuals making active, flexible use of their skills. Even the elderly have substantial intellectual reserves that can be called into operation through practice (although their reserves are less than those of young people, as shown by research that uses a 'testing-the-limits' strategy; see Baltes[11,12]). Physical disease is also relevant, with intellectual decline tending to be greater in those with marked hardening of the arteries. However, the development of Alzheimer's dementia makes the most difference; it occurs at a rate of about 5 per cent at seventy, 15 per cent at eighty and 30 per cent at ninety. A distinction needs to be drawn between normal ageing and pathological ageing.[11]

As with other life transitions that we have discussed, we need to consider not just when they occur and the extent of the change involved, but also the manner in which each individual copes with them. It might be thought that, although perhaps the ageing process is more variable and open to influence than used to be believed, nevertheless it is a fact that physical and mental prowess *does* go down with age, and surely that is bound to be quite demoralizing. Of course, no one likes to see their powers go, but there are many different ways of responding. Paul and Margret Baltes[12] quoted the example of the pianist Rubinstein, who in a television interview late in his life described how he dealt with the weaknesses associated with ageing. First, he reduced his repertoire, playing a smaller number of pieces (a selection strategy); second, he practised them more often (an 'optimization' strategy); and third, he slowed down his speed of playing just prior to fast movements, thereby producing a contrast effect that enhanced the impression of speed (the strategy of 'compensation'). By these means, he continued a successful concert career into old age. The Preservation Hall Jazz Band, with Percy and Willy Humphreys continuing acclaimed performances well into their eighties, provides another example.

The Baltes have argued convincingly that successful ageing resides in an individualized use of *'selective optimization with compensation'* as a means of coping with reductions in biological energy or mental reserves. It is obvious that people's skills in employing coping strategies to deal with the changes of old age are likely to have been shaped, in part, by their previous coping experiences and by their adaptational success or failure in dealing with earlier life transitions. It has to be admitted that there is a paucity of data on the extent to which these coping linkages over time exist but their investigation constitutes an important task on the research agenda for studies of ageing.

Before turning to continuities and discontinuities in psychosocial functioning, a further point needs to be made in relation to the goals of preventive gerontology. Fries[12] has emphasized that these should be posed in terms of a *compression of morbidity*, rather than an extension of the life span. Of course, improvements in overall health are likely to mean that people will live longer on average. Nevertheless, there does not seem to be much point in prolonging life if that means increasing dependency, worsening health, a prolonged vegetative existence and spiralling health-care costs. However, that need *not* be the usual consequence. Thus, we know that stopping smoking, increasing exercise and maintaining weight control provide a successful means of reducing cardiac morbidity (sickness). Interestingly, these steps make little difference to the overall mortality. As Fries[12] suggests, the aim needs to be to reduce the period of infirmity before death, rather than postponing death *per se*. Success lies in keeping fit and active until terminal illness comes; in other words reducing the period of infirmity before death. In the past, improvements in health have tended to mean an increasing life expectancy but, in industrialized countries, we are probably nearing the limit in expectancy. However, there remains a long way to go in reducing morbidity.

Psychosocial Functioning

A striking feature of the findings on life expectancy is that females outlive males by some seven years on average.[199] The sex difference in mortality begins before birth (more male foetuses miscarry) and extends throughout life (although the difference narrows in extreme old age). There has been much speculation on whether women die off at a slower rate because their way of life protects them but the evidence makes clear that, although this may play some role,[159] this cannot constitute the main explanation. The same sex difference applies to houseflies[199] and, for humans, it has been shown to apply to monks and nuns all living in a religious community and engaged in teaching or administration.[285] As we noted in Chapter 2, biologically speaking, the male is the weaker sex in most respects. One important consequence is that women are more likely than men to experience the death of their spouse and that the marriage market for widows is more restricted than that for widowers — a point to which we return.

Although a good deal is known about psychosocial functioning in later life and about mental disorders in old age,[36,37,432] there has been rather little systematic research into the continuities and discontinuities between early and late periods of life. However, there are several important long-term longitudinal studies that span the privileged and the disadvantaged. Vaillant[12] has followed a group of male Harvard University students from eighteen to sixty-five years of age. His results showed that the most powerful predictors of a good psychosocial outcome in later life included good physical health, cohesive family relationships in childhood, a lack of psychiatric problems in early adult life, a practical and organizing approach to life's challenges, a degree of self-discipline in coping with problems (meaning that they did *not* turn to tranquillizers or alcohol), exercise in early adult life and a stable marital relationship.

The findings show important patterns of continuity but it is necessary to underline the modest strength of the continuities. The correlation for psychosocial adjustment at age forty-seven and that between fifty and sixty-five was 0.44, but that from age twenty-nine was only 0.29 and that from age twenty-one even lower, at 0.16 (although all these correlations were statistically significant). The two most important features causing a shift from good to poor psychosocial adjustment were the onset of poor physical health or alcoholism. More interpretation is required in inferring the factors associated with improvements in psychosocial adjustment, but perseverance and self-control stood out, together with the capacity to postpone gratification, to see but not exaggerate the bright side of life. Good outcomes tended to be most evident in men thought to be 'dependable' and 'trustworthy' in college, and who tended not to stay at home from work with minor illnesses. As Vaillant put it, 'men who between twenty and forty had appeared disappointingly dull were often enjoying life at sixty-five more than some of the men with a far more colourful youthful adult adjustment' (p. 350).

Clausen's[94] findings from his analysis of the Californian longitudinal studies similarly emphasized the important mediating role of people's coping styles. He examined the association between planful competence as assessed in adolescence (meaning dependability, productivity, self-esteem and the ability to interact positively with others) and various outcomes at ages extending up to fifty-three to sixty-two years. Those individuals who showed high planful competence as teenagers tended to have higher educational attainments (after taking into account IQ and social background), were less likely to have had multiple marriages and, most strikingly, tended to show the greatest stability over time in their personality characteristics. Whatever its source, it seemed that an orientation to plan, in the context of high self-esteem, meant that long-term psychological outcomes tended to be better and that this also led to greater consistency in personality functioning over time. Men who had been in the top third on planful competence in adolescence showed a personality correlation of .56 between late adolescence and age fifty-three to sixty-two, compared with a correlation of .16 for those in the bottom third; the comparable figures for women were .40 and .18. As Clausen[94] put it (p. 836):

The success of early competence in predicting long-term outcomes, including personality continuity, derives both from the greater effectiveness of competent persons and from the greater ability of competent adolescents to make choices that would serve them well in their later careers. Competent men and women were better able to marshal, draw on and maintain social support and to achieve their objectives. They received positive feedback, confirming the persons that they were.

The findings bring us back to the point that we made in Chapters 2 and 3 that, to an important extent, people have an influence on their own development by virtue of their selection and shaping of their environments.

Elder and Liker's[138] analysis of the Californian longitudinal studies showed that mental health measures tended to show less stability over time in women than men. Whether this was because emotional problems in females during the child-bearing years are more subject to influences that are not applicable in old age is uncertain, but this might be the case. However, the findings are important in highlighting a social-class contrast in women's responses to the privations and stresses associated with the Depression. For those women in lower social groups the experiences were associated with *lower* morale and *greater* feelings of helplessness in old age. It seemed that the early hardships were too great and the experiences of not being able to cope satisfactorily led to lasting emotional ill-effects, albeit of only modest degree. By contrast, in the upper social groups, the reverse applied. Their experience of economic deprivation was less devastating and, compared with the non-deprived in the same group, they showed *better* emotional health in old age. It seemed that successful coping gave them inner strengths that enabled them to cope better with later life transitions. As one woman is quoted as saying, 'It's only when you have been through experiences and digested them that you acquire enough sense to know how to deal with them' (p. 267).

It should be remembered, too, that genetic factors also influence the ageing process and the individual variations in the pattern that it shows.[434] It has long been observed that if you wish to live to a ripe old age it is as well to choose long-lived parents! However, this familial association represents environmental, as well as genetic, effects; and genetic factors apply to far more than determination of the length of the life span. The Swedish adoption/twin study, described by Pedersen and Harris,[12] showed that genetic influences accounted for some 17–51 per cent of the variation in psychological characteristics in old age, as at younger age periods. Moreover, it was found that genetic factors were relatively stable over time and, if anything, tended to become slightly stronger in their effects with increasing age. However, we know very little about the relative importance of genetic and environmental influences on successful coping with ageing processes.

Bereavement

As mentioned earlier, the death of a spouse constitutes a powerful stressor. Grief reactions frequently last up to two years, and although only a minority amount to frank psychiatric disorder, there is a significant increase in overt depressive reactions and, indeed, an increased mortality during the six months following the bereavement, at least for men. Research findings show that some 5 per cent of older bereaved spouses become severely depressed and 10–17 per cent depressed to a clinically significant degree.[279] It is a highly stressful experience in most instances but many older surviving spouses are quite resilient and the profound loss may even be associated with positive feelings accompanying a pride in coping, as well as with the negative feelings of grief. Loneliness and problems associated with the tasks of daily living stand out as the major challenges for most people but there is a wide diversity in responses, with a tendency to gradual improvement after the early months. Although the increase in death rate following bereavement tends to be greater in men, depressive reactions are about equally common in both sexes. Perhaps the initial reaction tends to be more marked in men but those in women may last longer.[10] However, there is some difference in the ways in which men and women respond to bereavement; with men more likely to keep themselves busy as a means of diverting themselves from their grief and women more likely to want to talk.[279] Forewarning of the death (through illness) does not make much difference, although perhaps it helps a little; and religious beliefs are not strongly influential; but, (as in younger age groups), social support is helpful.[279] The specific coping mechanisms are not particularly influential, but self-efficacy, control, self-esteem and independence are important, as also are self-help competencies in daily tasks. There is a much greater tendency for people to remarry after divorce than after widowhood and, apart from in the youngest age groups, a marked tendency for men to be more likely than women to remarry. The survival rate of second marriages is not quite as great as that of first marriages but the difference is much less in older age groups.[10,490]

It is apparent that many of these considerations apply at all ages. However, there are some age-related features. Other things being equal, grief reactions tend to be less severe when the death is felt to be expected and normative. Thus, the death of loved ones in old age from natural causes tends to be less stressful than unexpected deaths in early life. This difference probably applies more to effects on the children than it does to those on the spouse because usually other things are not equal. Bereavement is most stressful when the person lacks other close social ties. If the elderly person is part of a close-knit supportive group, he or she is likely to cope better than if isolated and unsupported. Thus, old people are most at risk when their children have grown up and moved away, and when they have lost most of their friends through death or moving house. A related aspect of support concerns the ability to make relationships for emotional support. On the whole, men are less good at this than women, being less likely to have close, intimate, confiding friendships. Perhaps because of this, their initial reaction to bereavement tends to be somewhat more marked.

One aspect of bereavement is the acute effect of *loss*, but an equally important aspect is the chronic *lack* brought about by the death and by the other life changes that may follow the bereavement. In that connection, it is relevant that few of the elderly bereaved remarry. Men's greater tendency to remarry perhaps compensates for their lesser tendency to have confiding friendships.[2] The lack of a spouse may also make it more difficult for the elderly person to cope on their own, with the consequent further readaptation entailed in moving to stay with children or go into an old people's home.

As we have noted repeatedly, *Homo sapiens* is a social animal and the maintenance of social ties is important for mental health. Of course, individuals vary greatly in their emotional reliance on other people; unduly intrusive relationships can sometimes be quite stressful. Nevertheless, it is an unusual person who does not need any form of emotional tie. One consequence of growing old is that an increasing proportion of friends and acquaintances will have died or moved away. Their loss will also constitute a stressor. How much such losses will prove risky for mental health is likely to depend to an important extent on the existence of other social relationships and especially on the ease with which the person is able to develop new friendships. In fairly obvious ways, this is likely to be a function in part of personality characteristics and of social styles developed at an earlier age.

In considering therapeutic interventions to relieve grief reactions, several points are relevant.[339,365] There is immense individual variation in how people respond and there is no one 'healthy' way. There is equally great variation in the time taken to get over a bereavement. Also, the grieving process does not always, and need not, involve any overt depression. Indeed as Wortman and Silver[12] have pointed out, those people who do *not* develop depression in the period immediately following the loss probably have a better long-term prognosis.

Nevertheless, it does seem that some form of grieving 'process' usually occurs, in which the person accepts or comes to terms with the loss. This may involve the recognition of angry feelings about being left unsupported, or of guilt when the relationship before the death has been ambivalent (a risk factor for a more difficult grieving process). So-called 'guided' mourning may be helpful. This may take several different forms but what each approach has in common is that the person confronts the reality of what has happened and the reality of their own feelings. While emotional expression, or catharsis, is *not* in itself helpful, suppression of emotion may be damaging if it means a denial or a failure to cope with the situation. Emotional sharing can be quite supportive and self-help groups, such as Cruse in the UK and various similar widow-to-widow groups in the US, may be beneficial.

Traditionally, most therapeutic attention has focused on the loss but it is crucial to appreciate that the task for the bereaved person, and for the therapist, is to look forward as much as to look back. That is, a new life must be built and it is necessary to consider how best to help the person do that effectively. As Wortman and Silver[12] emphasized, in addition to grieving the loss of a spouse, widows may need to learn a new set of skills – such as managing financial affairs, arranging household maintenance and car repairs, and coping with the job market. Widowers face a comparable set of learning tasks. It is important to note that surveys have shown that most widows judge themselves to have become more competent and independent and only a small minority view the changes entirely in negative terms.

Retirement

Retirement is sometimes seen as a very stressful event leading to a deterioration in mental and physical health. However, the research evidence does *not* support this stereotype.[487] Some individuals react adversely, but most do not, and some experience an improvement in health. It is necessary to consider the various different elements that serve to determine whether the overall effect is positive or negative.[10,36,46]

First, there is the issue of expectability or the normative quality of the timing. It seems that retirement at the usual age is not necessarily stressful whereas forced redundancy usually is traumatic. Second, there is the question of whether the job before retirement was itself stressful, or boring, or excessively demanding; if it was, retirement may bring a welcome relief. Third, retirement may mean a substantial drop in income, with the consequent stresses that this may entail. Fourth, there is a potential loss of status, or of the meaning of life, or of work satisfaction. There is likely to be less stress if the retired person is able to maintain work interests or develop new ones. A somewhat related point is that, for men, retirement often means the loss or weakening of friendships because frequently they have been based in the work environment; this seems to be less true for women.[2] If retirement derives from ill-health, this may add to the strains but, paradoxically, sometimes it may help if it leads to increased social contacts, as can happen.

A further difficulty many couples face in retirement is the need to adjust to the greater amount of time spent together. The need for the wife to include her husband in her activities or relinquish some activities to spend time with him may require a major adaptation. If the marital relationship has not been a rewarding or harmonious one, this may not be satisfactorily resolved. This adjustment has been put traditionally in terms of the man's retirement but, of course, increasingly this is something that involves the woman as much as the man, with added complexities if both partners retire together.

Another change that complicates retirement for some people is a move to a retirement home or community, with the added need to develop new relationships in an unfamiliar setting. It is likely that if such a geographical move involving a break in social ties coincides with retirement, this may increase the likelihood of an adverse response.

As with other transitions, much will depend on the individual's personal resources and coping skills. Retirement may be a universal transition but it does not have a universal meaning. Its effects will be determined in part by its personal significance for the individual, the social context of the event and by the person's past experiences.

Most studies of retirement have been in men but the few on women bring out some relevant points of broader application. O'Rand and Henretta[333] showed that women who entered careers late, and who had children, were less likely than other women to retire early. This seemed to be both because they were more likely to be in jobs with limited earnings and pension options, and because their late start meant that they were out-of-step with career sequences and therefore not eligible for early retirement. The findings show the structural implications of an earlier life transition, namely the choice of job and timing of career entry, and the constraining effect of societal conditions.

The same study showed that women who married in late life, or those who were divorced or separated, or who became widowed in late life, were *more* likely to retire early. Again, the life situation makes an impact through both psychological and financial routes.

This chapter concludes our selective traverse of the life span from infancy to old age. It has been striking that many of the issues regarding transitions and turning-points, continuities and discontinuities, have applied in a broadly comparable fashion across different age periods. In the final chapter we need to round off our account of what is involved in development by returning to the general principles with which we started, in order to note briefly some of the main issues that have emerged from our review of research concepts and findings.

Chapter 10

Epilogue:
Transitions and Turning-points;
Continuities and Discontinuities

Individual Differences

Throughout the book, we have paid particular attention to individual differences, recognizing their universal occurrence and their importance both for an understanding of developmental processes and for applications to clinical issues. Relatively few individuals follow the pattern of age changes predicted from the assessment of averages; variation is an inherent feature of human functioning both in childhood and old age. Yet it is surprising how little attention has been paid to the causes of this variation. Thus, from a biological perspective, the menarche and menopause stand out as obvious life-span landmarks. All females experience these transitions but they do so at very varying ages and we know remarkably little about the causes of this variation. For example, it is commonly assumed by clinicians that stress can bring about a premature menopause, but we lack good evidence on whether or not that is so and, if it is, how great are the effects in different circumstances. If we are to understand what is involved in such life-span transitions it is crucial that we obtain a good appreciation of the factors affecting their *origin* as well as an understanding of their *effects*.

Individuality, however, needs to be considered, not only in terms of developmental pattern and timing, but also with respect to the features that most mark us out as separate personalities. In the past, trait psychologists have tended to focus on characteristics that are pervasive across situations – in terms of features such as sociability or anxiety or activity level. These attributes do indeed tell us something useful about how people function, but there has been a growing awareness that our individuality may be seen most clearly in challenging or stressful situations. Thus, it is no accident that the measurement of attachment insecurity by means of the 'strange situation' relies on experimentally manipulated brief separations to elicit the qualities of attachment behaviour (particularly as evident during reunion). Similarly, the measurement of behavioural inhibition relies on the physiological and behavioural evaluation of children's responses to socially challenging situations. Or again, children's social skills are often most evident when they are introduced into a new social group. Equally, children's thought processes may be tapped most effectively through experimental procedures that use deception or ambiguity – as in the tasks employed to assess 'theory of mind' or conservation skills. The non-experimental equivalents are evident in the appreciation of the value of using new situations (such as starting at a new school or the birth of a sibling) to bring out crucial aspects of psychological individuality. A further facet of the same general point about the stimulus-value of challenge situations is the recognition that *how* children – or adults – deal with, respond to or cope with the challenges may provide a very important reflection of the qualities that will matter most in their development. The current interest in self-esteem, self-efficacy and planful competence as key variables in protective and vulnerability mechanisms is part of this overall shift of paradigm.

Several further points need to be made about how to characterize psychological individuality. First, the usual approach has been to examine developmental trends in terms of specific traits. While that is a worthwhile approach, it has become clear that often it may be more useful to examine patterns or constellations of behaviours. Thus, we drew attention to Magnusson and Bergman's[375,406] finding that the predictive power for adult criminality lay in the *combination* of aggression, hyperactivity, inattention and poor peer relationships. Once individuals with this multi-trait combination had been removed from the group under study, the individual traits no longer predicted adult outcome. Similarly, Kagan and his colleagues[237,238] have shown that it is the combination of psychological and behavioural inhibition that is relatively stable over time. Second, it may be useful to subdivide behaviours by the *timing* of their onset, as well as by their qualities. Thus, unusually early onset conduct disturbance seems more likely to persist into adult life (see Farrington *et al.*[258]); disorders beginning in adolescence have a somewhat different set of correlates from those arising earlier in childhood;[393] and the fears arising at different ages differ in form and may differ in outcome (see Rutter and Garmezy[204]).

Third, psychological features may change their form to some extent over the course of development. For example, we drew attention to the evidence that intelligence in infancy may be best indexed by attentional qualities[45] whereas in later childhood verbal and problem-solving skills are more important. Similarly, conduct disturbance in childhood may be followed in adult life by a range of different disorders, including, but by no means restricted to, antisocial personality disorders (see Robins[331]); continuity may be heterotypic as well as homotypic.

Fourth, neither continuities nor discontinuities between normality and mental disorder should be assumed; both are known to be present. Thus, it is clear that severe mental retardation is discontinuous with the normal range of intelligence (both the causes and the consequences being different; see Rutter and Gould[417]). On the other hand, at least some varieties of conduct disturbance are likely to constitute just extremes of the normal distribution (see Plomin[90,415]). With other conditions there is greater uncertainty. For example, it appears quite likely that Alzheimer's dementia beginning unusually early (in the fifties and sixties) may prove to be genetically distinct from that beginning at the more usual time in advanced old age; however, opinions are divided on whether or not the latter represents an extreme version of the 'normal' cognitive ageing process or something quite different. It is necessary to keep both alternatives in mind when investigating the disorder.

Understanding Causal Mechanisms

At the beginning of the book we set ourselves the goal of understanding the causal mechanisms underlying developmental processes. It is clear that there is quite some way to go before that objective can be attained; nevertheless quite a lot is known, probably rather more than is generally realized. During their undergraduate training, all psychologists have it drummed into them that 'correlation does not mean causation', and often there is an emphasis on laboratory experiments with rats to show the importance of controlled procedures for the testing of laws of learning. The caution about correlations is necessary, to be sure, because it is so easy (and so frequently misleading) to assume that just because some circumstance A is associated with some outcome B, it means that A caused B, when the reality is that both A and B have been brought about by some third variable C which has not been taken into account. Also, the emphasis on the need for experimental designs is well targeted. If we are to understand how any system 'works', it is necessary to manipulate or change some element, in a controlled fashion in order to find out what effect the change brings about.

However, this traditional teaching carries with it the very real danger of creating a false impression that the only way to test causal hypotheses is through controlled experiments in the laboratory. Of course, such experiments are crucial for many purposes and we have made frequent mention of them at various places in our discussion of developmental issues. However, it is obvious that there are severe limitations to the applicability of laboratory experiments for the study of developmental processes, if only because there needs to be a focus on continuities and discontinuities across very long time spans. For obvious reasons, it is not practicable to undertake controlled experiments lasting, say, thirty years! The use of animal studies with species having much shorter life spans provides a partial answer, and one that has been very useful in some connections, but there are numerous difficulties in extrapolating across species with respect to psychological functions that are characteristically human, such as language, or to those where effects are very dependent on social meaning as, for example, with teenage pregnancy.

What, then, is the solution? As we have seen, the answer is to be found in the ingenuity with which researchers have identified 'natural' experiments which create the manipulations that are crucial to the experimental strategy. In essence, the crux of the experimental approach is to be found in its power to separate, or pull apart, variables that ordinarily go together. This separation is then used to manipulate one variable to see if, in effect, it causes the outcome of interest to 'move'. We have seen the force of this 'pulling apart of variables' strategy in the twin and adoptee studies that separate the effects of nature and nurture. The results have been as powerful in demonstrating the effects of environmental influences[77,433] as in testing genetic hypotheses.[414] But there are numerous other examples of the same general strategy. For example, we instanced the use of the one-year age span in school classes to contrast the relative effects on scholastic attainment of chronological age and duration of teaching;[74] the use of changes over time in the age of completing compulsory schooling to test whether schooling or chronological age might be more important in the crime peak seen in adolescence;[148] and the contrasting of parental death and parental divorce to test whether the main risk stemmed from family discord or the loss of a parent.[391]

For many purposes, however, three further elements are needed in order to put causal hypotheses to the test in a rigorous manner. First, longitudinal studies are necessary to ensure that the individuals in the contrasting situations were truly comparable beforehand *and* to determine that the key experience, internal or external, is followed by systematic changes within individuals in the relevant psychological function (see Farrington[406]). It is the existence of such longitudinal data that provides convincing evidence of the psychological risks associated with unemployment.[17,344]

Second, further information is provided by *reversal* of the key experience to see if that is followed by reversal of the psychological effects. Thus, the reduction in emotional disturbance in unemployed individuals when they get a job provides strong confirmatory evidence that the ill-effects do indeed stem from the unemployment.[245] The reversal may also allow a test of competing explanatory mechanisms. Thus, parental divorce is usually associated with a marked drop in living standards for the woman, and hence for the children, as she usually has their care. At one time, some researchers thought that the main psychological risks for the children stemmed from this associated socio-economic disadvantage, rather than from the family tensions and disruption that surround divorce. If that hypothesis was correct, parental remarriage should bring marked psychological benefits for the children because it usually markedly improves the financial situation. The fact that this does *not* usually occur points to the likelihood that the risks derive from some aspect of family relationships rather than economic factors.[205]

Reversal also serves another research purpose. Critics of the view that adverse early life experiences are usually followed by long-lasting psychological sequelae pointed out that most early adversities were followed by later adversities and that the ill-effects were just as likely to stem from the later adversities as from the early ones. Accordingly, it has been important to examine what happens when a seriously adverse early environment is followed by an ordinary, or better than average environment.[396] The results, for example, from the study of children rescued from extreme deprivation,[443] have shown substantial recovery when they are moved into an ordinary environment. However, there are important exceptions. Thus, the Hodges and Tizard[215,216] follow-up of children reared in a residential nursery for the first few years of their life showed persistent differences in the quality of their peer relationships in spite of a radical change in their later environment. In this instance, it seems that there may be a lasting effect associated with some kind of sensitive-period phenomenon.

The third research strategy involves intervention. For example, the suggestion that the osteoporosis that affects so many post-menopausal women is due to the reduction in oestrogens received powerful confirmation from the evidence that it could be prevented or arrested to a very considerable degree by hormone replacement therapy.[360] Similarly, the hypothesis that phonological deficits underlie many reading difficulties was supported by the evidence that relevant teaching focused on rhyme and alliteration fostered reading skills, but made no difference to attainment in mathematics.[177]

These few examples serve as reminders of the rich array of experimental approaches that have been employed in developmental research and which have provided the means for a hardheaded testing of causal hypotheses. The key issue for us to consider here in conclusion is what has been learned from this extensive body of research.

Age as a Non-explanation

The first point is that age does not in itself provide an explanation for development.[407] We need to go on to ask what it is about age that is bringing the observed effects. Life-span researchers in the field of ageing were among the first to highlight this as an issue through their pointing out that cross-sectional studies of intellectual decline with increasing age were open to possible biases stemming from a generation effect in which older people tended to be less well-educated and less healthy. Similarly Kreitman's[252] finding that the rise in suicide with age is largely a function of family circumstances illustrates the importance of disaggregating age effects; as does Farrington's[148] demonstration that the age peak for crime has changed markedly over the years. It is chastening that some of the best examples of the testing of age effects come from research in adult life rather than in childhood. So far as childhood and adolescence are concerned, it is obvious that there are some striking age trends that remain unexplained – for example, the rise in depression during the years of adolescence. The means to test competing hypotheses on the mechanisms underlying this trend – and others – are available, but the necessary research has still to be undertaken.

Of course, this is not to deny the reality of biological maturation in development or of biological decline in ageing. Both are real and important. Nevertheless, chronological age rarely provides a sufficient explanation for changes in psychological functioning. Moreover, neither early nor late in life can maturation and ageing be considered unitary processes. Quite often one particular biological feature may be crucial. For example, this is evident with respect to the role of oestrogens and exercise in osteoporosis. At all ages, too, there is a close ongoing interplay between structure and function, and between psyche and soma. Just as visual input is necessary for the normal development of the visual cortex in infancy, so exercise is necessary for the optimal maintenance of cardiovascular and musculoskeletal function in old age. Testosterone increases sex drive but also sexual activity increases testosterone levels. The popular view portrays development as a process of incremental growth, and old age as one of progressive decline. Neither is wholly correct. Brain development involves a crucial subtractive phase in early life in which loss of neurones serves to fine-tune brain functions. Similarly, children lose some skills as a result of gaining others; and middle life involves an increase in some cognitive functions at the same time as there is some loss in others.

Transitions and Turning-points

One of our starting-points was the recognition that we are social animals and, therefore, that it was likely that social experiences would affect psychological functioning and personal development. Much research, of which we have provided just a few examples, shows that such effects are real and substantial. The 'natural experiments' to which we have referred, together with longitudinal research designs, provide convincing evidence that causal influences do occur and, at least with extreme environmental conditions, do matter. However, several key issues arise with respect to the mechanisms involved. To begin with, there are very few major life transitions that make the same impact on everyone. Thus, it is clear on the one hand that the mere fact of marriage has no appreciable predictive power for psychological functioning. On the other hand, it is equally clear that the experience of marriage can and does have a major effect in some circumstances. The effects stem from *when* a person marries, *whom* a person marries, the *quality* of the relationship formed and whether or not *changes* in social group and life patterns are involved. At first sight, all of that sounds too complicated to give rise to any meaningful generalizations, but that is not the case. Thus, teenage marriage to a psychologically deviant spouse, a discordant marital relationship and continuation in a delinquent social group all carry risks that have been well documented in several different studies.

The second issue is that there is substantial individual variability in people's susceptibility to the effects of major social experiences. In that connection, we need to differentiate between stressful or challenging experiences and experiences that alter life circumstances in other ways. With respect to the former, it is evident that individuals already showing mild problems are those most likely to be affected adversely. This has been shown, for example, in relation to unemployment, pregnancy, economic deprivation, early puberty (in girls) and a discordant marriage. Both genetic background and prior experiences play a role in creating this increased psychological vulnerability. Experiences that alter life circumstances in other ways operate somewhat differently. If the environmental change is for the better, rather than for the worse, the benefits are likely to be greatest in the case of those individuals for whom the change makes most difference. Thus, particularly good experiences at school made little difference to children from ordinary backgrounds but carried substantial benefits for institutional children in the Quinton and Rutter[361] study. The implication was that if children had many good experiences at home, one more at school made little difference, but, for those individuals lacking positive relationships at home good schooling could make a decisive difference. Similarly, Elder[135] found that entering the army created a beneficial turning-point for disadvantaged youths – not because of the joys of army life but because it served to further their education and make it more likely that they would marry someone from a less disadvantaged background.

The third issue concerns the nature of the effects of these major life experiences. Following Elder and Caspi[137] we have pointed to the accentuation principle by which stressful or challenging events mainly accentuate the personal or relationship qualities that were already present. When this is the consequence, the experience can be viewed as a provoking agent for emotional distress or psychological disorder but not a turning-point. However, the second class of major experiences to which we have referred, namely those that alter life circumstances for the better in some way, may reasonably be thought of as turning-points, the operation of which involves a different set of mechanisms from those that apply to stressful life events. Also, of course, although stresses impinge most on the psychologically vulnerable, severe stressors can be damaging to anyone and, when that occurs, they constitute a negative turning-point.

The fourth issue has been rather neglected up to now, but may turn out to be most important, namely what causes differences in people's exposure to psychologically beneficial and risky environments. We have drawn attention to the evidence that, to a very considerable extent, experiences in adult life are predictable on the basis of a person's circumstances and behaviour in childhood. The very high rate of stressful life events that occur to adults who showed conduct disorder as children provides a striking example of this effect. What we do, how we behave and how we relate with other people all serve to select and shape the environments that we experience. However, it is a mistake to see this as just an active process. It is often the *lack* of planning that creates the risk and the presence of planful competence that proves protective in the long-term.[94,361] Moreover, as we have noted, adult environments are shaped, too, by social and economic forces outside our personal control. The effects of racial discrimination and high unemployment attest to the importance of these broader forces.

That issue emphasizes the importance of a developmental perspective in considering how life experiences arise; the same perspective is also needed in considering how the effects are carried forward. The need is not just to determine the degree of persistence of sequelae, or even to chart their patterns and causes, but also to find out how the experience alters a person's *reaction* to some later circumstance. That this happens is well documented in biology. We mentioned the affects of early physical stress on the neuroendocrine system and thereby on later resistance to stress, but there are many others.[42] We are all familiar with the effects of exposure to pathogens in building up immunity to infections and of exposure to allergens in creating sensitization to their ill-effects, and we drew attention to Barker's finding[42] that low weight in infancy increased the risk for coronary artery disease in adult life, possibly because in some way it made individuals more vulnerable to the ill-effects of over-rich diets in middle age. The question is what are the psychological equivalents of these 'steeling' and 'sensitizing' effects, and what are the mechanisms by which they operate? This is the issue on which we know least, and clearly it warrants research investment because such knowledge is needed for the planning of effective policies of prevention and intervention. The evidence so far demonstrates the reality of long-term sequelae from, for example, early family adversity or teenage pregnancy, but we have only a limited understanding of the processes involved.

Continuities and Discontinuities

Finally, we need to summarize a few key issues that apply to continuities and discontinuities. As we have emphasized throughout, there are strong biological reasons for expecting both substantial changes *and* substantial continuities in development across the life span and in ageing processes. To begin with, changes will occur because function is based on structure. The workings of the mind will alter just because maturation of the brain proceeds through childhood and because somatic changes in the brain are part of growing old. But, also, discontinuities will arise because development is influenced by a host of experiences, both internal and external, physical and psychosocial. Thus, it is to be expected that puberty and the climacteric will have some psychological impact. The effect will not be the same in everyone, however, because the impact will be influenced by variations in timing and in social meaning. Similarly, patterns of upbringing, the experience of abuse or neglect, bereavement, unemployment and other major life experiences – positive or negative – will bring their effects. Again, the effects will not be uniform; even with the same experience, there is marked individual variability in susceptibility and in the varied ways in which apparently the same experience impinges on the different children in the same family. Also, however, individuals vary greatly in whether or not they *have* such experiences. Many new experiences occur throughout life, and some key experiences such as marriage or child-rearing do not usually arise until adulthood. As a result, psychological change is to be expected in the middle years as well as during childhood. Moreover, changing psychological functions are to be expected because the effects of many experiences will fade with time if they are not repeated or reinforced, and because some life events constitute turning-points in which a lasting change in the environment may result in an alteration of life trajectory. Such turning-points may arise from an opening up or closing down of opportunities (as with education or work careers), or because there is a major change in social group or social circumstances (as with marriage or divorce). It has to be remembered, too, that genetic factors bring about variations in developmental course as well as stability in behavioural expression.

Continuities, equally, are to be expected, for several rather different reasons. To begin with, for many characteristics, the genetic factors that are influential at one age are the same ones that are operative at later ages, so that genetic continuities will predispose to psychological continuities. But, in addition, it is important that for most people there is considerable continuity in environmental influences and these, too, will foster consistency in psychological functioning. Children born into social disadvantage all too often continue to experience psychosocial adversity when they grow up. Similarly, those reared in privilege tend to go on to experience above average environments during their adult lives. The continuities in environments arise through a variety of mechanisms, but, as we commented, one reason is that people act – or fail to act – in ways that serve to 'select' the environments that they will experience. To an important extent, individual variations in experiences are determined by behavioural tendencies that have developed as a consequence of both genetic and environmental effects operating at an earlier age.

New environments may also serve to promote continuities. As we have noted, stress experiences often seem to accentuate previous personal and interpersonal characteristics and, in so doing, they too will promote psychological consistency over time – the accentuation principle as it has been called. In addition, experiences may have long-lasting effects because they influence the biological substrate, affect underlying organizing psychological structures or lead to overlearned habits, attitudes or styles of interaction or response.

Finally, as our choice of title, 'Developing Minds', indicates, we are all thinking, feeling beings and our thought processes in terms of self-images, self-concepts, internal working models and attributional styles will influence how we deal with life transitions and challenges. Because such thought processes are both, to a degree, self-perpetuating (through habit and practice) and also open to change (through the effects of new and different experiences), they will, in different circumstances, predispose to either continuity or discontinuity.

List of References

1. Achenbach, T.M., and Edelbrock, C.S. (1978) The classification of child psychopathology: a review and analysis of empirical efforts. *Psychological Bulletin, 85*, 1275–1301.
2. Adams, R.G., and Blieszner, R., eds. (1989) *Older adult friendship: structure and process*. London: Sage.
3. Adelstein, A.M., Downham, D.Y., Stein, Z. and Susser, M.W. (1968) The epidemiology of mental illness in an English city. *Social Psychiatry, 3*, 47–59.
4. Ainsworth, M.D., Blehar, M.C., Waters, E., and Wall, S. (1978) *Patterns of attachment*. Hillsdale, NJ: Erlbaum.
5. Alexander, C.S., Ensminger, M.E., Young, J.K., Smith, B.J., Johnson, K.E., and Dolan, L.J. (1989) Early sexual activity among adolescents in small towns and rural areas: race and gender patterns. *Family Planning Perspectives, 21*, 261–6.
6. Asher, S.R., and Coie, J.D., eds. (1990) *Peer rejection in childhood*. New York: Cambridge University Press.
   (Coie and Koeppl; Mize and Ladd; Rubin)
7. Astington, J.W., Harris, P.L., and Olson, D.R., eds. (1988) *Developing theories of mind*. Cambridge: Cambridge University Press.
8. Attie, I., and Brooks-Gunn, J. (1989) Development of eating problems in adolescent girls: a longitudinal study. *Developmental Psychology, 25*, 70–79.
9. Baber, R., Abdalla, H., and Studd, J. (1991) The premature menopause. In J. Studd, ed., *Progress in obstetrics and gynaecology, Vol. 9*. London: Churchill Livingstone.
10. Bahr, S.J., and Peterson, E.T., eds. (1989) *Aging in the family*. Lexington, Mass.: D.C. Heath.
11. Baltes, P.B. (1991) Many faces of human aging. *Psychological Medicine, 21*, 837–54.
12. Baltes, P.B., and Baltes, M.M., eds. (1990) *Successful aging: Perspectives from the behavioral sciences*. Cambridge: Cambridge University Press.

(Baltes and Baltes; Ericsson; Fries; Pedersen and Harris; Schaie; Vaillant; Wortman and Silver)

13. Bancroft, J. (1989) *Human sexuality and its problems* (2nd edn). Edinburgh: Churchill Livingstone.

14. Bancroft, J. and Reinisch, J.M., eds. (1990) *Adolescence and puberty*. New York/Oxford: Oxford University Press.
   (Forrest; Rubin; Rutter)

15. Bandura, A. (1986) *Social foundations of thought and action: a social cognitive theory*. Englewood Cliffs, NJ: Prentice-Hall.

16. Bandura, A. (1989) Regulation of cognitive processes through perceived self-efficacy. *Developmental Psychology, 25,* 729–35.

17. Banks, M.H., and Ullah, P. (1988) *Youth unemployment in the 1980s: its psychological effects*. London: Croom Helm.

18. Barlow, D.H. (1988) *Anxiety and its disorders: the nature and treatment of anxiety and panic*. New York: Guilford Press.

19. Baron-Cohen, S. (1990) Autism: a specific cognitive disorder of 'mind-blindness'. *International Review of Psychiatry, 2,* 79–88.

20. Baron-Cohen, S., Leslie, A.M., and Frith, U. (1985) Does the autistic child have a 'theory of mind'? *Cognition, 21,* 37–46.

21. Bates, E., Bretherton, I., and Snyder, L. (1988) *From first words to grammar: individual differences and dissociable mechanisms*. Cambridge: Cambridge University Press.

22. Bateson, P. (1966) The characteristics and context of imprinting. *Biological Reviews, 41,* 177–211.

23. Bateson, P. (1990) Is imprinting such a special case? *Philosophical Transactions of the Royal Society of London, 329,* 125–31.

24. Baumrind, D. (1971) Current patterns of parental authority. *Developmental Psychology Monograph, 4* (1, Pt 2).

25. Bebbington, P.E., Tennant, C., and Hurry, J. (1991) Adversity in groups with an increased risk of minor affective disorder. *British Journal of Psychiatry, 158,* 33–40.

26. Bell, R.Q. (1968) A reinterpretation of the direction of effects in studies of socialization. *Psychological Review, 75,* 81–95.

27. Bell, R.Q., and Chapman, M. (1986) Child effects in studies using experimental or brief longitudinal approaches to socialization. *Developmental Psychology, 22,* 595–603.

28. Belle, D., ed. (1982) *Lives in stress: women and depression*. Beverly Hills, Calif.: Sage Publications.

29. Belsky, J. (1988) Infant day care and socioemotional development: the United States. *Journal of Child Psychology and Psychiatry, 29,* 397–406.

30. Belsky, J., and Nezworski, T. (1988) *Clinical implications of attachment*. Hillsdale, NJ: Erlbaum.
   (Crittenden; Sroufe)
31. Bengtson, V.L., and Robertson, J.F., eds. (1985) *Grandparenthood*. Beverly Hills, CA: Sage Publications.
32. Berger, M., Yule, W., and Rutter, M. (1975) Attainment and adjustment in two geographical areas. II. The prevalence of specific reading retardation. *British Journal of Psychiatry, 126,* 510–19.
33. Bernstein, B. (1965) A socio-linguistic approach to social learning. In J. Gould, ed. *Penguin survey of the social sciences*. Penguin.
34. Berreuta-Clement, J.R., Schweinart, L.J., Barnett, W.C., Epstein, A.S., and Weikart, D.P. (1984) *Changed lives: the effects of the Perry Pre-school Program on youths through age 19*. Ypsilanti: High Scope.
35. Bertenthal, B.L., and Campos, J.J. (1987) New directions in the study of early experience. *Child Development, 58,* 560–67.
36. Birren, J.E., and Schaie, K.W., eds. (1985) *Handbook of the psychology of the aging* (2nd edn). New York: Van Nostrand Reinholt.
37. Birren, J.E., and Sloane, R.B., eds. (1980) *Handbook of mental health and aging*. Englewood Cliffs, NJ: Prentice Hall.
38. Bishop, D., and Adams, C. (1990) A prospective study of the relationship between specific language impairment, phonological disorders and reading retardation. *Journal of Child Psychology and Psychiatry, 31,* 1027–50.
39. Blacher, J., and Meyers, C.E. (1983) Review of attachment formation and disorder of handicapped children. *American Journal of Mental Deficiency, 87,* 359–71.
40. Block, J. (1971) *Lives through time*. Berkeley: Bancroft Books.
41. Block, J.H., Block, J., and Gjerde, P.F. (1986) The personality of children prior to divorce: a prospective study. *Child Development, 57,* 827–40.
42. Bock, G.R., and Whelan, J., eds. (1991) *The childhood environment and adult disease*. Ciba Foundation Symposium No. 156. Chichester: Wiley.
   (Barker; Blakemore; Caspi; Mott *et al.*; Murray *et al.*; Rutter; Suomi)
43. Bolton, W., and Oatley, K. (1987) A longitudinal study of social support and depression in unemployed men. *Psychological Medicine, 17,* 453–60.
44. Bornstein, M.H., and Lamb, M.E., eds. (1988) *Perceptual, cognitive and linguistic development* (Part II of *Developmental psychology: an advanced textbook*, 2nd edn). Hillsdale, NJ: Erlbaum.
   (Sternberg)

45. Bornstein, M.H., and Sigman, M.D. (1986) Continuity in mental development from infancy. *Child Development*, 57, 251–74.

46. Botwinick, J. (1984) *Aging and behavior: a comprehensive integration of research findings* (3rd edn). New York: Springer.

47. Bower, G.N. (1981) Mood and memory. *American Psychologist*, 36, 129–48.

48. Bowlby, J. (1951) *Maternal care and mental health*. Geneva: World Health Organization.

49. Bowlby, J. (1969) *Attachment and loss*, Vol. 1, *Attachment*. London: Hogarth Press.

50. Bowlby, J. (1973) *Attachment and loss*, Vol. 2, *Separation, anxiety and anger*. London: Hogarth Press.

51. Bowlby, J. (1980) *Attachment and loss*, Vol. 3, *Loss, sadness and depression*. New York: Basic Books.

52. Bowlby, J. (1988) *A secure base: clinical applications of attachment theory*. London: Routledge.

53. Bretherton, I., and Waters, E., eds. (1985) *Growing points of attachment theory and research* (Child Development Monographs, 209, No. 1–2). University of Chicago Press.
(Bretherton and Waters; Main)

54. Brewin, C. (1985) Depression and causal attributions: what is their relation? *Psychological Bulletin*, 98, 297–309.

55. Brim, Jr, O.G., and Kagan, J., eds. (1980) *Constancy and change in human development*. Cambridge, Mass.: Harvard University Press.
(Kagan; Moss and Susman)

56. Briscoe, M. (1982) *Sex differences in psychological wellbeing* (Psychological Medicine Monograph Supplement 1). Cambridge: Cambridge University Press.

57. Bronfenbrenner, U. (1979) *The ecology of human development: experiments by nature and design*. Cambridge, Mass.: Harvard University Press.

58. Brooks-Gunn, J., and Petersen, A.C., eds. (1983) *Girls at puberty: biological and psychosocial perspectives*. New York: Plenum.

59. Brown, C. (1984) *Black and white Britain: the third PSI survey*. London: Heinemann.

60. Brown, G.W., and others (1990) Self-esteem and depression. I. Measurement issues and prediction of onset. II. Social correlates of self-esteem. III. Aetiological issues. IV. Effect on course and recovery. *Social Psychiatry and Psychiatric Epidemiology*, 25, 200–209, 225–34, 235–43, 244–9.

61. Brown, G.W., and Harris, T.O. (1978) *Social origins of depression: a study of psychiatric disorder in women*. London: Tavistock.

62. Brown, G.W., and Harris, T. (1986) Stressor, vulnerability and depression: a question of replication. *Psychological Medicine, 16*, 739–44.

63. Brown, G.W., and Harris, T.O. (1989) *Life events and illness*. New York: Guilford.

64. Brown, G.W., and Wing, J.K. (1962) A comparative clinical and social survey of three mental hospitals. *Sociological Review Monograph, 5*, 145–71.

65. Bruck, M. (1985) The adult functioning of children with specific learning disabilities. In I. Sigel, ed., *Advances in applied developmental psychology*, Vol. 1. Norwood, NJ: Ablex. Pp. 91–120.

66. Bruck, M. (1990) Word-recognition skills of adults with childhood diagnoses of dyslexia. *Developmental Psychology, 26*, 439–54.

67. Brunk, M.A., and Henggeler, S.W. (1984) Child influences on adult controls: an experimental investigation. *Developmental Psychology, 20*, 1074–81.

68. Bryant, P.E. (1974) *Perception and understanding in young children*. London: Methuen.

69. Burgoyne, J., Ormrod, R., and Richards, M. (1987) *Divorce matters*. Harmondsworth, Middx: Penguin.

70. Bury, J.K. (1986) Teenagers and contraception. *British Journal of Family Planning, 12*, 11–14.

71. Buss, A.H., and Plomin, R. (1984) *Temperament: early developing personality traits*. Hillsdale, NJ: Erlbaum.

72. Cadoret, R.J. (1985) Genes, environment and their interaction in the development of psychopathology. In T. Sakai and T. Tsuboi, eds., *Genetic aspects of human behavior*. Tokyo: Igaku-Shoin. Pp. 165–75.

73. Cadoret, R.J., and Cain, C. (1980) Sex differences in predictors of antisocial behavior in adoptees. *Archives of General Psychiatry, 37*, 1171–5.

74. Cahan, S., and Cohen, N. (1989) Age versus schooling effects on intelligence development. *Child Development, 60*, 1239–49.

75. Cairns, R. (1983) The emergence of developmental psychology. In W. Kessen, ed., *History, theory, and methods* (Vol. 1 of *Mussen's handbook of child psychology*, 14th edn). New York: Wiley. Pp. 41–102.

76. Caplan, M.Z., and Hay, D.F. (1989) Preschoolers' responses to peers; distress and beliefs about bystander intervention. *Journal of Child Psychology and Psychiatry, 30*, 231–42.

77. Capron, C., and Duyme, M. (1989) Assessment of effects of socio-economic status on IQ in a full cross-fostering study. *Nature, 340,* 552–4.

78. Carmichael, L. (1926) The development of behavior in vertebrates experimentally removed from the influence of external stimulation. *Psychological Review, 33,* 51–8.

79. Carraher, T.N., Carraher, D.W., and Schliemann, A.D. (1985) Mathematics in the streets and in the schools. *British Journal of Developmental Psychology, 3,* 21–9.

80. Caspi, A., and Herbener, E.S. (1990) Continuity and change: assortative marriage and the consistency of personality in adulthood. *Journal of Personality and Social Psychology, 58,* 250–8.

81. Caspi, A., Lynam, D., Moffitt, T.E., and Silva, P.A. (in press) Unraveling girls' delinquency: biological, dispositional and contextual contributions to adolescent misbehavior. *Developmental Psychology.*

82. Caspi, A., and Moffitt, T.E. (1991) Individual differences are accentuated during periods of social change: the sample case of girls at puberty. *Journal of Personality and Social Psychology, 61,* 157–68.

83. Chase-Lansdale, P.L., and Hetherington, E.M. (1990) The impact of divorce on life-span development: short and long term effects. In P.B. Baltes, D.L. Featherman and R.M. Lerner, eds. *Life-span development and behavior,* Vol. 10. Hillsdale, NJ: Erlbaum. Pp. 107–50.

84. Cherry, N. (1984a) Nervous strain, anxiety and symptoms amongst 32-year-old men at work in Britain. *Journal of Occupational Psychology, 57,* 95–105.

85. Cherry, N. (1984b) Women and work stress: evidence from the 1946 birth cohort. *Ergonomics, 27,* 519–26.

86. Chomsky, N. (1959) A review of B.F. Skinner's *Verbal Behaviour. Language, 35,* 26–58.

87. Christenson, C.V., and Gagnon, J.H. (1965) Sexual behavior in a group of older women. *Journal of Gerontology, 20,* 351–6.

88. Christensen, H.T. (1960) Cultural relativism and premarital sex norms. *American Sociological Review, 25,* 31–9.

89. Cicchetti, D., and Carlson, V., eds. (1989) *Child maltreatment.* New York: Cambridge University Press.
   (Rutter)

90. Cicchetti, D., and Toth, S.L., eds. (1991) *Internalizing and externalizing expressions of dysfunction: Rochester Symposium on Developmental Psychopathology,* Vol. 2. Hillsdale, NJ: Erlbaum.

(Campbell; Plomin *et al.*)

91. Clark, D.M. (1990) Cognitive therapy for depression and anxiety: is it better than drug treatment in the long-term? In K. Hawton and P. Cowen, eds., *Dilemmas and difficulties in the management of psychiatric patients*. Oxford: Oxford University Press.

92. Clark, D.M., and Ehlers, A. (in press) Empirical status of the cognitive theory and treatment of panic disorder. *Applied and Preventative Psychology*.

93. Clarke, A.M., and Clarke, A.D.B. (1976) *Early experience: myth and evidence*. London: Open Books.
(Koluchova)

94. Clausen, J.S. (1991) Adolescent competence and the shaping of the life course. *American Journal of Sociology*, *96*, 805–42.

95. Clemens, A.W., and Axelson, L.J. (1985) The not-so-empty nest: the return of the fledgling adult. *Family Relations*, *34*, 259–64.

96. Coie, J.D., and Kupersmidt, J.B. (1983) A behavioral analysis of emerging social status in boys' groups. *Child Development*, *54*, 1400–1416.

97. Coleman, J.C., and Hendry, L. (1990) *The nature of adolescence* (2nd edn). London: Routledge.

98. Condry, J., and Condry, S. (1976) Sex differences: a study of the eye of the beholder. *Child Development*, *47*, 812–19.

99. Conel, J.L. (1939 and 1951) *The postnatal development of the human cerebral cortex*, Vol.1, *The cortex of the newborn* and Vol. 4, *The cortex of the six-month infant*. Cambridge, Mass.: Harvard University Press.

100. Connolly, K.J., and Prechtl, H.F.R., eds. (1981) *Maturation and development: Biological and psychological perspectives* (Clinics in Developmental Medicine No. 77/78). London: SIMP/Heinemann; Philadelphia: Lippincott.

101. Costa, Jr., P.T., and McCrae, R.R. (1980) Still stable after all these years: personality as a key to some issues in adulthood and old age. In P.B. Baltes and O.G. Brim, Jr, eds., *Life-span development and behavior*, Vol. 3. New York: Academic Press. Pp. 65–102.

102. Cowan, P.A. and Hetherington, E.M., eds. (1991) *Family transitions*. Hillsdale, NJ: Erlbaum.
(Cowan *et al.*; Hetherington)

103. Craighead, L.W., Stunkard, A.J., and O'Brien, R.M. (1981) Behavior therapy and pharmacotherapy for obesity. *Archives of General Psychiatry*, *38*, 763–8.

104. Crain, S.M., Bornstein, M.B., and Peterson, E.R. (1968) Maturation of cultured embryonic CNS tissues during chronic exposure

to agents which prevent bioelectric activity. *Brain Research*, *8*, 363–72.

105. Cromer, R.E. (1991) *Language and thought in normal and handicapped children*. Oxford: Basil Blackwell.

106. Crowe, R.R. (1974) An adoption study of antisocial personality. *Archives of General Psychiatry*, *31*, 785–91.

107. Cummings, E.M. (1987) Coping with background anger in early childhood. *Child Development*, *58*, 976–84.

108. Cummings, E.M., Vogel, D., Cummings, J.S., and El-Sheikh, M. (1989) Children's responses to different forms of expressions of anger between adults. *Child Development*, *60*, 1392–1404.

109. Cummings, J.S., Pellegrini, D.S., Notarius, C.I., and Cummings, E.M. (1989) Children's responses to angry adult behavior as a function of marital distress and history of inter-parent hostility. *Child Development*, *60*, 1035–43.

110. Daniel, W.W. (1968) *Racial discrimination in England*. Harmondsworth, Middx: Penguin.

111. Daniels, P. and Weingarten, K. (1982) *The timing of parenthood in adult lives*. New York: Norton.

112. David, H.P. Dytrych, Z., Matejcek, Z. and Schüller, V., eds. (1988) *Born unwanted: Developmental effects of denied abortion*. Prague: Avicenum, Szechoslovak Medical Press.

113. Davies, D.L. (1956) Psychiatric illness in those engaged to be married. *British Journal of Preventive and Social Medicine*, *10*, 123–7.

114. Demetriou, A. (Special Issue Editor) (1987) The Neo-Piagetian theories of cognitive development: toward an integration. *International Journal of Psychology*, *22*, nos. 5/6.
(Case; Desen and de Ribaupierre; Pascual-Leone; Siegler)

115. Deykin, E.Y., and MacMahon, B. (1979) The incidence of seizures among children with autistic symptoms. *American Journal of Psychiatry*, *136*, 1310–12.

116. DiLalla, L.F., and Gottesman, I.I. (1989) Heterogeneity of causes for delinquency and criminality: lifespan perspectives. *Development and Psychopathology*, *1*, 339–49.

117. Dodge, K.A. (1980) Social cognition and children's aggressive behavior. *Child Development*, *51*, 1386–99.

118. Dodge, K.A. (1983) Behavioral antecedents of peer social status. *Child Development*, *54*, 1386–99.

119. Dodge, K.A., Bates, J.E., and Pettit, G.S. (1990) Mechanisms in the cycle of violence. *Science*, *250*, 1678–83.

120. Dodge, K.A., Coie, J.D., Pettit, G.S. and Price, J.M. (1990) Peer

status and aggression in boys' groups: developmental and contextual analyses. *Child Development*, *61*, 1289–1309.

121. Dodge, K.A., and Frame, C.L. (1982) Social cognitive biases and deficits in aggressive boys. *Child Development*, *53*, 620–35.

122. Dodge, K.A., Pettit, G.S., McClaskey, C.L., and Brown, M. (1986) Social competence in children. *Monographs of the Society for Research in Child Development*, *51* (2, Serial No. 213).

123. Donaldson, M. (1978) *Children's Minds*. London: Fontana/Collins.

124. Downey, G., and Walker, E. (1989) Social cognition and adjustment in children at risk for psychopathology. *Developmental Psychology*, *25*, 835–45.

125. Duck, S., ed. (1988) *Handbook of personal relationships: theory, research and interventions*. Chichester/New York: Wiley.
    (Dunn; Gotlib and Hooley; Hendrick; Nash)

126. Dunn, J. (1988) *The beginnings of social understanding*. Oxford: Blackwell.

127. Dunn, J., and Kendrick, C. (1982) *Siblings: love, envy and understanding*. Cambridge, Mass: Harvard University Press; London: Grant McIntyre.

128. Dunn, J., and Plomin, R. (1990) *Separate lives: why siblings are so different*. New York: Basic Books. ·

129. Dunn, J., Stocker, C., and Plomin, R. (1990) Nonshared experiences within the family: correlates of behavioral problems in middle childhood. *Development and Psychopathology*, *2*, 113–26.

130. Earls, F. (1987) Sex differences in psychiatric disorders: origins and developmental influences. *Psychiatric Developments*, *1*, 1–23.

131. Eisen, M., Zellman, G.L., and McAlister, A.L. (1990) Evaluating the impact of a theory-based sexuality and contraceptive education program. *Family Planning Perspectives*, *22*, 261–71.

132. Eisenberg, N., and Strayer, J., eds. (1987) *Empathy and its development*. Cambridge: Cambridge University Press.

133. Elder, Jr, G.H. (1979) Historical change in life patterns and personality. In P. Baltes and O.G. Brim, eds. *Life span development and behavior*, Vol.2. New York: Academic Press.

134. Elder, Jr, G.H., ed. (1985) *Life course dynamics: trajectories and transitions, 1968–1980*. Ithaca: Cornell University Press.
    (Elder; Hofferth; Moen)

135. Elder, Jr, G.H. (1986) Military times and turning points in men's lives. *Developmental Psychology*, *22*, 233–45.

136. Elder, Jr, G.H., and Caspi, A. (1988) Human development and

social change: an emerging perspective on the life course. In N. Bolger, A. Caspi, G. Downey and M. Moorehouse, eds., *Persons in context: developmental processes.* Cambridge: Cambridge University Press. Pp. 77–113.

137. Elder, Jr, G.H., and Caspi, A. (in press) Studying lives in a changing society: sociological and personological explorations. In A.I. Rabin, R.A. Zucker, S. Frank and R.A. Emmons, eds., *Studying persons and lives.* New York: Springer.

138. Elder, Jr, G.H. and Liker, J.K. (1990) Hard times in women's lives: historical influences across 40 years. *American Journal of Sociology, 88,* 241–69.

139. Elder, Jr, G.H., Liker, J., and Cross, C. (1984) Parent–child behavior in the Great Depression: life course and intergenerational influences. In P.B. Baltes and O.G. Brim, Jr, eds., *Life-span development and behavior. Vol. 6.* New York: Academic Press. Pp. 109–58.

140. Elliott, D.S., and Voss, H.L. (1974) *Delinquency and dropout.* Toronto and London: Lexington Books.

141. Ellis, P.L. (1982) Empathy: a factor in antisocial behavior. *Journal of Abnormal Child Psychology, 10,* 123–34.

142. Emery, R.E. (1988) *Marriage, divorce, and children's adjustment.* Newbury Park: Sage Publications.

143. Entwisle, S., and Doering, S. (1981) *The first birth: a family turning point.* Baltimore, Maryland: Johns Hopkins University Press.

144. Epstein, E., and Guttman, R. (1984) Mate selection in man: evidence, theory, and outcome. *Social Biology, 31,* 243–78.

145. Erikson, E. (1968) *Identity, youth, and crisis.* New York: Norton.

146. Eysenck, H.J. (1977) *Crime and personality.* London: Paladin.

147. Fagot, B.I., and Kavanagh, K. (1990) The prediction of antisocial behavior from avoidant attachment classifications. *Child Development, 61,* 864–73.

148. Farrington, D.P. (1986) Age and crime. In M. Tonry and N. Morris, eds., *Crime and justice,* Vol.7. Chicago: Chicago University Press.

149. Farrington, D.P., Gallagher, B., Morley, L., St Ledger, R.J. and West, D.J. (1988) A 24 year follow-up of men from vulnerable backgrounds. In R.L. Jenkins and W.K. Brown, eds., *The abandonment of delinquent behavior: promoting the turnaround.* New York: Praeger. Pp. 115–73.

150. Farrington, D.P., Gallagher, B., Morley, L., St Ledger, R.J., and West, D.J. (1986) Unemployment, school leaving and crime. *British Journal of Criminology, 26,* 335–56.

151. Feldman, S.S., and Elliott, G.R., eds. (1990) *At the threshold: the developing adolescent.* Cambridge, Mass.: Harvard University Press. (Harter; Henderson and Dweck; Keating; Modell and Goodman; Savin-Williams and Berndt; Steinberg)

152. Field, T. (1989) Maternal depression effects on infant interaction and attachment behavior. In D. Cicchetti, ed., *The emergence of a discipline: Rochester Symposium on Developmental Psychopathology, Vol.1.* Hillsdale, NJ: Erlbaum. Pp. 139–63.

153. Fischer, K.W., and Lamborn, S.D. (1989) Mechanisms of variation in developmental levels: cognitive and emotional transitions during adolescence. In A. de Ribaupierre, ed., *Transition mechanisms in child development: the longitudinal perspective.* Cambridge: Cambridge University Press. Pp. 33–67.

154. Flavell, J.H. (1982) Structures, stages and sequences in cognitive development. In W.A. Collins, ed., *The concept of development* (Minnesota symposia on child psychology, Vol. 15). Hillsdale, NJ: Erlbaum. Pp. 1–28.

155. Flavell, J.H., and Markman, E.M., eds. (1983) *Cognitive development* (Vol. 3 of *Mussen's handbook of child psychology,* 4th edn). New York: Wiley. (Brown *et al.*; Gelman and Baillargeon; Maratsos; Sternberg and Powell)

156. Floeter, M.K., Greenough, W.T. (1979) Cerebellar plasticity: modification of Purkinje cell structure by differential rearing in monkeys. *Science, 206,* 227–9.

157. Floud, J.E., Halsey, A.H., and Martin, F.M. (1956) *Social class and educational opportunity.* London: Heinemann.

158. Fox, N.A., Kimmerly, N.L., and Schafer, W.D. (1991) Attachment to mother/attachment to father: a meta-analysis. *Child Development, 62,* 210–25.

159. Frankenhaeuser, M., Lundberg, U., and Chesney, M. (1991) *Women, work, and health: stress and opportunities.* New York: Plenum. (Frankenhaeuser; Sarrel; Wortman *et al.*)

160. Franz, C.E., McClelland, D.C., and Weinberger, T. (1991) Childhood antecedents of conventional social accomplishment in midlife adults: a 36 year prospective study. *Journal of Personality and Social Psychology, 60,* 586–95.

161. Freud, A. (1958) Adolescence. *Psychoanalytic Study of the Child, 13,* 255–78.

162. Frith, U. (1989) *Autism: explaining the enigma.* Oxford: Basil Blackwell.

163. Furstenberg, Jr, F.F., Brooks-Gunn, S., and Morgan, S.P. (1987) *Adolescent mothers in later life*. Cambridge: Cambridge University Press.

163a. Furstenberg, Jr, F.F., Morgan, S.P., Moore, K.A., and Peterson, J.L. (1987) Race differences in the timing of adolescent intercourse. *American Sociological Review*, *52*, 511–18.

164. Galaburda, A.M., Corsiglia, J., Rosen, G.D., and Sherman, G.F. (1987) Planum temporale asymmetry, reappraisal since Geschwind and Levitsky. *Neuropsychologia*, *25*, 853–68.

165. Garber, H.L. (1988) *The Milwaukee Project: preventing mental retardation in children at risk*. Washington, DC: American Association on Mental Retardation.

166. Garber, J., and Dodge, K., eds. (1991) *The development of emotion and dysregulation*. Cambridge: Cambridge University Press.
(Rutter)

167. Gargiulo, J., Attie, I., Brooks-Gunn, J., and Warren, M.P. (1987) Girls' dating behavior as a function of social context and maturation. *Developmental Psychology*, *23*, 730–37.

168. Garrison, W., and Earls, F. (1987) *Temperament and child psychopathology*. Newbury Park: Sage.

169. Gerstel, N., Riessman, C.K., and Rosenfield, S. (1985) Explaining the symptomatology of separated and divorced women and men: the role of material conditions and social networks. *Social Forces*, *64*, 84–101.

170. Gibbons, M. (1984) Psychiatric sequelae of induced abortion: a review. *Journal of the Royal College of General Practitioners*, *34*, Appendix 2D.

171. Gittelman, R., ed. (1986) *Anxiety disorders of childhood*. Chichester: Wiley.

172. Goldberg, S. (1983) Parent–infant bonding: another look. *Child Development*, *54*, 1355–82.

173. Goldstein, M.J. (1988) The family and psychopathology. *Annual Review of Psychology*, *39*, 283–99.

174. Goodenough, F.L. (1931) *Anger in young children*. Minneapolis: University of Minnesota Press.

175. Goodman, R. (1990) Technical note: are perinatal complications causes or consequences of autism? *Journal of Child Psychology and Psychiatry*, *31*, 809–12.

176. Goswami, U. (1991) Analogical reasoning: what develops? a review of research and theory. *Child Development*, *62*, 1–22.

177. Goswami, U., and Bryant, P. (1990) *Phonological skills and learning to read*. Hove, East Sussex: Erlbaum.

178. Gottlieb, G. (1981) Roles of early experience in species-specific perceptual development. In R.N. Aslin, J.R. Alberts and M.R. Petersen, eds., *Development of perception*, Vol. 1. New York: Academic Press.

179. Gove, W.B. (1978) Sex differences in mental illness among adult men and women: an evaluation of four questions raised regarding the evidence on the higher rates of women. *Social Science and Medicine, 12B*, 187–98.

180. Gove, W.B., and Tudor, J.F. (1973) Adult sex roles and mental illness. *American Journal of Sociology, 78*, 812–35.

181. Grantham-McGregor, S.M. (1990) Malnutrition and mental function. In R. Suskind, ed., *The malnourished child*. New York: Raven Press. Pp. 197–212.

182. Gray, G., Smith, A., and Rutter, M. (1980) School attendance and the first year of employment. In L. Hersov and I. Berg, eds., *Out of school: modern perspectives in truancy and school refusal*. Chichester: Wiley. Pp. 343–70.

183. Gray, J.A. (1987) *The psychology of fear and stress*. Cambridge: Cambridge University Press.

184. Greenberg, M.T., Cicchetti, D., and Cummings, E.M., eds. (1990) *Attachment in the preschool years: theory, research, and intervention*. Chicago: University of Chicago Press.

185. Greene, J.G. (1984) *The social and psychological origins of the climacteric syndrome*. Aldershot, Hants: Gower.

186. Greenough, W.T., Black, J.E., and Wallace, C.S. (1987) Experience and brain development. *Child Development, 58*, 539–59.

187. Gregory, R.L. (1966) *Eye and brain: the psychology of seeing*. London: World University Library.

188. Gregory, R.L., and Wallace, J.G. (1963) Recovery from early blindness: a case study (Experimental Psychology Monograph, No. 2), Cambridge: Heffer.

189. Grych, J.H., and Fincham, F.D. (1990) Marital conflict and children's adjustment: a cognitive-contextual framework. *Psychological Bulletin, 108*, 267–90.

190. Haith, M.M., and Campos, J.J., eds., *Infancy and developmental psychobiology* (Vol. 2, *Mussen's handbook of child psychology*, 4th edn). New York: Wiley.
(Aslin *et al.*; Banks and Salapatek; Campos *et al.*; Clarke-Stewart and Fein; Golman-Rakic *et al.*; Gottlieb; Hinde; Scarr and Kidd)

191. Hahn, M.E., Hewitt, J.K., Henderson, N.D., and Benno, R., eds. (1990) *Developmental behavior genetics: neural, biometrical, and evolutionary approaches*. New York: Oxford University Press. (Matheny)

192. Hall, V.C., and Kaye, D.B. (1978) The necessity of logical necessity in Piaget's theory. In L.S. Siegel and C.J. Brainerd, eds., *Alternatives to Piaget*. New York: Academic Press. Pp. 153–67.

193. Hareven, T.K., ed. (1978) *Transitions: the family and the life course in historical perspective*. New York: Academic Press.

194. Harlow, H.F., and Harlow, M.K. (1969) Effects of various mother–infant relationships on rhesus monkey behaviours. In B.M. Foss, ed., *Determinants of infant behaviour*, Vol. 4. London: Methuen.

195. Harrington, R., Fudge, H., Rutter, M., Pickles, A., and Hill, J. (1990) Adult outcome of childhood and adolescent depression. I. Psychiatric status. *Archives of General Psyciatry*, *47*, 465–73. II. Links with antisocial disorder. *Journal of the American Academy of Child and Adolescent Psychiatry*, *30*, 434–9.

196. Harris, P.L. (1989) *Children and emotion: the development of psychological understanding*. Oxford: Basil Blackwell.

197. Haspels, A.A., and Musaph, H., eds. (1979) *Psychosomatics in perimenopause*. Lancaster: MTP Press. (Severne)

198. Hayes, C.D., ed. (1987) *Risking the future: adolescent sexuality, pregnancy, and childbearing* Vol. 1. Washington, DC: National Academy Press.

199. Hazzard, W.R. (1986) Biological basis of the sex differential in longevity. *Journal of the American Geriatrics Society*, *34*, 455–71.

200. Held, R. (1965) Plasticity in sensory-motor systems. *Scientific American*, *213*, 84–94.

201. Hennessey, J.W., and Levine, S. (1979) Stress, arousal, and the pituitary-adrenal system: a psychoendocrine hypothesis. In J.M. Sprague and A.N. Epstein, eds., *Progress in psychobiology and physiological psychology*. New York: Academic Press.

202. Hermelin, B., and O'Connor, N. (1970) *Psychological experiments with autistic children*. Oxford: Pergamon.

203. Hermelin, B., and O'Connor, N. (1986) Idiot savant calendrical calculators: rules and regularities. *Psychological Medicine*, *16*, 885–93.

204. Hetherington, E.M., ed. (1983) *Socialization, personality and social development*, Vol. 4 of *Mussen's handbook of child development* (4th edn). New York: Wiley.

(Campos *et al.*; Dweck and Elliot; Harter; Hartup; Huston; Maccoby and Martin; Parke and Slaby; Radke-Yarrow *et al.*; Rutter and Garmezy)

205. Hetherington, E.M. (1989) Coping with family transitions: winners, losers, and survivors. *Child Development, 60,* 1–14.

206. Hetherington, E.M., Cox, M., and Cox, R. (1979) Play and social interaction in children following divorce. *Journal of Social Issues, 35,* 26–49.

207. Higgins, E.T., Ruble, D.N., and Hartup, W.W., eds. (1983) *Social cognition and social development: a sociocultural perspective.* New York: Cambridge University Press.

208. Hinde, R.A. (1979) *Towards understanding relationships.* London: Academic Press.

209. Hinde, R.A. (1990) The Croonian lecture: the interdependence of the behavioural sciences. *Philosophical Transactions of the Royal Society, 329,* 217–27.

210. Hinde, R.A., and Bateson, P. (1985) Discontinuities versus continuities in behavioral development and the neglect of process. *International Journal of Behavioural Development, 7,* 129–43.

211. Hinde, R., and Stevenson-Hinde, J. (1988) *Relationships within families: mutual influences.* Oxford: Clarendon Press.
(Caspi and Elder; Dunn, Engfer, Radke-Yarrow *et al.*; Rutter; Sroufe and Fleeson; Stevenson-Hinde)

212. Hirschi, T., and Gottfredson, M. (1983) Age and the explanation of crime. *American Journal of Sociology, 89,* 552–84.

213. Hobson, R.P. (1989) Beyond cognition: a theory of autism. In G. Dawson, ed. *Autism: nature, diagnosis, and treatment.* New York: Guilford Press. Pp. 22–48.

214. Hobson, R.P., Ouston, J., and Lee, A. (1988) What's in a face? The case of autism. *British Journal of Psychology, 79,* 441–53.

215. Hodges, J., and Tizard, B. (1989a) IQ and behavioural adjustment of ex-institutional adolescents. *Journal of Child Psychology and Psychiatry, 30,* 53–75.

216. Hodges, J., and Tizard, B. (1989b) Social and family relationships of ex-institutional adolescents. *Journal of Child Psychology and Psychiatry, 30,* 77–97.

217. Hofferth, S.L., and Hayes, C.D., eds. (1987) *Risking the future: adolescent sexuality, pregnancy, and childbearing,* Vol. 2. Working papers and statistical appendixes. Washington, DC: National Academy Press.

218. Hofferth, S.L., Kahn, J.R., and Baldwin, W. (1987) Premarital sexual activity among US teenage women over the past three decades. *Family Planning Perspectives*, *19*, 46–53.

219. Hook, E.B. (1981) Rates of chromosome abnormalities at different maternal ages. *Obstetrics and Gynecology*, *58*, 282–5.

220. Horn, G. (1990) Neural bases of recognition memory investigated through an analysis of imprinting. *Philosophical Transactions of the Royal Society*, *329*, 133–42.

221. Horn, J.L., and Cattell, R.B. (1966) Refinement and test of the theory of fluid and crystallized general intelligences. *Journal of Educational Psychology*, *57*, 253–70.

222. Houts, A.C., Shutty, M.S., and Emery, R. (1985) The impact of children on adults. In B.B. Lahey and A.E. Kazdin, eds., *Advances in clinical child psychology*, Vol. 8. New York: Plenum. Pp. 267–307.

223. Hull, M.G.R., Glazener, C.M.A., Kelly, N.J., Conway, D.I., Foster, P.A., Hinton, R.A., Coulson, C., Lambert, P.A., Watt, E.M., and Desai, K.M. (1985) Population study of causes, treatment, and outcome of infertility. *British Medical Journal*, *291*, 1693–7.

224. Hunt, J.McV. (1979) Psychological development: early experience. *Annual Review of Psychology*, *30*, 103–43.

225. Hyde, J.S. (1984) How large are gender differences in aggression? A developmental meta-analysis. *Journal of Psychology*, *20*, 722–36.

226. Istvan, J. (1986) Stress, anxiety, and birth outcomes: a critical review of the evidence. *Psychological Bulletin*, *100*, 331–48.

227. Izard, C.E., Hembree, E.A., and Huebner, R.R. (1987) Infants' emotional expressions to acute pain: developmental change and stability of individual differences. *Developmental Psychology*, *23*, 105–13.

228. Jahoda, M. (1981) Work, employment, and unemployment: values, theories, and approaches in social research. *American Psychologist*, *36*, 184–91.

229. Jenkins, J.M., and Smith, M.A. (1990) Factors protecting children living in disharmonious homes: maternal reports. *Journal of the American Academy of Child and Adolescent Psychiatry*, *29*, 60–69.

230. Jensen, A.R. (1969) How much can we boost IQ and scholastic achievement? *Harvard Educational Review*, *39*, 1–123.

231. Joffe, J.M. (1969) *Prenatal determinants of behaviour.* Oxford: Pergamon.

232. John, E.R. (1989) *Neurometric evaluation of brain function in normal*

and learning disabled children. Ann Arbor: University of Michigan Press.

233. Johnson-Laird, P.N., Legrenzi, P., and Legrenzi, M.S. (1972) Reasoning and a sense of reality. *British Journal of Psychology, 63,* 395–400.

234. Kagan, J. (1981) *The second year: the emergence of self-awareness.* Cambridge, Mass.: Harvard University Press.

235. Kagan, J. (1982) The emergence of self. *Journal of Child Psychology and Psychiatry, 23,* 363–81.

236. Kagan, J. (1984) *The nature of the child.* New York: Basic Books.

237. Kagan, J., and Klein, R.E. (1973) Cross-cultural perspectives on early development. *American Psychologist, 28,* 947–61.

238. Kagan, J., Reznick, J.S., and Gibbons, J. (1989) Inhibited and uninhibited types of children. *Child Development, 60,* 838–45.

239. Kagan, J., Reznick, J.S., and Snidman, N. (1987) The physiology and psychology of behavioral inhibition in children. *Child Development, 58,* 1459–73.

240. Kay, D.W.K., and Bergmann, K. (1980) Epidemiology of mental disorders among the aged in the community. In J.E. Birren and R.B. Sloane, eds., *Handbook of mental health and aging.* Englewood Cliffs, NJ: Prentice-Hall. Pp. 34–56.

241. Kelvin, P. (1969) *The bases of social behaviour: an approach in terms of order and value.* London: Holt, Rinehart and Winston.

242. Kendell, R.E., Chalmers, J.C., and Platz, C. (1987) Epidemiology of puerperal psychoses. *British Journal of Psychiatry. 150,* 662–73.

243. Kendell, R.E., Mackenzie, W.E., West, C., McGuire, R.J., and Cox, J.L. (1984) Day-to-day mood changes after childbirth: further data. *British Journal of Psychiatry, 145,* 620–25.

244. Kessler, R.C., Turner, J.B., and House, J.S. (1987) Intervening processes in the relationship between unemployment and health. *Psychological Medicine, 17,* 949–61.

245. Kessler, R.C., Turner, J.B., and House, J.S. (1989) Unemployment, reemployment, and emotional functioning in a community sample. *American Sociological Review, 54,* 648–57.

246. King, N.J., Hamilton, D.I., and Ollendick, T.H. (1988) *Children's phobias: a behavioural perspective.* Chichester: Wiley.

247. Klinnert, M.D., Campos, J.J., Sorce, J.F., Emde, R.N., and Svejda, M. (1983) Emotions as behavior regulators: social referencing in infancy. In R. Plutchik and H. Kellerman, eds., *Emotion: theory, research, and experience,* Vol. 2, *Emotions in early development.* New York: Academic Press.

248. Klinteberg, B., and Magnusson, D. (1989) Aggressiveness and hyperactive behaviour as related to adrenaline excretion. *European Journal of Personality*, *3*, 81–93.

249. Knight, B.J., Osborn, S.G., and West, D.J. (1977) Early marriage and criminal tendency in males. *British Journal of Criminology*, *17*, 348–60.

250. Kolvin, I., Miller, F.J.W., Scott, D.M., Gatzanis, S.R.M., and Fleeting, M. (1990) *Continuities of deprivation? The Newcastle 1000 family study*. Aldershot, Hants: Avebury.

251. Kohnstamm, G.A., Bates, J.E., and Rothbart, M.K., eds. (1989) *Temperament in childhood*. Chichester: Wiley.
(Higley and Suomi; Kagan; Rutter)

252. Kreitman, N. (1988) Suicide, age and marital status. *Psychological Medicine*, *18*, 121–8.

253. Kuh, D., and Maclean, M. (1990) Women's childhood experience of parental separation and their subsequent health and socio-economic status in childhood. *Journal of Biosocial Science*, *22*, 121–35.

254. Kumar, R., and Robson, K. (1978) Previous induced abortion and antenatal depression in primiparae: preliminary report of a survey of mental health in pregnancy. *Psychological Medicine*, *8*, 711–15.

255. Kupersmidt, J.B., and Coie, J.D. (1990) Preadolescent peer status, aggression, and school adjustment as predictors of externalizing problems in adolescence. *Child Development*, *61*, 1350–62.

256. LaFreniere, P.J., and Sroufe, L.A. (1985) Profiles of peer competence in the preschool: interrelations between measures, influences of social ecology and relation to attachment history. *Developmental Psychology*, *24*, 56–69.

257. Lahey, B.B., and Kazdin, A.E., eds. (1988) *Advances in clinical child psychology*, Vol. 11. New York: Plenum.
(Coie *et al*; Loeber; Patzer and Burke; Silverman *et al*.)

258. Lahey, B.B., and Kazdin, A.E., eds. (1990) *Advances in clinical child psychology*, Vol. 13. New York: Plenum.
(Barden; Farrington *et al*.; Hammen)

259. Lamb, M., ed. (1986) *The father's role: applied perspectives*. New York: Wiley.
(Harrington; Russell)

260. Lamb, M.E., Thompson, R.A., Gardner, W., Charnov, E.L., and Estes, D. (1984) Security of infantile attachment as assessed in the 'Strange Situation'; its study and biological interpretation. *Behavior and Brain Sciences*, *7*, 127–47.

261. Lane, N.E., Bloch, D.A., Jones, H.H., Marshall, W.H., Wood,

P.D., and Fries, J.F. (1986) Long-distance running, bone density, and osteoarthritis. *Journal of the American Medical Association*, *255*, 1147–51.

262. Lane, N.E., Bloch, D.A., Wood, P.D., and Fries, J.F. (1987) Aging, long-distance running and the development of musculoskeletal disability: a controlled study. *American Journal of Medicine*, *82*, 722–80.

263. Langdell, T. (1978) Recognition of faces: an approach to the study of autism. *Journal of Child Psychology and Psychiatry*, *19*, 255–68.

264. Lazar, I., and Darlington, R. (1982) Lasting effects of early education: a report from the consortium for longitudinal studies. *Monographs of the Society for Research in Child Development*, Serial No. 195, *47*, 2–3.

265. Lee, C.L., and Bates, J.E. (1985) Mother–child interaction at age two years and perceived difficult temperament. *Child Development*, *56*, 1314–25.

266. Leff, J.P., and Vaughn, C. (1985) *Expressed emotion in families: its significance for mental illness*. New York: Guilford Press.

267. Lerner, R.M., and Hultsch, D.F. (1983) *Human development: a life-span perspective*. New York: McGraw-Hill.

268. Leslie, A.M., and Frith, U. (1990) Prospects for a cognitive neuropsychology of autism: Hobson's choice. *Psychological Review*, *97*, 122–31.

269. Levinson, D.J. in collaboration with Darrow, C.N., Klein, E.B., Levinson, M.H., and McKee, B. (1978) *The seasons of a man's life*. New York: Knopf.

270. Levy, D.M. (1943) *Maternal over-protection*. New York: Columbia University Press.

271. Levy, D.M. (1960) The infants' earliest memory of inoculation: a contribution to public health procedures. *Journal of Genetic Psychology*, *96*, 3–46.

272. Levy, V. (1987) The maternity blues in post-partum and post-operative women. *British Journal of Psychiatry*, *151*, 368–72.

273. Lewis, M., and Miller, S.M., eds., *Handbook of developmental psychopathology*. New York: Plenum.
(Eron and Huesmann; Plomin *et al.*; Smetana)

274. Lewis, S.N.C., and Cooper, C.L. (1988) The transition to parenthood in dual-earner couples. *Psychological Medicine*, *18*, 477–86.

275. Lippitt, R., and White, R.K. (1958) An experimental study of leadership and group life. In E.E. Maccoby, T.M. Newcomb and

E.L. Hartley, eds., *Readings in social psychology*. New York: Holt. Pp. 496–511.

276. Locurto, C. (1990) The malleability of IQ as judged from adoption studies. *Intelligence, 14*, 275–90.

277. Loeber, R., and Stouthamer-Loeber, M. (1986) Family factors as correlates and predictors of juvenile conduct problems and delinquency. In M. Tonry and N. Morris, eds., *Crime and Justice*, Vol. 7. Chicago: University of Chicago Press. Pp. 219–37.

278. Loeber, R., Tremblay, R.E., Gagnon, C., and Charlebois, P. (1989) Continuity and desistance in disruptive boys' early fighting at school. *Development and Psychopathology, 1*, 39–50.

279. Lund, D.A., ed. (1989) *Older bereaved spouses: research with practical applications*. New York: Hemisphere Publishing.

280. Lütkenhaus, P., Grossmann, K.E., and Grossmann, K. (1985) Infant–mother attachment at twelve months and style of interaction with a stranger at the age of three years. *Child Development, 56*, 1538–42.

281. Maccoby, E.E. (1988) Gender as a social category. *Developmental Psychology, 24*, 755–65.

282. Maccoby, E.E. (1990) Gender and relationships: a developmental account. *American Psychologist, 45*, 513–20.

283. Maccoby, E.E., and Jacklin, C.N. (1974) *The psychology of sex differences*. Stanford, Calif.: Stanford University Press.

284. Maccoby, E.E., and Jacklin, C.N. (1980) Sex differences in aggression: a rejoinder and reprise. *Child Development, 51*, 964–80.

285. Madigan, F.C. (1957) Are sex mortality differentials biologically caused? *Milbank Memorial Fund Quarterly, 35*, 202–23.

286. Magnusson, D., Stattin, H., and Allen, V.L. (1986) Differential maturation among girls and its relation to social adjustment: a longitudinal perspective. In P.B. Baltes, D. Featherman and R.M. Lerner, eds., *Life-span development*, Vol. 7. New York: Academic Press. Pp. 136–72.

287. Mansfield, P., and Collard, J. (1988) *The beginning of the rest of your life? A portrait of newly-wed marriage*. London: Macmillan.

288. Marks, I.M. (1987) *Fears, phobias and rituals; panic, anxiety and their disorders*. Oxford: Oxford University Press.

289. Marks, I.M. (1987) The development of normal fear: a review. *Journal of Child Psychology and Psychiatry, 28*, 667–97.

290. Markson, E.Q., ed. (1983) *Older women: issues and prospects*. Lexington, Mass.: D.C. Heath.

291. Martin, T.C., and Bumpass, L.L. (1989) Recent trends in marital disruption. *Demography*, 26, 37–51.

292. Mascie-Taylor, C.G.N., and Vandenberg, S.G. (1988) Assortative mating for IQ and personality due to propinquity and personal preference. *Behavior Genetics*, 18, 339–45.

293. Masten, A.S., and Garmezy, N. (1985) Risk, vulnerability, and protective factors in developmental psychopathology. In B.B. Lahey and A.E. Kazdin, eds., *Advances in clinical child psychology*, Vol. 8. New York: Plenum. Pp. 1–52.

294. Masters, W.H., and Johnson, V. (1966) *Human sexual response*. London: Churchill.

295. Matheny, A.P. (1989) Children's behavioral inhibition over age and across situations: genetic similarity for a trait during change. *Journal of Personality*, 57, 215–35.

296. Maughan, B., and Rutter, M. (1987) Pupil progress in selective and non-selective schools. *Schools Organization*, 7, 50–68.

297. McCall, R.B. (1979) The development of intellectual functioning in infancy and the prediction of later IQ. In J.D. Osofsky, ed., *Handbook of infant development*. New York: Wiley. Pp. 707–41.

298. McCartney, K., and Galanopoulos, A. (1988) Child care and attachment: a new frontier the second time around. *American Journal of Orthopsychiatry*, 58, 16–24.

299. McCluskey, K.A., Killarney, J., and Papini, D.R. (1983) Adolescent pregnancy and parenthood: implications for development. In E.J. Callahan and K.A. McCluskey, eds., *Life-span developmental psychology: nonnormative life events*. New York: Academic Press. Pp. 69–113.

300. McGuffin, P., and Katz, R. (1986) Nature, nurture and affective disorder. In J.F.W. Deakin, ed., *The biology of depression*. London: Royal College of Psychiatrists/Gaskell Press. Pp. 26–52.

301. McGuffin, P., and Murray, R., eds. (1991) *The new genetics of mental illness*. London: Butterworth-Heinemann.
(Goodman; Jones and Murray; Rutter)

302. McRae, Jr. J.A., and Brody, C.J. (1989) The differential importance of marital experiences for the well-being of women and men: a research note. *Social Science Research*, 18, 237–48.

303. Mednick, S.A., Moffitt, T.E., and Stack, S.A., eds. (1987) *The causes of crime: new biological approaches*. Cambridge: Cambridge University Press.
(Cloninger and Gottesman; Rubin; Venables)

304. Merikangas, K.R. (1982) Assortative mating for psychiatric dis-

orders and psychological traits. *Archives of General Psychiatry, 39,* 1173–80.

305. Michaels, G.Y., and Goldberg, W.A. (1988) *The transition to parenthood: Current theory and research.* Cambridge: Cambridge University Press.

306. Moffitt, T.E. (1990) The neuropsychology of juvenile delinquency: a critical review. In M. Tonry and N. Morris, eds., *Crime and Justice,* Vol. 12. Chicago: University of Chicago Press. Pp. 99–169.

307. Moffitt, T.E., Caspi, A., Belsky, J., and Silva, P.A. (1992) Childhood experience and the onset of menarche: a test of a sociobiological model. *Child Development, 63,* 47–58.

308. Moffitt, T.E., and Henry, B. (1989) Neuropsychological assessment and external functions in self-reported delinquents. *Development and Psychopathy,* I, 105–18.

309. Moore, K.A. (1989, 1990) *Facts at a glance.* Washington, DC: Child Trends Inc.

310. Moos, R.H., ed. (1986) *Coping with life crises: an integrated approach.* New York: Plenum.
(Robinson and Thurnher)

311. Morris, R.G., Morris, L.W., and Britton, P.G. (1988) Factors affecting the emotional wellbeing of the caregivers of dementia sufferers. *British Journal of Psychiatry, 153,* 147–56.

312. Mortimore, P., Sammons, P., Stoll, L., Lewis, D., and Ecob, R. (1988) *School Matters: the junior years.* Wells, Somerset: Open Books.

313. Moss, P., Bolland, G., Foxman, R., and Owen, C. (1986) Marital relations during the transition to parenthood. *Journal of Reproductive and Infant Psychology, 4,* 57–67.

314. Murphy, G.E., Simons, A.D., Wetzel, R.D., and Lustman, P.J. (1984) Cognitive theory and pharmacotherapy: single and together in the treatment of depression. *Archives of General Psychiatry, 41,* 33–41.

315. Myers, B.J. (1984) Mother–infant bonding: the status of this critical period hypothesis. *Developmental Review, 4,* 240–74.

316. Neugarten, B.L., and Weinstein, K.K. (1964) The changing American grandparent. *Journal of Marriage and the Family, 26,* 199–204.

317. Northcott, J. (1991) *Britain in 2010.* London: Policy Studies Institute.

318. Nottelman, E.D. (1987) Competence and self-esteem during transi-

tion from childhood to adolescence. *Developmental Psychology, 23,* 441–50.

319. Novak, M.A. (1979) Social recovery of monkeys isolated for the first year of life. II. Long term assessment. *Developmental Psychology, 15,* 50–61.

320. Novak, M.A., and Harlow, H.F. (1975) Social recovery of monkeys isolated for the first year of life: I. Rehabilitation and therapy. *Developmental Psychology, 11,* 453–65.

321. O'Connor, N., and Hermelin, B. (1963) *Speech and thought in severe subnormality.* Oxford: Pergamon Press.

322. O'Connor, N., and Hermelin, B. (1987) *Seeing and hearing and space and time.* London: Academic Press.

323. O'Connor, N., and Hermelin, B. (1987) Visual and graphic abilities of the idiot-savant artist. *Psychological Medicine, 17,* 79–90.

324. O'Connor, N., and Hermelin, B. (1991) Talents and preoccupations in idiot savants. *Psychological Medicine, 21,* 959–64.

325. Offer, D. (1969) *The psychological world of the teenager.* London: Basic Books.

326. *Office of Population and Census Statistics Monitor* (1990), 30 October, Pp. 13–14.

327. Ollendick, T.H., Yule, W., and Ollier, K. (1991) Fears in British children and their relationship to manifest anxiety and depression. *Journal of Child Psychology and Psychiatry, 32,* 321–31.

328. Olson, R.K., Wise, B.W., and Rack, J.P. (1989) Dyslexia: deficits, genetic aetiology, and computer-based remediation. *Irish Journal of Psychology, 10,* 494–508.

329. Olweus, D. (1979) Stability of aggressive reaction patterns in males: a review. *Psychological Bulletin, 86,* 852–75.

330. Olweus, D. (1989) Bully/victim problems among schoolchildren: basic facts and effects of a school based intervention program. In D. Petler and K.H. Rubin, eds., *The development and treatment of childhood aggression.* Hillsdale, NJ: Erlbaum.

331. Olweus, D., Block, J., and Radke-Yarrow, M., eds. (1986) *Development of antisocial and prosocial behavior: research, theories, and issues.* Orlando: Academic Press. (Farrington; Maccoby; Pulkkinen; Robins)

332. Oppel, W.C., Harper, P.A., and Rider, R.V. (1968) The age of attaining bladder control. *Pediatrics, 42,* 614–26.

333. O'Rand, A.M., and Henretta, J.C. (1982) Delayed career entry, industrial pension structure, and early retirement in a cohort of unmarried women. *American Sociological Review, 47,* 365–73.

334. Osofsky, J.D., ed. (1987) *Handbook of infant development* (2nd edn). New York: Wiley.
(Bretherton; Field; Izard; Lewis; Rovee-Collier; Rutter)

335. Ozonoff, S., Pennington, B.F. and Rogers, S.J. (1991) Executive function deficits in high-functioning autistic individuals: relationship to theory of mind. *Journal of Child Psychology and Psychiatry, 32*, 1081–1105.

336. Ozonoff, S., Rogers, S.J., and Pennington, B.F. (1991) Asperger's syndrome: evidence of an empirical distinction from high-functioning autism. *Journal of Child Psychology and Psychiatry, 32*, 1107–1122.

337. Parke, R.D., ed. *Review of child development research*, Vol.7, *The family*. Chicago: University of Chicago Press.
(Elder, Osofsky and Osofsky)

338. Parker, J.G., and Asher, S.R. (1987) Peer relations and later personal adjustment: are low-accepted children at risk? *Psychological Bulletin, 102*, 357–89.

339. Parkes, C.M. (1986) *Bereavement: studies of grief in adult life* (2nd edn). Harmondsworth, Middx.: Penguin.

340. Parkes, C.M., and Stevenson-Hinde, J., eds. (1982) *The place of attachment in human behavior*. London: Tavistock.
(Hinde)

341. Parkes, C.M., Stevenson-Hinde, J., and Marris, P., eds. (1991) *Attachment across the life cycle*. London: Tavistock/Routledge.
(Hinde)

342. Parten, M.B. (1932) Social participation among preschool children. *Journal of Abnormal and Social Psychology, 27*, 243–69.

343. Patterson, G.R. (1982) *Coercive family process*. Eugene, Oregon: Castalia.

344. Patton, W., and Noller, P. (1984) Unemployment and youth: a longitudinal study. *Australian Journal of Psychology, 36*, 399–413.

345. Pedersen, E., Faucher, T.A., and Eaton, W.W. (1978) A new perspective on the effects of first grade teachers on children's subsequent adult status. *Harvard Education Review, 48*, 1–31.

346. Perlmutter, M., ed. (1986) *Cognitive perspectives on children's social and behavioral development* (Minnesota symposia on child psychology, Vol. 18). Hillsdale, NJ: Erlbaum.
(Dodge; Rubin and Krasnor)

347. Petersen, A.C. (1988) Adolescent development. *Annual Review of Psychology, 39*, 583–607.

348. Phillips, K., Fulker, D.W., Carey, G., and Nagoshi, C.T. (1988)

Direct marital assortment for cognitive and personality variables. *Behavior Genetics, 18*, 347–56.

349. Pickles, A., and Rutter, M. (1991) Statistical and conceptual models of 'turning points' in developmental processes. In D.Magnusson, L.R.Bergman, G.Rudinger and B. Törestad, eds., *Problems and methods in longitudinal research: stability and change*. Cambridge: Cambridge University Press.

350. Plomin, R. (1986) *Development, genetics and psychology*. Hillsdale, NJ: Erlbaum.

351. Plomin, R., and Bergeman, C.S. (1991) The nature of nurture: genetic influence on 'environmental' measures. *Behavioral and Brain Sciences, 14*, 373–86.

352. Plomin, R., and Daniels, D. (1987) Why are children in the same family so different from one another? *Behavioral and Brain Sciences, 10*, 1–15.

353. Plomin, R., DeFries, J.C., and Fulker, D.W. (1988) *Nature and nurture during infancy and early childhood*. New York: Cambridge University Press.

354. Pope, A.W., Bierman, K.L., and Mumma, G.H. (1989) Relations between hyperactive and aggressive behavior and peer relations at three elementary grade levels. *Journal of Abnormal Child Psychology, 17*, 253–67.

355. Porter, R., O'Connor, M., and Whelan, J., eds. (1984) *Mechanisms of alcohol damage in utero* (Ciba Symposium No. 105). London: Pitman.

356. Post, R.M., and Goodwin, F.K. (1973) Simulated behaviour states: an approach to specificity in psychobiological research. *British Journal of Psychiatry, 7*, 237–54.

357. Puig-Antich, J., Lukens, E., Davies, M., Goetz, D., Brennan-Quattrock, J., and Todak, G. (1985) Psychosocial functioning in prepubertal major depressive disorder. I. Interpersonal relationships during the depressive episode. II. Interpersonal relationships after sustained recovery from affective episode. *Archives of General Psychiatry, 42*, 500–507; 511–17.

358. Putallaz, M., and Gottman, J. (1983) Social relationship problems in children: an approach to intervention. In B.B. Lahey and A.E. Kazdin, eds. *Advances in clinical child psychology*, Vol. 6. New York: Plenum. Pp. 1–43.

359. Quay, H.C. (1965) Psychopathic personality as pathological stimulation-seeking. *American Journal of Psychiatry, 122*, 180–83.

360. Quigley, M.E.T., Martin, P.L., Burnier, A.M., and Brooks, P.

(1987) Estrogen therapy arrests bone loss in elderly women. *American Journal of Obstetrics and Gynecology, 156,* 1516–23.

361. Quinton, D., and Rutter, M. (1988) *Parenting breakdown: the making and breaking of inter-generational links.* Aldershot: Avebury.

362. Rachman, D. (1977) The conditioning theory of fear acquisition: a critical examination. *Behaviour Research and Therapy, 15,* 375–89.

363. Rajecki, D.W., Lamb, M.E., and Obmascher, P. (1978) Toward a theory of infantile attachment: a comparative review of aspects of the social bond. *Behavioral and Brain Sciences, 1,* 417–36.

364. Ramey, C.T., and Campbell, F.A. (1984) Preventive education for high risk children: cognitive consequences of the Carolina Abercedarian project. *American Journal of Mental Deficiency, 88,* 515–24.

365. Raphael, B. (1984) *The anatomy of bereavement: a handbook for the caring professions.* London: Hutchinson.

366. Reinisch, J.M., and Sanders, S.A. (1987) Behavioral influences of prenatal hormones. In C.B. Nemeroff and P.T. Loosen, eds., *Handbook of clinical psychoneuroendocrinology.* New York: Guilford Press. Pp. 431–48.

367. Remschmidt, H., and Schmidt, M., eds. (1990) *Anorexia nervosa.* Toronto: Hogrefe & Huber.

368. Richards, M.H., Boxer, A.M., Petersen, A.C., and Albrecht, R. (1990) Relation of weight to body image in pubertal girls and boys from two communities. *Developmental Psychology, 26,* 313–21.

369. Richman, N., Stevenson, J., and Graham, P. (1982) *Pre-school to school: a behavioural study.* London: Academic Press.

370. Riessman, C.K., and Gerstel, N. (1985) Marital dissolution and health: do males or females have greater risk? *Social Science and Medicine, 20,* 627–35.

371. Robertson, J., and Robertson, J. (1971) Young children in brief separation: a fresh look. *Psychoanalytic Study of the Child, 26,* 264–315.

372. Robins, L. (1966) *Deviant children grown up.* Baltimore: Williams & Wilkins.

373. Robins, L. (1978) Sturdy childhood predictors of adult antisocial behaviour: replications from longitudinal studies. *Psychological Medicine, 8,* 611–22.

374. Robins, L., and Hill, S.Y. (1966) Assessing the contributions of family structure, class and peer groups to juvenile delinquency. *Journal of Crime, Law, Criminology and Police Science, 57,* 325–34.

375. Robins, L., and Rutter, M., eds. (1990) *Straight and devious pathways from childhood to adulthood.* New York: Cambridge University Press.
(Cadoret *et al.*; Cannon *et al.*; Erlenmeyer-Kimling *et al.*; Farrington *et al.*; LeBlanc; Magnusson and Bergman; Robins and McEvoy; Rodgers; Rutter *et al.*)

376. Rolf, J., Masten, A., Cicchetti, D., Nuechterlein, K., and Weintraub, S., eds. (1990) *Risk and protective factors in the development of psychopathology.* New York: Cambridge University Press.
(Kagan *et al.*; Rutter)

377. Rollins, B.C., and Feldman, H. (1970) Marital satisfaction over the family life cycle. *Journal of Marriage and the Family, 32,* 20–28.

378. Rose, R.M. (1980) Endocrine responses to stressful psychological events. *Psychiatric Clinics of North America, 2,* 53–71.

379. Rose, R.M., Holaday, J.W., and Bernstein, I.S. (1971) Plasma testosterone, dominance risk and aggressive behaviour in male rhesus monkeys. *Nature, 231,* 366–8.

380. Rosenbaum, J.F., Biederman, J., Gersten, M., Hirschfeld, D.R., Menninger, S.R., Herman, J.B., Kagan, J., Reznick, S., and Snidman, N. (1988) Behavioral inhibition in children of parents with panic disorder and agoraphobia. A controlled study. *Archives of General Psychiatry, 45,* 463–70.

381. Rosenzweig, M.R., and Bennett, E.L. (1977) Effects of environmental enrichment or impoverishment on learning and on brain values in rodents. In A. Oliviero, ed., *Genetics, environment and intelligence.* Amsterdam: North-Holland. Pp.163–96.

382. Rowe, D.C., Rodgers, J.L., and Meseck-Busheys, S. (1989) An 'epidemic' model of sexual intercourse prevalences for black and white adolescents. *Social Biology, 36,* 127–45.

383. Rubin, K., and Asendorpf, J.S. (in press) *Shyness, inhibition and social withdrawal.* Chicago: University of Chicago Press.
(Engfer)

384. Rubin, L.B. (1979) *Women of a certain age: the midlife search for self.* New York: Harper & Row.

385. Ruble, D.N., and Brooks-Gunn, J. (1982) The experience of menarche. *Child Development, 53,* 1557–66.

386. Rumsey, J.M., and Hamburger, S.D (1990) Neuropsychological divergence of high-level autism and severe dyslexia. *Journal of Autism and Developmental Disorders, 20,* 155–68.

387. Runciman, W.G. (1972) *Relative deprivation and social justice.* Harmondsworth, Middx: Penguin Books.

388. Ruppenthal, G.C., Arling, G.L., Harlow, H.F., Sackett, G.P., and Suomi, S.J. (1976) A 10-year perspective of motherless-mother monkey behavior. *Journal of Abnormal Psychology, 85*, 341–9.

389. Rutter, M. (1966) *Children of sick parents: an environmental and psychiatric study* (Maudsley Monograph No. 16). Oxford: Oxford University Press.

390. Rutter, M. (1970) Autistic children: Infancy to adulthood. *Seminars in Psychiatry, 2*, 435–50.

391. Rutter, M. (1971) Parent–child separation: psychological effects on the children. *Journal of Child Psychology and Psychiatry, 12*, 233–60.

392. Rutter, M. (1976) Family, area and school influences in the genesis of conduct disorders. In L. Hersov, M. Berger and D. Shaffer, eds., *Aggression and antisocial behavior in childhood and adolescence* (Journal of Child Psychology and Psychiatry, Book Series No.1). Oxford: Pergamon.

393. Rutter, M. (1979) *Changing youth in a changing society: patterns of adolescent development and disorder.* London: Nuffield Provincial Hospitals Trust (1980, Cambridge, Mass: Harvard Press).

394. Rutter, M. (1979) Protective factors in children's responses to stress and disadvantage. In M.W. Kent and J.E. Rolf, eds., *Primary prevention of psychopathology*, Vol.3, *Social competence in children.* Hanover, New Hampshire: University Press of New England. Pp. 49–74.

395. Rutter, M., ed., (1980) *Scientific foundations of developmental psychiatry.* London: Heinemann Medical.
(Howlin; Madge and Tizard; Rutter on 'Attachment'.)

396. Rutter, M. (1981) *Maternal deprivation reassessed* (2nd edn). Harmondsworth, Middx: Penguin Books.

397. Rutter, M. (1981) Epidemiological/longitudinal strategies and causal research in child psychiatry. *Journal of the American Academy of Child Psychiatry, 20*, 513–44.

398. Rutter, M. (1982) Prevention of children's psychosocial disorders. *Pediatrics, 70*, 883–94.

399. Rutter, M. (1983) School effects on pupil progress: research findings and policy implications. *Child Development, 54*, 1–29.

400. Rutter, M., ed. (1983) *Developmental neuropsychiatry.* New York: Guilford Press.
(Cravioto and Arrieta; Rourke and Strang; Rutter)

401. Rutter, M. (1985) Family and school influences on cognitive development. *Journal of Child Psychology and Psychiatry, 26*, 683–704.

402. Rutter, M. (1985) Family and school influences on behavioural development. *Journal of Child Psychology and Psychiatry, 26*, 349–68.

403. Rutter, M. (1986) Meyerian psychobiology, personality development and the role of life experience. *American Journal of Psychiatry, 143*, 1077–87.

404. Rutter, M. (1987) The role of cognition in child development and disorder. *British Journal of Medical Psychology, 60*, 1–16.

405. Rutter, M. (1987) Temperament, personality and personality disorder. *British Journal of Psychiatry, 150*, 443–58.

406. Rutter, M., ed. (1988) *Studies of psychosocial risk: the power of longitudinal data.* Cambridge: Cambridge University Press. (Farrington; Hinde; Magnusson and Bergman; Rutter)

407. Rutter, M. (1989) Age as an ambiguous variable in developmental research: some epidemiological considerations from developmental psychopathology. *International Journal of Behavioral Development, 12*, 1–34.

408. Rutter, M. (1989) Pathways from childhood to adult life. *Journal of Child Psychology and Psychiatry, 30*, 23–51.

409. Rutter, M. (1989) Psychiatric disorder in parents as a risk factor for children. In D. Shaffer, I. Philips and N.B. Enzer, eds., *Prevention of mental disorders, alcohol and other drug use in children and adolescents* (OSAP Prevention Monograph 2). Rockville, Maryland: Office for Substance Abuse Prevention, US Department of Health and Human Services. Pp.157–89.

410. Rutter, M. (1989) Annotation: child psychiatric disorders in ICD–10. *Journal of Child Psychology and Psychiatry, 30*, 499–513.

411. Rutter, M. (1991) Nature, nurture, and psychopathology: a new look at an old topic. *Development and Psychopathology, 3*, 125–36.

412. Rutter, M. (1991) A fresh look at 'maternal deprivation'. In P. Bateson, ed., *The development and integration of behaviour.* Cambridge: Cambridge University Press. Pp. 331–74.

413. Rutter, M. (1991) Pathways from childhood to adult life: the role of schooling. *Pastoral Care in Education, 9*, 3–10.

414. Rutter, M., et al. (1990) Genetic factors in child psychiatric disorder: I. A review of research strategies. II. Empirical findings. *Journal of Child Psychology and Psychiatry, 31*, 3–37; 39–83.

415. Rutter, M., and Casaer, P., eds. (1991) *Biological risk factors for psychosocial disorders.* Cambridge: Cambridge University Press. (Bancroft; Casaer *et al.*; Goodman; Plomin; Rutter and Mawhood; Swaab)

416. Rutter, M., and Giller, H. (1983) *Juvenile delinquency: trends and perspectives*. Harmondsworth, Middx: Penguin Books.

417. Rutter, M., and Hersov, L., eds. (1985) *Child and adolescent psychiatry: modern approaches* (2nd edn). Oxford: Blackwell Scientific. (Garmezy and Rutter; Graham and Rutter; Hersov; Hobson; McGuffin and Gottesman; Rutter; Rutter and Gould; Wolkind and Rutter; Yule and Rutter)

418. Rutter, M., Izard, C.E., and Read, P.B., eds. (1986) *Depression in young people: developmental and clinical perspectives*. New York: Guilford Press.
(Brown *et al.*; Izard; Rutter)

419. Rutter, M., and Madge, N. (1976) *Cycles of disadvantage: a review of research*. London: Heinemann.

420. Rutter, M., Maughan, B., Mortimore, P., and Ouston, J., with Smith, A. (1979) *Fifteen thousand hours: secondary schools and their effects on children*. London: Open Books (1980: Cambridge, Mass: Harvard University Press).

421. Rutter, M., and Pickles, A. (1991) Person–environment interactions: concepts, mechanisms and implications for data analysis. In T. Wachs and R. Plomin, eds., *Conceptualization and measurement of organism–environment interaction*. Washington, DC: American Psychological Association, pp. 105–41.

422. Rutter, M., and Quinton, D. (1977) Psychiatric disorder – ecological factors and concepts of causation. In H. McGurk, ed., *Ecological factors in human development*. Amsterdam: North Holland. Pp. 173–87.

423. Rutter, M., and Redshaw, J. (1991) Growing up as a twin: twin-singleton differences in psychological development. *Journal of Child Psychology and Psychiatry, 32*, 885–895.

424. Rutter, M., Tizard, J., and Whitmore, K., eds. (1970) *Education, health and behaviour*. London: Longmans (reprinted, 1981, Krieger, Melbourne, FA).

425. Rutter, M., Tuma, A.H., and Lann, I.S. (1988) *Assessment and diagnosis in child psychopathology*. New York: Guilford Press.

426. Rutter, M., Yule, B., Quinton, D., Rowlands, O., Yule, W., and Berger, M. (1975) Attainment and adjustment in two geographical areas. III. Some factors accounting for area differences. *British Journal of Psychiatry, 126*, 520–33.

427. Saarni, C., and Harris, P.L., eds. (1989) *Children's understanding of emotion*. Cambridge: Cambridge University Press.

428. St Claire, L., and Osborn, A.F. (1987) The ability and behaviour

of children who have been 'in care' or separated from their parents. Report from the Economic and Social Research Council. *Early Child Development and Care, 28*, No.3 – Monograph.

429. Sampson. R.J., and Laub, J.H. (1990) Crime and deviance over the life course: the salience of adult social bonds. *American Sociological Review, 55*, 609–27.

430. Scarbourough, H.S. (1990) Very early language deficits in dyslexic children. *Child Development, 61*, 1728–43.

431. Scarr, S., and McCartney, K. (1983) How people make their own environments: a theory of genotype → environmental effects. *Child Development, 54*, 424–35.

432. Schaie, K.W., and Willis, S.L. (1986) *Adult development and aging* (2nd edn). Boston: Little, Brown & Company.

433. Schiff, M., and Lewontin, R. (1986) *Education and class: the irrelevance of IQ genetic studies*. Oxford: Clarendon.

434. Schneider, E.L., and Rowe, J.W., eds. (1990) *Handbook of the biology of aging* (3rd edn). San Diego: Academic Press. *cf.* Brock.

435. Schwartz, D., and Mayaux, M.J. (1982) Female fecundity as a function of age. *New England Journal of Medicine, 306*, 404–6.

436. Shankweiler, D., and Lieberman, I.Y., eds. (1989) *Phonology and reading disability: solving the reading puzzle*. Ann Arbor: University of Michigan Press.
(Hanson)

437. Sherif, M., Harvey, O.J., White, B.J., Hood, W.R., and Sherif, C.W. (1961) *Intergroup conflict and cooperation: the Robbers' Cave experiment*. Norman, Oklahoma: University of Oklahoma Press.

438. Shields, J. (1962) *Monozygotic twins brought up apart and brought up together*. London: Oxford University Press.

439. Sigman, M., Mundy, P., Sherman, T., and Ungerer, J. (1986) Social interactions of autistic, mentally retarded and normal children and their caregivers. *Journal of Child Psychology and Psychiatry, 27*, 647–55.

440. Sigman, M., and Ungerer, J.A. (1984) Attachment behaviors in autistic children. *Journal of Autism and Developmental Disorders, 14*, 231–44.

441. Simmons, R.G., and Blyth, D.A. (1987) *Moving into adolescence: the impact of pubertal change and school context*. New York: Aldine de Gruyter.

442. Skinner, B.F. (1957) *Verbal Behavior*. New York: Appleton Century Crofts.

443. Skuse, D. (1984) Extreme deprivation in early childhood. II.

Theoretical issues and a comparative review. *Journal of Child Psychology and Psychiatry, 25,* 543–72.

444. Skuse, D., Pickles, A., Wolke, D., and Reilly, S. (submitted) Postnatal growth and mental development: evidence for a 'sensitive period'.

445. Smedslund, J. (1961) The acquisition of conservation of substance and weight in children. III. Extinction of conservation of weight acquired 'normally' and by means of empirical controls on a balance. *Scandinavian Journal of Psychology, 2,* 85–7.

446. Smith, C., and Lloyd, B. (1978) Maternal behavior and the perceived sex of infant: revisited. *Child Development, 49,* 1263–6.

447. Smith, D.J., and Tomlinson, S. (1989) *The school effect: a study of multi-racial comprehensives.* London: Policy Studies Institute.

448. Smith, P.K., ed. (1991) *The psychology of grandparenthood: an international perspective.* London: Routledge.

449. Snowling, M. (1987) *Dyslexia: a cognitive developmental perspective.* Oxford: Basil Blackwell.

450. Snowling, M. (1991) Developmental reading disorders. *Journal of Child Psychology and Psychiatry, 32,* 49–77.

451. Sorenson, R.C. (1973) *Adolescent sexuality in contemporary America: personal values and sexual behavior ages thirteen to nineteen.* New York: World Publishing.

452. Sroufe, L.A. (1983) Infant–caregiver attachment and patterns of adaptation in preschool: the roots of maladaptation and competence. In M. Perlmutter, ed., *Minnesota symposia on child psychology,* Vol. 16. Hillsdale, NJ: Erlbaum. Pp. 41–81.

453. Sroufe, L.A., Egeland, B., and Kreutzer, T. (1991) The fate of early experience following developmental change: longitudinal approaches to individual adaptation in childhood. *Child Development, 61,* 1363–73.

454. Sroufe, L.A., Fox, N., and Pancake, V. (1983) Attachment and dependency in developmental perspective. *Child Development, 55,* 17–29.

455. Sroufe, L.A., Jacobvitz, J., Mangelsdorf, S., DeAngelo, E., and Ward, M.J. (1985) Generational boundary dissolution between mothers and their preschool children: a relationships systems approach. *Child Development, 56,* 317–25.

456. Sroufe, L.A., and Waters, E. (1976) The ontogenesis of smiling and laughter: a perspective on the organization of development in infancy. *Psychological Review, 83,* 173–89.

457. Stanton, A.L., and Dunkel-Schetter, C., eds. (1991) *Infertility: perspectives from stress and coping research*. New York: Plenum.

458. Stattin, H., and Magnusson, D. (1990) *Pubertal maturation in female development*. Hillsdale, NJ: Erlbaum.

459. Stern, D.N. (1985) *The interpersonal world of the infant: a view from psychoanalysis and developmental psychology*. New York: Basic Books.

460. Stevenson, H.W., Lee, S-Y., Chen, C., Lummis, M., Stigler, J.W., Liu, F., and Fang, G. (1990) Mathematics achievement of children in China and the United States. *Child Development, 61,* 1053–66.

461. Stevenson, H.W., Lee, S-Y., with Chen, C., Stigler, J.W., Hsu, C.-C., and Kitamura, S. (1990) Contexts of achievement. *Monographs of the Society for Research in Child Development*, Serial No. 221, 55, 1–2.

462. Stevenson, H.W., Stigler, J.W., Lucker, G.W., and Lee, S.-Y. (1982) Reading disabilities: the case of Chinese, Japanese, and English. *Child Development, 53,* 1164–81.

463. Stillwell, R., and Dunn, J. (1985) Continuities in sibling relationships: patterns of aggression and friendliness. *Journal of Child Psychology and Psychiatry, 26,* 627–37.

464. Stout, J.W., and Rivara, F.P. (1989) Schools and sex education: does it work? *Pediatrics, 83,* 375–9.

465. Sussman, M.B., and Steinmetz, S.K., eds. (1987) *Handbook of marriage and the family*. New York: Plenum.

466. Szmukler, G.I., Eisler, I., Gillies, C., and Hayward, M.E. (1985) The implications of anorexia nervosa in a ballet school. *Journal of Psychiatric Research, 19,* 177–81.

467. Tallal, P. (1985) Neuropsychological foundations of specific developmental disorders of speech and language: implications for theories of hemispheric specialization. In J.O. Cavenar, JR, ed., *Psychiatry*, Vol. 3. Philadelphia: Lippincott. Pp. 1–15.

468. Tanner, J.M. (1962) *Growth at adolescence* (2nd edn). Oxford: Blackwell Scientific.

469. Tanner, J.M. (1973) Growing up. *Scientific American, 229,* 34–43.

470. Tanner, J.M. (1986) Growth as a target-seeking function: catch-up and catch-down growth in man. In F. Falkner and J.M. Tanner, eds., *Human growth: a comprehensive treatise*, Vol. 1, *Developmental biology and prenatal growth* (2nd edn). New York: Plenum. Pp. 167–79.

471. Taylor, E., Sandberg, S., Thorley, G., and Giles, S. (1991) *The*

epidemiology of childhood hyperactivity (Maudsley Monograph No. 33). Oxford: Oxford University Press.

472. Thomas, A., Chess, S., and Birch, H. (1968) *Temperament and behavioral disorders in childhood*. New York: New York University Press.

473. Thomas, L. (1979) *The medusa and the snail: more notes of a biology watcher*. New York: Viking Press.

474. Thompson, R.A., Connell, J.P., and Bridges, L.J. (1988) Temperament, emotion, and social interactive behavior in the strange situation: a component process analysis of attachment system functioning. *Child Development, 59*, 1102–10.

475. Thornes, B., and Collard, J. (1979) *Who divorces?* London: Routledge & Kegan Paul.

476. Tizard, B., and Hodges, J. (1978) The effect of early institutional rearing on the development of eight-year-old children. *Journal of Child Psychology and Psychiatry, 19*, 99–118.

477. Tizard, B., and Hughes, M. (1984) *Young children learning: talking and thinking at home and at school*. London: Fontana.

478. Tizard, B., and Rees, J. (1975) The effect of early institutional rearing on the behaviour problems and affectional relationships of four-year-old children. *Journal of Child Psychology and Psychiatry, 16*, 61–74.

479. Tizard, J. (1975) Race and IQ: the limits of probability? *New Behaviour, 1*, 6–9.

480. Townsend, P., and Davidson, N. (1982) *Inequalities in health: the Black Report*. Harmondsworth, Middx: Penguin.

481. Trabasso, T.R. (1975) Representation, memory and reasoning: how do we make transitive inferences? In Pick, A.D., ed., *Minnesota symposia on child psychology*, Vol. 9. Minneapolis: University of Minnesota Press.

482. Treffert, D.A. (1989) *Extraordinary people*. London: Bantam Press.

483. Vaillant, G. (1977) *Adaptation to life: how the best and brightest came of age*. Boston: Little Brown.

484. Vandenberg, S.G. (1972) Assortative mating, or who marries whom? *Behavior Genetics, 2*, 127–57.

485. Wallerstein, J.S., and Blakeslee, S. (1989) *Second chances: men, women and children a decade after divorce*. Uxbridge, Middx: Bantam Press.

486. Wallerstein, J.S., and Kelly, J.B. (1980) *Surviving the breakup*. London: Grant McIntyre.

487. Warr, P. (1987) *Work, unemployment and mental health*. Oxford: Clarendon Press.

488. Warr, P., and Payne, R.L. (1983) Affective outcomes of paid employment in a random sample of British workers. *Journal of Occupational Behaviour, 4,* 91–104.

489. Wasik, B.H., Ramey, C.T., Bryant, D.M., and Sparling, J.J. (1990) A longitudinal study of two early intervention strategies: Project CARE. *Child Development, 61,* 1682–96.

490. Weg, R.B. (1983) *Sexuality in the later years: roles and behavior.* New York: Academic Press.

491. Weinberger, D.R. (1987) Implications of normal brain development for the pathogenesis of schizophrenia. *Archives of General Psychiatry, 44,* 660–69.

492. Werner, E.E. (1984) *Child care: kith, kin and hired hands.* Baltimore: University Park Press.

493. Werner, E.E., and Smith, R.S. (1977) *Kauai's children come of age.* Honolulu: University Press of Hawaii.

494. Werner, E.E., and Smith, R.S. (1982) *Vulnerable, but invincible: a longitudinal study of resilient children and youth.* New York: McGraw-Hill.

495. West, D. (1982) *Delinquency: its roots, careers and prospects.* London: Heinemann.

496. West, D.J., and Farrington, D.P. (1973) *Who becomes delinquent?* London: Heinemann Educational.

497. White, L.K. (1990) Determinants of divorce: a review of research in the eighties. *Journal of Marriage and the Family, 52,* 904–12.

498. White, M., and McRae, S. (1989) *Young adults and long-term unemployment.* London: Policy Studies Institute Publications.

499. Whiten, A., ed. (1991) *Natural theories of mind.* Oxford: Basil Blackwell.

500. Wimmer, H., and Perner, J. (1983) Beliefs about beliefs: representation and constraining function of wrong beliefs in young children's understanding of deception. *Cognition, 13,* 103–28.

501. Witelson, S.F. (1987) Neurobiological aspects of language in children. *Child Development, 58,* 653–88.

502. Wolff, S. (1981) *Children under stress* (2nd edn). Harmondsworth, Middx: Penguin.

503. Wolkind, S.N. (1974) The components of 'affectionless psychopathy' in institutionalized children. *Journal of Child Psychology and Psychiatry, 15,* 215–20.

504. Woodhead, M. (1985) Pre-school education has long-term effects: but can they be generalised? *Oxford Review of Education, 11,* 133–55.

505. World Health Organization (1981) *Research on the menopause* (Technical Report Series, 670). Geneva: World Health Organization.

506. Yule, W., and Rutter, M., eds. (1987) *Language development and disorders* (Clinics in Developmental Medicine, No. 101/102). London/Oxford: Mac Keith Press/Blackwell Scientific; Philadelphia: Lippincott.
(Goodman; Puckering and Rutter)

507. Yule, W., Udwin, O., and Murdoch, K. (1990) The 'Jupiter' sinking: effects on children's fears, depression and anxiety. *Journal of Child Psychology and Psychiatry, 31,* 1051–61.

508. Zigler, E.F., and Gordon, E.W., eds. (1982) *Day care: Scientific and social policy issues.* Boston, Mass.: Auburn.

509. Zoccolillo, M., Pickles, A., Quinton, D., and Rutter, M. (in press) The outcome of conduction disorder: implications for defining adult personality disorder. *Psychological Medicine.*

Index